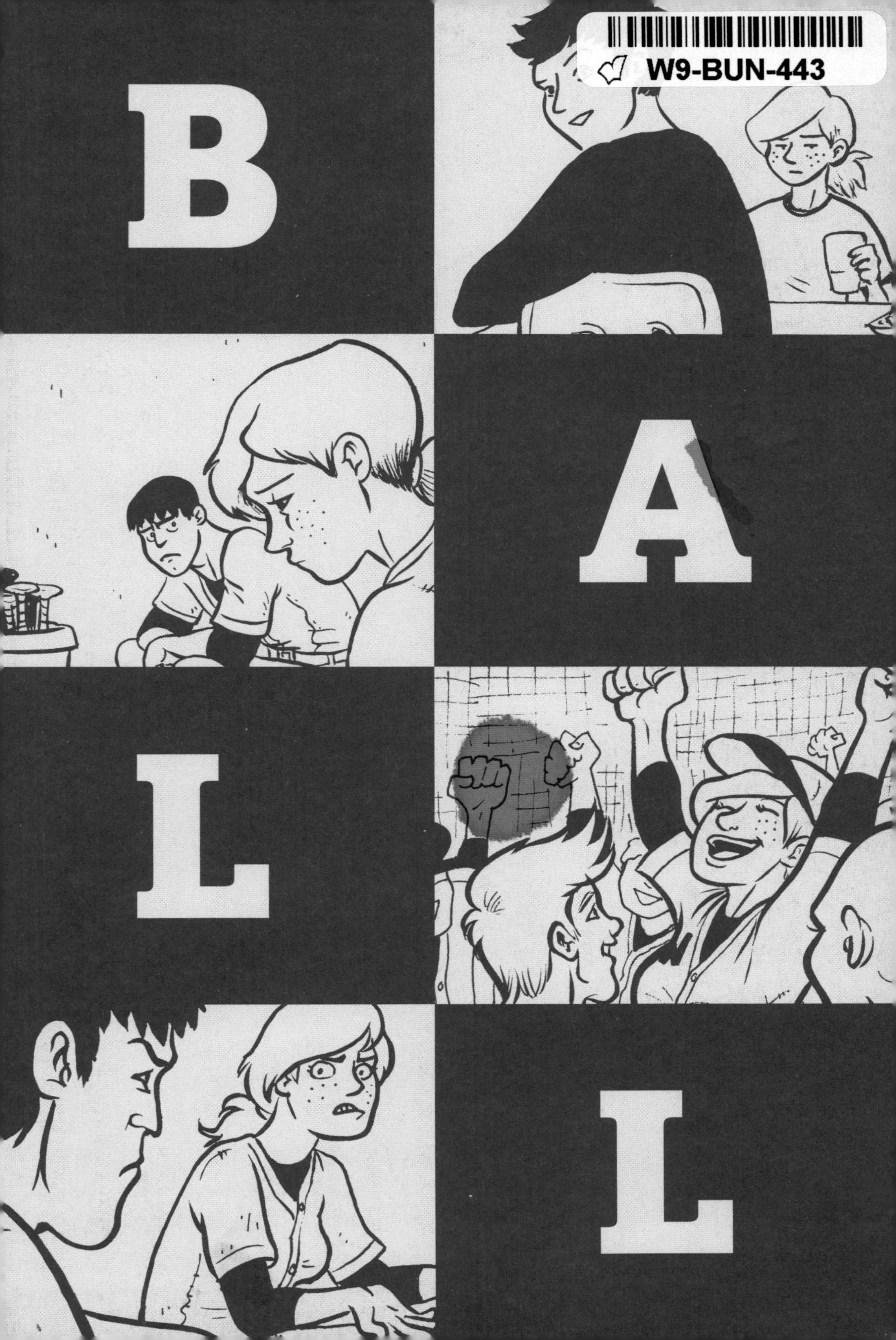
B
A
L
L

AN ONI PRESS PUBLICATION

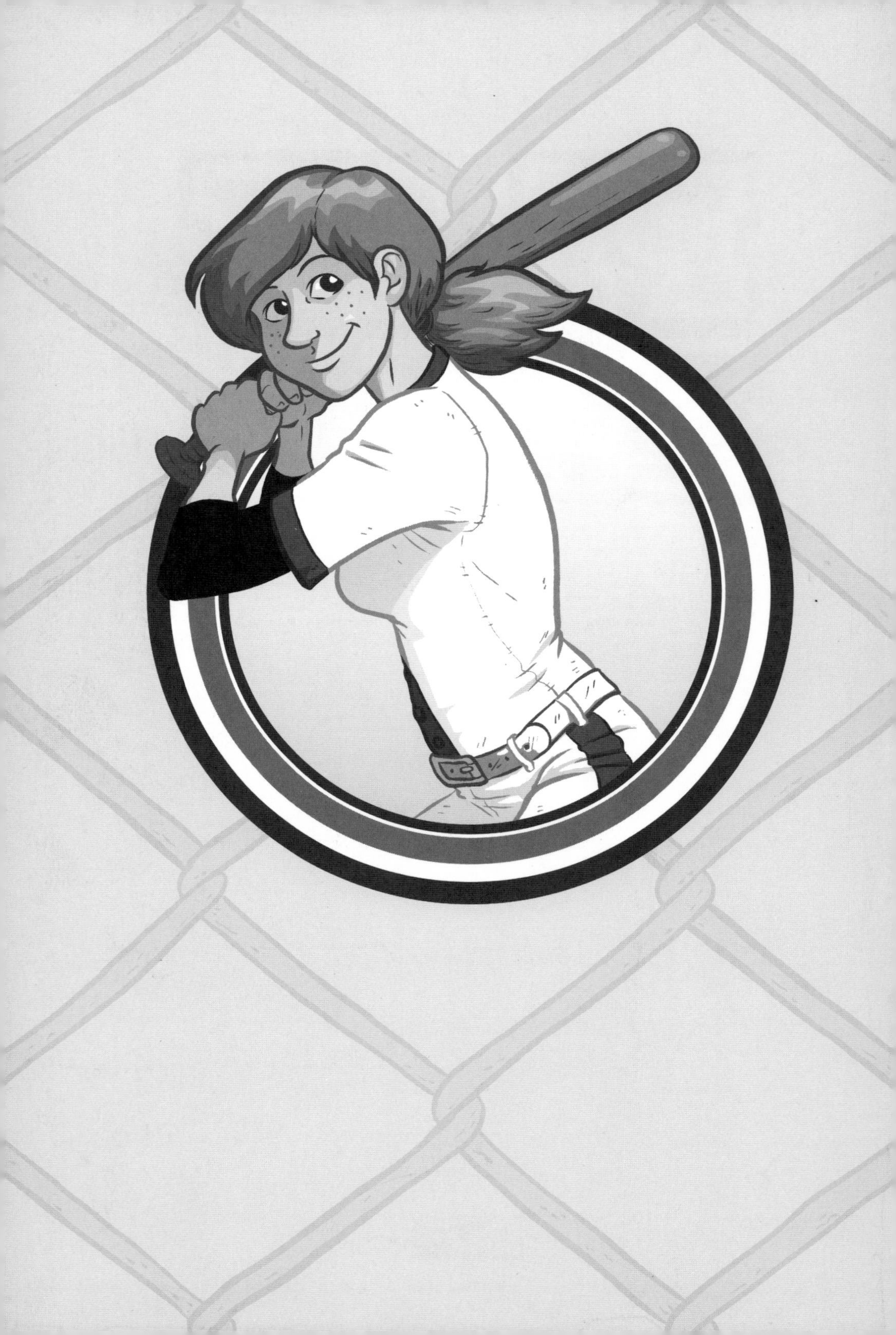

PLAY BALL

WRITTEN BY
NUNZIO DEFILIPPIS
AND
CHRISTINA WEIR

ILLUSTRATED BY
JACKIE LEWIS

COVER COLORS BY
DAN JACKSON

LETTERED BY
DOUGLAS E. SHERWOOD

DESIGN BY
KEITH WOOD

EDITED BY
JILL BEATON

Oni Press, Inc.

JOE NOZEMACK *publisher*

JAMES LUCAS JONES *editor in chief*

CORY CASONI *director of marketing*

KEITH WOOD *art director*

GEORGE ROHAC *operations director*

JILL BEATON *editor*

CHARLIE CHU *editor*

TROY LOOK *digital prepress lead*

Play Ball, April 2012. Published by Oni Press, Inc. 1305 SE Martin
Luther King Jr. Blvd., Suite A, Portland, OR 97214. Play Ball is ™ & ©
2012 Nunzio DeFilippis and Christina Weir. All rights reserved. Unless
otherwise specified, all other material © 2012 Oni Press, Inc. Oni Press
logo and icon ™ & © 2012 Oni Press, Inc. Oni Press logo and icon
artwork created by Keith A. Wood. The events, institutions, and char-
acters presented in this book are fictional. Any resemblance to actual
persons, living or dead, is purely coincidental. No portion of this
publication may be reproduced, by any means, without the express
written permission of the copyright holders.

1305 SE Martin Luther King Jr. Blvd.
Suite A
Portland, OR 97214

www.onipress.com

First Edition: April 2012

ISBN 978-1-934964-79-8
ISBN 978-1-62010-020-2 (eBook)

1 3 5 7 9 10 8 6 4 2

Library of Congress Control Number: 2011933142

Printed in China.

For our nieces and god-daughters:
Alexa, Eva, Marley, and Dashiell

Smart little girls never let anyone else tell
them what they can or can't do.

– Nunzio and Christina

For my mother, without whom I would
never have achieved so much.

– Jackie

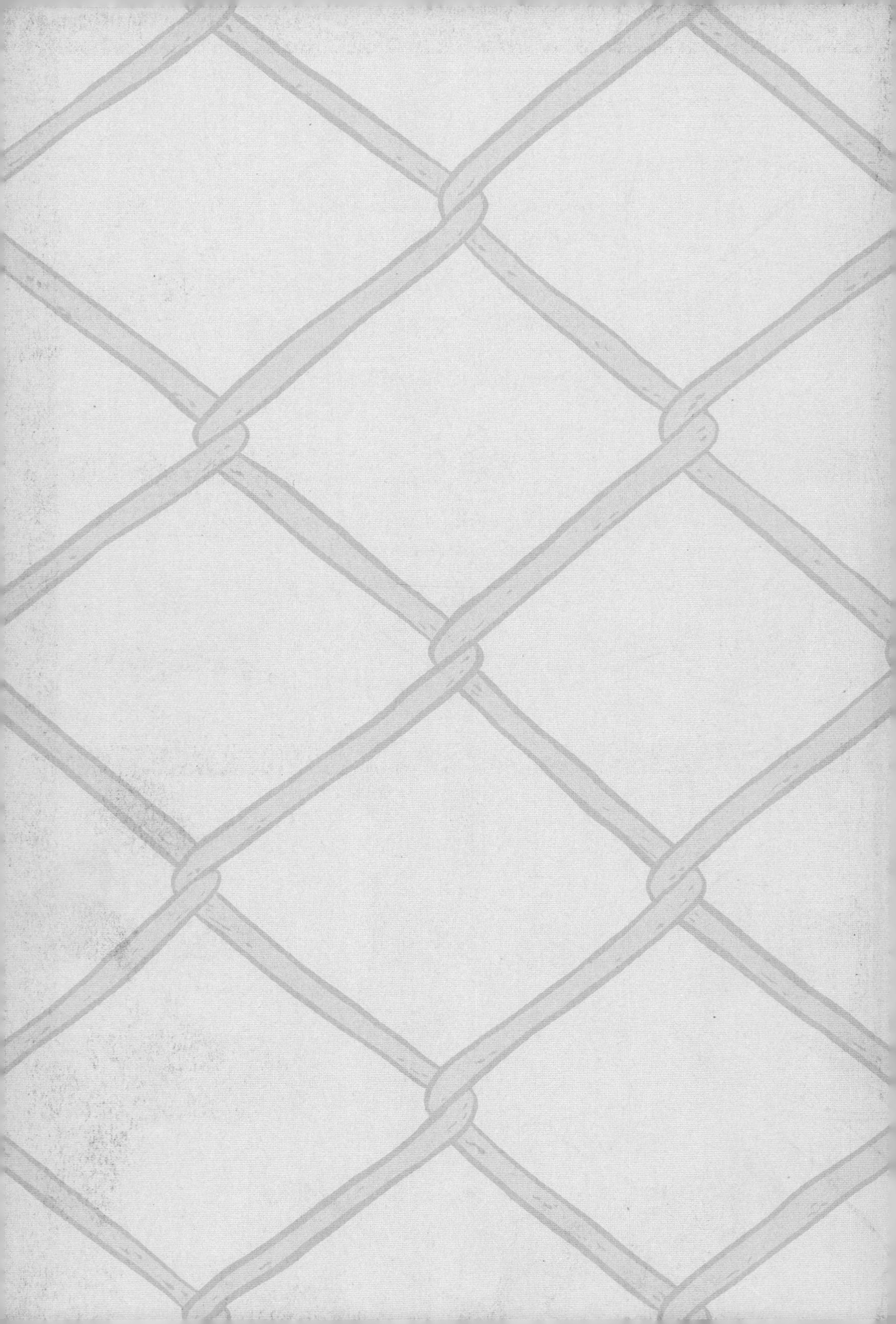

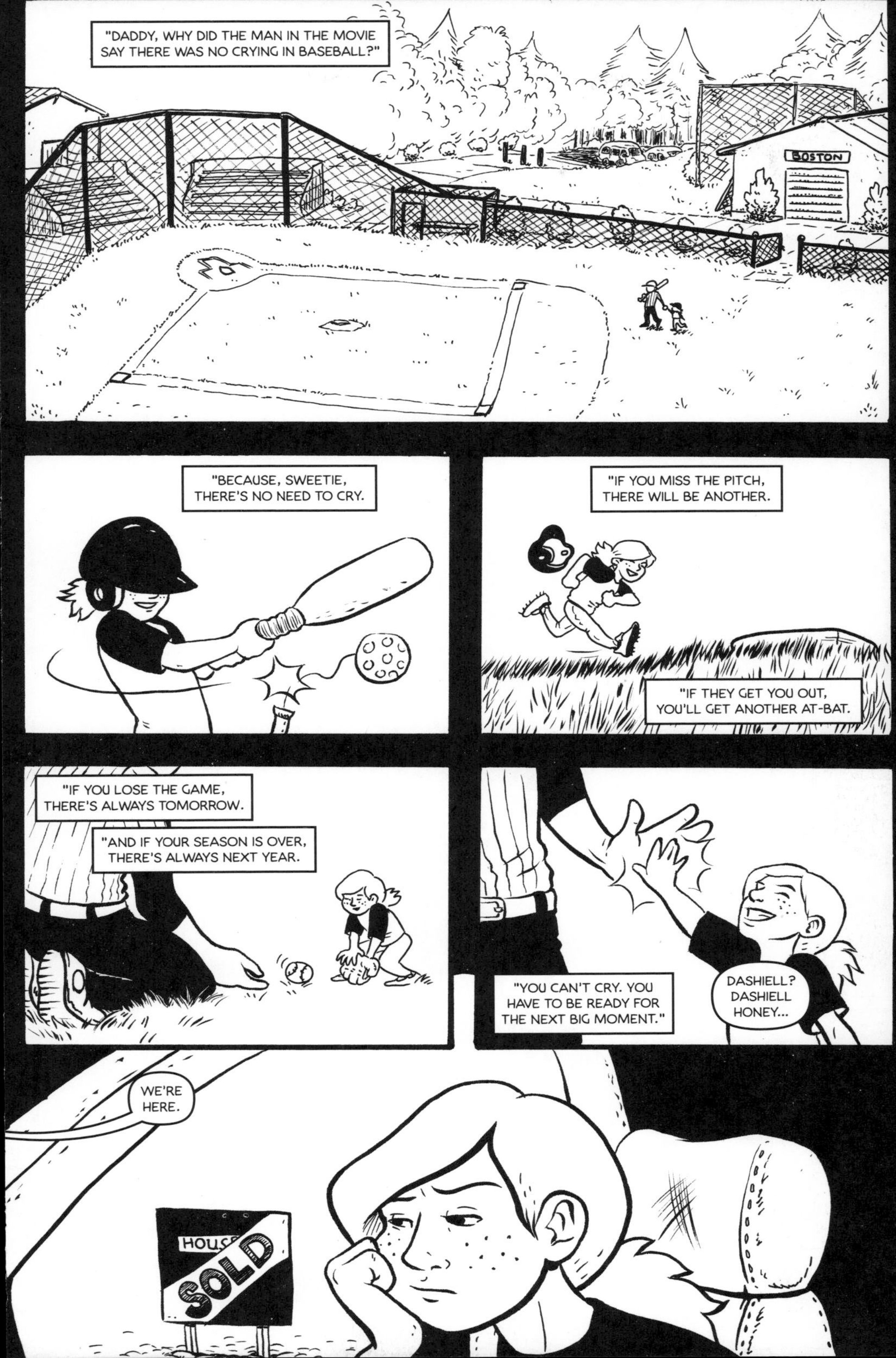
"DADDY, WHY DID THE MAN IN THE MOVIE SAY THERE WAS NO CRYING IN BASEBALL?"
BOSTON
"BECAUSE, SWEETIE, THERE'S NO NEED TO CRY.
"IF YOU MISS THE PITCH, THERE WILL BE ANOTHER.
"IF THEY GET YOU OUT, YOU'LL GET ANOTHER AT-BAT.
"IF YOU LOSE THE GAME, THERE'S ALWAYS TOMORROW.
"AND IF YOUR SEASON IS OVER, THERE'S ALWAYS NEXT YEAR.
"YOU CAN'T CRY. YOU HAVE TO BE READY FOR THE NEXT BIG MOMENT."
DASHIELL? DASHIELL HONEY...
WE'RE HERE.
SOLD

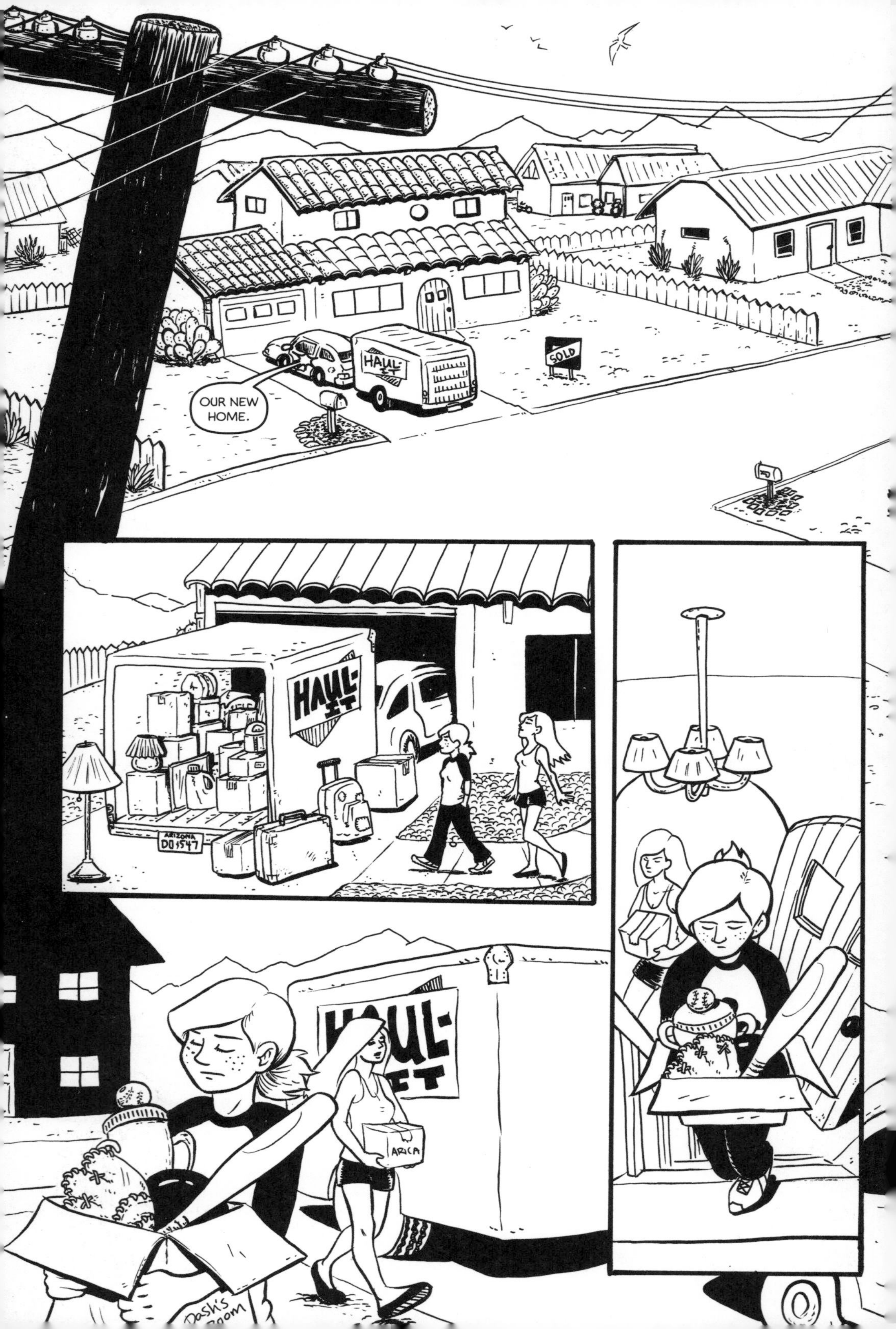
OUR NEW HOME.
HAUL-IT
SOLD
ARIZONA
DO 1547
ARICA

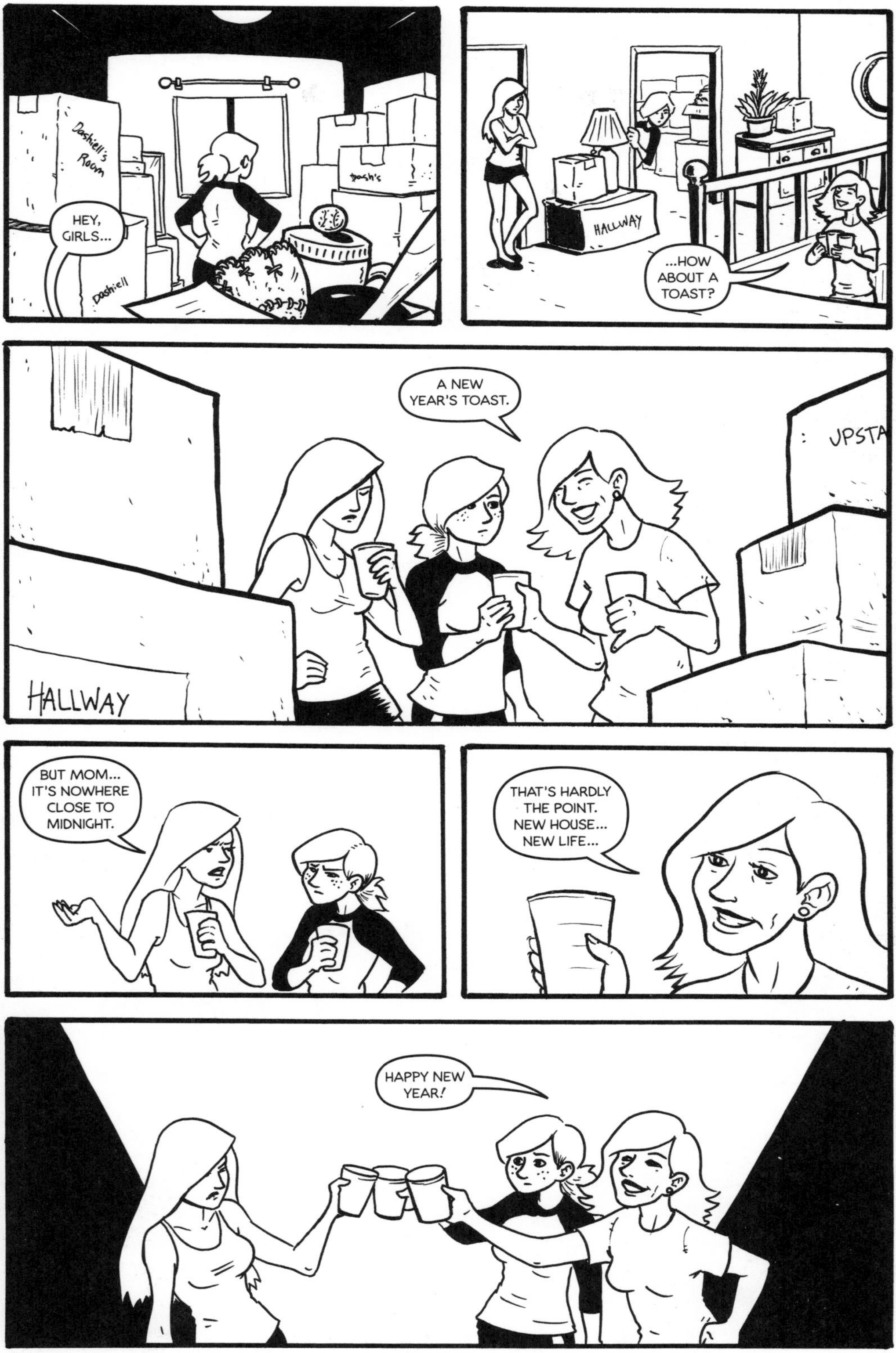
HEY, GIRLS...
Dashiell's Room
Dash's
Dashiell
HALLWAY
...HOW ABOUT A TOAST?
A NEW YEAR'S TOAST.
HALLWAY
BUT MOM... IT'S NOWHERE CLOSE TO MIDNIGHT.
THAT'S HARDLY THE POINT. NEW HOUSE... NEW LIFE...
HAPPY NEW YEAR!

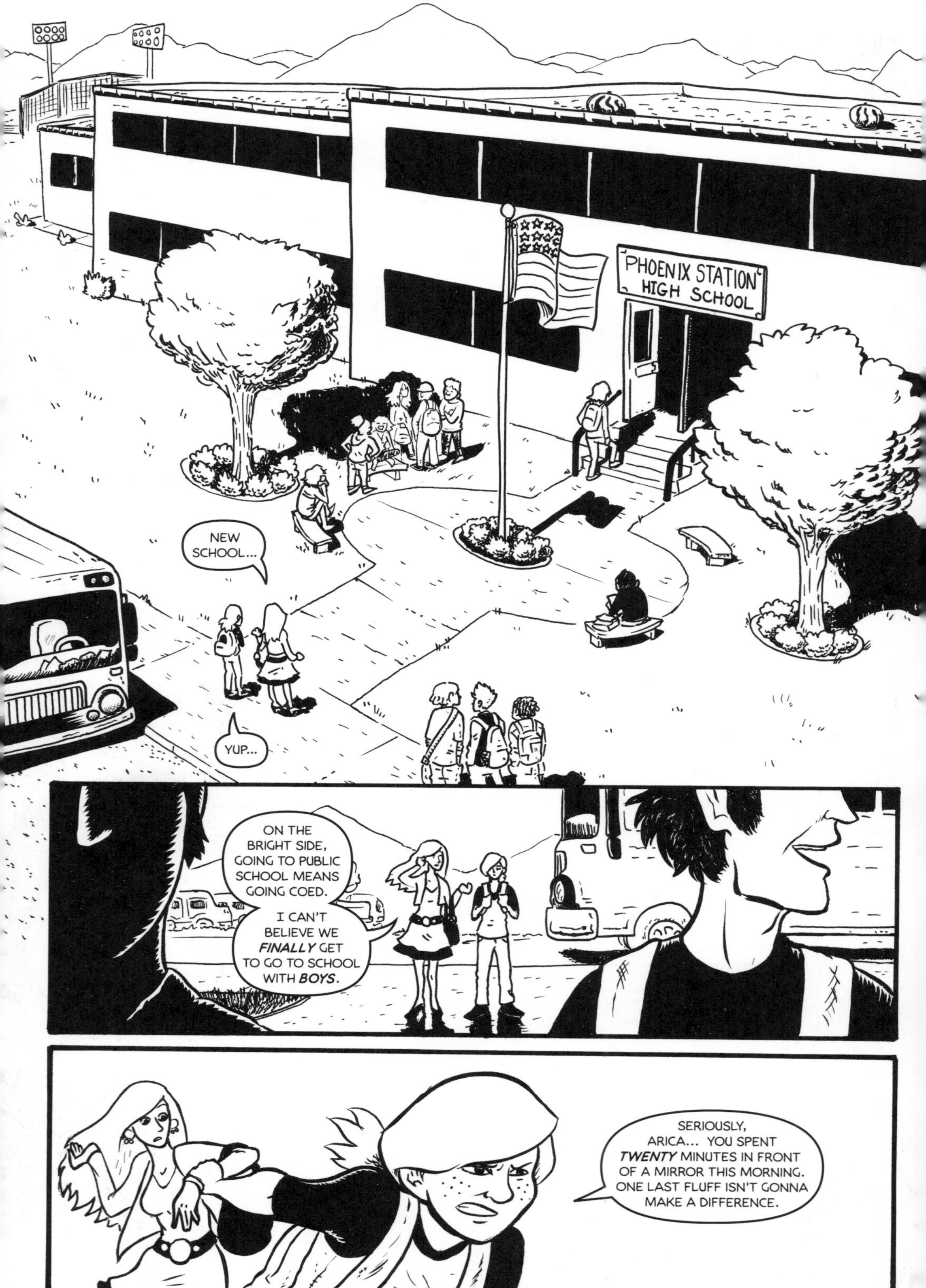
PHOENIX STATION HIGH SCHOOL
NEW SCHOOL...
YUP...
ON THE BRIGHT SIDE, GOING TO PUBLIC SCHOOL MEANS GOING COED.
I CAN'T BELIEVE WE *FINALLY* GET TO GO TO SCHOOL WITH *BOYS*.
SERIOUSLY, ARICA... YOU SPENT *TWENTY* MINUTES IN FRONT OF A MIRROR THIS MORNING. ONE LAST FLUFF ISN'T GONNA MAKE A DIFFERENCE.

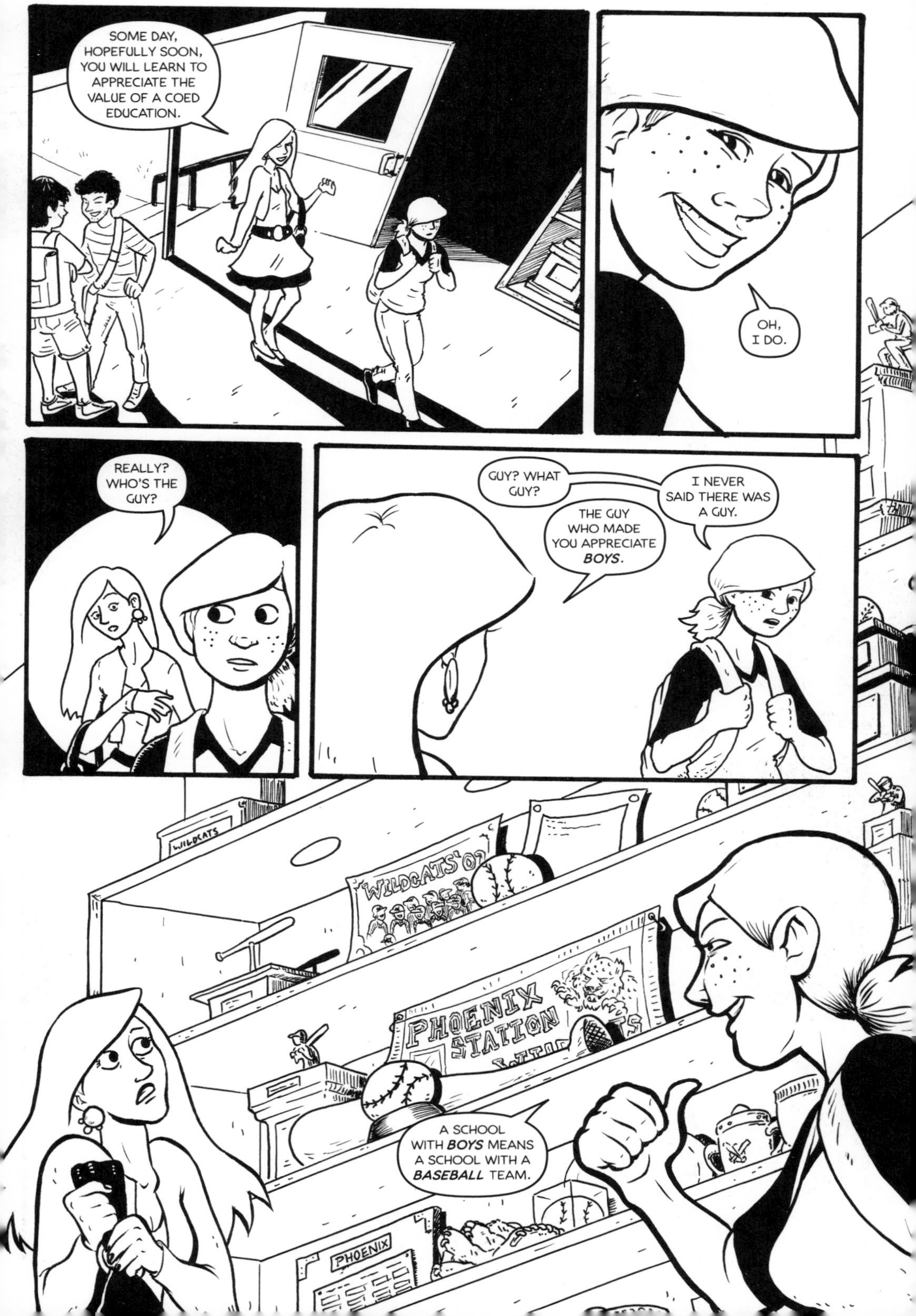
SOME DAY, HOPEFULLY SOON, YOU WILL LEARN TO APPRECIATE THE VALUE OF A COED EDUCATION.
OH, I DO.
REALLY? WHO'S THE GUY?
GUY? WHAT GUY?
I NEVER SAID THERE WAS A GUY.
THE GUY WHO MADE YOU APPRECIATE *BOYS*.
WILDCATS
WILDCATS '07
PHOENIX STATION
A SCHOOL WITH *BOYS* MEANS A SCHOOL WITH A *BASEBALL* TEAM.
PHOENIX

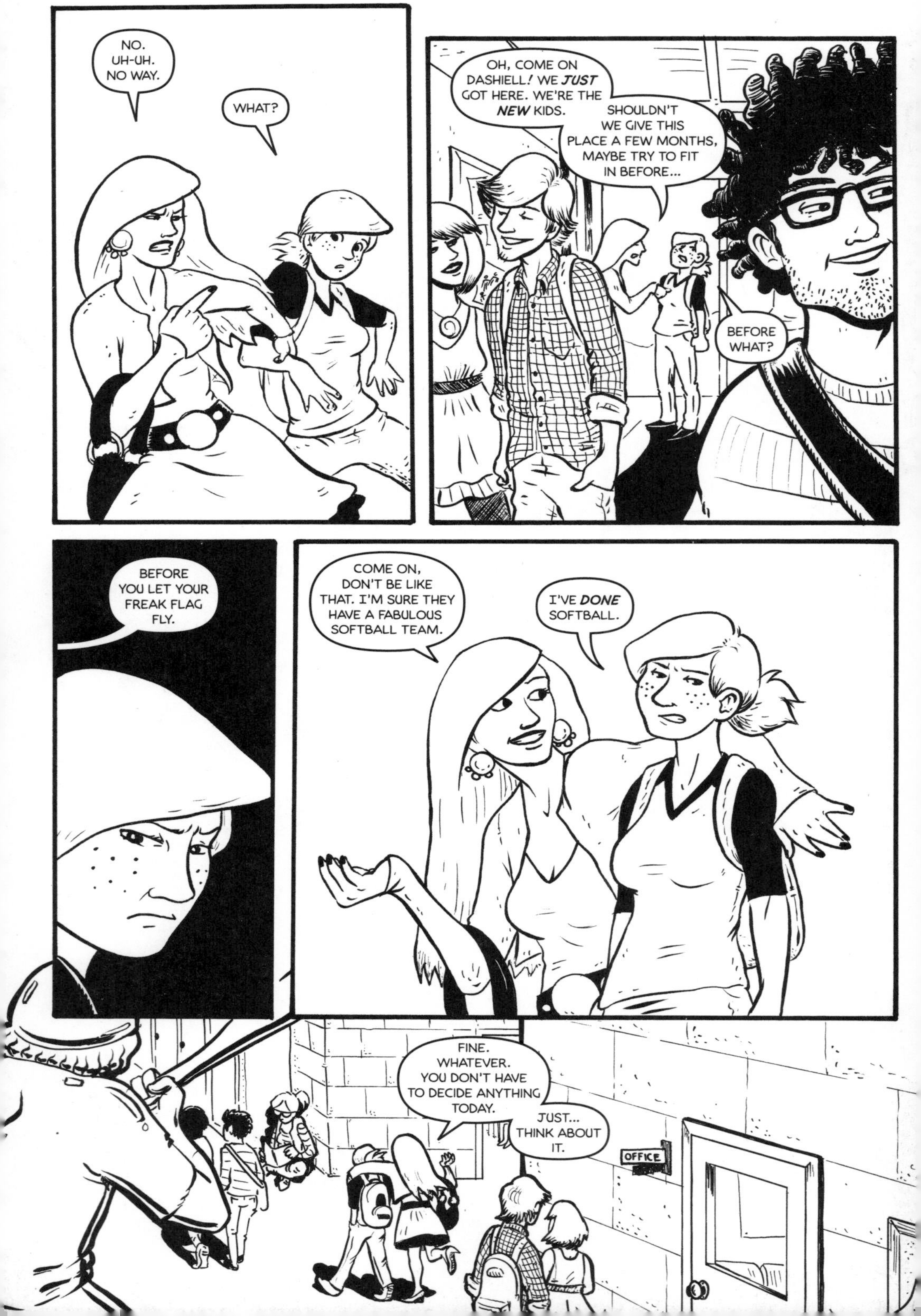
NO. UH-UH. NO WAY.
WHAT?
OH, COME ON DASHIELL! WE *JUST* GOT HERE. WE'RE THE *NEW* KIDS.
SHOULDN'T WE GIVE THIS PLACE A FEW MONTHS, MAYBE TRY TO FIT IN BEFORE...
BEFORE WHAT?
BEFORE YOU LET YOUR FREAK FLAG FLY.
COME ON, DON'T BE LIKE THAT. I'M SURE THEY HAVE A FABULOUS SOFTBALL TEAM.
I'VE *DONE* SOFTBALL.
FINE. WHATEVER. YOU DON'T HAVE TO DECIDE ANYTHING TODAY.
JUST... THINK ABOUT IT.
OFFICE

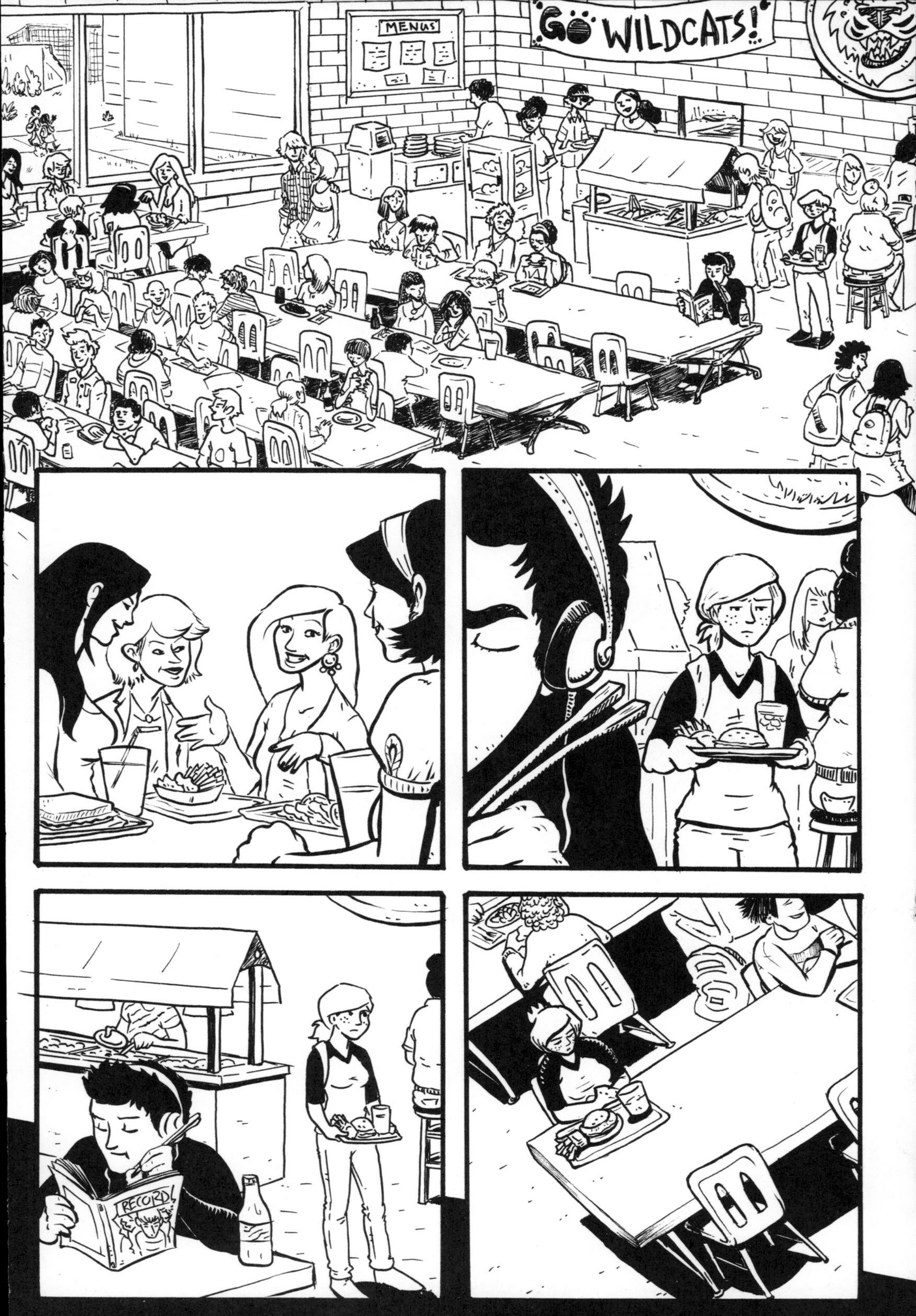
MENUS
GO WILDCATS!
RECORD

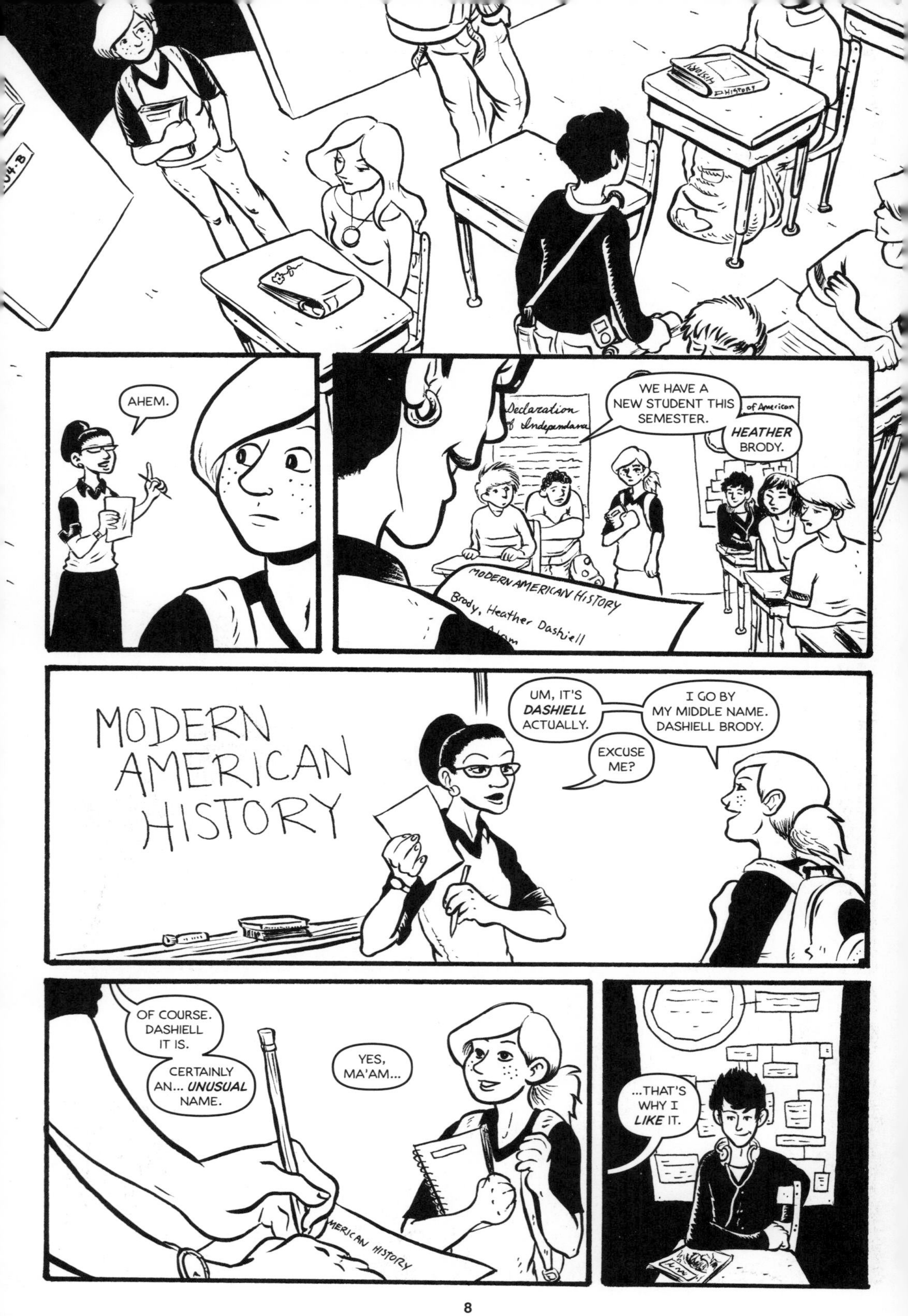
04-B
HISTORY
HISTORY
AHEM.
Declaration of Independance
WE HAVE A NEW STUDENT THIS SEMESTER.
of American
HEATHER BRODY.
MODERN AMERICAN HISTORY
Brody, Heather Dashiell
MODERN AMERICAN HISTORY
UM, IT'S DASHIELL ACTUALLY.
EXCUSE ME?
I GO BY MY MIDDLE NAME. DASHIELL BRODY.
OF COURSE. DASHIELL IT IS.
CERTAINLY AN... UNUSUAL NAME.
YES, MA'AM...
MERICAN HISTORY
...THAT'S WHY I LIKE IT.

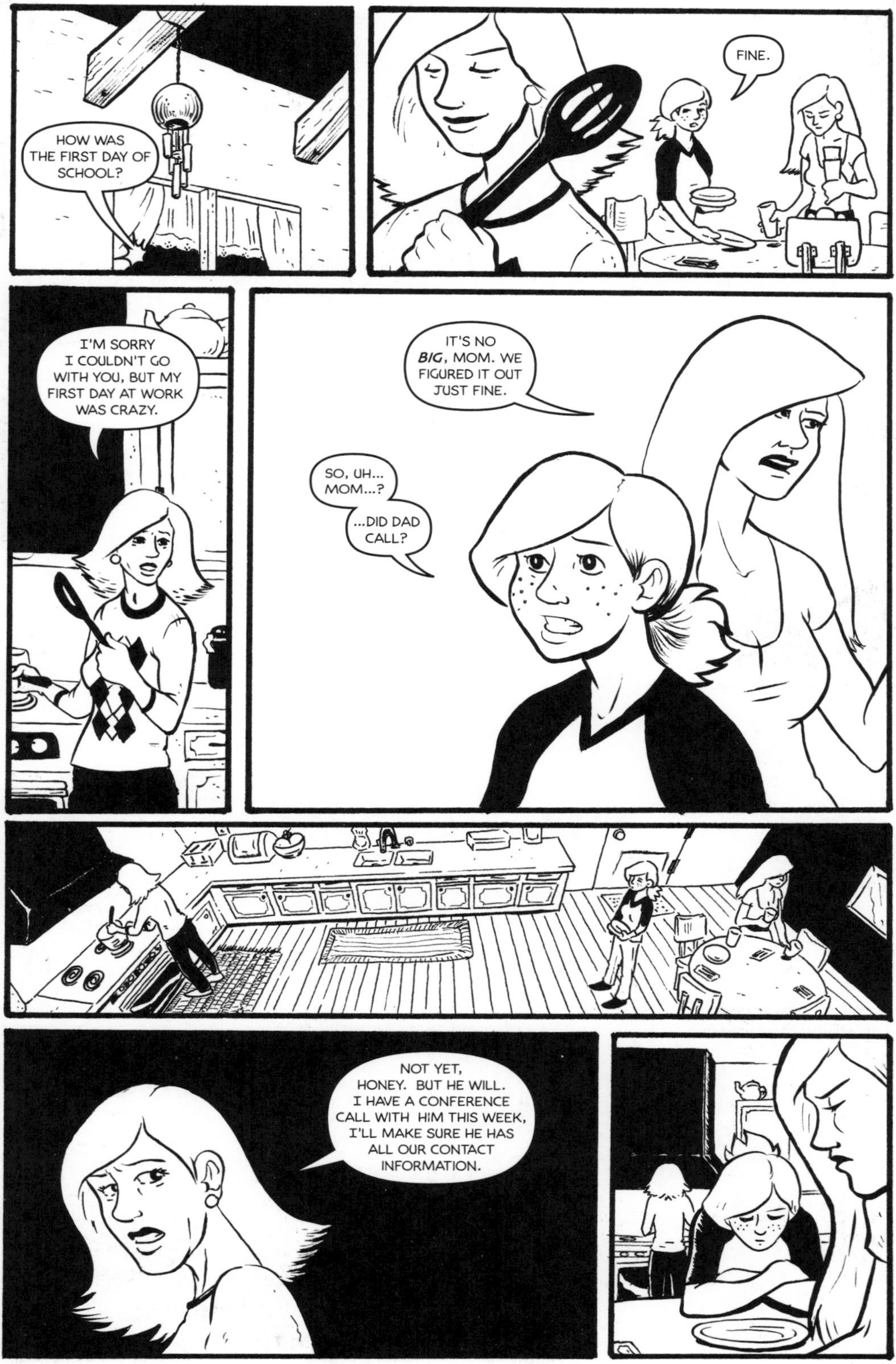
HOW WAS THE FIRST DAY OF SCHOOL?
FINE.
I'M SORRY I COULDN'T GO WITH YOU, BUT MY FIRST DAY AT WORK WAS CRAZY.
IT'S NO BIG, MOM. WE FIGURED IT OUT JUST FINE.
SO, UH... MOM...?
...DID DAD CALL?
NOT YET, HONEY. BUT HE WILL. I HAVE A CONFERENCE CALL WITH HIM THIS WEEK, I'LL MAKE SURE HE HAS ALL OUR CONTACT INFORMATION.

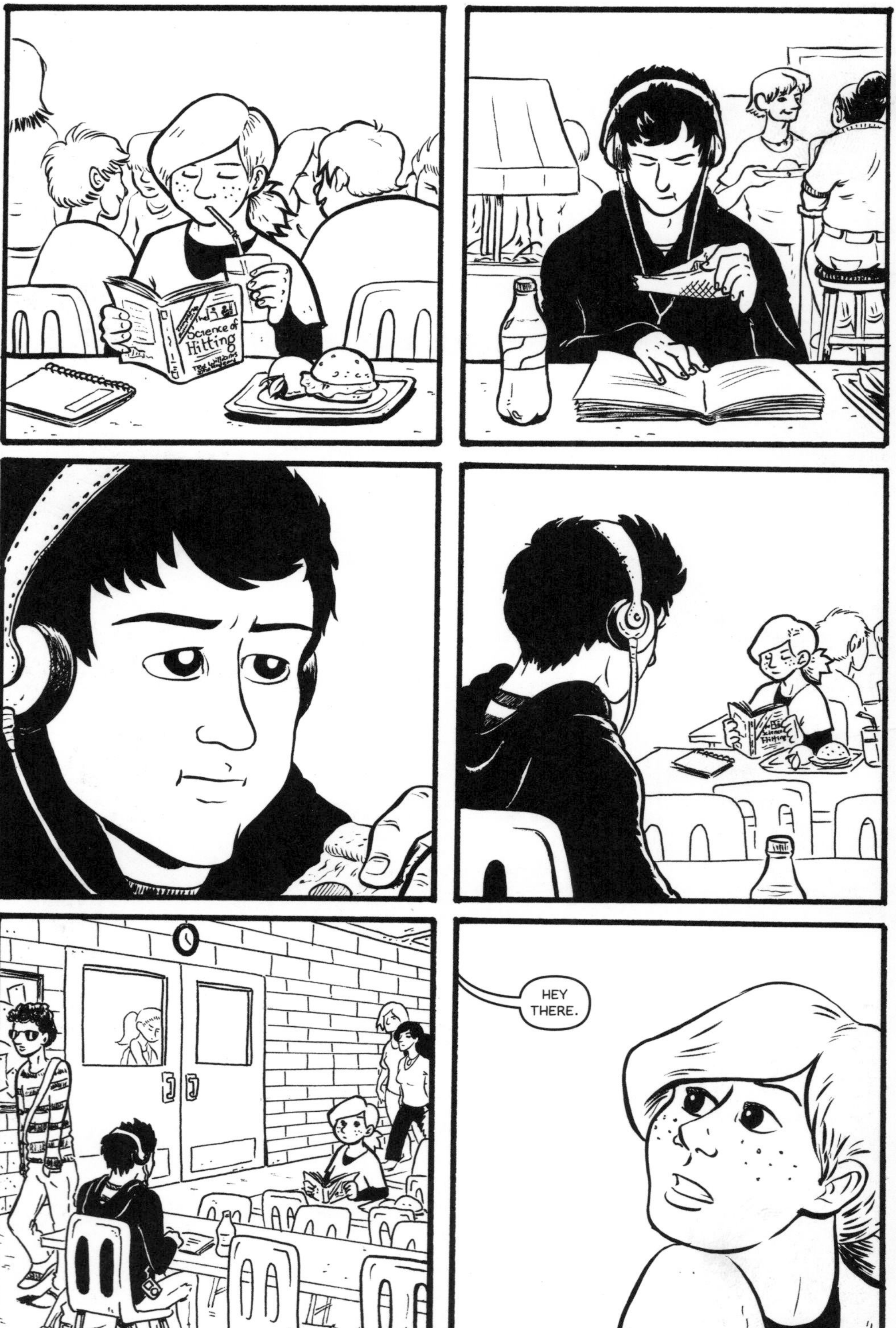
Science of Hitting
Ted Williams
HEY THERE.

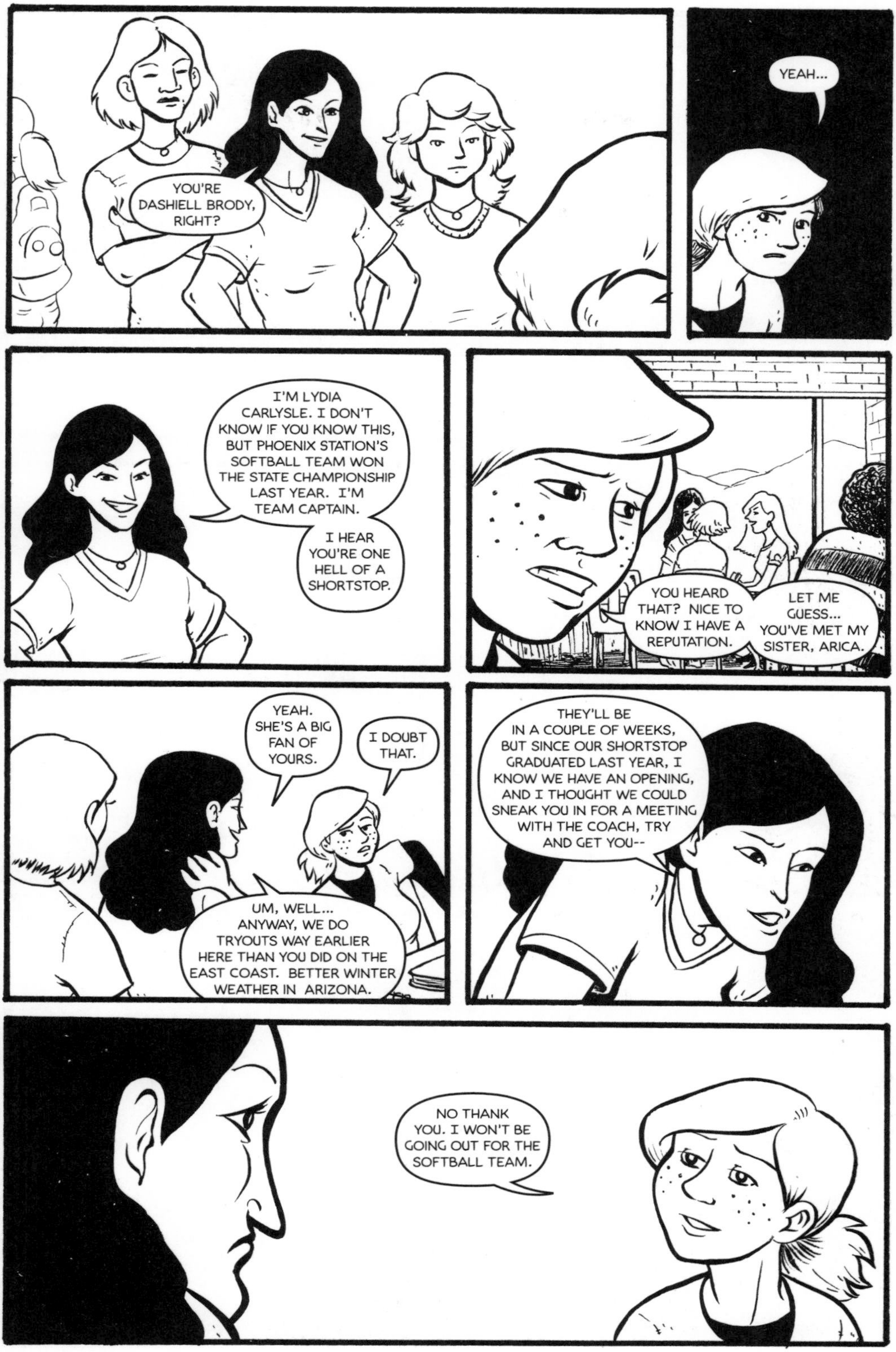

YOU'RE DASHIELL BRODY, RIGHT?
YEAH...
I'M LYDIA CARLYSLE. I DON'T KNOW IF YOU KNOW THIS, BUT PHOENIX STATION'S SOFTBALL TEAM WON THE STATE CHAMPIONSHIP LAST YEAR. I'M TEAM CAPTAIN.
I HEAR YOU'RE ONE HELL OF A SHORTSTOP.
YOU HEARD THAT? NICE TO KNOW I HAVE A REPUTATION.
LET ME GUESS... YOU'VE MET MY SISTER, ARICA.
YEAH. SHE'S A BIG FAN OF YOURS.
I DOUBT THAT.
UM, WELL... ANYWAY, WE DO TRYOUTS WAY EARLIER HERE THAN YOU DID ON THE EAST COAST. BETTER WINTER WEATHER IN ARIZONA.
THEY'LL BE IN A COUPLE OF WEEKS, BUT SINCE OUR SHORTSTOP GRADUATED LAST YEAR, I KNOW WE HAVE AN OPENING, AND I THOUGHT WE COULD SNEAK YOU IN FOR A MEETING WITH THE COACH, TRY AND GET YOU--
NO THANK YOU. I WON'T BE GOING OUT FOR THE SOFTBALL TEAM.

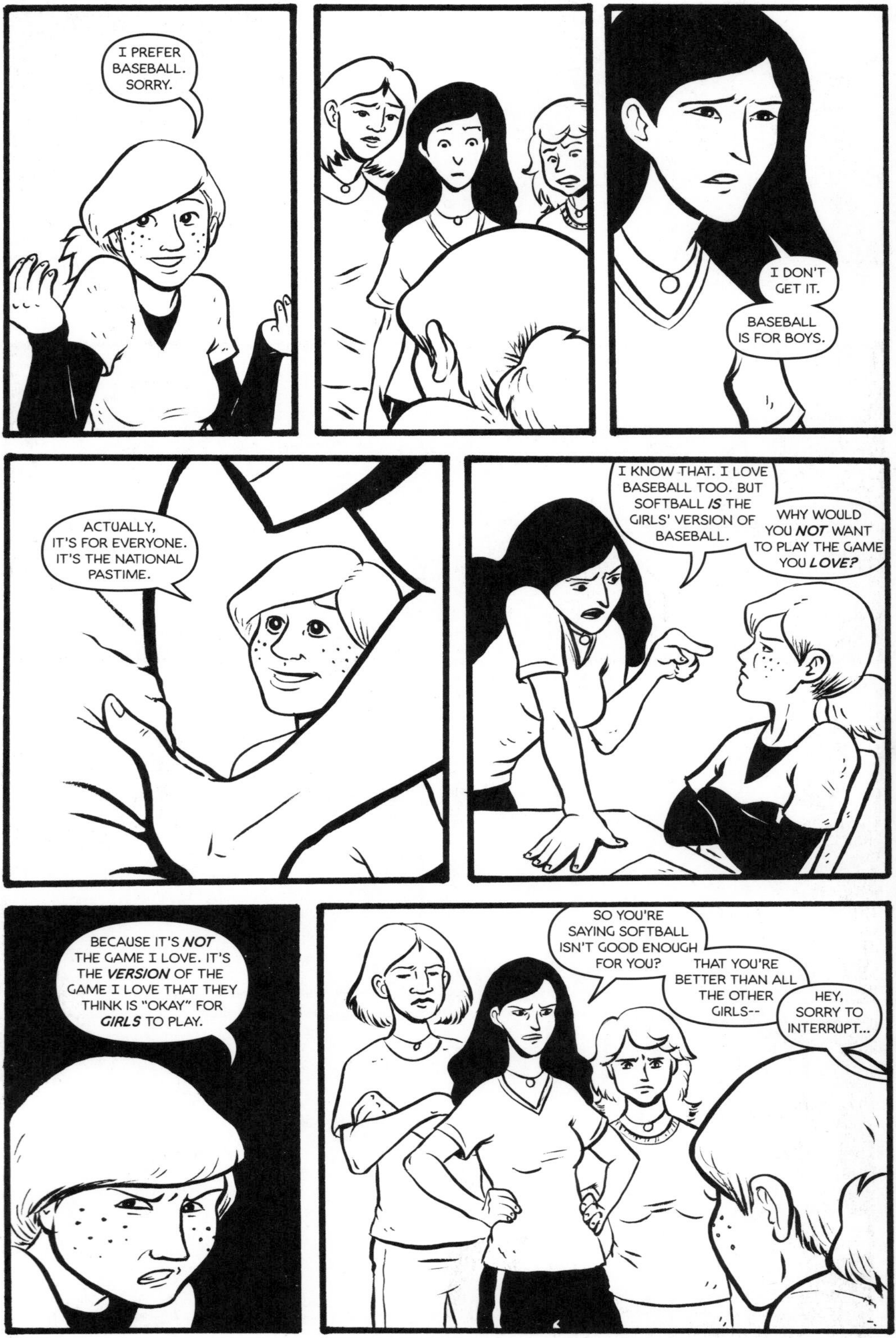
I PREFER BASEBALL. SORRY.
I DON'T GET IT.
BASEBALL IS FOR BOYS.
ACTUALLY, IT'S FOR EVERYONE. IT'S THE NATIONAL PASTIME.
I KNOW THAT. I LOVE BASEBALL TOO. BUT SOFTBALL *IS* THE GIRLS' VERSION OF BASEBALL.
WHY WOULD YOU *NOT* WANT TO PLAY THE GAME YOU *LOVE?*
BECAUSE IT'S *NOT* THE GAME I LOVE. IT'S THE *VERSION* OF THE GAME I LOVE THAT THEY THINK IS "OKAY" FOR *GIRLS* TO PLAY.
SO YOU'RE SAYING SOFTBALL ISN'T GOOD ENOUGH FOR YOU?
THAT YOU'RE BETTER THAN ALL THE OTHER GIRLS--
HEY, SORRY TO INTERRUPT...

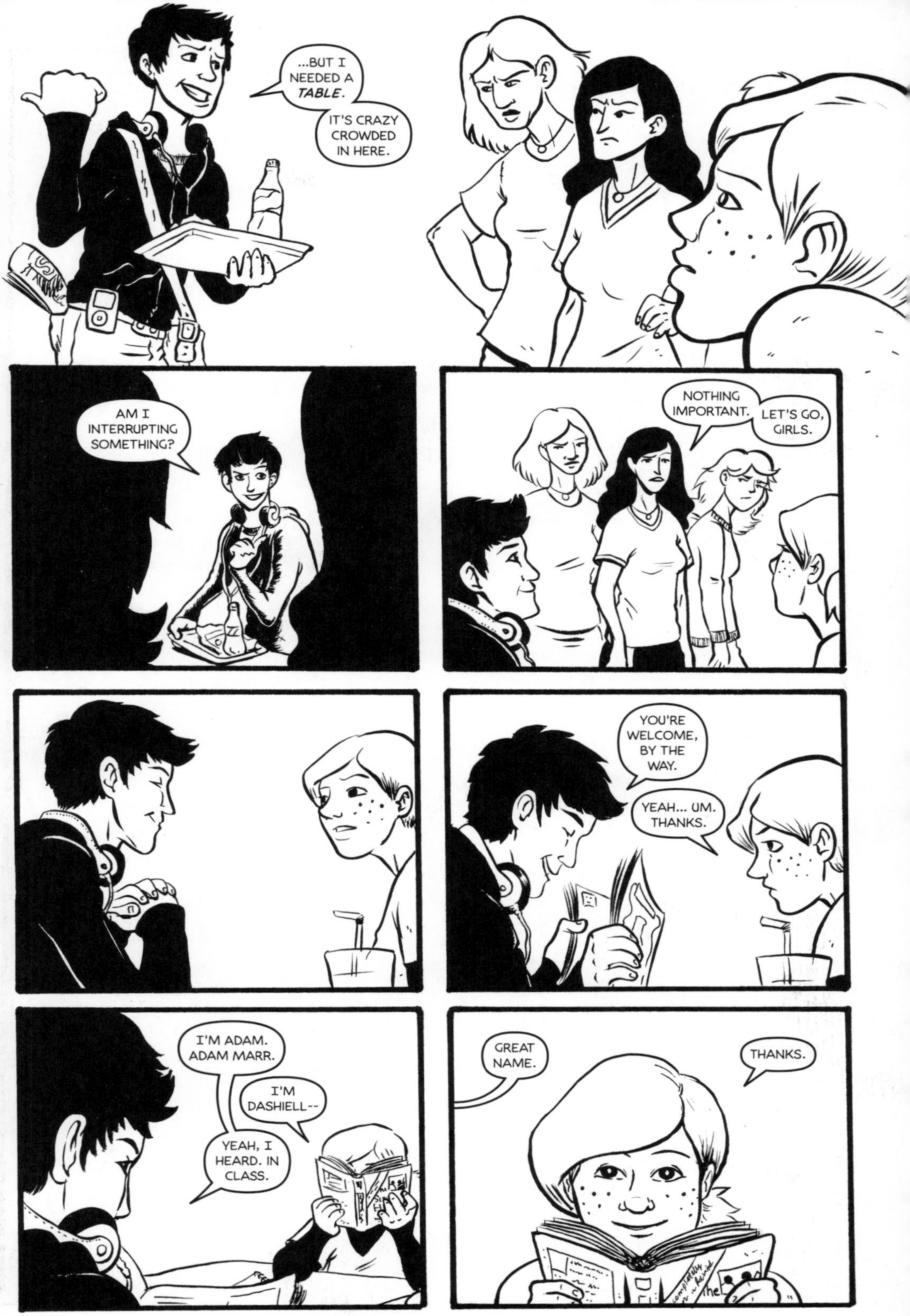

...BUT I NEEDED A *TABLE*.
IT'S CRAZY CROWDED IN HERE.
AM I INTERRUPTING SOMETHING?
NOTHING IMPORTANT.
LET'S GO, GIRLS.
YOU'RE WELCOME, BY THE WAY.
YEAH... UM. THANKS.
I'M ADAM. ADAM MARR.
I'M DASHIELL--
YEAH, I HEARD. IN CLASS.
GREAT NAME.
THANKS.

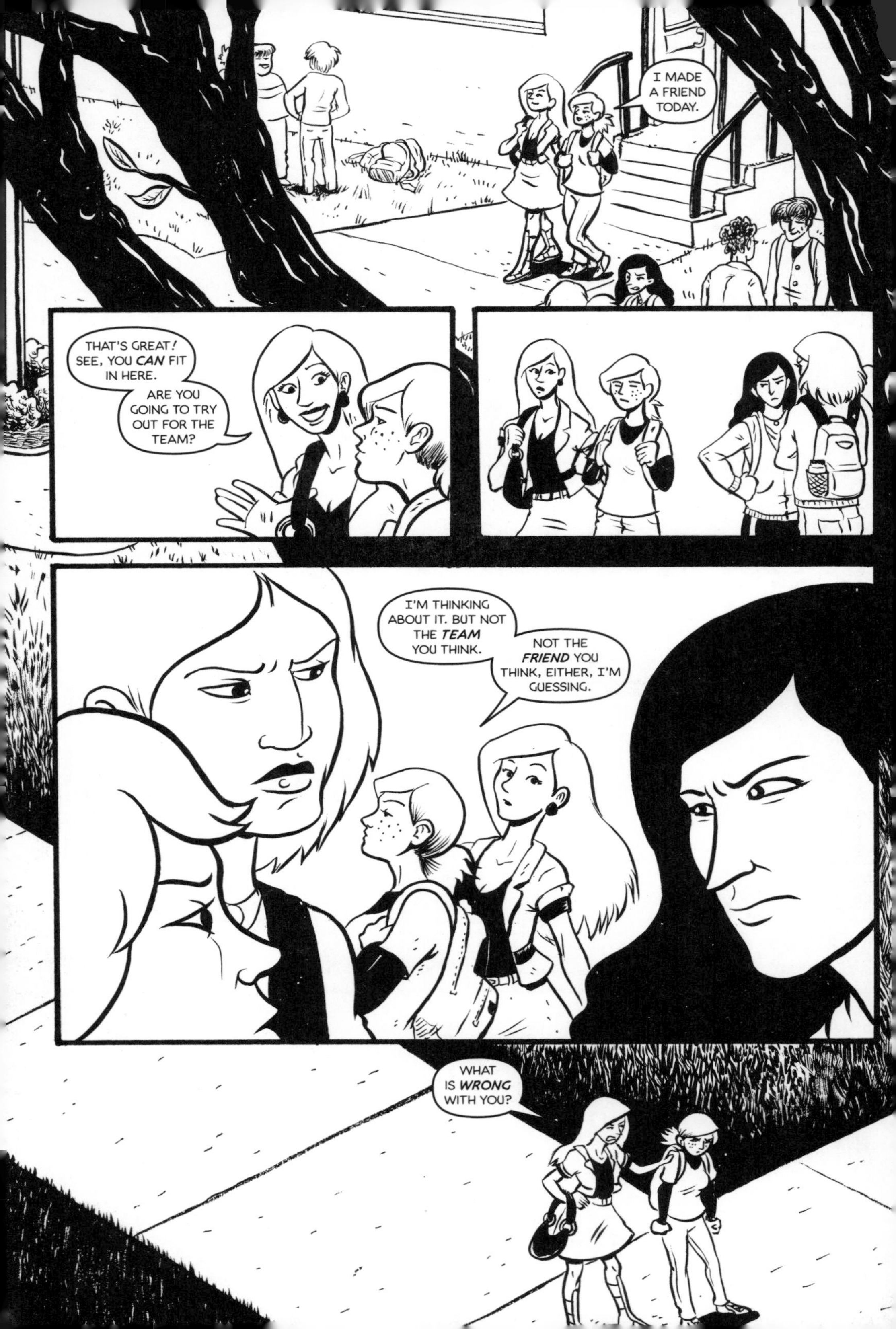
I MADE A FRIEND TODAY.
THAT'S GREAT! SEE, YOU CAN FIT IN HERE.
ARE YOU GOING TO TRY OUT FOR THE TEAM?
I'M THINKING ABOUT IT. BUT NOT THE TEAM YOU THINK.
NOT THE FRIEND YOU THINK, EITHER, I'M GUESSING.
WHAT IS WRONG WITH YOU?

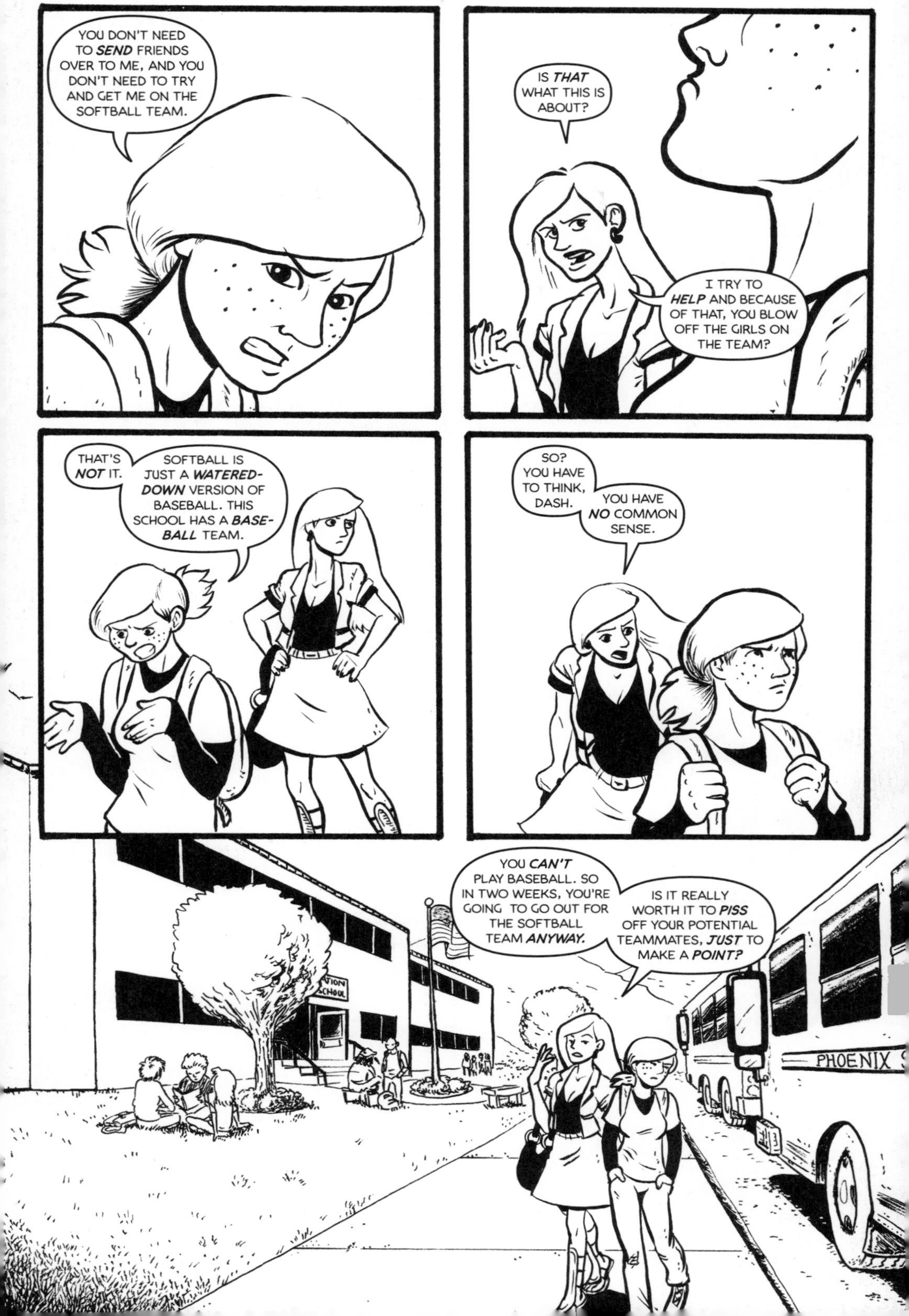
YOU DON'T NEED TO SEND FRIENDS OVER TO ME, AND YOU DON'T NEED TO TRY AND GET ME ON THE SOFTBALL TEAM.
IS THAT WHAT THIS IS ABOUT?
I TRY TO HELP AND BECAUSE OF THAT, YOU BLOW OFF THE GIRLS ON THE TEAM?
THAT'S NOT IT.
SOFTBALL IS JUST A WATERED-DOWN VERSION OF BASEBALL. THIS SCHOOL HAS A BASEBALL TEAM.
SO? YOU HAVE TO THINK, DASH.
YOU HAVE NO COMMON SENSE.
YOU CAN'T PLAY BASEBALL. SO IN TWO WEEKS, YOU'RE GOING TO GO OUT FOR THE SOFTBALL TEAM ANYWAY.
IS IT REALLY WORTH IT TO PISS OFF YOUR POTENTIAL TEAMMATES, JUST TO MAKE A POINT?
PHOENIX

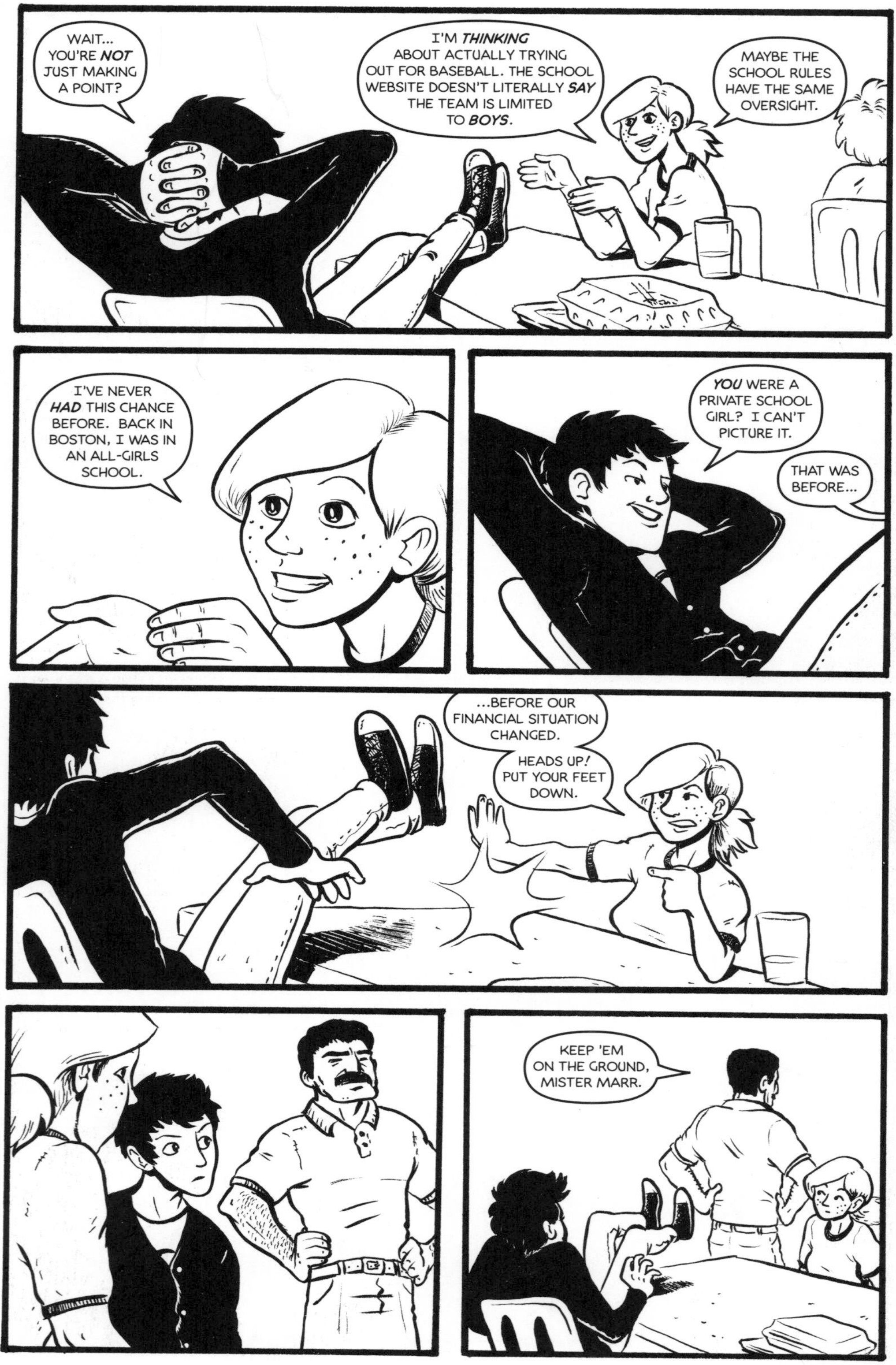
WAIT... YOU'RE **NOT** JUST MAKING A POINT?
I'M **THINKING** ABOUT ACTUALLY TRYING OUT FOR BASEBALL. THE SCHOOL WEBSITE DOESN'T LITERALLY **SAY** THE TEAM IS LIMITED TO **BOYS**.
MAYBE THE SCHOOL RULES HAVE THE SAME OVERSIGHT.
I'VE NEVER **HAD** THIS CHANCE BEFORE. BACK IN BOSTON, I WAS IN AN ALL-GIRLS SCHOOL.
YOU WERE A PRIVATE SCHOOL GIRL? I CAN'T PICTURE IT.
THAT WAS BEFORE...
...BEFORE OUR FINANCIAL SITUATION CHANGED.
HEADS UP! PUT YOUR FEET DOWN.
KEEP 'EM ON THE GROUND, MISTER MARR.

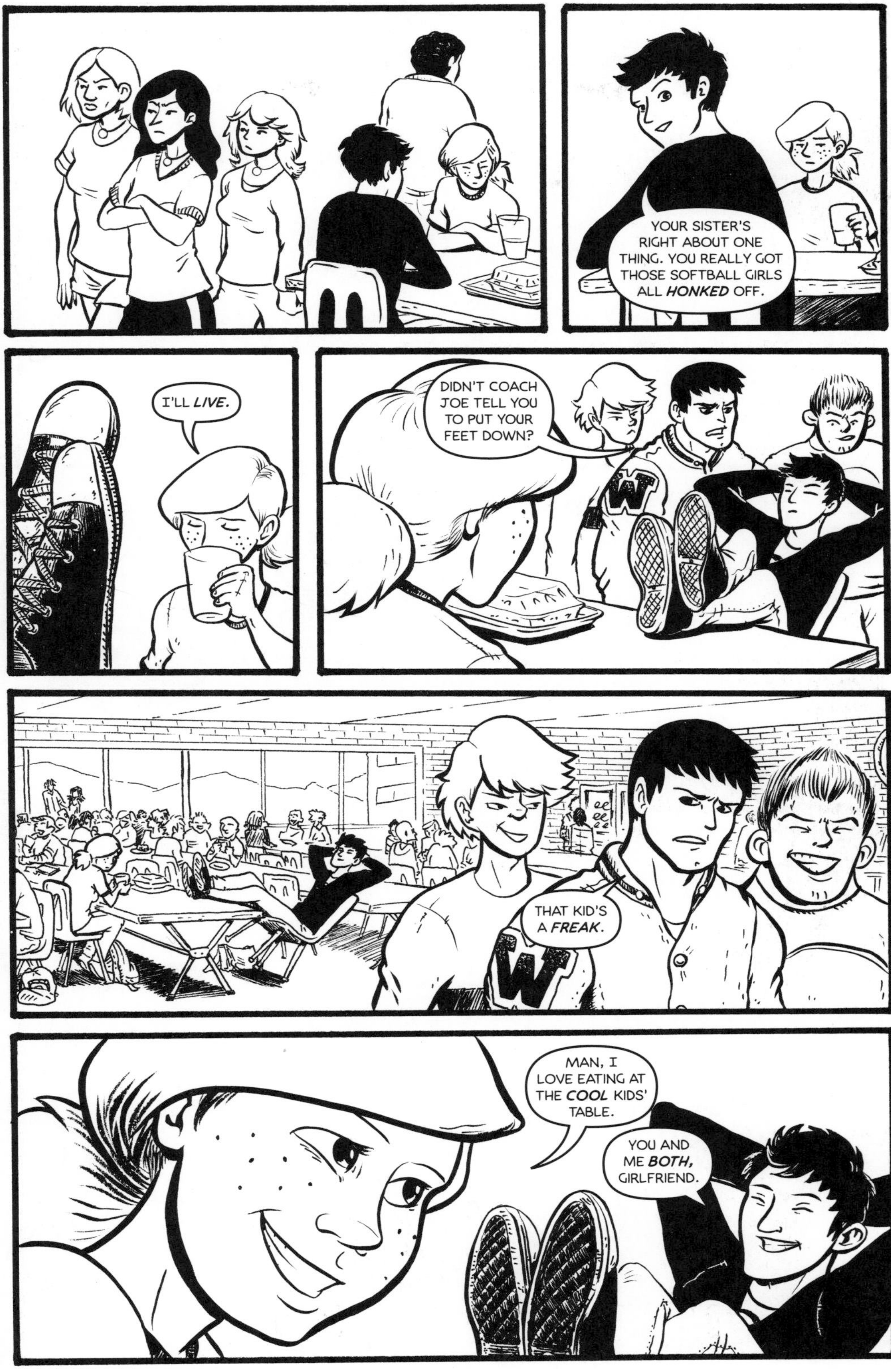
YOUR SISTER'S RIGHT ABOUT ONE THING. YOU REALLY GOT THOSE SOFTBALL GIRLS ALL HONKED OFF.
I'LL LIVE.
DIDN'T COACH JOE TELL YOU TO PUT YOUR FEET DOWN?
THAT KID'S A FREAK.
MAN, I LOVE EATING AT THE COOL KIDS' TABLE.
YOU AND ME BOTH, GIRLFRIEND.

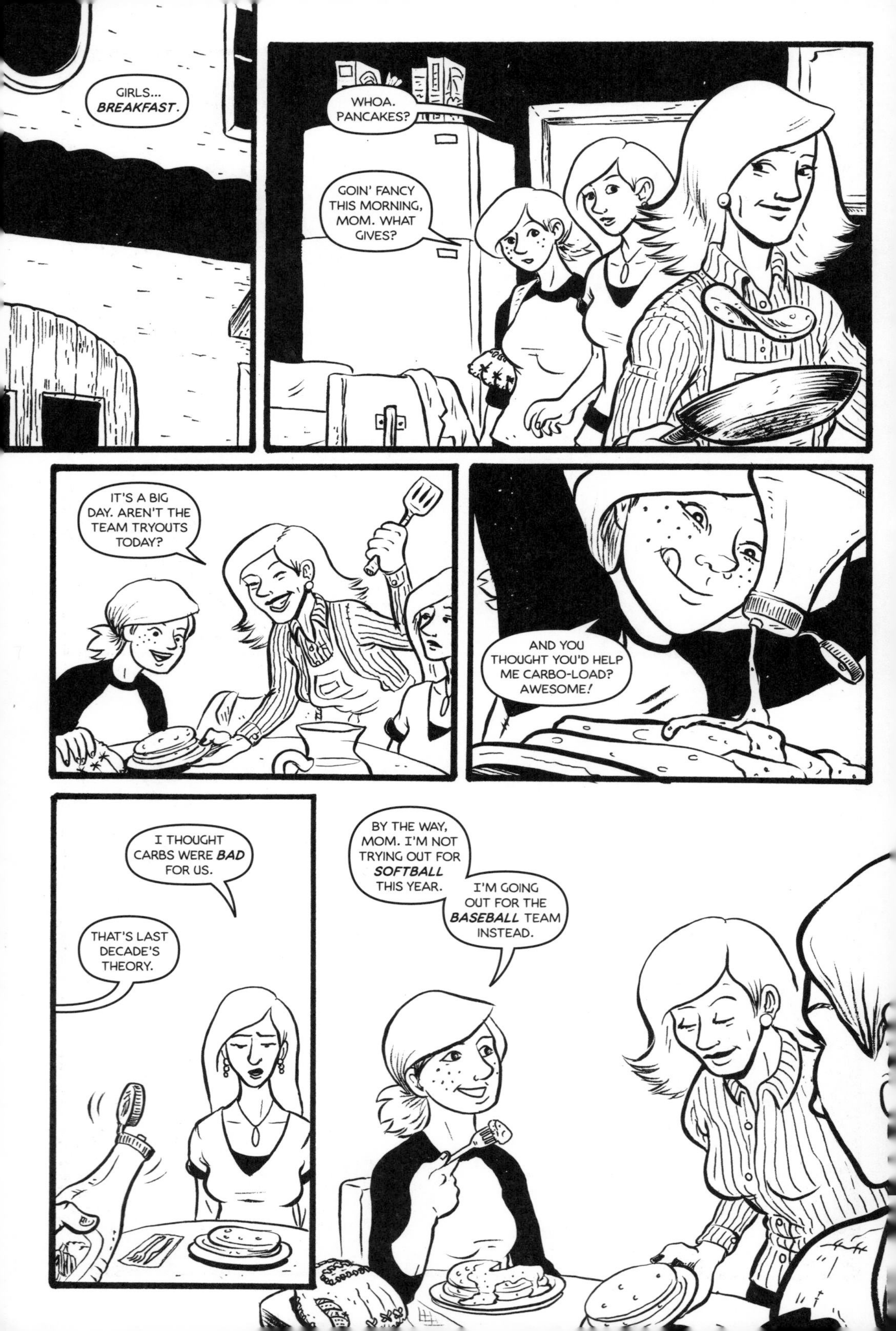
GIRLS... **BREAKFAST**.
WHOA. PANCAKES?
GOIN' FANCY THIS MORNING, MOM. WHAT GIVES?
IT'S A BIG DAY. AREN'T THE TEAM TRYOUTS TODAY?
AND YOU THOUGHT YOU'D HELP ME CARBO-LOAD? AWESOME!
I THOUGHT CARBS WERE **BAD** FOR US.
THAT'S LAST DECADE'S THEORY.
BY THE WAY, MOM. I'M NOT TRYING OUT FOR **SOFTBALL** THIS YEAR.
I'M GOING OUT FOR THE **BASEBALL** TEAM INSTEAD.

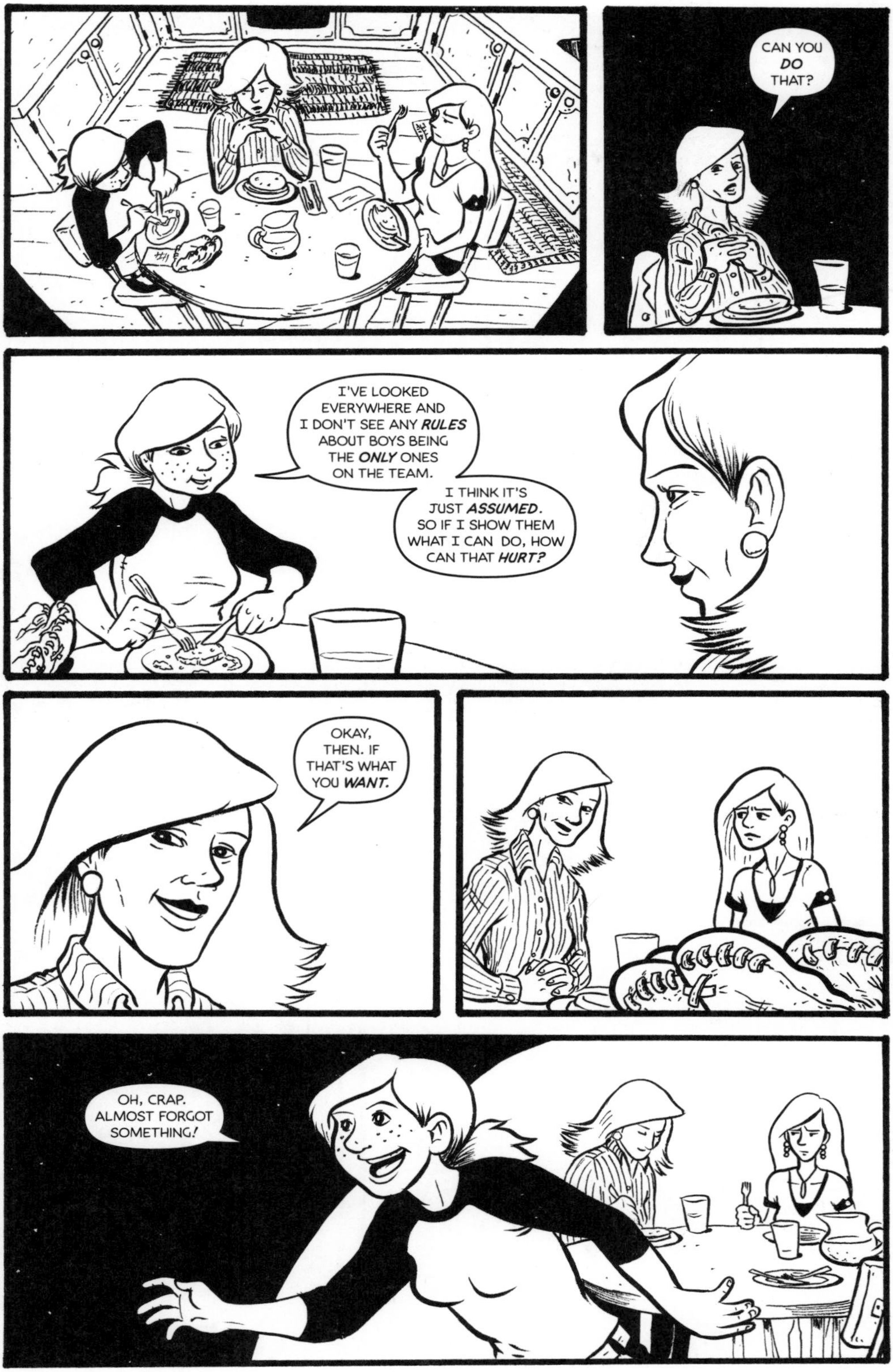
CAN YOU DO THAT?
I'VE LOOKED EVERYWHERE AND I DON'T SEE ANY RULES ABOUT BOYS BEING THE ONLY ONES ON THE TEAM.
I THINK IT'S JUST ASSUMED. SO IF I SHOW THEM WHAT I CAN DO, HOW CAN THAT HURT?
OKAY, THEN. IF THAT'S WHAT YOU WANT.
OH, CRAP. ALMOST FORGOT SOMETHING!

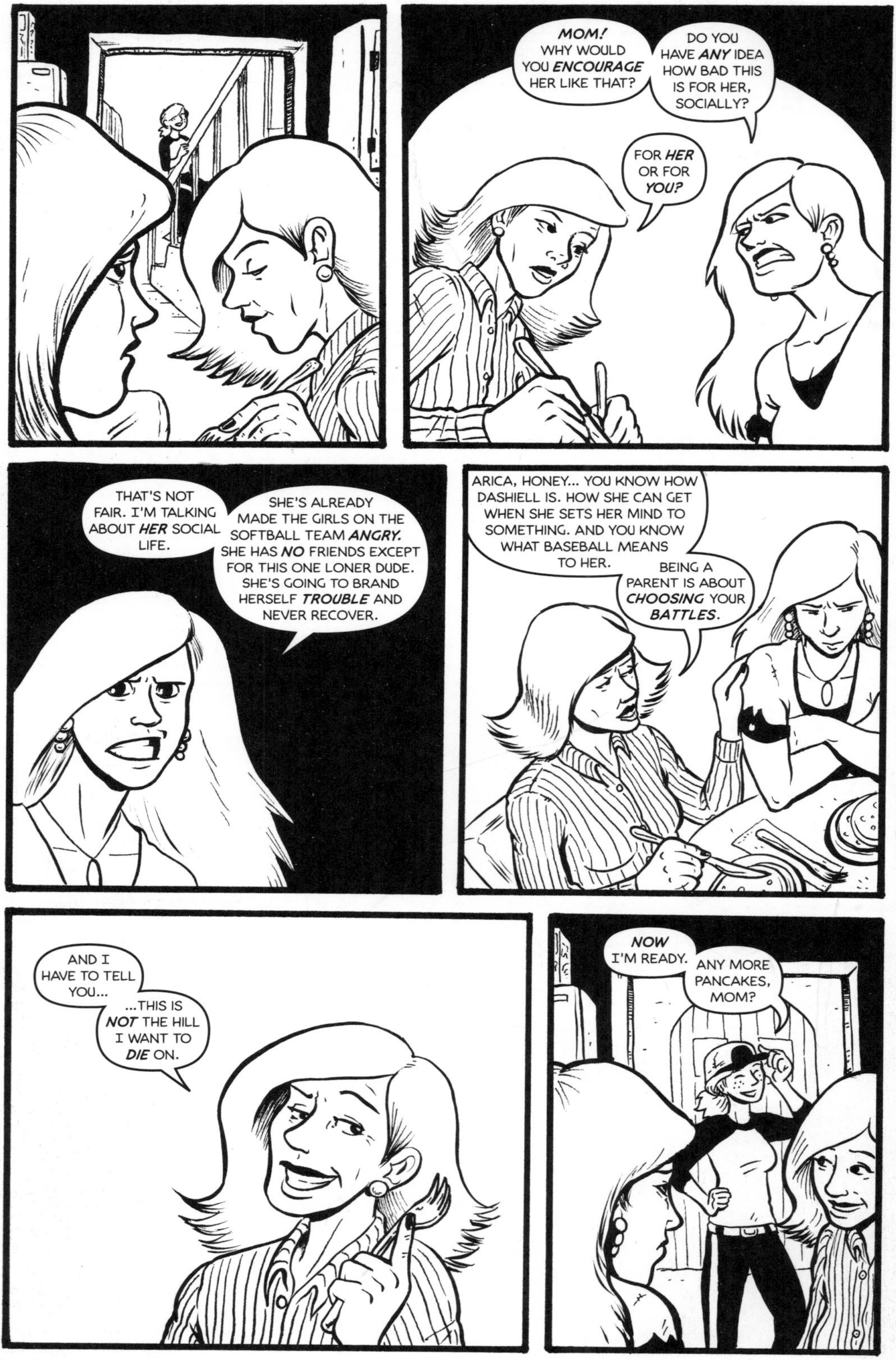
MOM! WHY WOULD YOU ENCOURAGE HER LIKE THAT?
DO YOU HAVE ANY IDEA HOW BAD THIS IS FOR HER, SOCIALLY?
FOR HER OR FOR YOU?
THAT'S NOT FAIR. I'M TALKING ABOUT HER SOCIAL LIFE.
SHE'S ALREADY MADE THE GIRLS ON THE SOFTBALL TEAM ANGRY. SHE HAS NO FRIENDS EXCEPT FOR THIS ONE LONER DUDE. SHE'S GOING TO BRAND HERSELF TROUBLE AND NEVER RECOVER.
ARICA, HONEY... YOU KNOW HOW DASHIELL IS. HOW SHE CAN GET WHEN SHE SETS HER MIND TO SOMETHING. AND YOU KNOW WHAT BASEBALL MEANS TO HER.
BEING A PARENT IS ABOUT CHOOSING YOUR BATTLES.
AND I HAVE TO TELL YOU...
...THIS IS NOT THE HILL I WANT TO DIE ON.
NOW I'M READY.
ANY MORE PANCAKES, MOM?

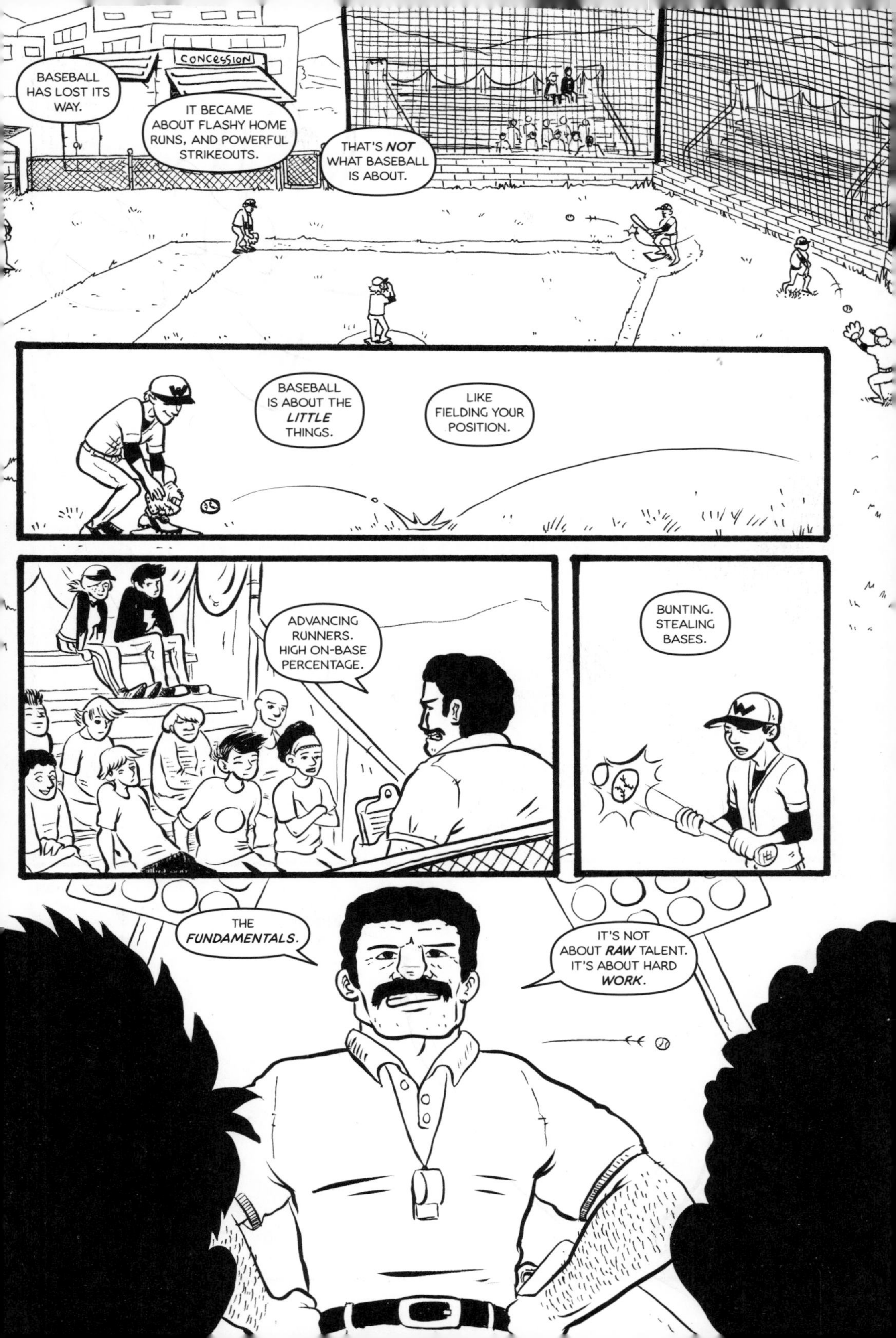
CONCESSION
BASEBALL HAS LOST ITS WAY.
IT BECAME ABOUT FLASHY HOME RUNS, AND POWERFUL STRIKEOUTS.
THAT'S *NOT* WHAT BASEBALL IS ABOUT.
BASEBALL IS ABOUT THE *LITTLE* THINGS.
LIKE FIELDING YOUR POSITION.
ADVANCING RUNNERS. HIGH ON-BASE PERCENTAGE.
BUNTING. STEALING BASES.
THE *FUNDAMENTALS*.
IT'S NOT ABOUT *RAW* TALENT. IT'S ABOUT HARD *WORK*.

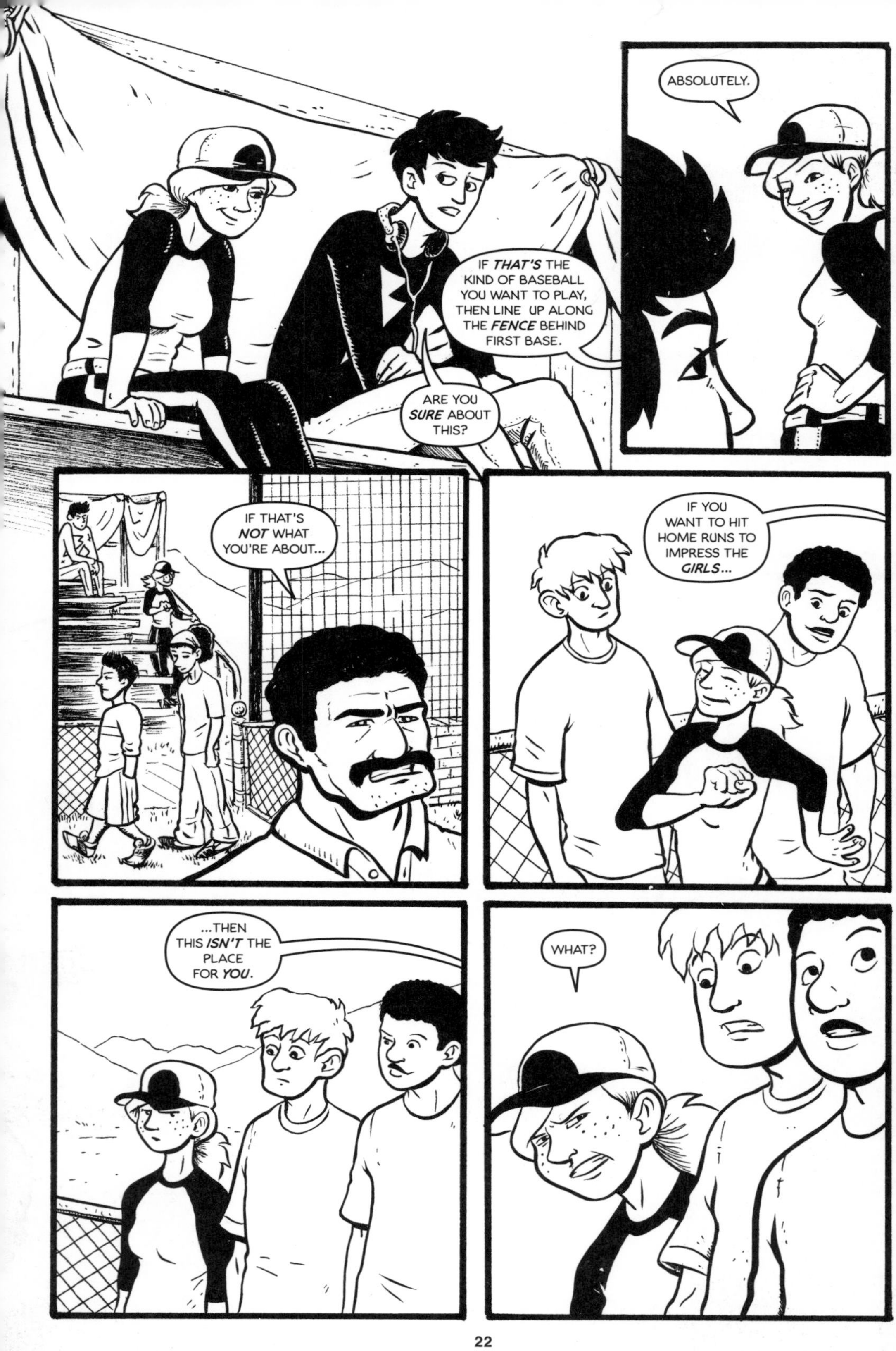
IF *THAT'S* THE KIND OF BASEBALL YOU WANT TO PLAY, THEN LINE UP ALONG THE *FENCE* BEHIND FIRST BASE.
ARE YOU *SURE* ABOUT THIS?
ABSOLUTELY.
IF THAT'S *NOT* WHAT YOU'RE ABOUT...
IF YOU WANT TO HIT HOME RUNS TO IMPRESS THE *GIRLS*...
...THEN THIS *ISN'T* THE PLACE FOR *YOU*.
WHAT?

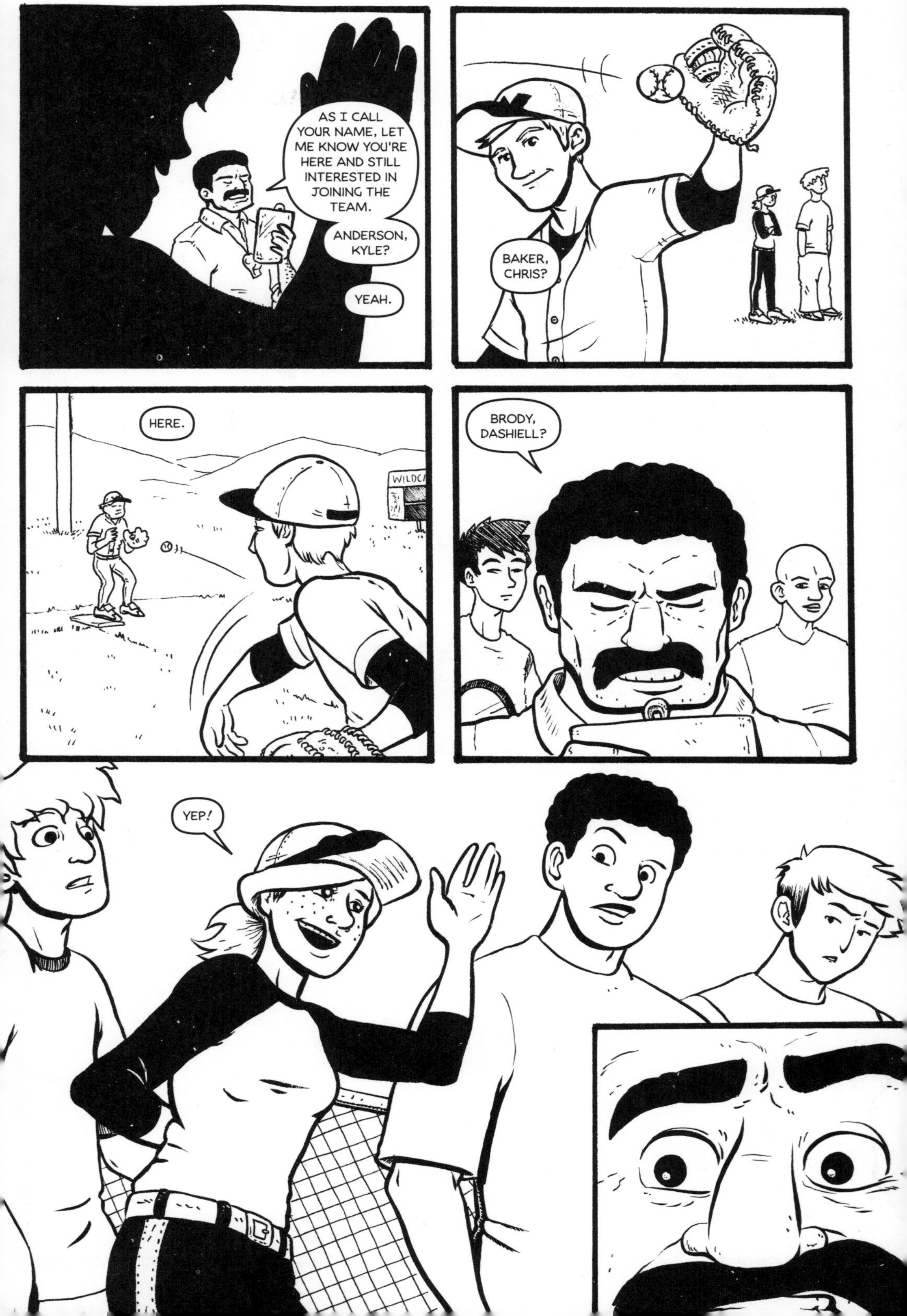

AS I CALL YOUR NAME, LET ME KNOW YOU'RE HERE AND STILL INTERESTED IN JOINING THE TEAM.
ANDERSON, KYLE?
YEAH.
BAKER, CHRIS?
HERE.
BRODY, DASHIELL?
YEP!

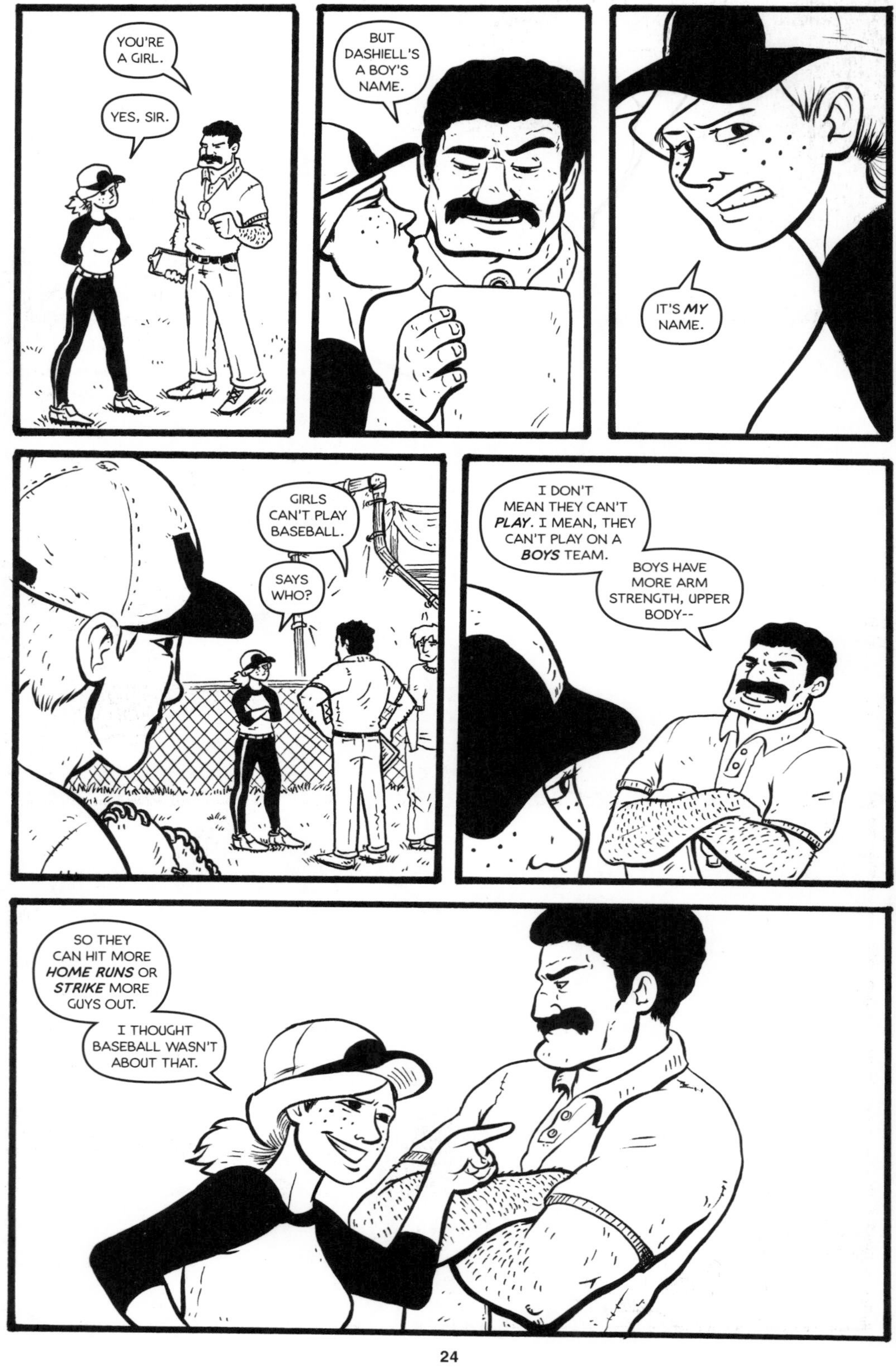
YOU'RE A GIRL.
YES, SIR.
BUT DASHIELL'S A BOY'S NAME.
IT'S *MY* NAME.
GIRLS CAN'T PLAY BASEBALL.
SAYS WHO?
I DON'T MEAN THEY CAN'T *PLAY*. I MEAN, THEY CAN'T PLAY ON A *BOYS* TEAM.
BOYS HAVE MORE ARM STRENGTH, UPPER BODY--
SO THEY CAN HIT MORE *HOME RUNS* OR *STRIKE* MORE GUYS OUT.
I THOUGHT BASEBALL WASN'T ABOUT THAT.

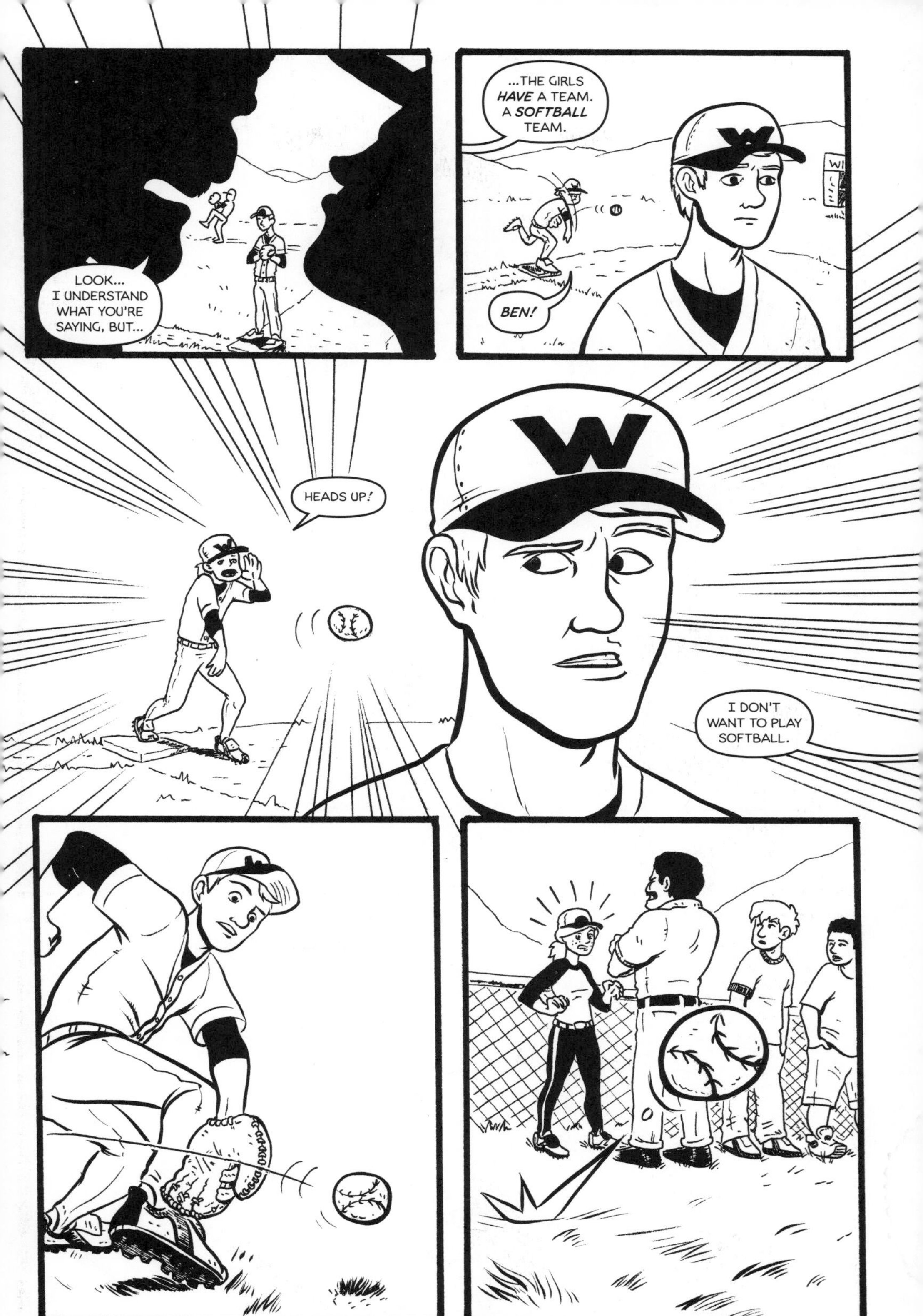
LOOK... I UNDERSTAND WHAT YOU'RE SAYING, BUT...
...THE GIRLS *HAVE* A TEAM. A *SOFTBALL* TEAM.
BEN!
HEADS UP!
I DON'T WANT TO PLAY SOFTBALL.

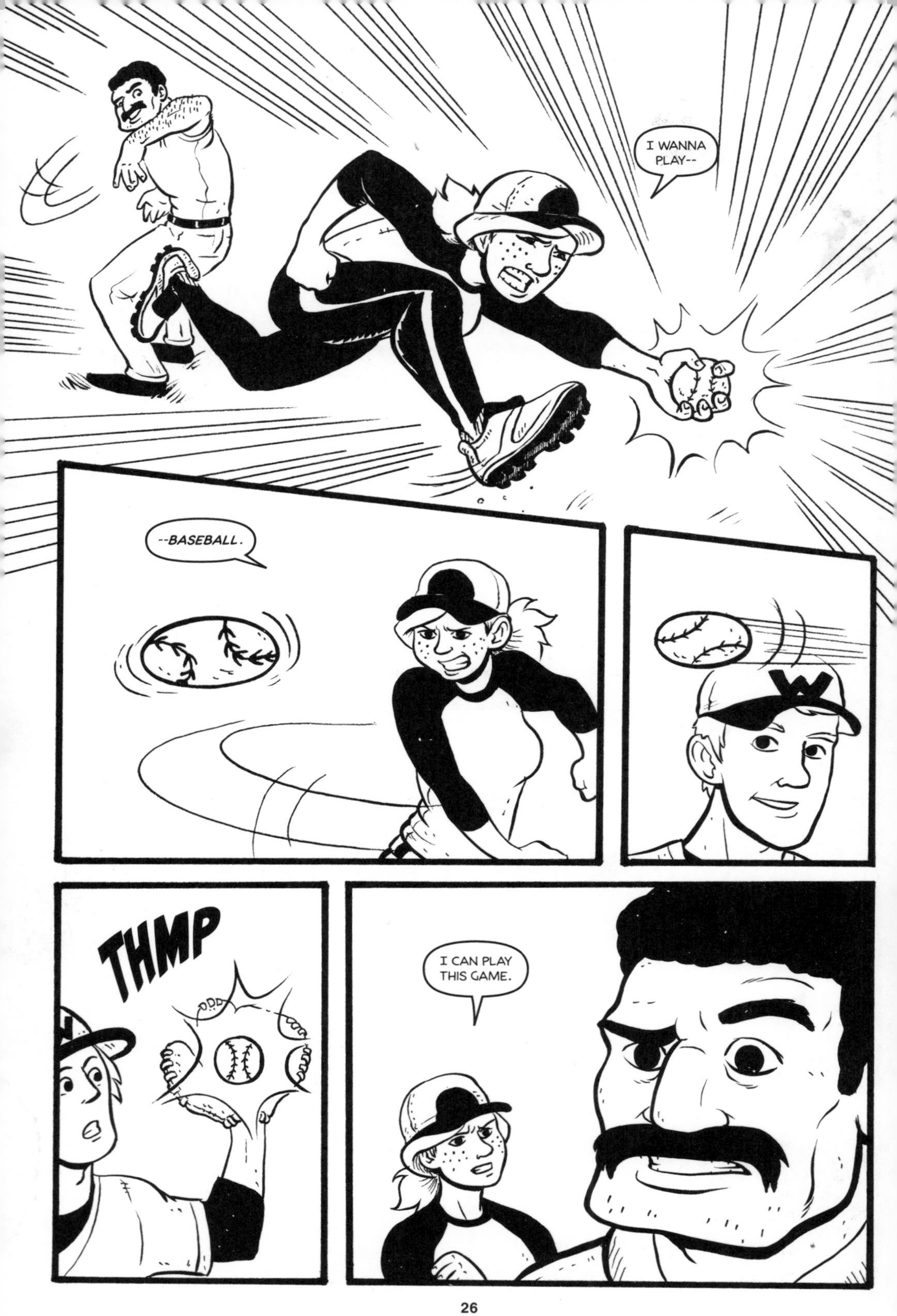
I WANNA PLAY--
--BASEBALL.
THMP
I CAN PLAY THIS GAME.

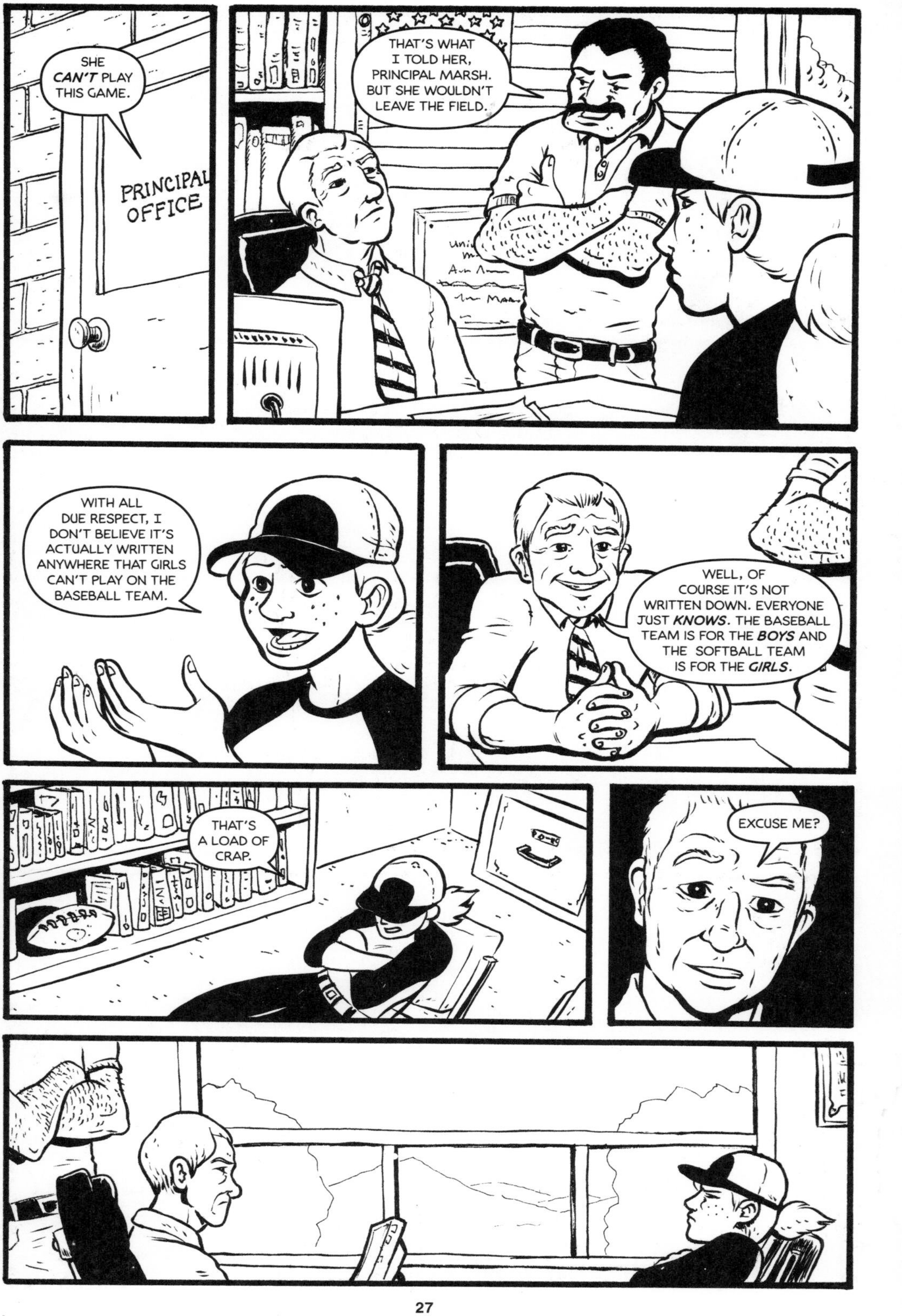
SHE CAN'T PLAY THIS GAME.
PRINCIPAL OFFICE
THAT'S WHAT I TOLD HER, PRINCIPAL MARSH. BUT SHE WOULDN'T LEAVE THE FIELD.
WITH ALL DUE RESPECT, I DON'T BELIEVE IT'S ACTUALLY WRITTEN ANYWHERE THAT GIRLS CAN'T PLAY ON THE BASEBALL TEAM.
WELL, OF COURSE IT'S NOT WRITTEN DOWN. EVERYONE JUST KNOWS. THE BASEBALL TEAM IS FOR THE BOYS AND THE SOFTBALL TEAM IS FOR THE GIRLS.
THAT'S A LOAD OF CRAP.
EXCUSE ME?

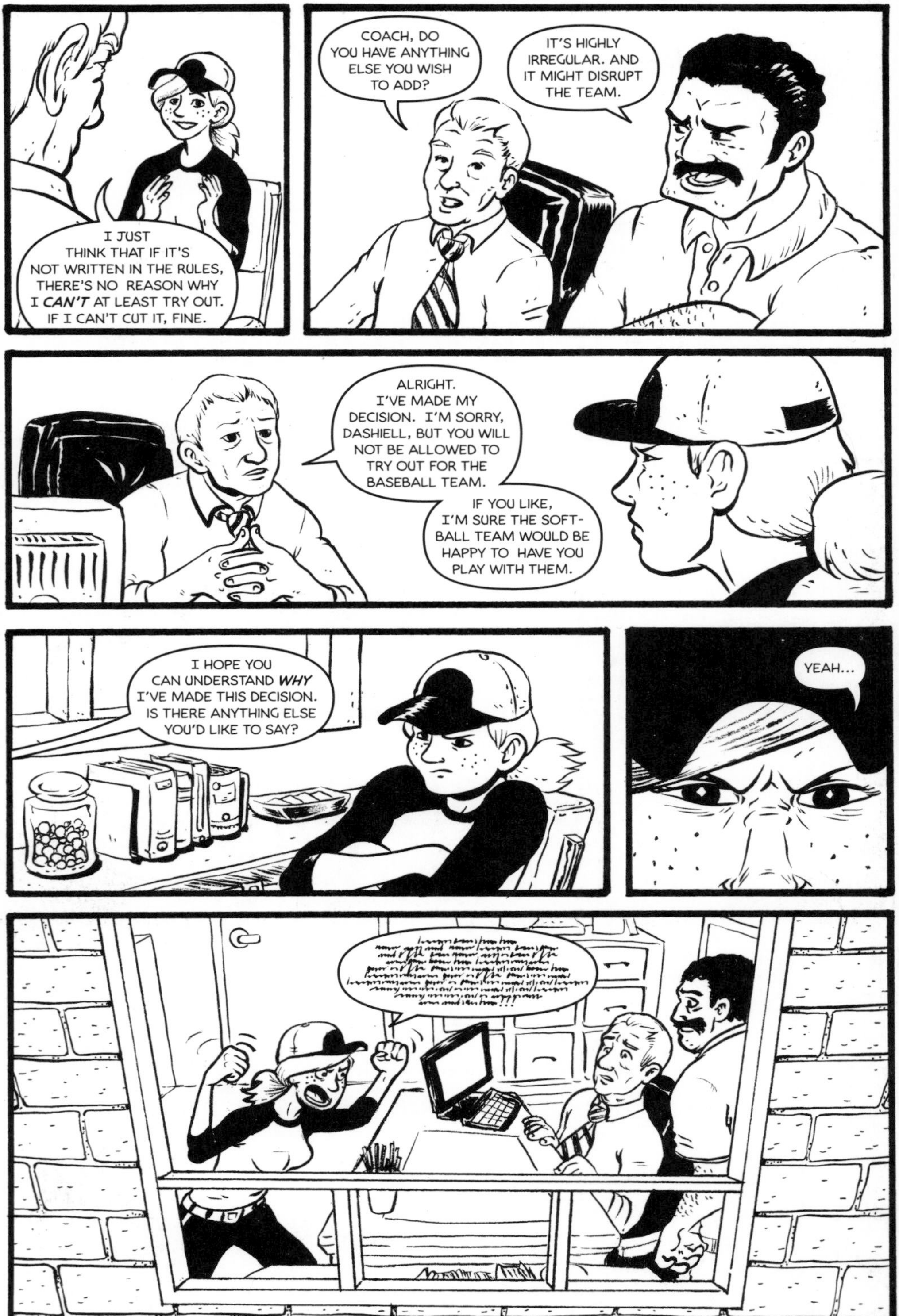
I JUST THINK THAT IF IT'S NOT WRITTEN IN THE RULES, THERE'S NO REASON WHY I *CAN'T* AT LEAST TRY OUT. IF I CAN'T CUT IT, FINE.
COACH, DO YOU HAVE ANYTHING ELSE YOU WISH TO ADD?
IT'S HIGHLY IRREGULAR. AND IT MIGHT DISRUPT THE TEAM.
ALRIGHT. I'VE MADE MY DECISION. I'M SORRY, DASHIELL, BUT YOU WILL NOT BE ALLOWED TO TRY OUT FOR THE BASEBALL TEAM.
IF YOU LIKE, I'M SURE THE SOFT-BALL TEAM WOULD BE HAPPY TO HAVE YOU PLAY WITH THEM.
I HOPE YOU CAN UNDERSTAND *WHY* I'VE MADE THIS DECISION. IS THERE ANYTHING ELSE YOU'D LIKE TO SAY?
YEAH...

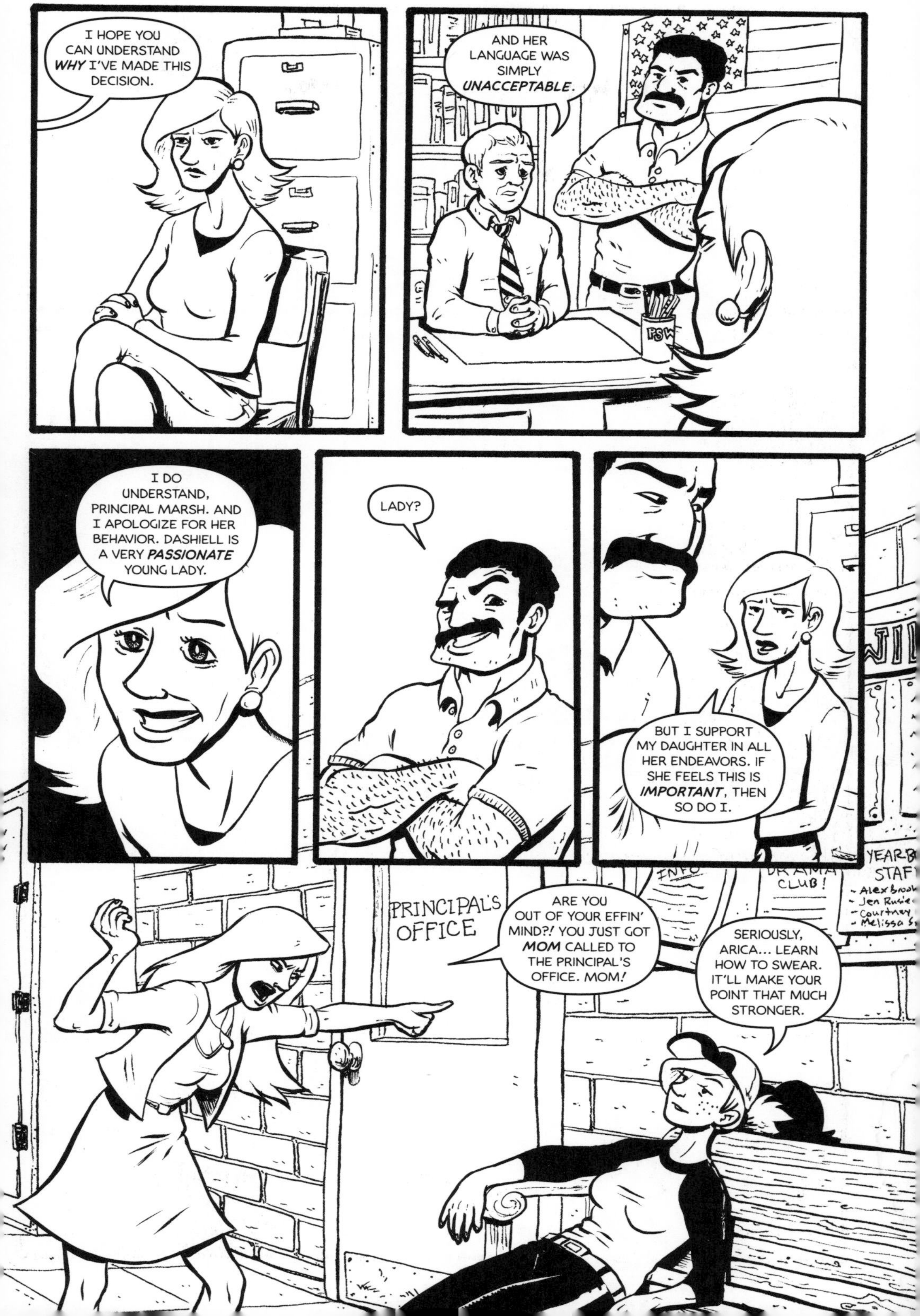

I HOPE YOU CAN UNDERSTAND *WHY* I'VE MADE THIS DECISION.
AND HER LANGUAGE WAS SIMPLY *UNACCEPTABLE*.
I DO UNDERSTAND, PRINCIPAL MARSH. AND I APOLOGIZE FOR HER BEHAVIOR. DASHIELL IS A VERY *PASSIONATE* YOUNG LADY.
LADY?
BUT I SUPPORT MY DAUGHTER IN ALL HER ENDEAVORS. IF SHE FEELS THIS IS *IMPORTANT*, THEN SO DO I.
PRINCIPAL'S OFFICE
INFO
ARE YOU OUT OF YOUR EFFIN' MIND?! YOU JUST GOT *MOM* CALLED TO THE PRINCIPAL'S OFFICE. MOM!
SERIOUSLY, ARICA... LEARN HOW TO SWEAR. IT'LL MAKE YOUR POINT THAT MUCH STRONGER.

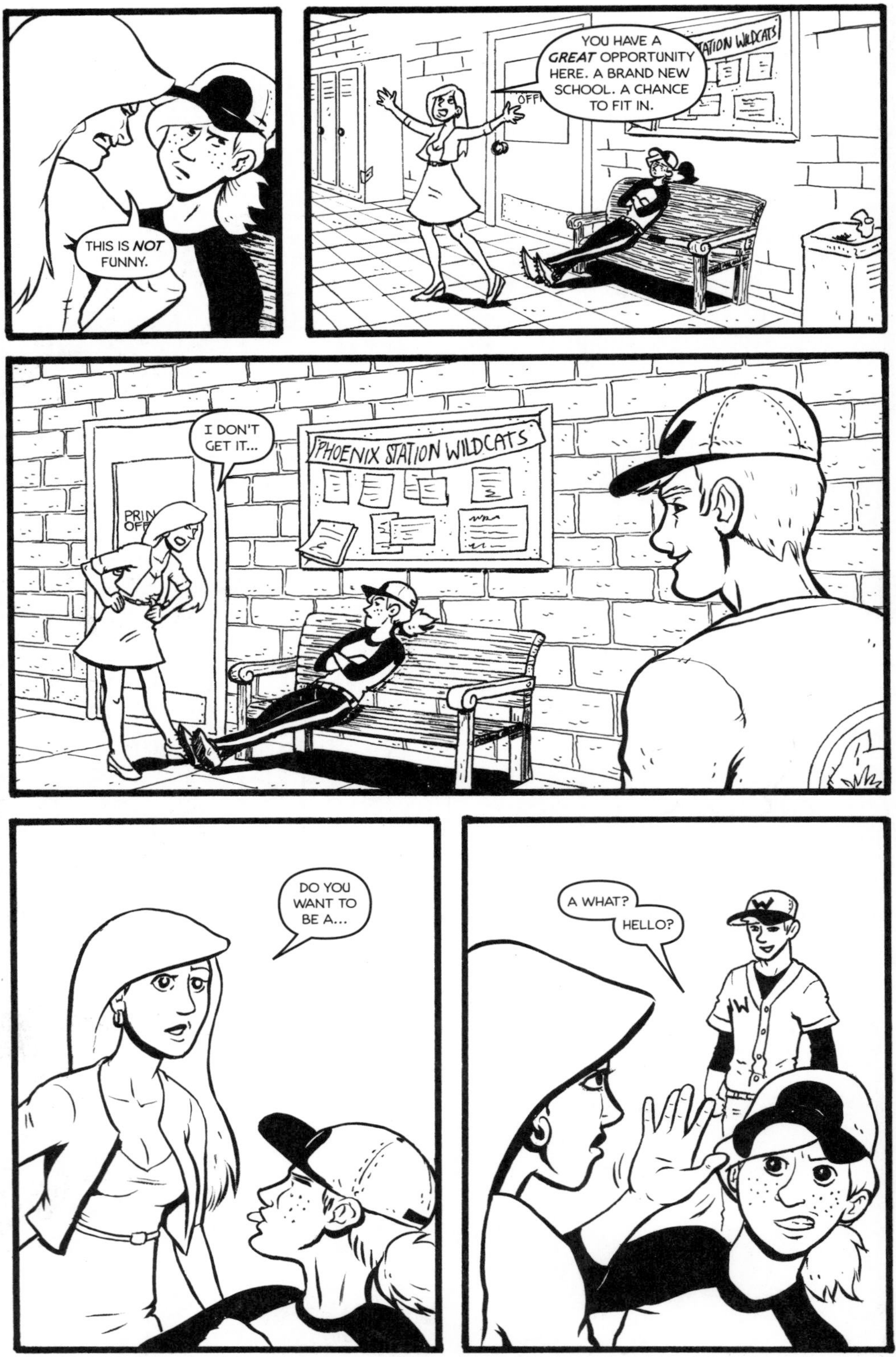
THIS IS NOT FUNNY.
YOU HAVE A GREAT OPPORTUNITY HERE. A BRAND NEW SCHOOL. A CHANCE TO FIT IN.
I DON'T GET IT...
PHOENIX STATION WILDCATS
DO YOU WANT TO BE A...
A WHAT?
HELLO?

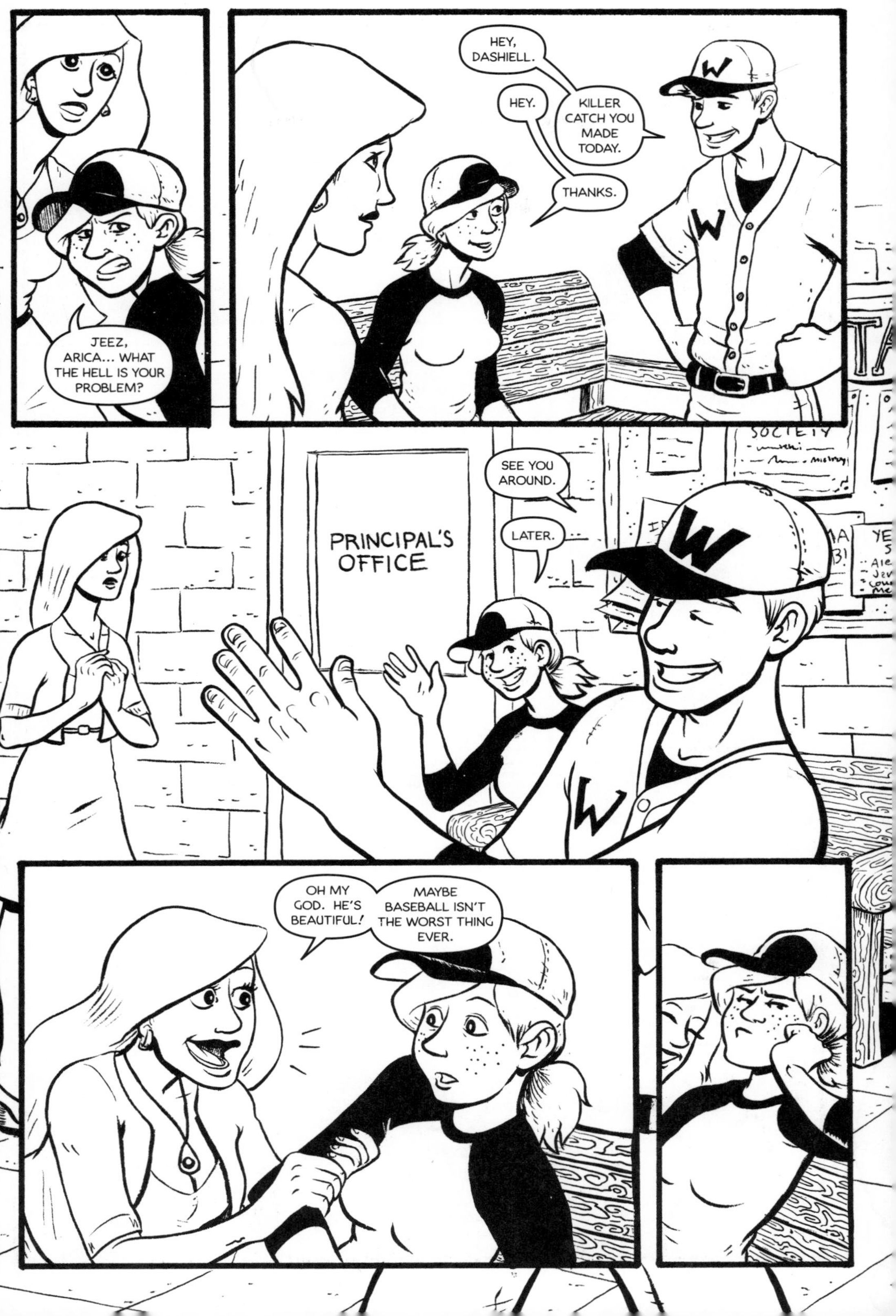
JEEZ, ARICA... WHAT THE HELL IS YOUR PROBLEM?
HEY, DASHIELL.
KILLER CATCH YOU MADE TODAY.
HEY.
THANKS.
SEE YOU AROUND.
LATER.
PRINCIPAL'S OFFICE
OH MY GOD. HE'S BEAUTIFUL!
MAYBE BASEBALL ISN'T THE WORST THING EVER.

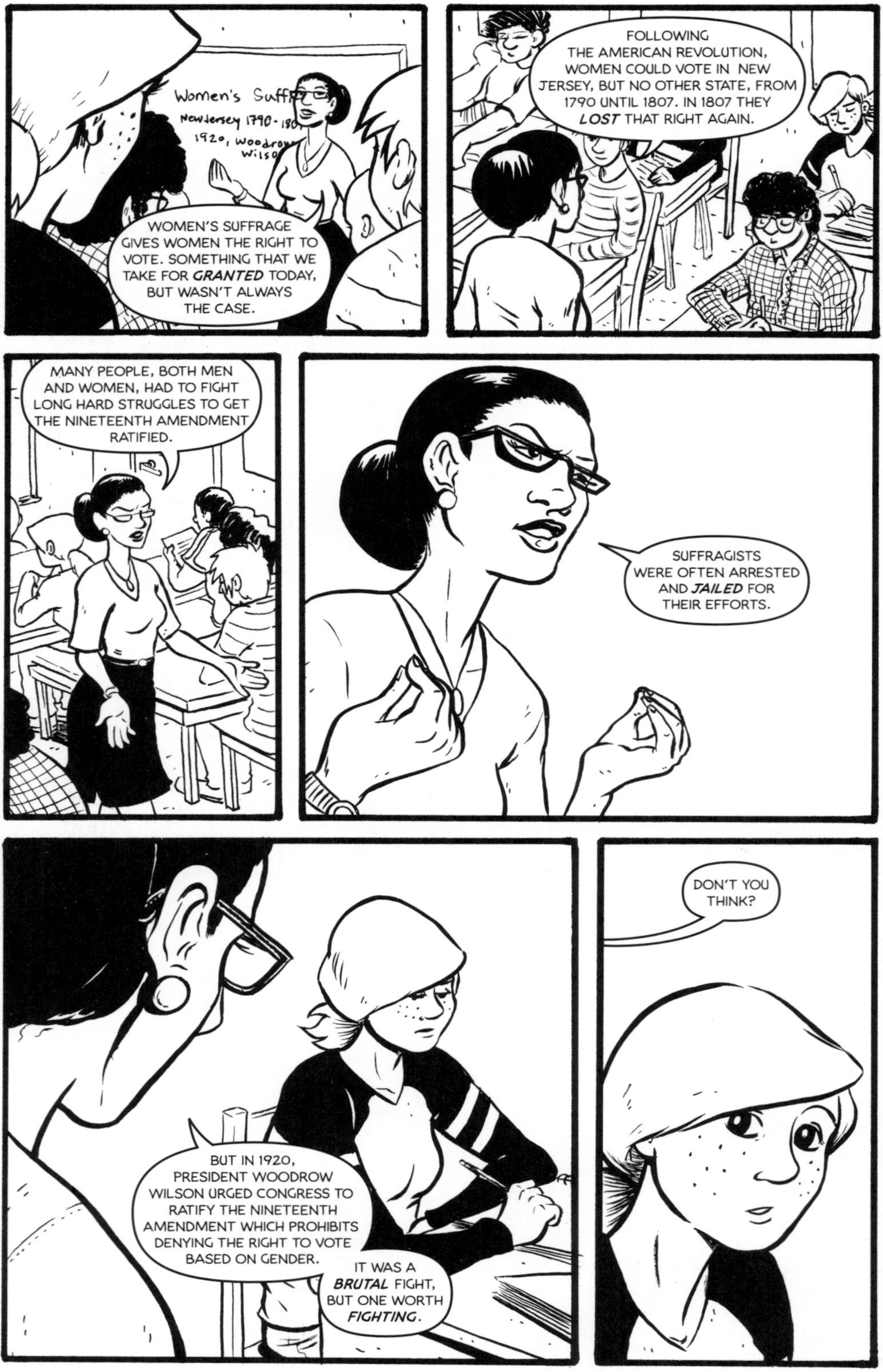
WOMEN'S SUFFRAGE GIVES WOMEN THE RIGHT TO VOTE. SOMETHING THAT WE TAKE FOR *GRANTED* TODAY, BUT WASN'T ALWAYS THE CASE.
FOLLOWING THE AMERICAN REVOLUTION, WOMEN COULD VOTE IN NEW JERSEY, BUT NO OTHER STATE, FROM 1790 UNTIL 1807. IN 1807 THEY *LOST* THAT RIGHT AGAIN.
MANY PEOPLE, BOTH MEN AND WOMEN, HAD TO FIGHT LONG HARD STRUGGLES TO GET THE NINETEENTH AMENDMENT RATIFIED.
SUFFRAGISTS WERE OFTEN ARRESTED AND *JAILED* FOR THEIR EFFORTS.
BUT IN 1920, PRESIDENT WOODROW WILSON URGED CONGRESS TO RATIFY THE NINETEENTH AMENDMENT WHICH PROHIBITS DENYING THE RIGHT TO VOTE BASED ON GENDER.
IT WAS A *BRUTAL* FIGHT, BUT ONE WORTH *FIGHTING*.
DON'T YOU THINK?

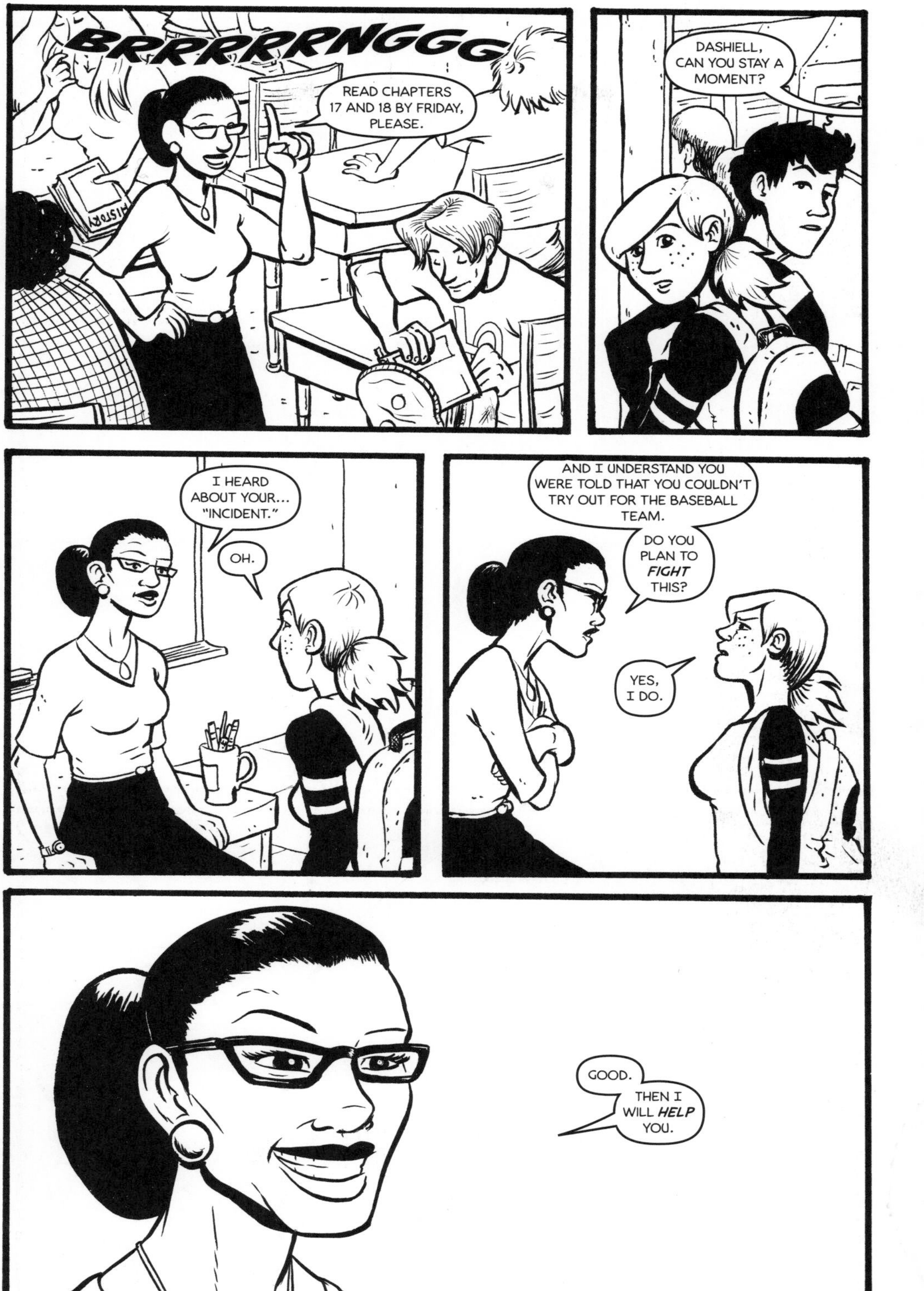
BRRRRRNGGG
READ CHAPTERS 17 AND 18 BY FRIDAY, PLEASE.
HISTORY
DASHIELL, CAN YOU STAY A MOMENT?
I HEARD ABOUT YOUR... "INCIDENT."
OH.
AND I UNDERSTAND YOU WERE TOLD THAT YOU COULDN'T TRY OUT FOR THE BASEBALL TEAM.
DO YOU PLAN TO *FIGHT* THIS?
YES, I DO.
GOOD.
THEN I WILL *HELP* YOU.

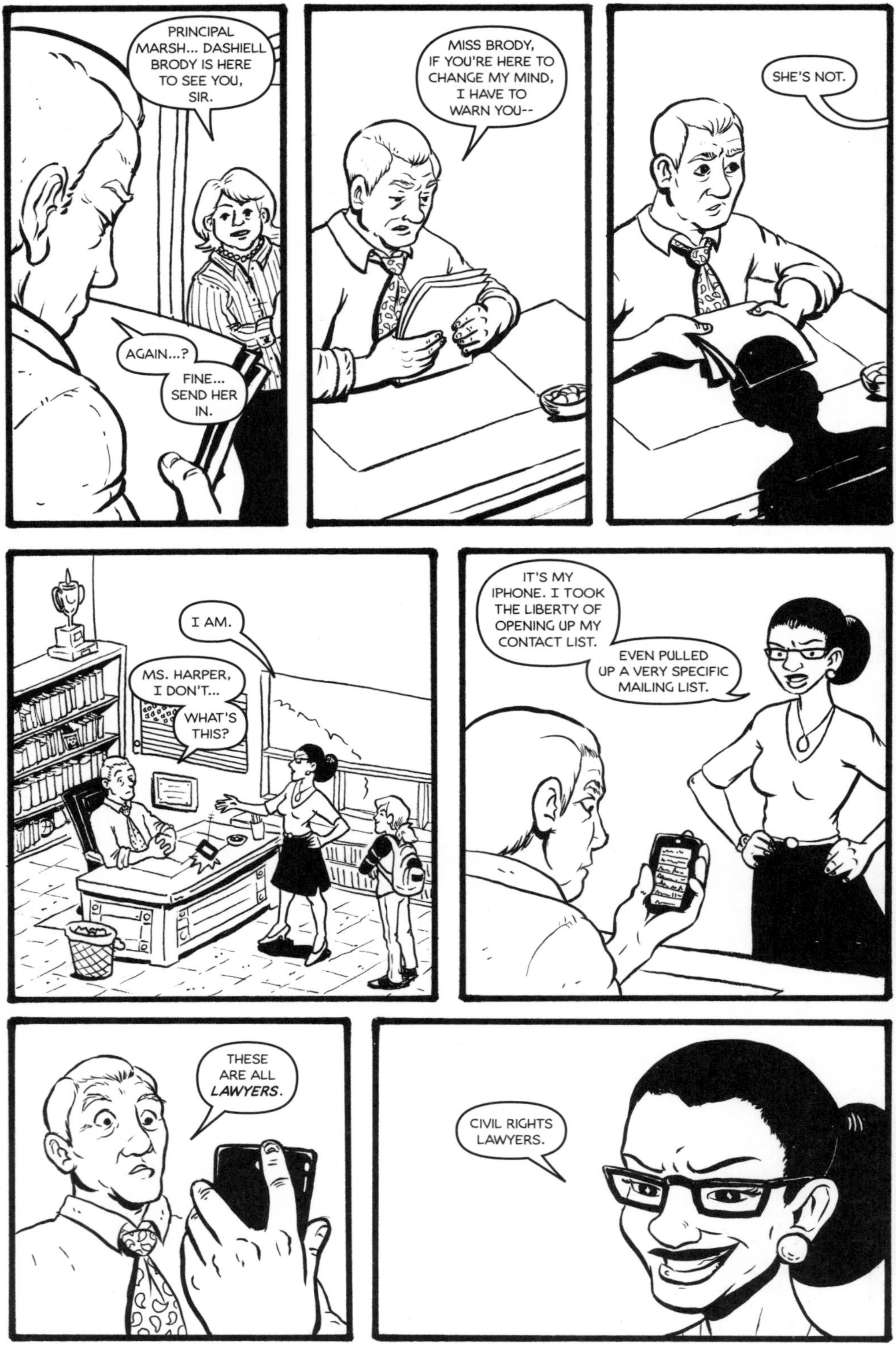
PRINCIPAL MARSH... DASHIELL BRODY IS HERE TO SEE YOU, SIR.
AGAIN...?
FINE... SEND HER IN.
MISS BRODY, IF YOU'RE HERE TO CHANGE MY MIND, I HAVE TO WARN YOU--
SHE'S NOT.
I AM.
MS. HARPER, I DON'T...
WHAT'S THIS?
IT'S MY IPHONE. I TOOK THE LIBERTY OF OPENING UP MY CONTACT LIST.
EVEN PULLED UP A VERY SPECIFIC MAILING LIST.
THESE ARE ALL *LAWYERS*.
CIVIL RIGHTS LAWYERS.

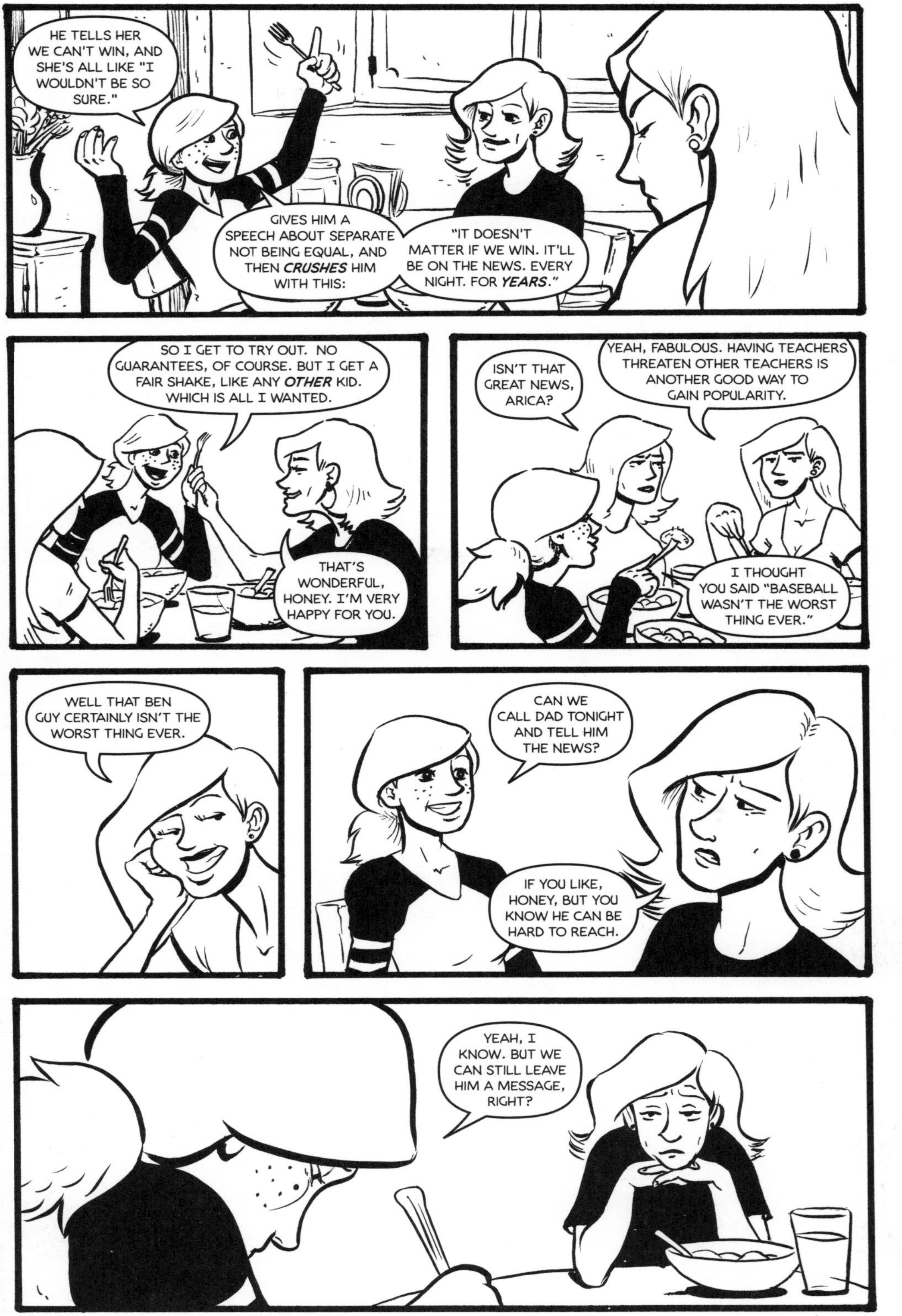
HE TELLS HER WE CAN'T WIN, AND SHE'S ALL LIKE "I WOULDN'T BE SO SURE."
GIVES HIM A SPEECH ABOUT SEPARATE NOT BEING EQUAL, AND THEN *CRUSHES* HIM WITH THIS:
"IT DOESN'T MATTER IF WE WIN. IT'LL BE ON THE NEWS. EVERY NIGHT. FOR *YEARS*."
SO I GET TO TRY OUT. NO GUARANTEES, OF COURSE. BUT I GET A FAIR SHAKE, LIKE ANY *OTHER* KID. WHICH IS ALL I WANTED.
THAT'S WONDERFUL, HONEY. I'M VERY HAPPY FOR YOU.
ISN'T THAT GREAT NEWS, ARICA?
YEAH, FABULOUS. HAVING TEACHERS THREATEN OTHER TEACHERS IS ANOTHER GOOD WAY TO GAIN POPULARITY.
I THOUGHT YOU SAID "BASEBALL WASN'T THE WORST THING EVER."
WELL THAT BEN GUY CERTAINLY ISN'T THE WORST THING EVER.
CAN WE CALL DAD TONIGHT AND TELL HIM THE NEWS?
IF YOU LIKE, HONEY, BUT YOU KNOW HE CAN BE HARD TO REACH.
YEAH, I KNOW. BUT WE CAN STILL LEAVE HIM A MESSAGE, RIGHT?

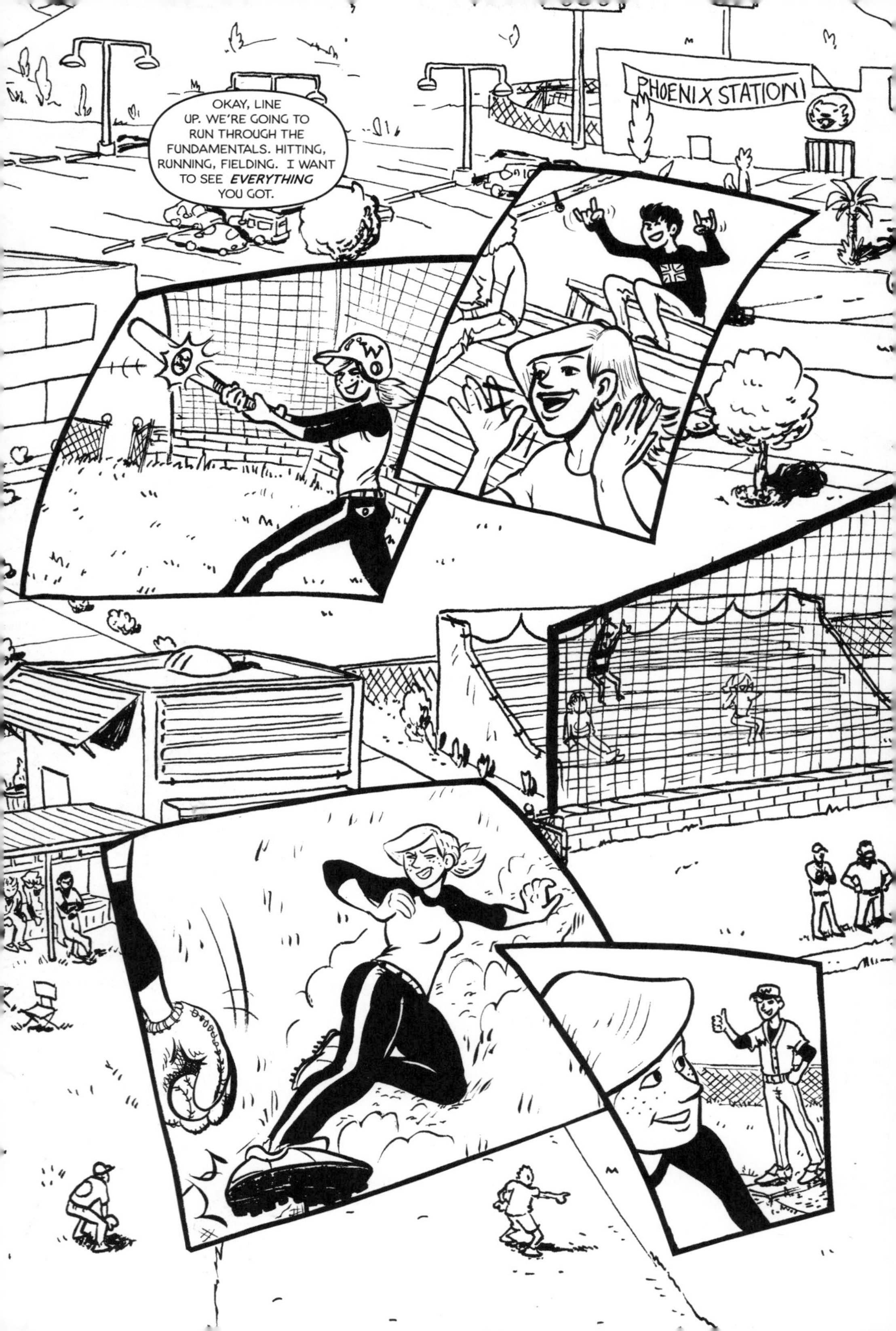

OKAY, LINE UP. WE'RE GOING TO RUN THROUGH THE FUNDAMENTALS. HITTING, RUNNING, FIELDING. I WANT TO SEE EVERYTHING YOU GOT.
PHOENIX STATION

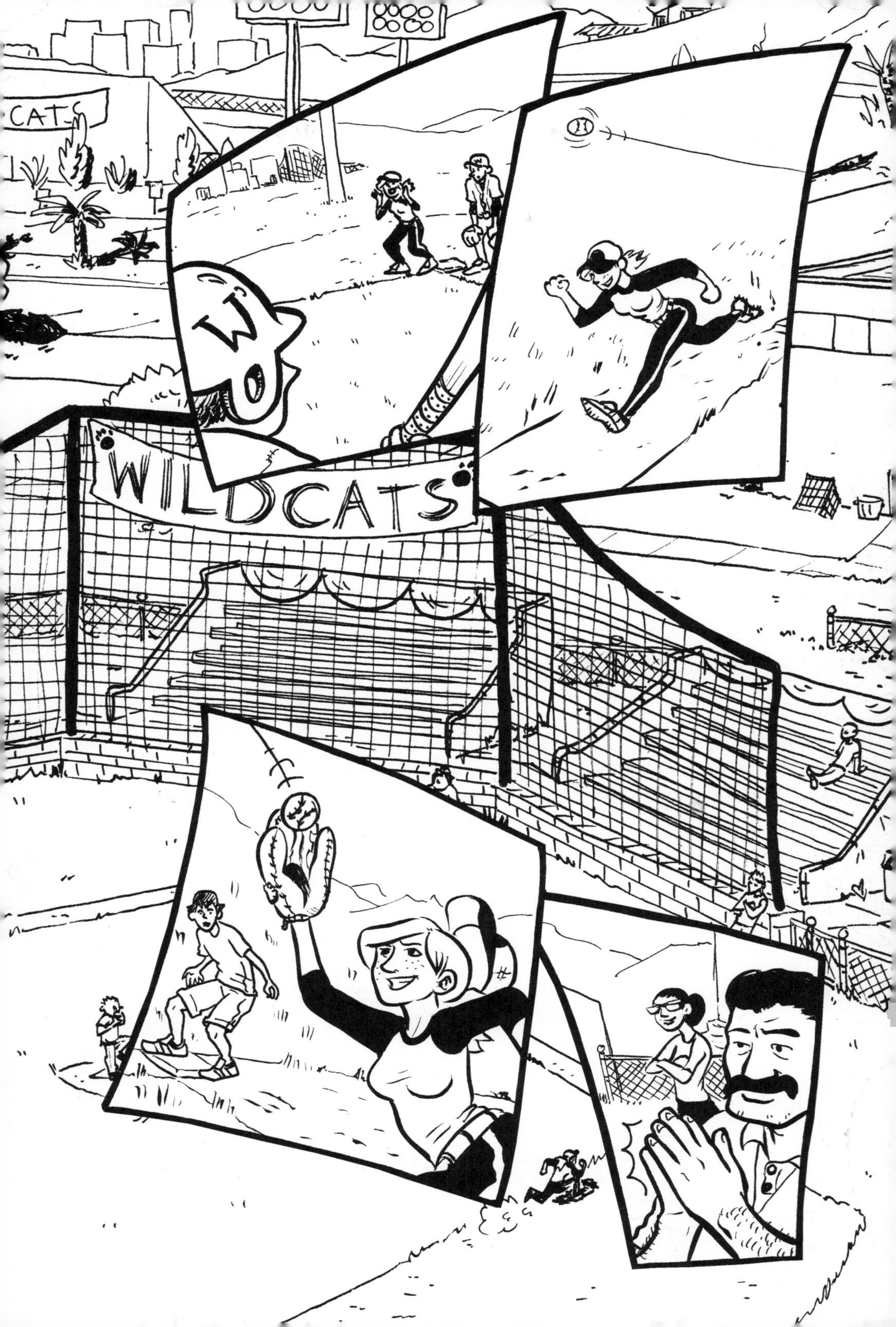
CATS
WILDCATS

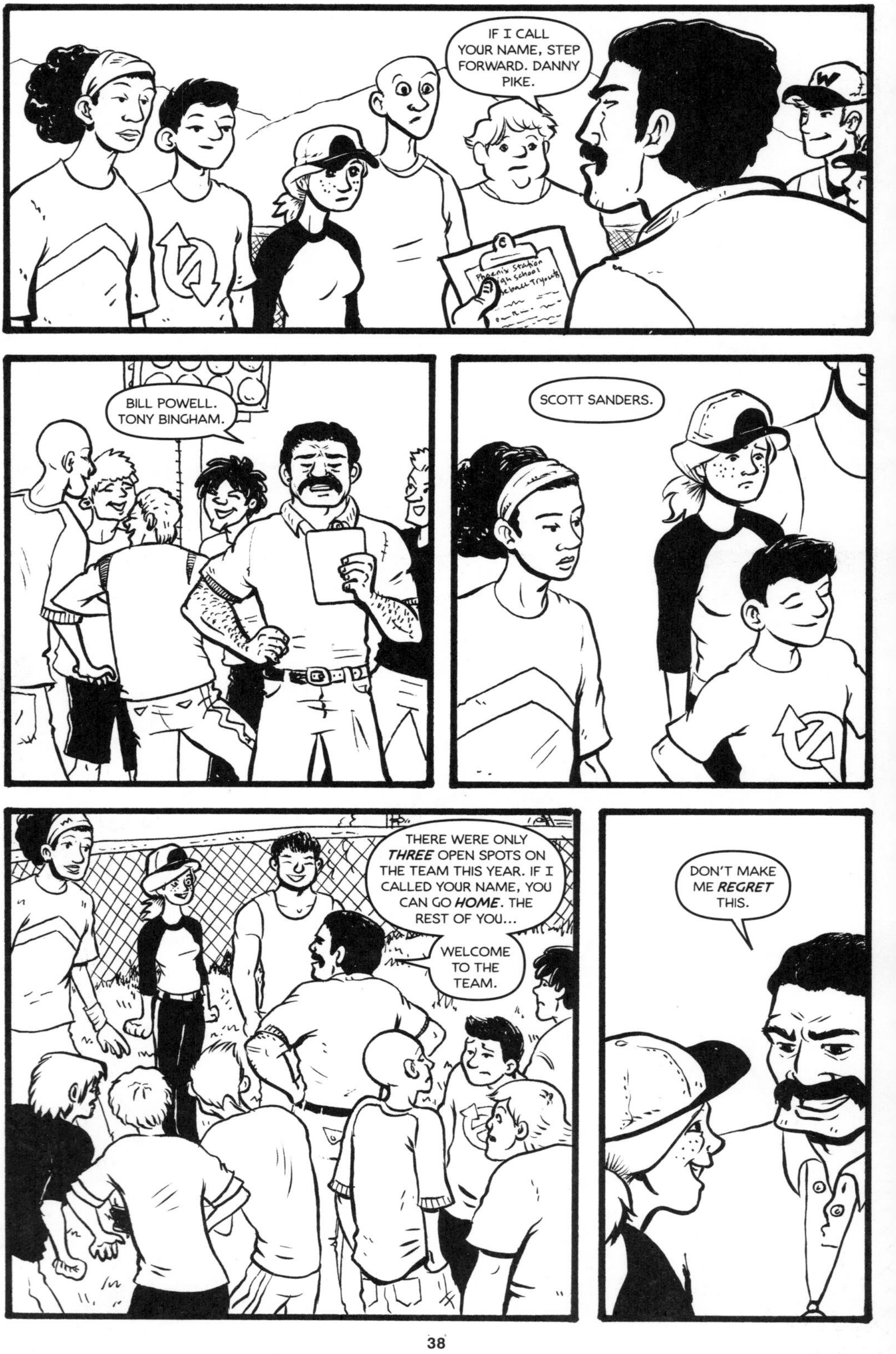
IF I CALL YOUR NAME, STEP FORWARD. DANNY PIKE.
Phoenix Station
BILL POWELL. TONY BINGHAM.
SCOTT SANDERS.
THERE WERE ONLY *THREE* OPEN SPOTS ON THE TEAM THIS YEAR. IF I CALLED YOUR NAME, YOU CAN GO *HOME*. THE REST OF YOU...
WELCOME TO THE TEAM.
DON'T MAKE ME *REGRET* THIS.

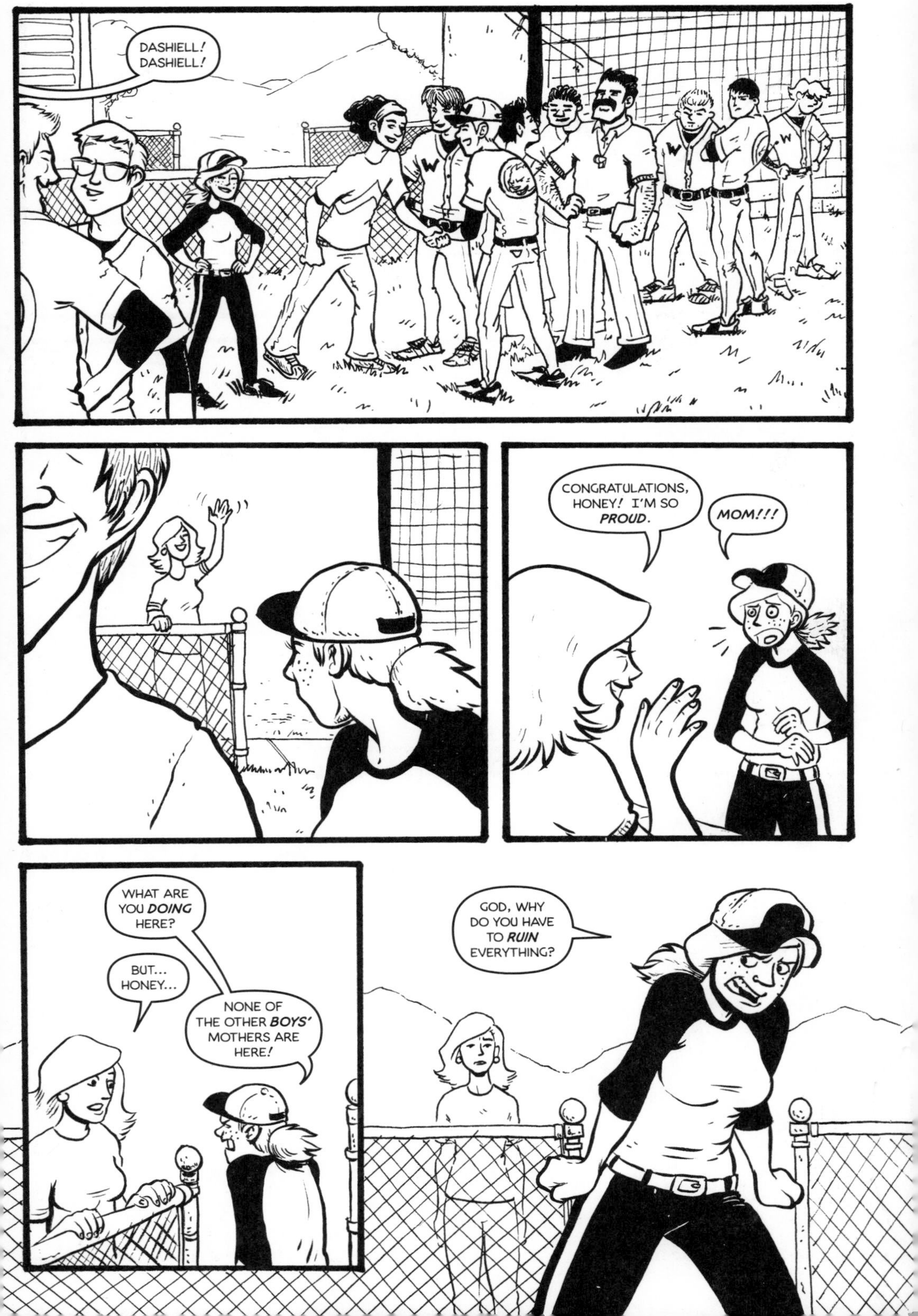
DASHIELL! DASHIELL!
CONGRATULATIONS, HONEY! I'M SO PROUD.
MOM!!!
WHAT ARE YOU DOING HERE?
BUT... HONEY...
NONE OF THE OTHER BOYS' MOTHERS ARE HERE!
GOD, WHY DO YOU HAVE TO RUIN EVERYTHING?

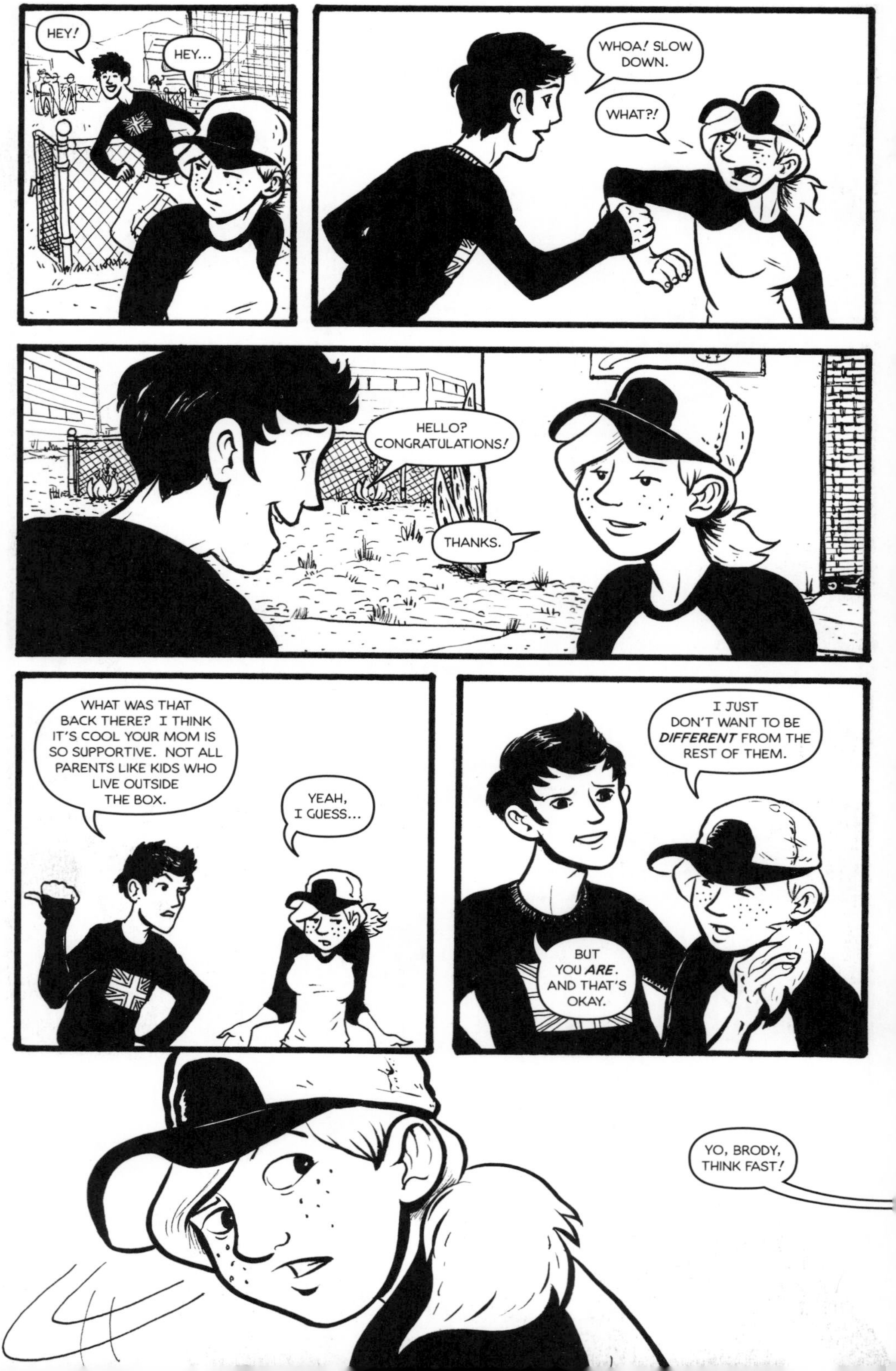
HEY!
HEY...
WHOA! SLOW DOWN.
WHAT?!
HELLO? CONGRATULATIONS!
THANKS.
WHAT WAS THAT BACK THERE? I THINK IT'S COOL YOUR MOM IS SO SUPPORTIVE. NOT ALL PARENTS LIKE KIDS WHO LIVE OUTSIDE THE BOX.
YEAH, I GUESS...
I JUST DON'T WANT TO BE *DIFFERENT* FROM THE REST OF THEM.
BUT YOU *ARE*. AND THAT'S OKAY.
YO, BRODY, THINK FAST!

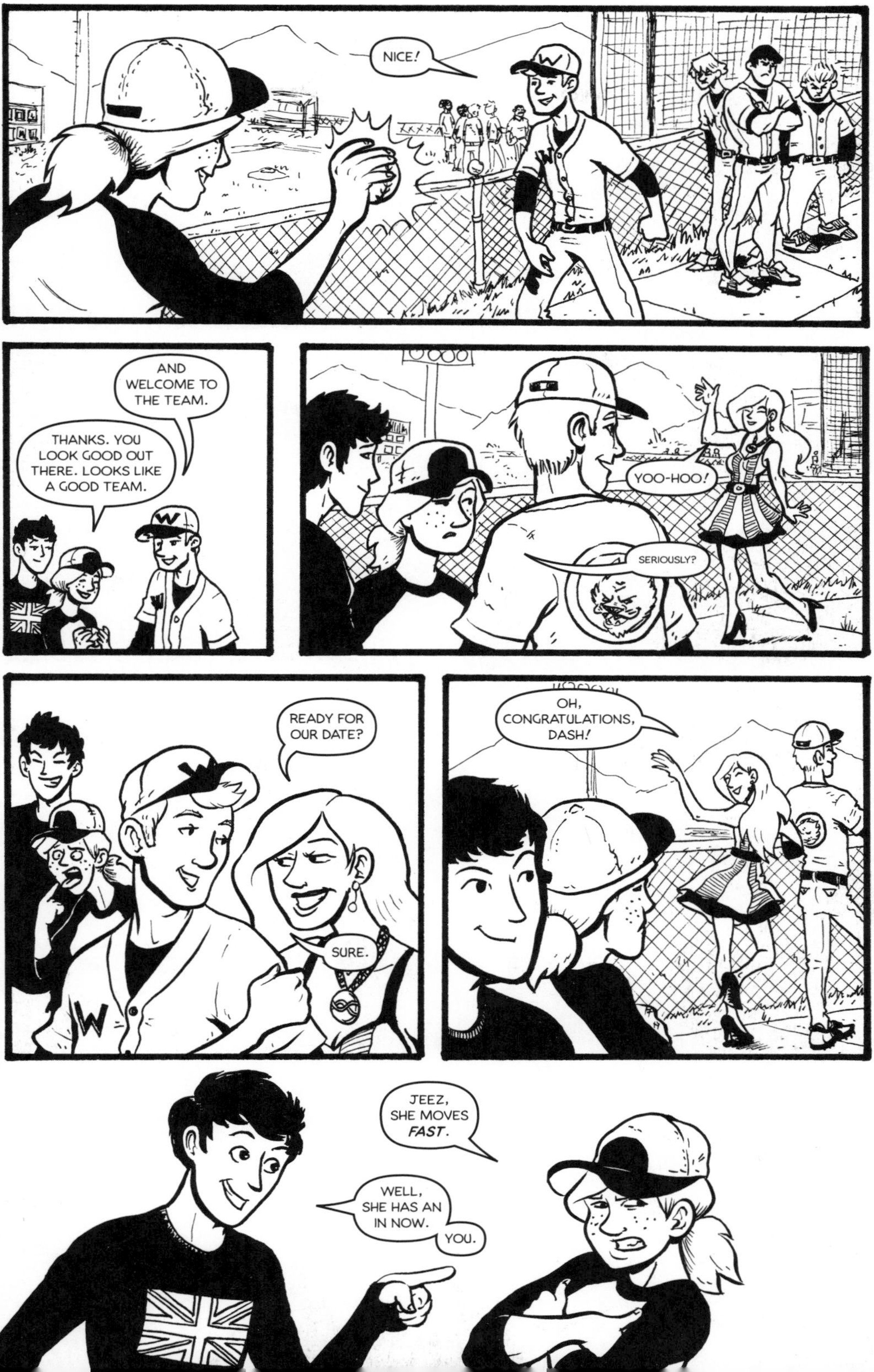
NICE!
AND WELCOME TO THE TEAM.
THANKS. YOU LOOK GOOD OUT THERE. LOOKS LIKE A GOOD TEAM.
YOO-HOO!
SERIOUSLY?
READY FOR OUR DATE?
SURE.
OH, CONGRATULATIONS, DASH!
JEEZ, SHE MOVES *FAST*.
WELL, SHE HAS AN IN NOW.
YOU.

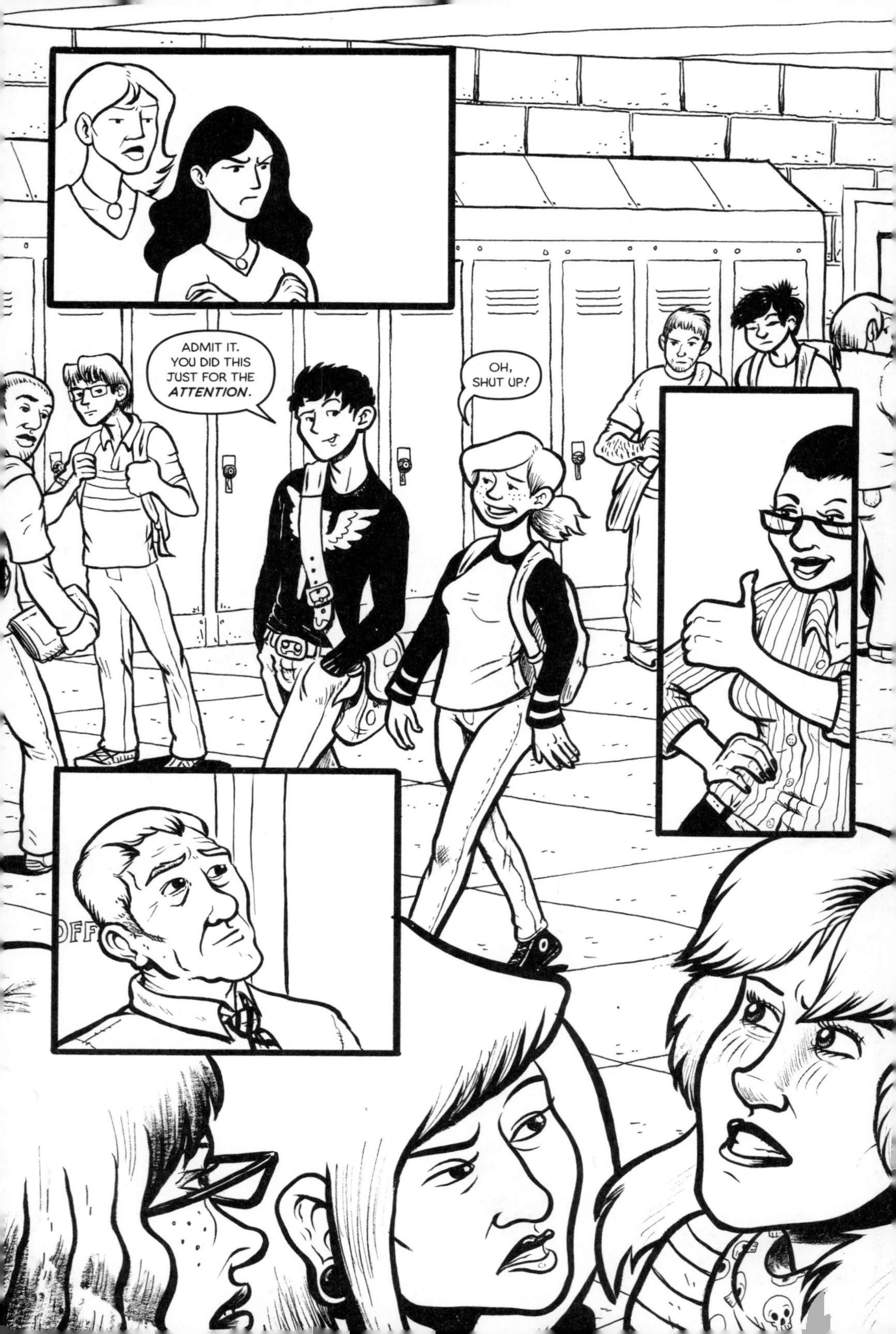
ADMIT IT. YOU DID THIS JUST FOR THE *ATTENTION*.
OH, SHUT UP!
OFF

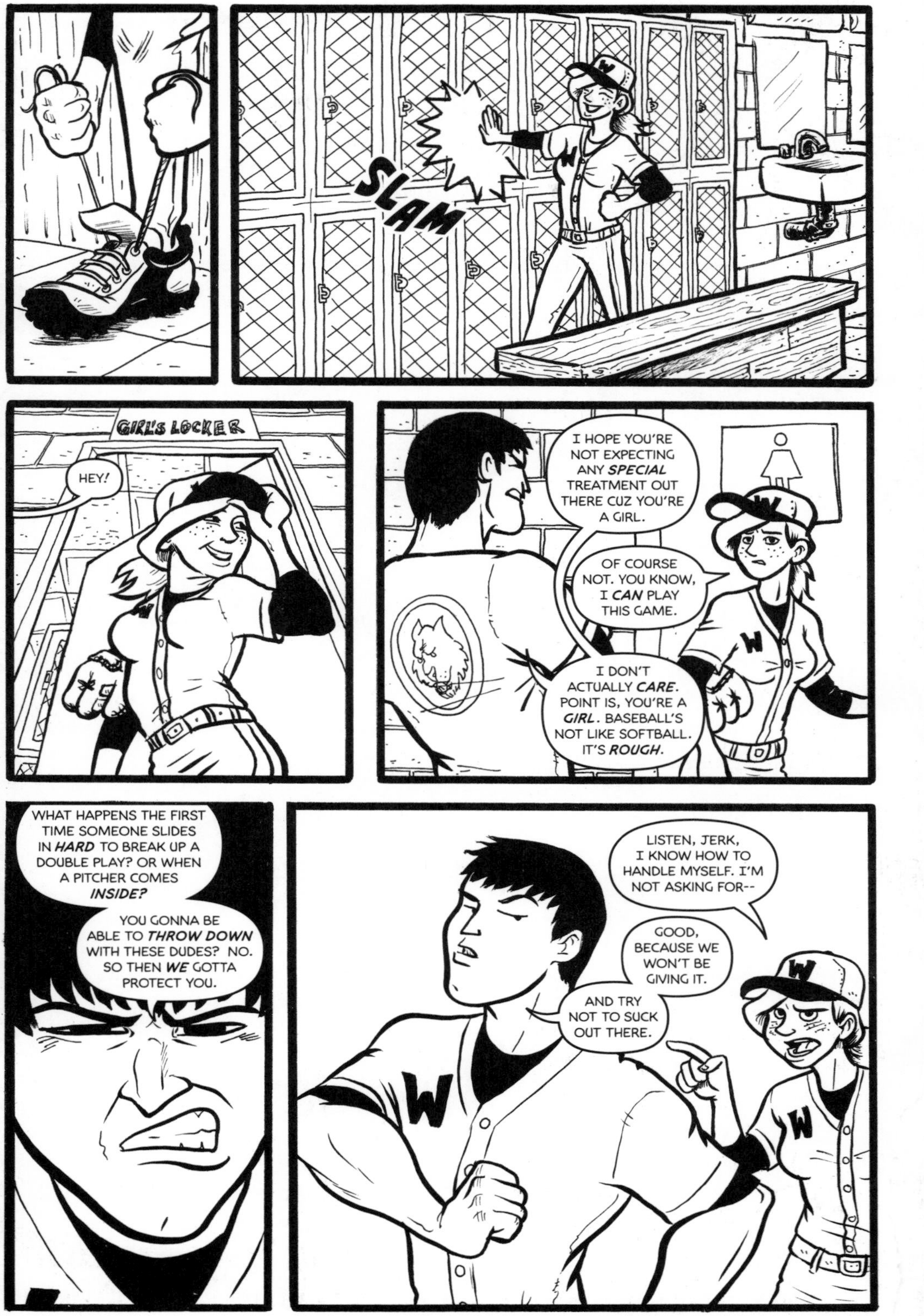
SLAM
GIRL'S LOCKER
HEY!
I HOPE YOU'RE NOT EXPECTING ANY SPECIAL TREATMENT OUT THERE CUZ YOU'RE A GIRL.
OF COURSE NOT. YOU KNOW, I CAN PLAY THIS GAME.
I DON'T ACTUALLY CARE. POINT IS, YOU'RE A GIRL. BASEBALL'S NOT LIKE SOFTBALL. IT'S ROUGH.
WHAT HAPPENS THE FIRST TIME SOMEONE SLIDES IN HARD TO BREAK UP A DOUBLE PLAY? OR WHEN A PITCHER COMES INSIDE?
YOU GONNA BE ABLE TO THROW DOWN WITH THESE DUDES? NO. SO THEN WE GOTTA PROTECT YOU.
LISTEN, JERK, I KNOW HOW TO HANDLE MYSELF. I'M NOT ASKING FOR--
GOOD, BECAUSE WE WON'T BE GIVING IT.
AND TRY NOT TO SUCK OUT THERE.

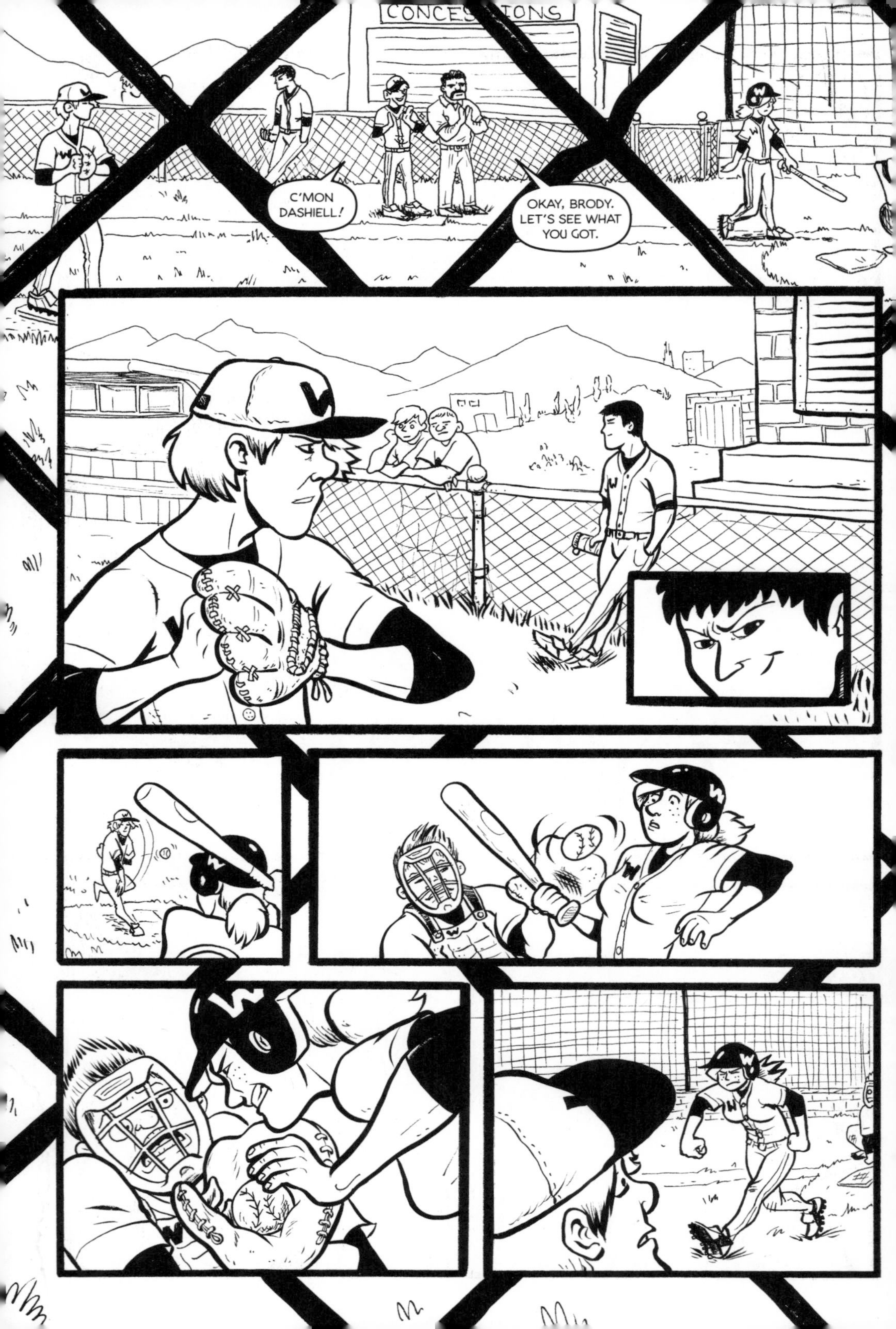
CONCES IONS
C'MON DASHIELL!
OKAY, BRODY. LET'S SEE WHAT YOU GOT.

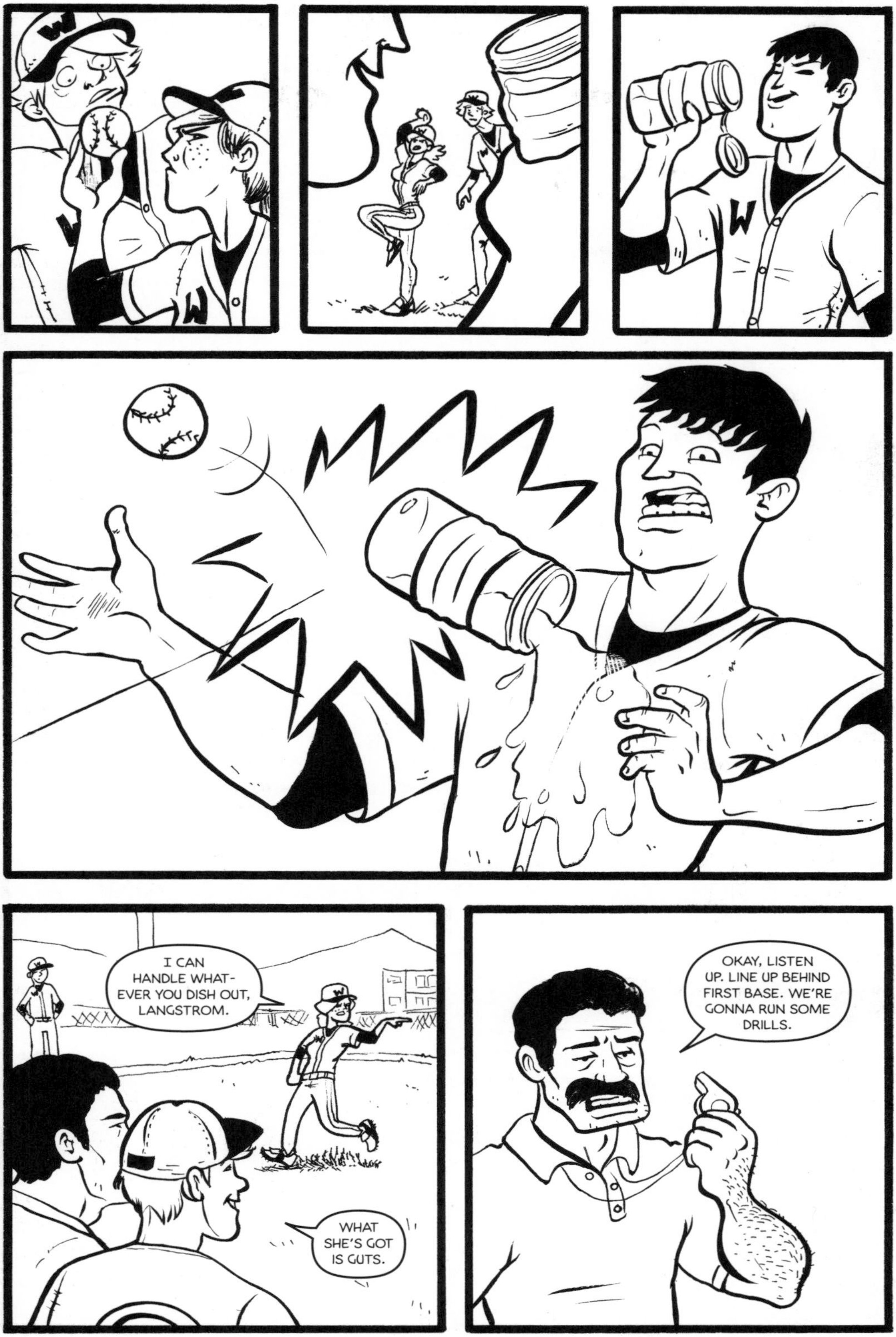
I CAN HANDLE WHAT-EVER YOU DISH OUT, LANGSTROM.
WHAT SHE'S GOT IS GUTS.
OKAY, LISTEN UP. LINE UP BEHIND FIRST BASE. WE'RE GONNA RUN SOME DRILLS.

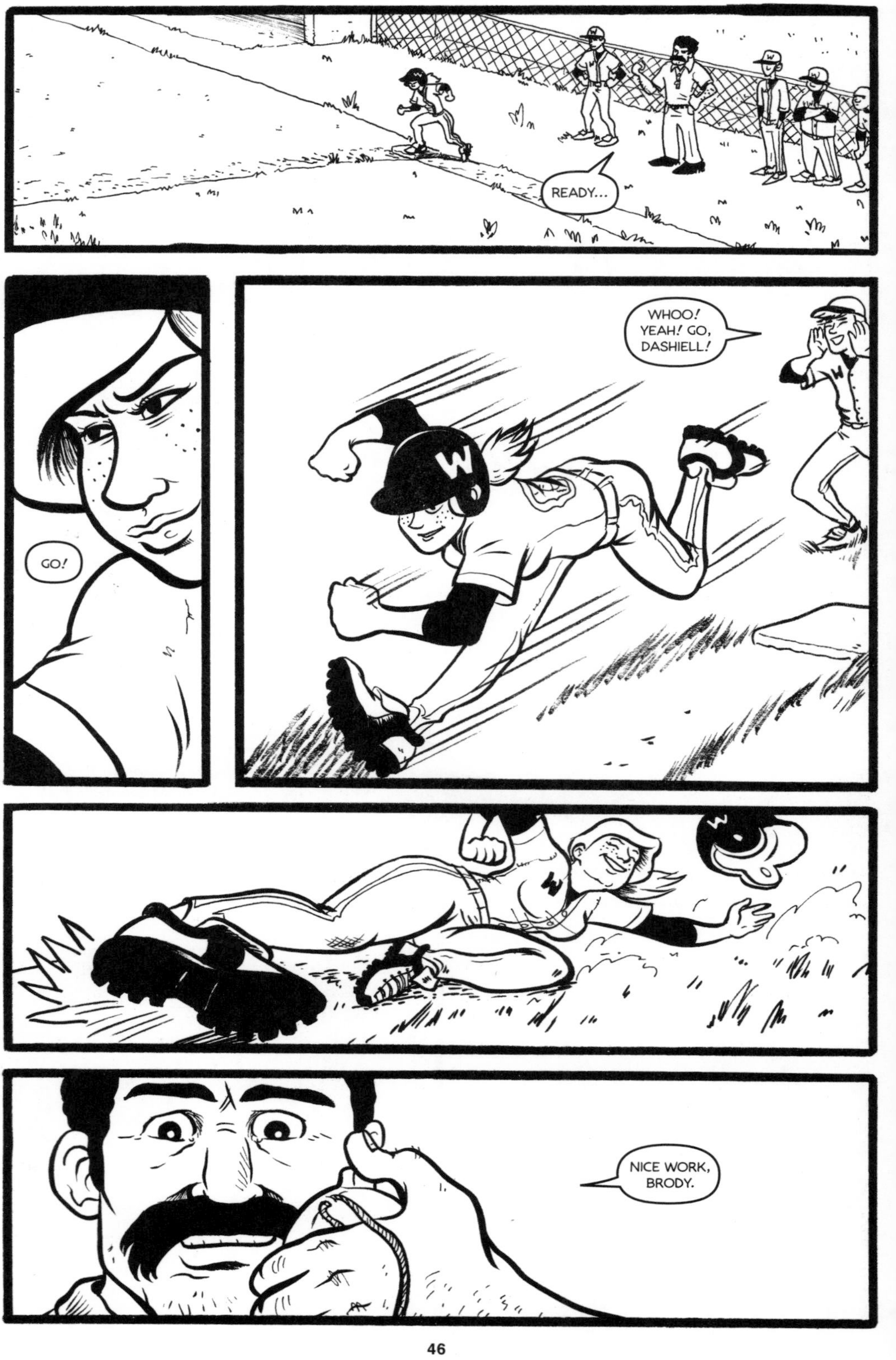
READY...
GO!
WHOO! YEAH! GO, DASHIELL!
NICE WORK, BRODY.

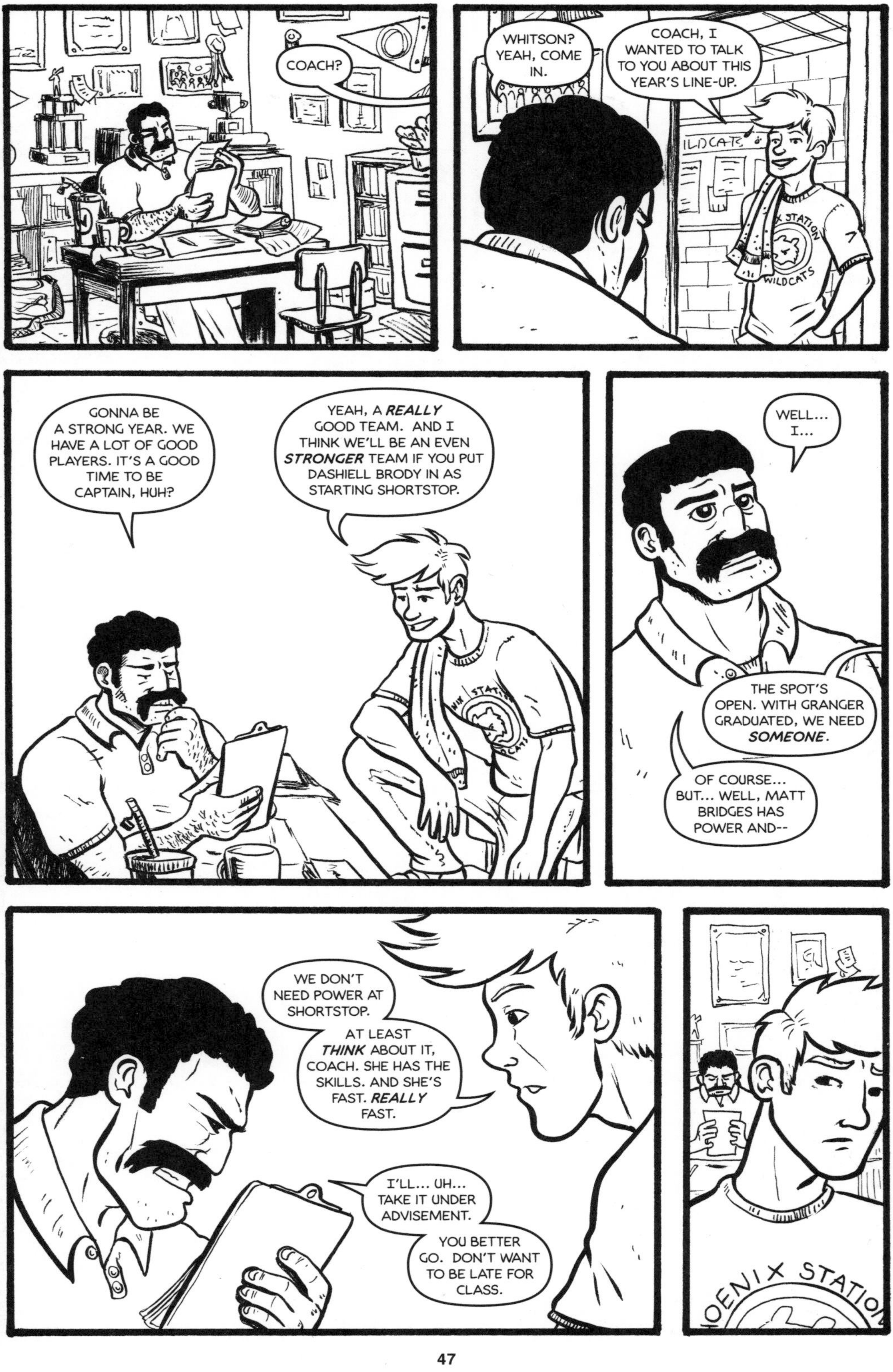
COACH?
WHITSON? YEAH, COME IN.
COACH, I WANTED TO TALK TO YOU ABOUT THIS YEAR'S LINE-UP.
WILDCATS
GONNA BE A STRONG YEAR. WE HAVE A LOT OF GOOD PLAYERS. IT'S A GOOD TIME TO BE CAPTAIN, HUH?
YEAH, A **REALLY** GOOD TEAM. AND I THINK WE'LL BE AN EVEN **STRONGER** TEAM IF YOU PUT DASHIELL BRODY IN AS STARTING SHORTSTOP.
WELL... I...
THE SPOT'S OPEN. WITH GRANGER GRADUATED, WE NEED **SOMEONE**.
OF COURSE... BUT... WELL, MATT BRIDGES HAS POWER AND--
WE DON'T NEED POWER AT SHORTSTOP.
AT LEAST **THINK** ABOUT IT, COACH. SHE HAS THE SKILLS. AND SHE'S FAST. **REALLY** FAST.
I'LL... UH... TAKE IT UNDER ADVISEMENT.
YOU BETTER GO. DON'T WANT TO BE LATE FOR CLASS.
OENIX STATIO

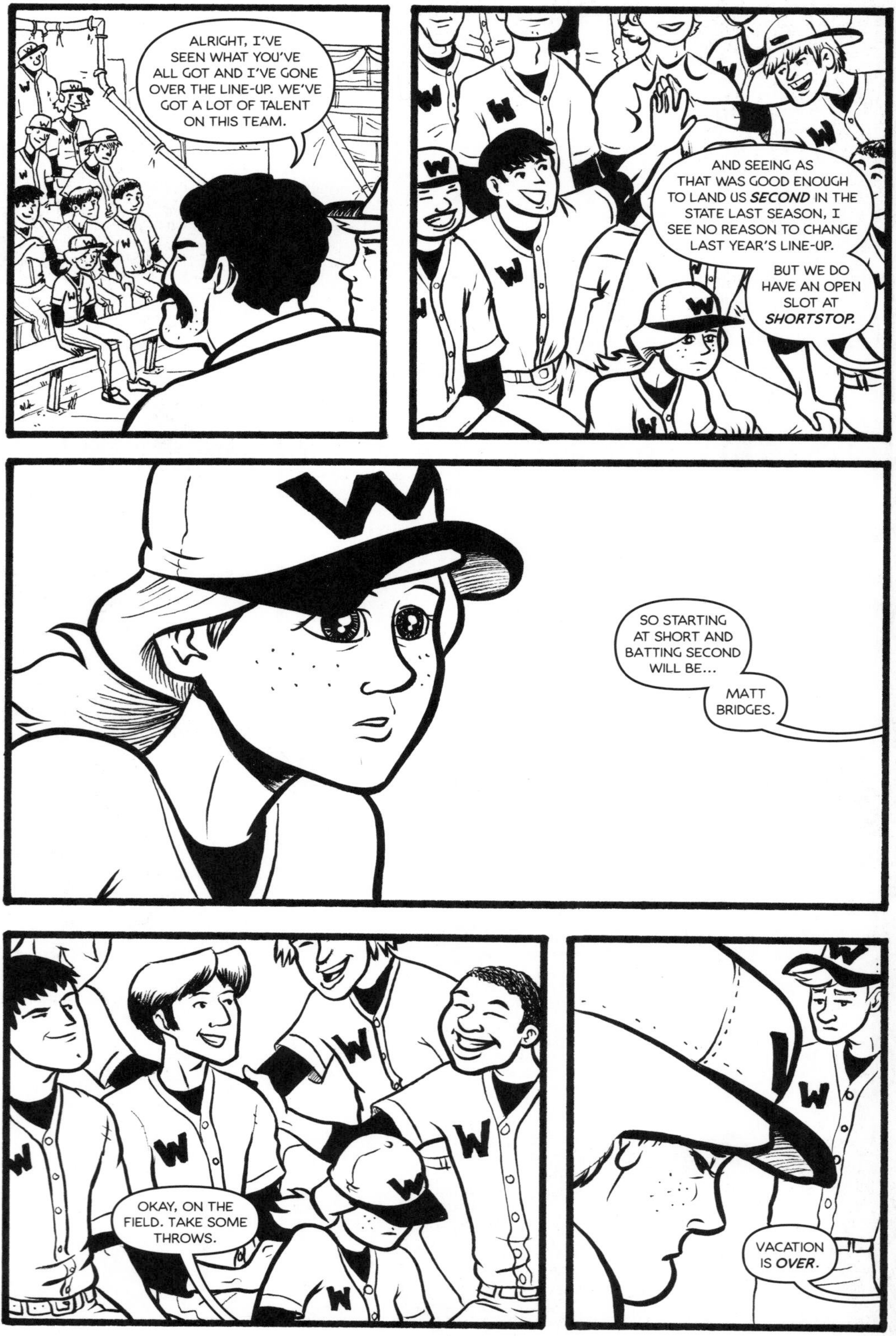
ALRIGHT, I'VE SEEN WHAT YOU'VE ALL GOT AND I'VE GONE OVER THE LINE-UP. WE'VE GOT A LOT OF TALENT ON THIS TEAM.
AND SEEING AS THAT WAS GOOD ENOUGH TO LAND US *SECOND* IN THE STATE LAST SEASON, I SEE NO REASON TO CHANGE LAST YEAR'S LINE-UP.
BUT WE DO HAVE AN OPEN SLOT AT ***SHORTSTOP.***
SO STARTING AT SHORT AND BATTING SECOND WILL BE...
MATT BRIDGES.
OKAY, ON THE FIELD. TAKE SOME THROWS.
VACATION IS ***OVER***.

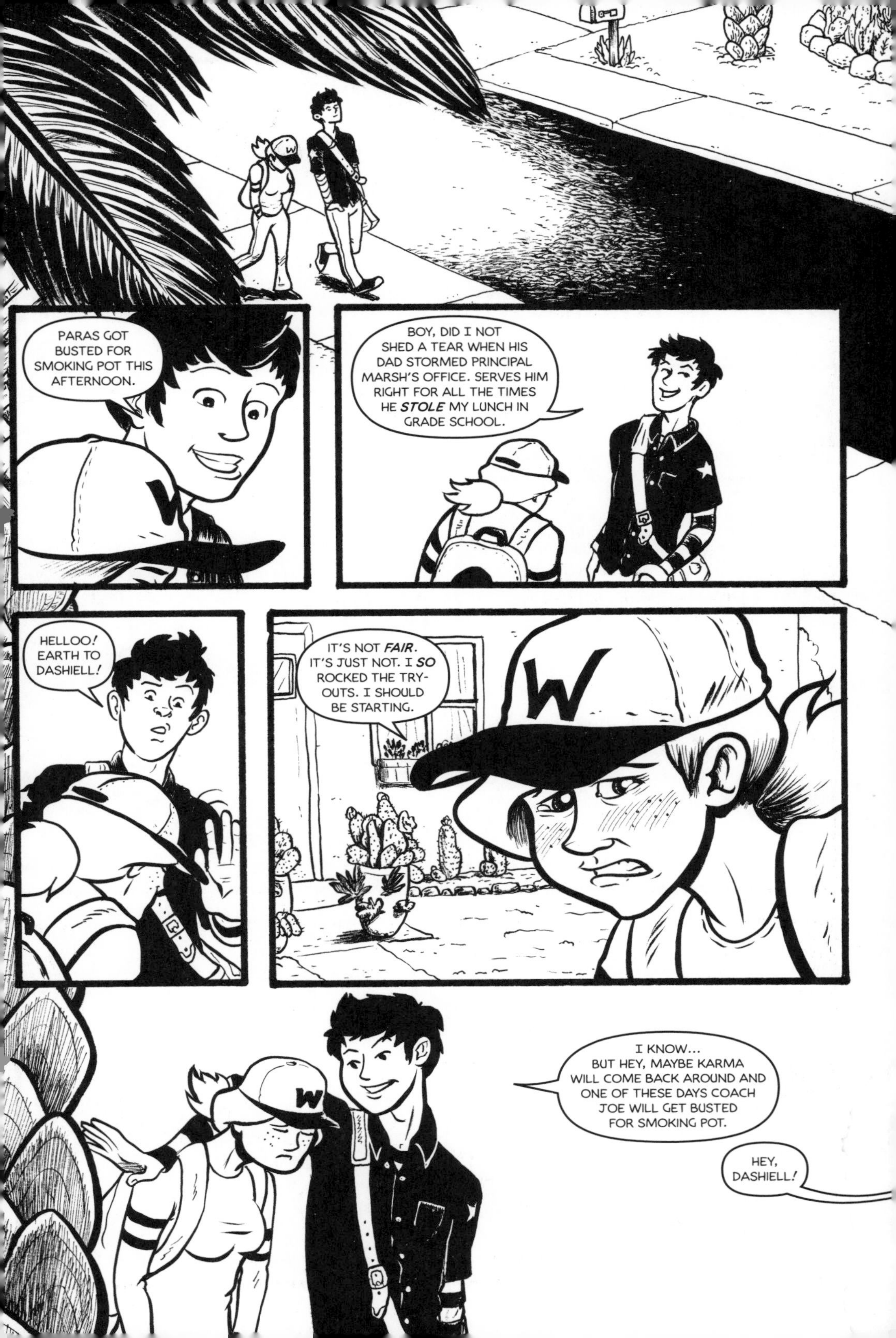
PARAS GOT BUSTED FOR SMOKING POT THIS AFTERNOON.
BOY, DID I NOT SHED A TEAR WHEN HIS DAD STORMED PRINCIPAL MARSH'S OFFICE. SERVES HIM RIGHT FOR ALL THE TIMES HE *STOLE* MY LUNCH IN GRADE SCHOOL.
HELLOO! EARTH TO DASHIELL!
IT'S NOT *FAIR*. IT'S JUST NOT. I *SO* ROCKED THE TRY-OUTS. I SHOULD BE STARTING.
I KNOW... BUT HEY, MAYBE KARMA WILL COME BACK AROUND AND ONE OF THESE DAYS COACH JOE WILL GET BUSTED FOR SMOKING POT.
HEY, DASHIELL!

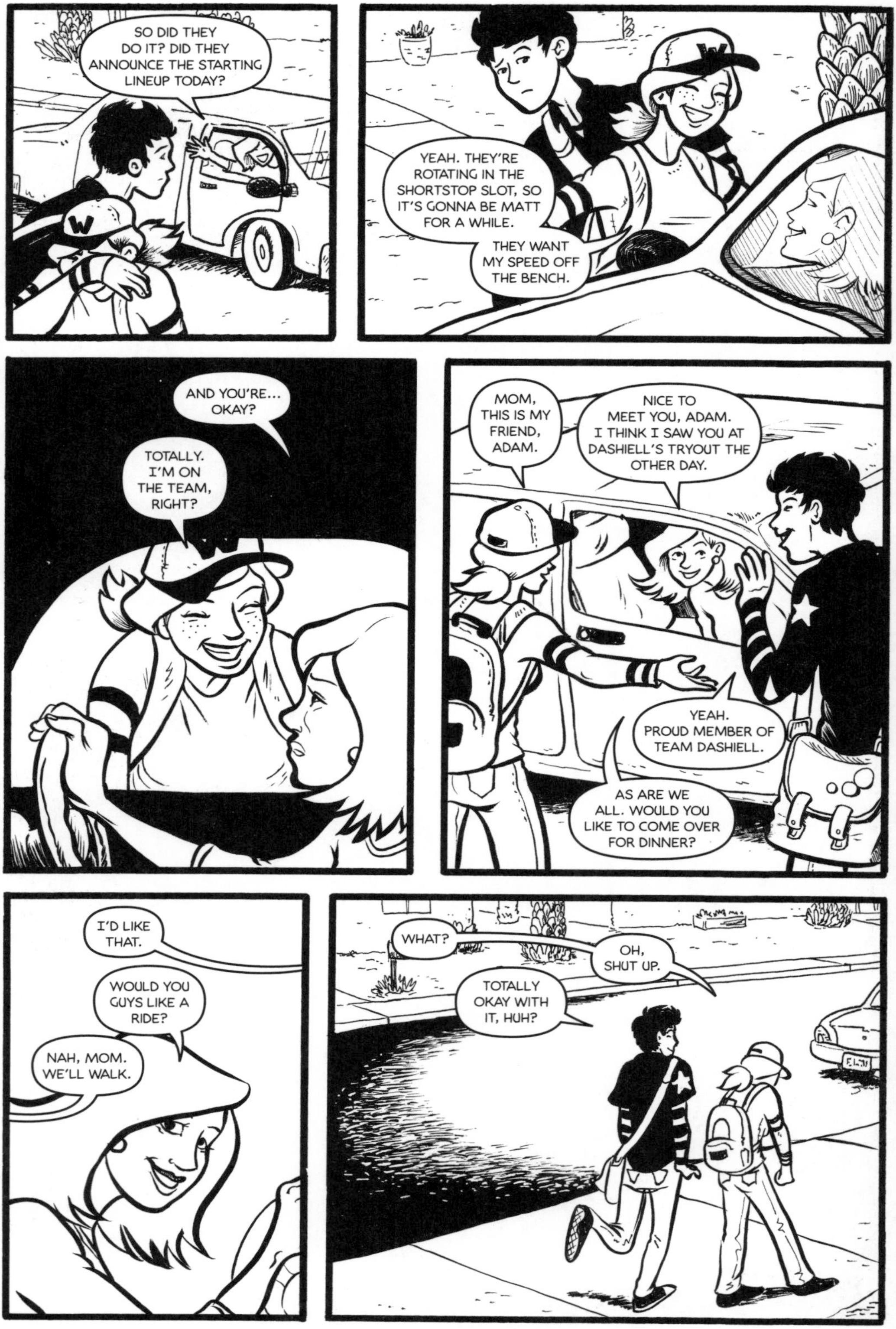

SO DID THEY DO IT? DID THEY ANNOUNCE THE STARTING LINEUP TODAY?
YEAH. THEY'RE ROTATING IN THE SHORTSTOP SLOT, SO IT'S GONNA BE MATT FOR A WHILE.
THEY WANT MY SPEED OFF THE BENCH.
AND YOU'RE... OKAY?
TOTALLY. I'M ON THE TEAM, RIGHT?
MOM, THIS IS MY FRIEND, ADAM.
NICE TO MEET YOU, ADAM. I THINK I SAW YOU AT DASHIELL'S TRYOUT THE OTHER DAY.
YEAH. PROUD MEMBER OF TEAM DASHIELL.
AS ARE WE ALL. WOULD YOU LIKE TO COME OVER FOR DINNER?
I'D LIKE THAT.
WOULD YOU GUYS LIKE A RIDE?
NAH, MOM. WE'LL WALK.
WHAT?
OH, SHUT UP.
TOTALLY OKAY WITH IT, HUH?

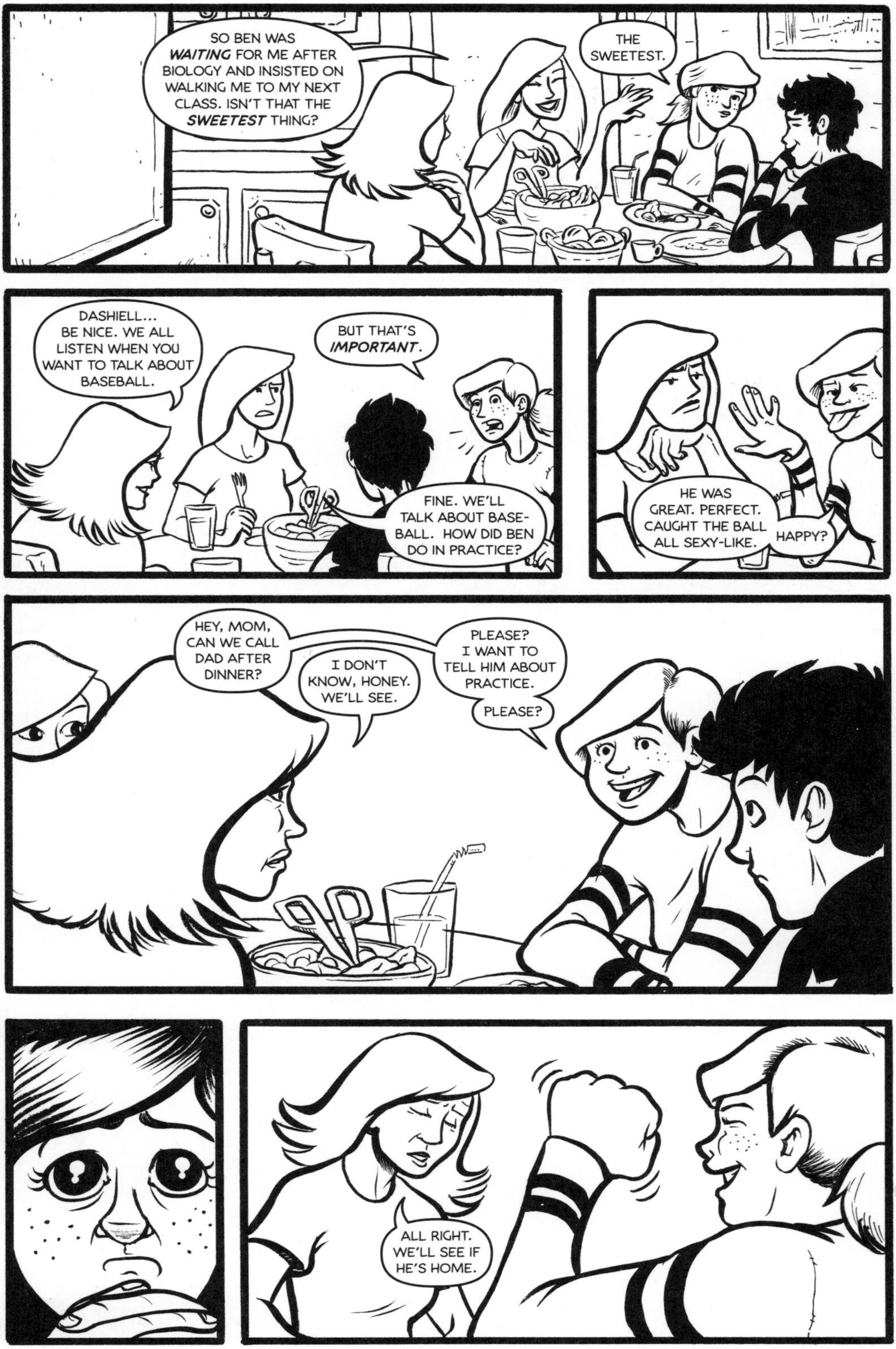
SO BEN WAS WAITING FOR ME AFTER BIOLOGY AND INSISTED ON WALKING ME TO MY NEXT CLASS. ISN'T THAT THE SWEETEST THING?
THE SWEETEST.
DASHIELL... BE NICE. WE ALL LISTEN WHEN YOU WANT TO TALK ABOUT BASEBALL.
BUT THAT'S IMPORTANT.
FINE. WE'LL TALK ABOUT BASE-BALL. HOW DID BEN DO IN PRACTICE?
HE WAS GREAT. PERFECT. CAUGHT THE BALL ALL SEXY-LIKE.
HAPPY?
HEY, MOM, CAN WE CALL DAD AFTER DINNER?
I DON'T KNOW, HONEY. WE'LL SEE.
PLEASE? I WANT TO TELL HIM ABOUT PRACTICE.
PLEASE?
ALL RIGHT. WE'LL SEE IF HE'S HOME.

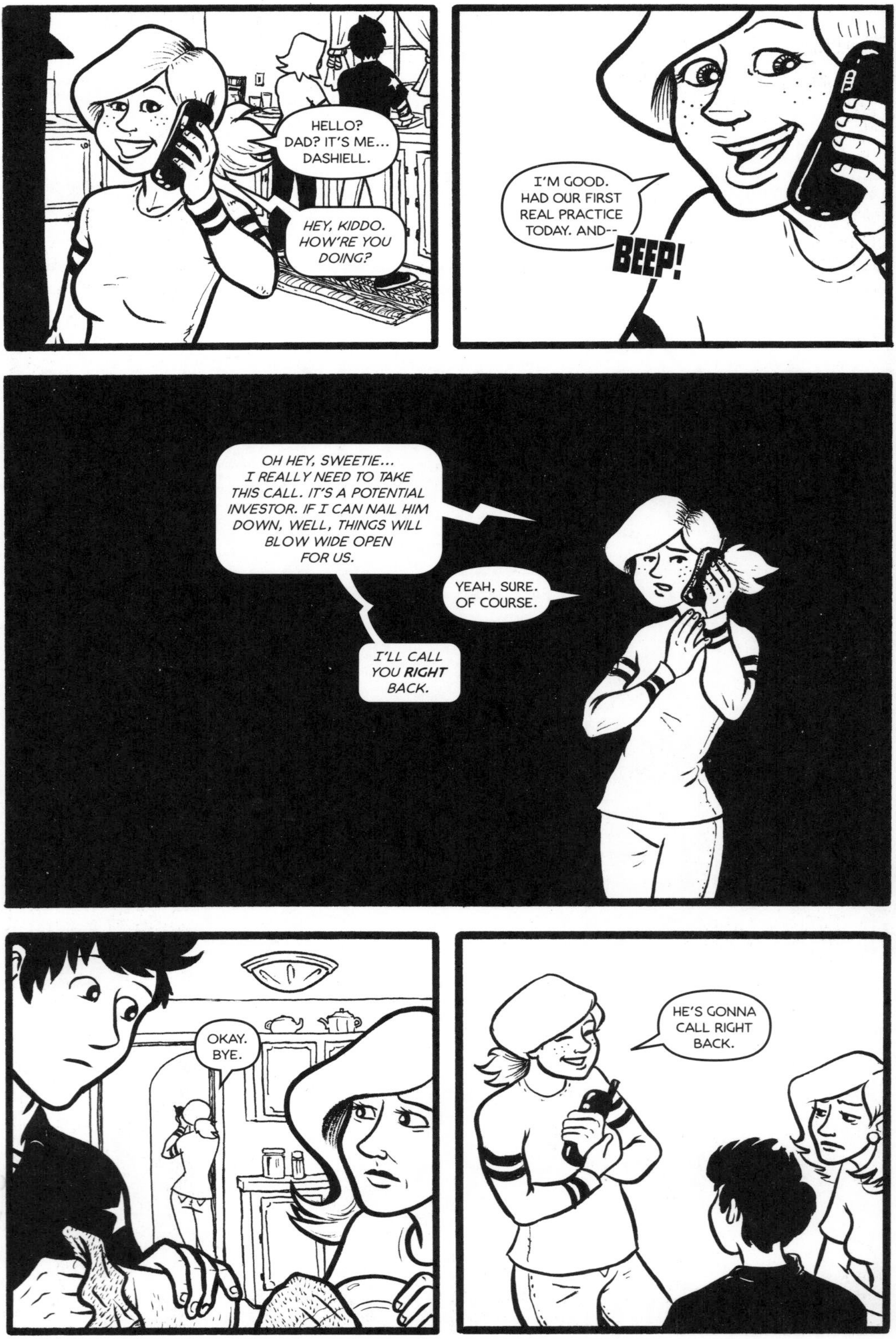
HELLO? DAD? IT'S ME... DASHIELL.
HEY, KIDDO. HOW'RE YOU DOING?
I'M GOOD. HAD OUR FIRST REAL PRACTICE TODAY. AND--
BEEP!
OH HEY, SWEETIE... I REALLY NEED TO TAKE THIS CALL. IT'S A POTENTIAL INVESTOR. IF I CAN NAIL HIM DOWN, WELL, THINGS WILL BLOW WIDE OPEN FOR US.
YEAH, SURE. OF COURSE.
I'LL CALL YOU RIGHT BACK.
OKAY. BYE.
HE'S GONNA CALL RIGHT BACK.

SOX
SOX
Dashiell
Brody
SOX
Dashiell
Brody
SOX
Dashiell
Brody

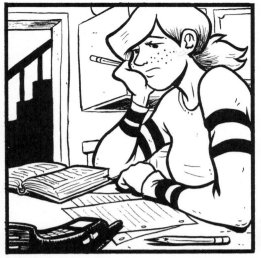

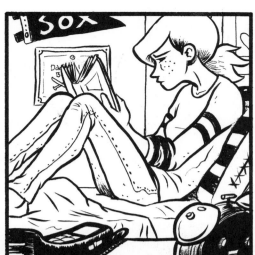

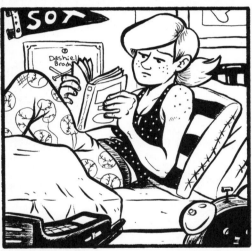

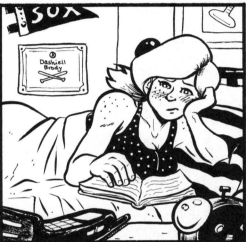

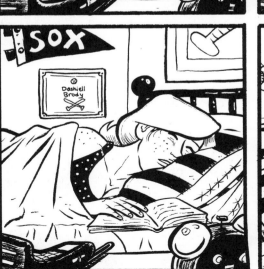

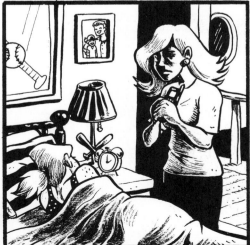

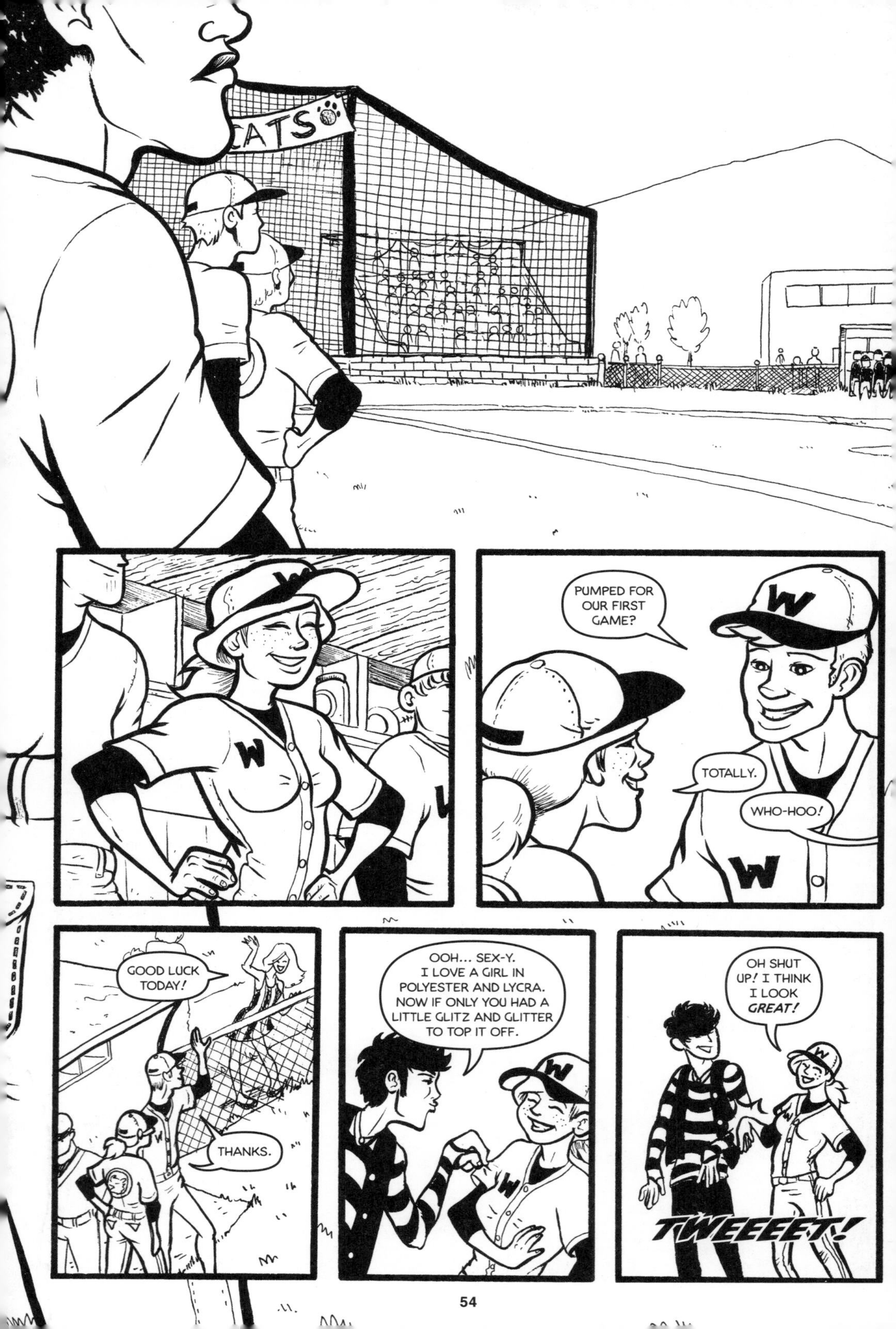
CATS
PUMPED FOR OUR FIRST GAME?
TOTALLY.
WHO-HOO!
GOOD LUCK TODAY!
THANKS.
OOH... SEX-Y. I LOVE A GIRL IN POLYESTER AND LYCRA. NOW IF ONLY YOU HAD A LITTLE GLITZ AND GLITTER TO TOP IT OFF.
OH SHUT UP! I THINK I LOOK *GREAT!*
TWEEEEET!

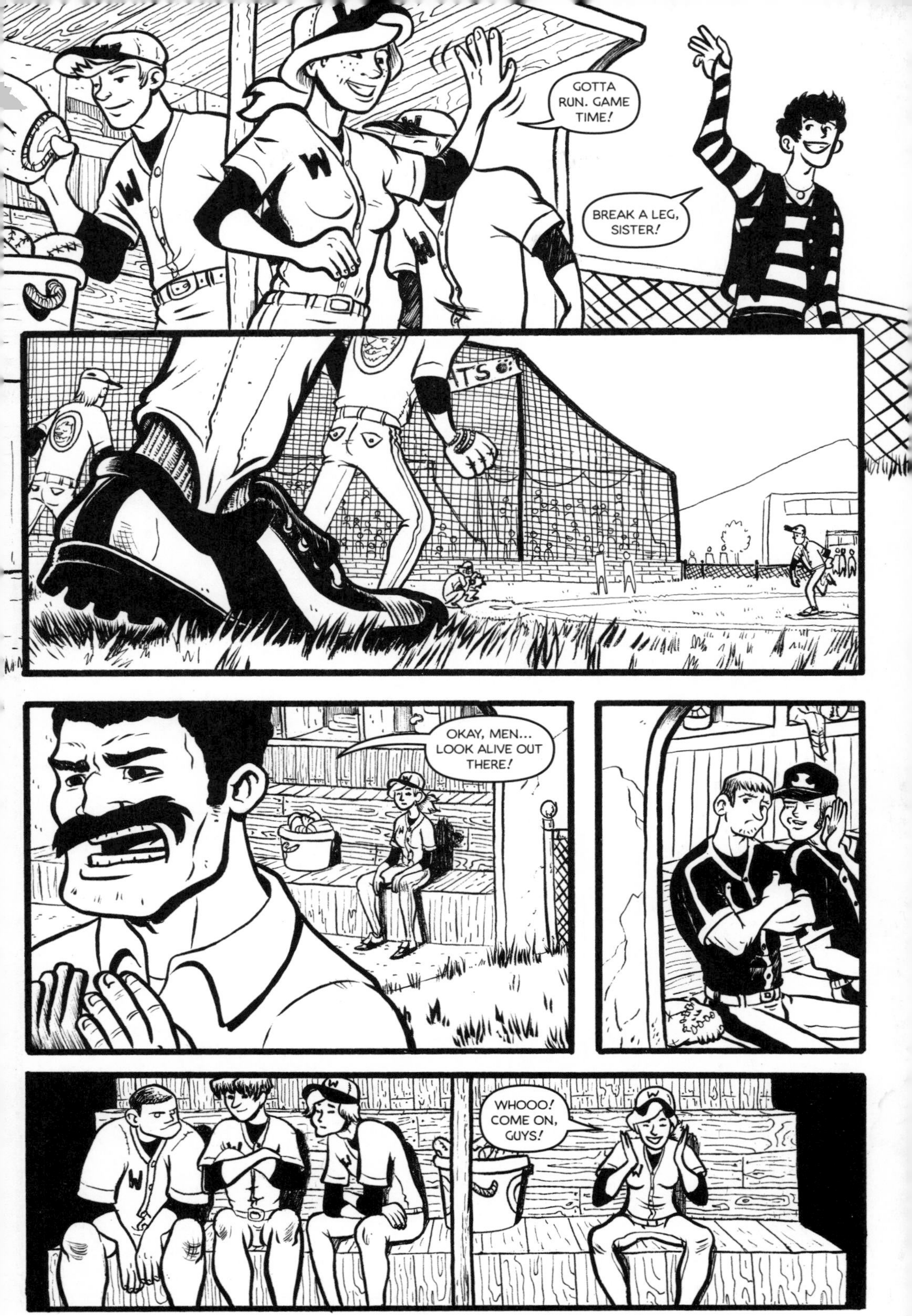
GOTTA RUN. GAME TIME!
BREAK A LEG, SISTER!
ATS
OKAY, MEN... LOOK ALIVE OUT THERE!
WHOOO! COME ON, GUYS!

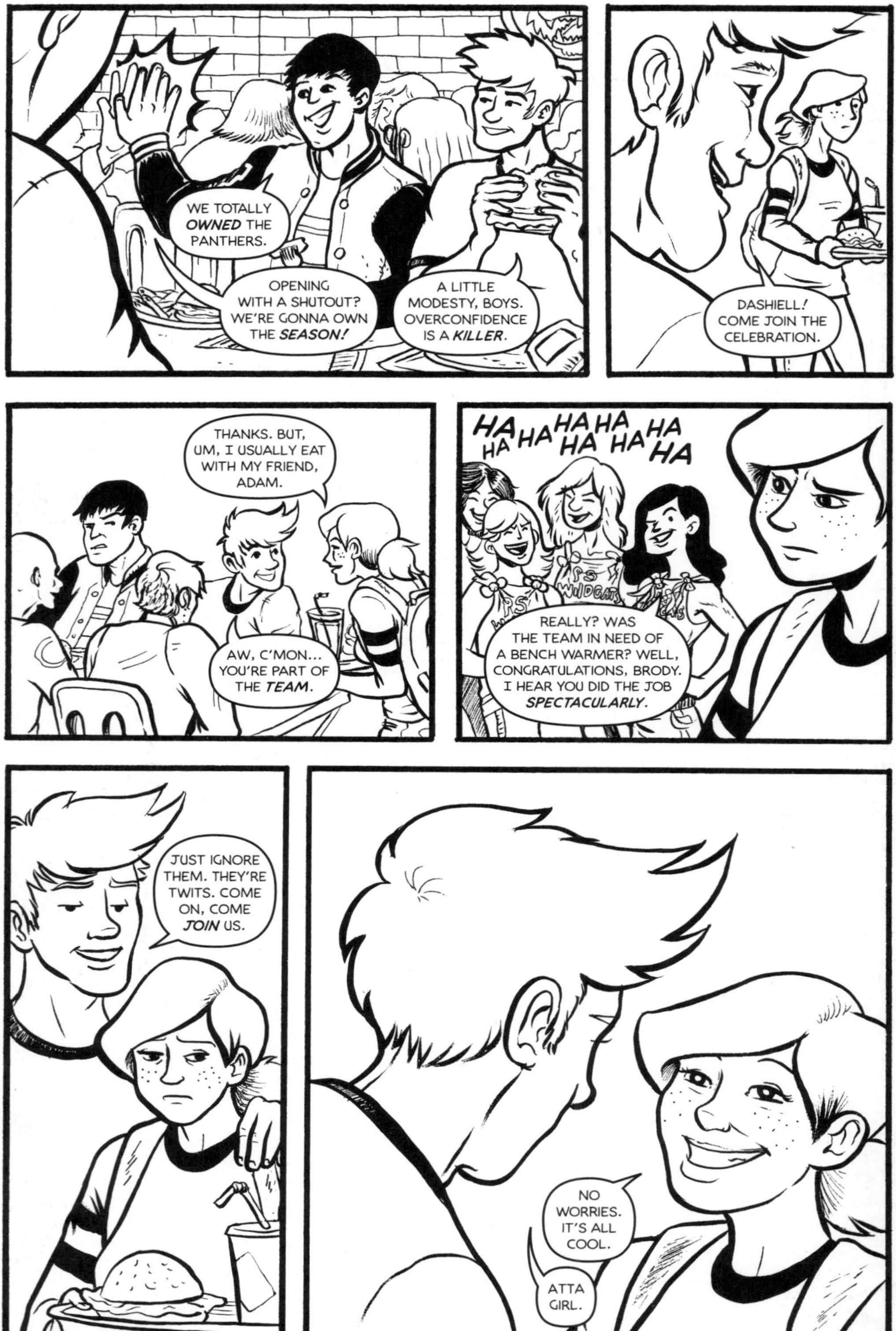
WE TOTALLY OWNED THE PANTHERS.
OPENING WITH A SHUTOUT? WE'RE GONNA OWN THE SEASON!
A LITTLE MODESTY, BOYS. OVERCONFIDENCE IS A KILLER.
DASHIELL! COME JOIN THE CELEBRATION.
THANKS. BUT, UM, I USUALLY EAT WITH MY FRIEND, ADAM.
AW, C'MON... YOU'RE PART OF THE TEAM.
HA HA HA HA HA HA HA HA HA HA
REALLY? WAS THE TEAM IN NEED OF A BENCH WARMER? WELL, CONGRATULATIONS, BRODY. I HEAR YOU DID THE JOB SPECTACULARLY.
JUST IGNORE THEM. THEY'RE TWITS. COME ON, COME JOIN US.
NO WORRIES. IT'S ALL COOL.
ATTA GIRL.

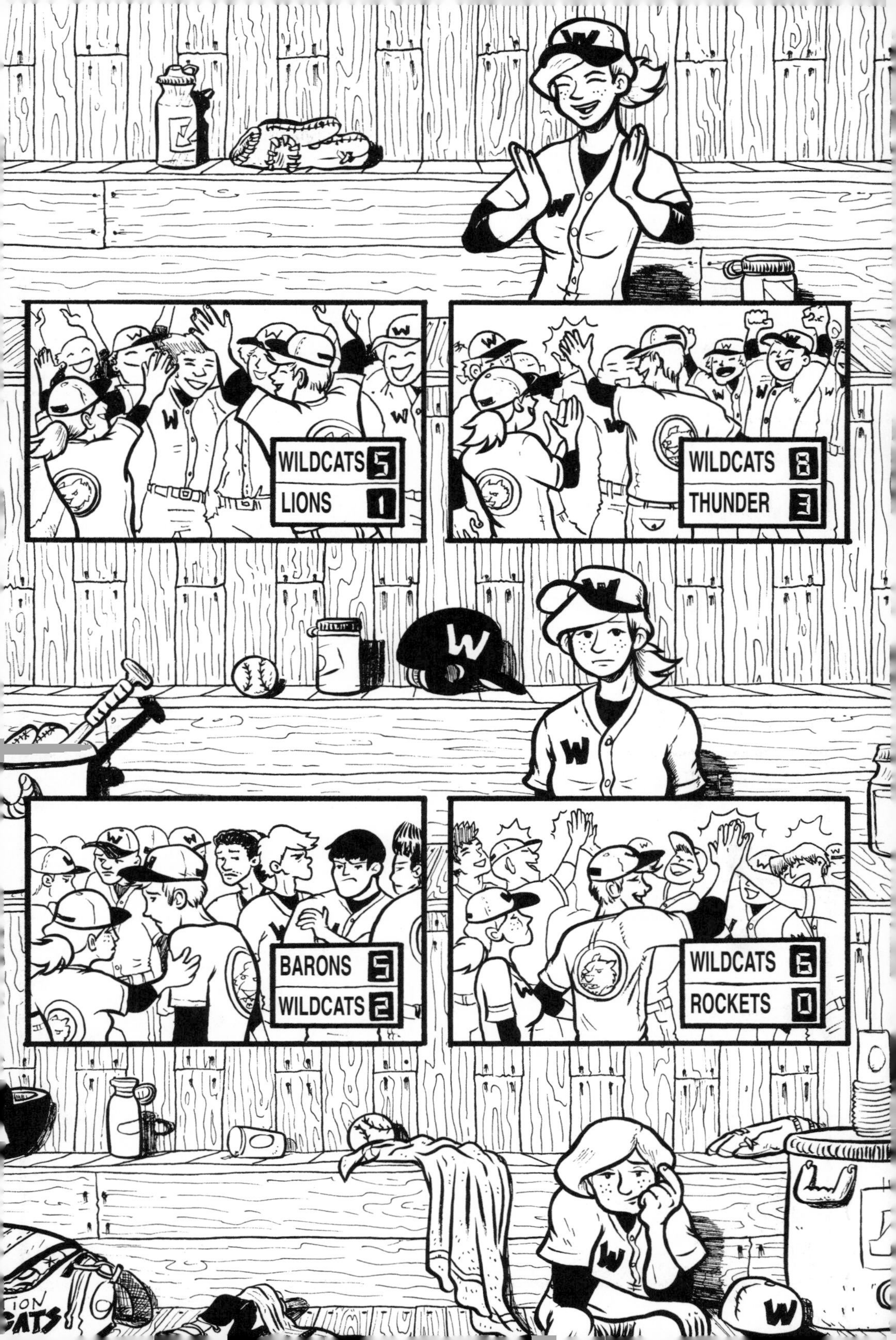
WILDCATS 5
LIONS 1
WILDCATS 8
THUNDER 3
BARONS 5
WILDCATS 2
WILDCATS 6
ROCKETS 0

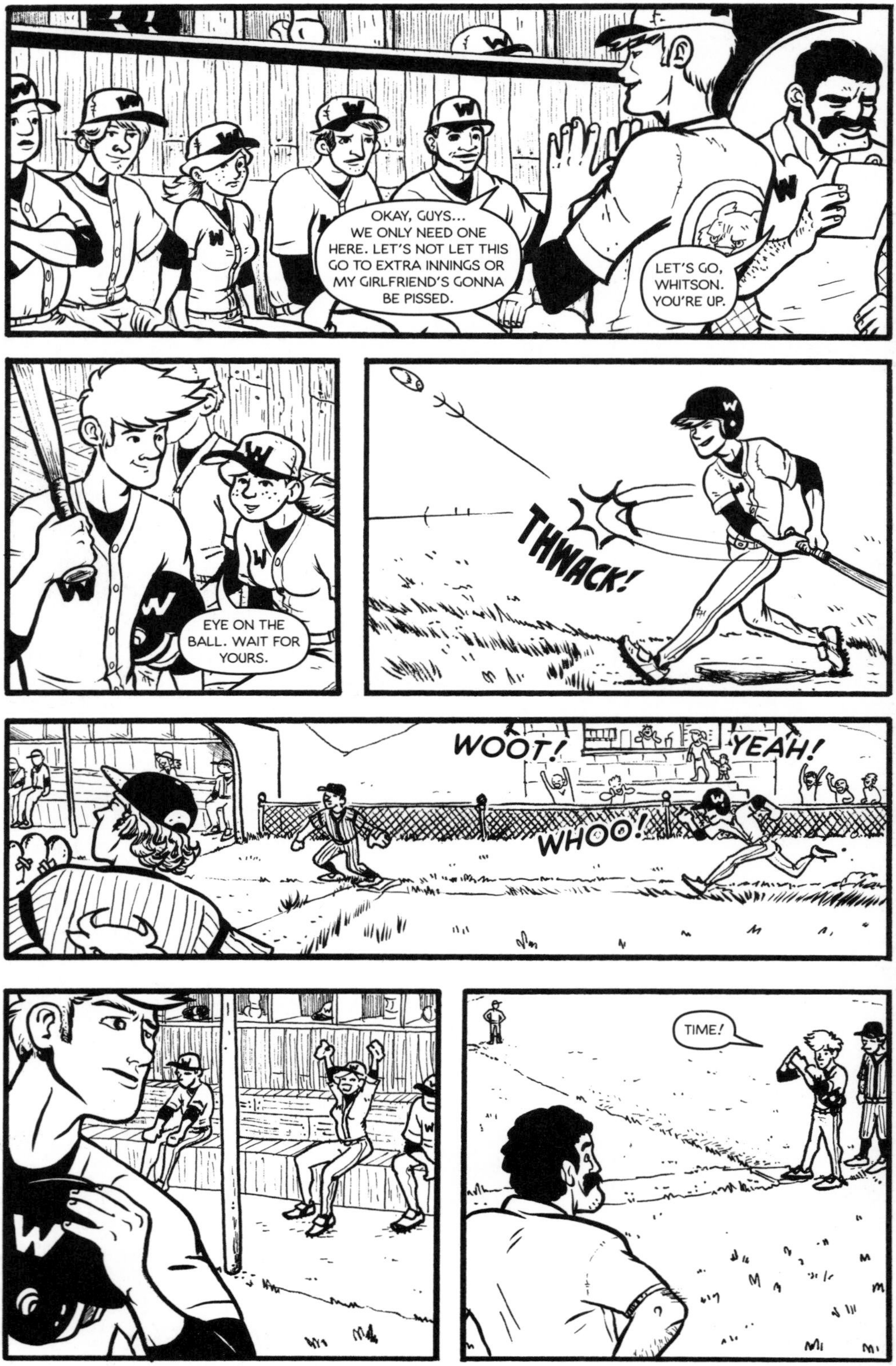

OKAY, GUYS... WE ONLY NEED ONE HERE. LET'S NOT LET THIS GO TO EXTRA INNINGS OR MY GIRLFRIEND'S GONNA BE PISSED.
LET'S GO, WHITSON. YOU'RE UP.
EYE ON THE BALL. WAIT FOR YOURS.
THWACK!
WOOT!
YEAH!
WHOO!
TIME!

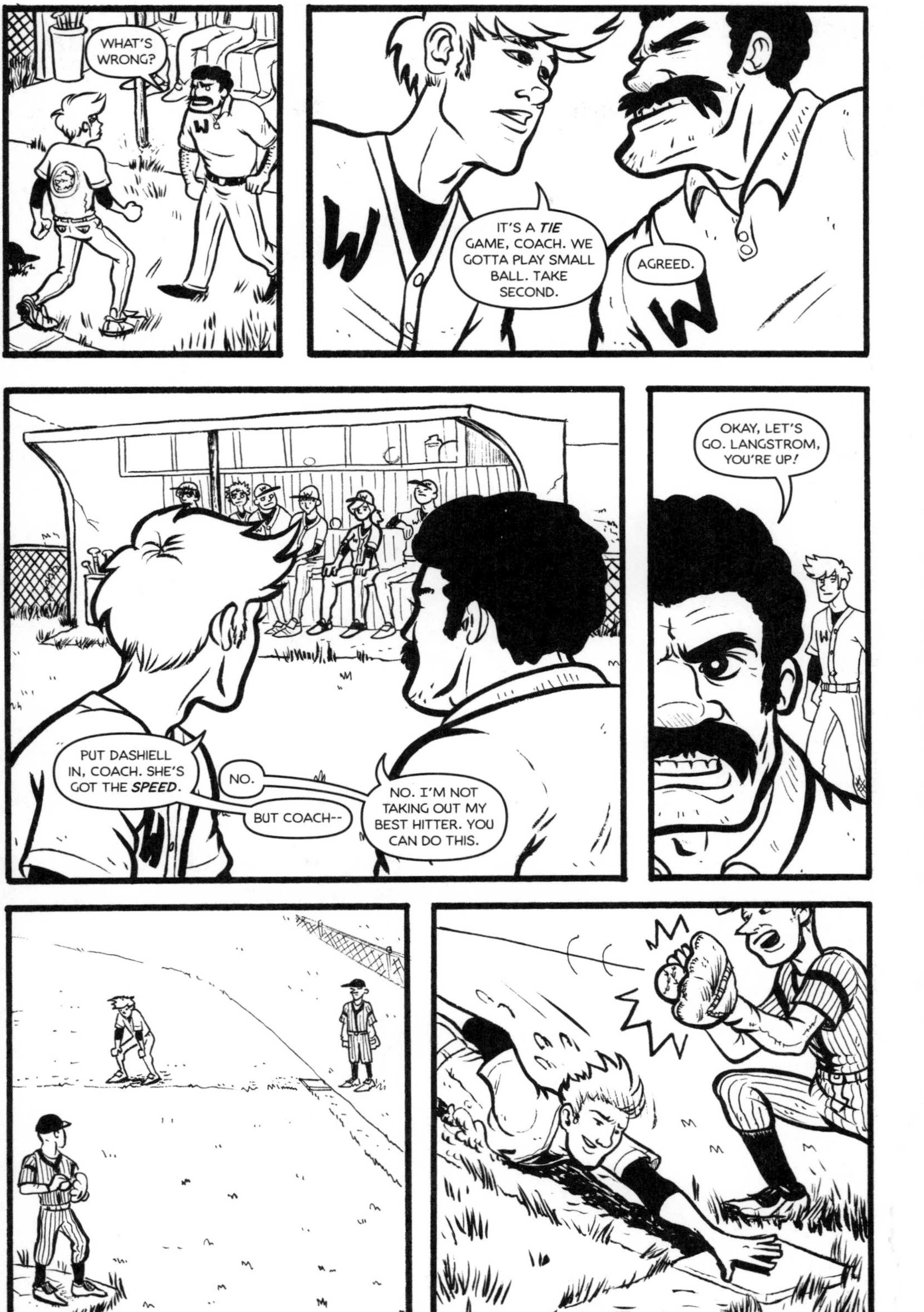
WHAT'S WRONG?
IT'S A *TIE* GAME, COACH. WE GOTTA PLAY SMALL BALL. TAKE SECOND.
AGREED.
PUT DASHIELL IN, COACH. SHE'S GOT THE *SPEED*.
NO.
BUT COACH--
NO. I'M NOT TAKING OUT MY BEST HITTER. YOU CAN DO THIS.
OKAY, LET'S GO. LANGSTROM, YOU'RE UP!

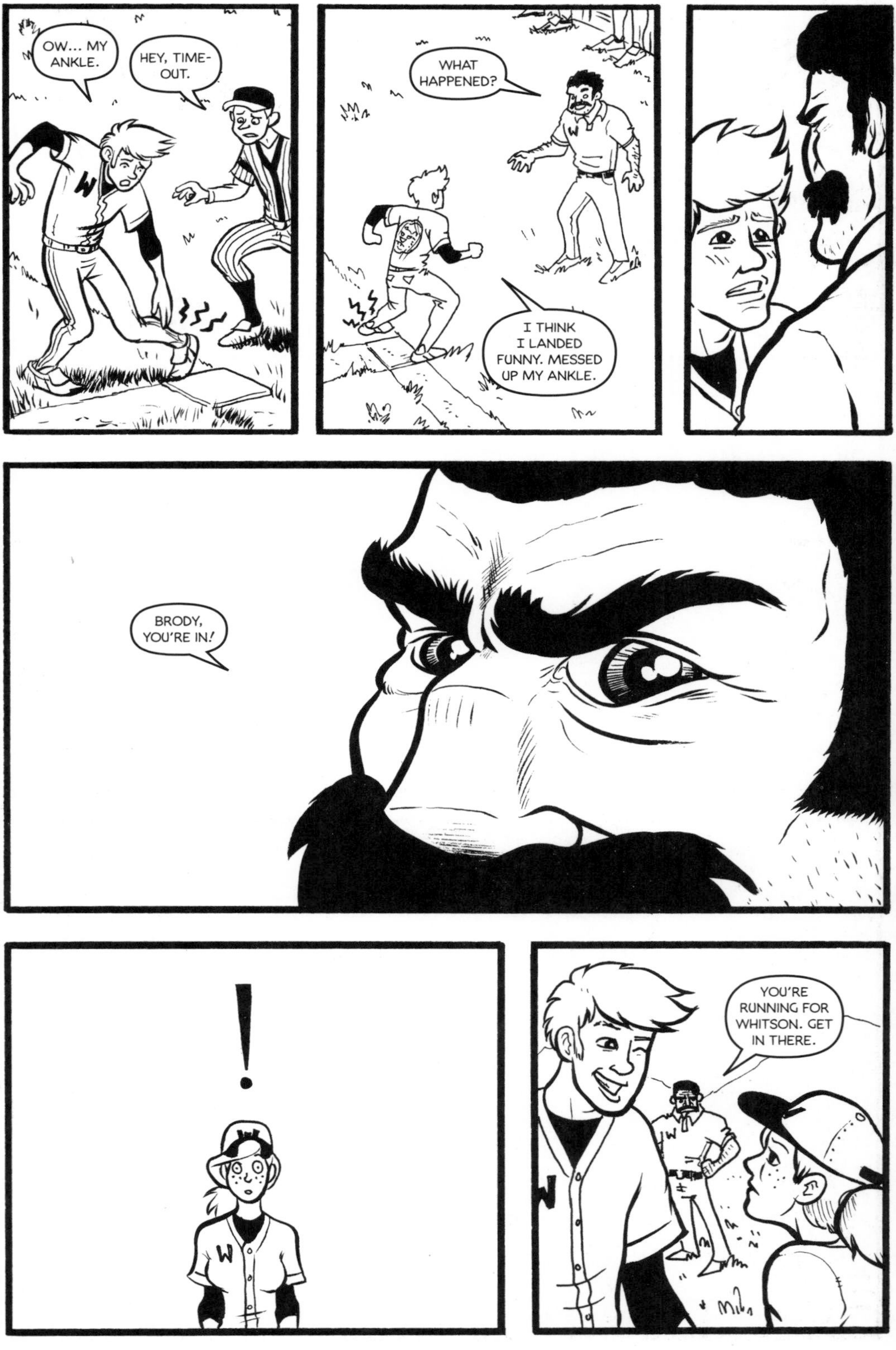
OW... MY ANKLE.
HEY, TIME-OUT.
WHAT HAPPENED?
I THINK I LANDED FUNNY. MESSED UP MY ANKLE.
BRODY, YOU'RE IN!
!
YOU'RE RUNNING FOR WHITSON. GET IN THERE.

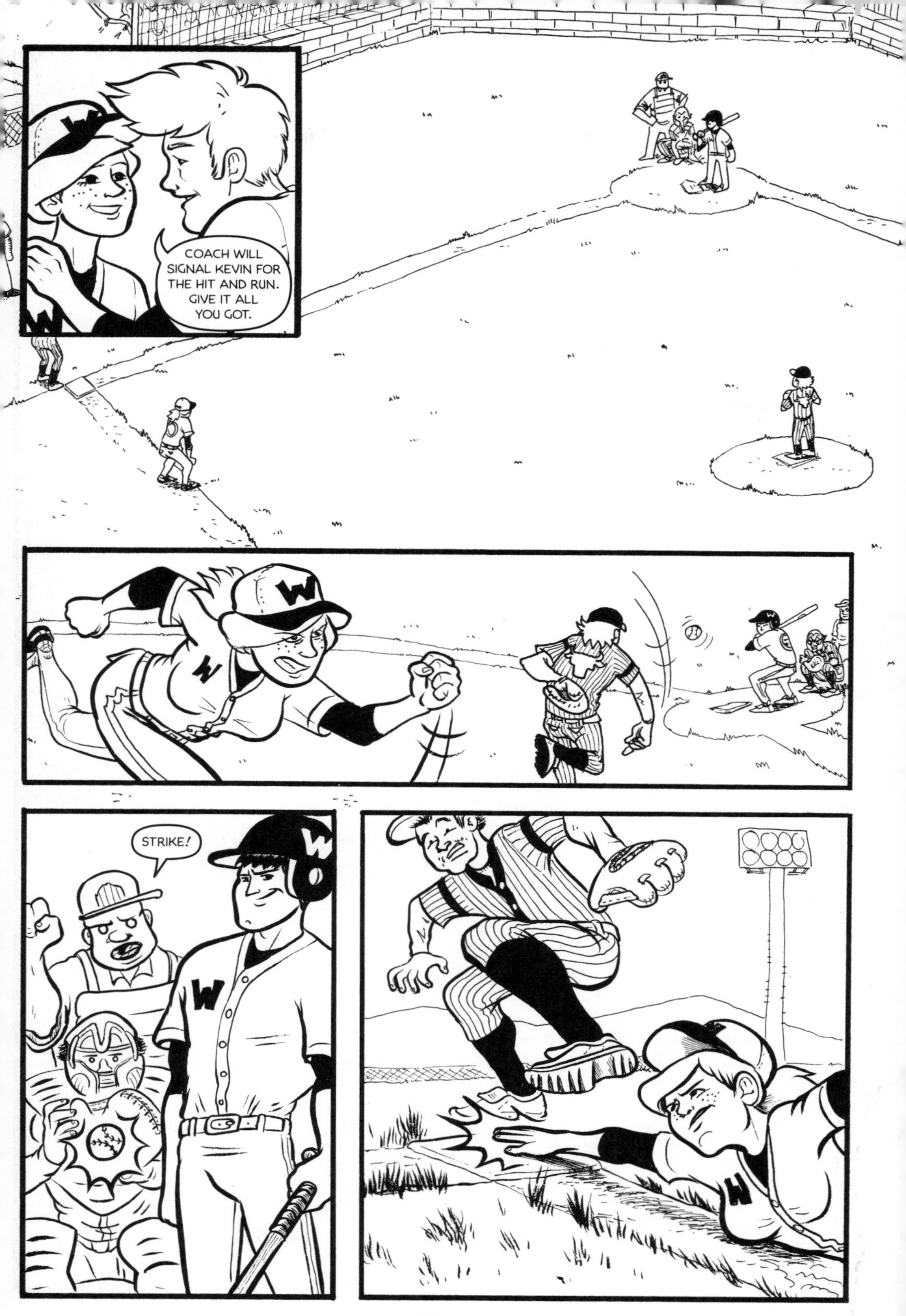
COACH WILL SIGNAL KEVIN FOR THE HIT AND RUN. GIVE IT ALL YOU GOT.
STRIKE!

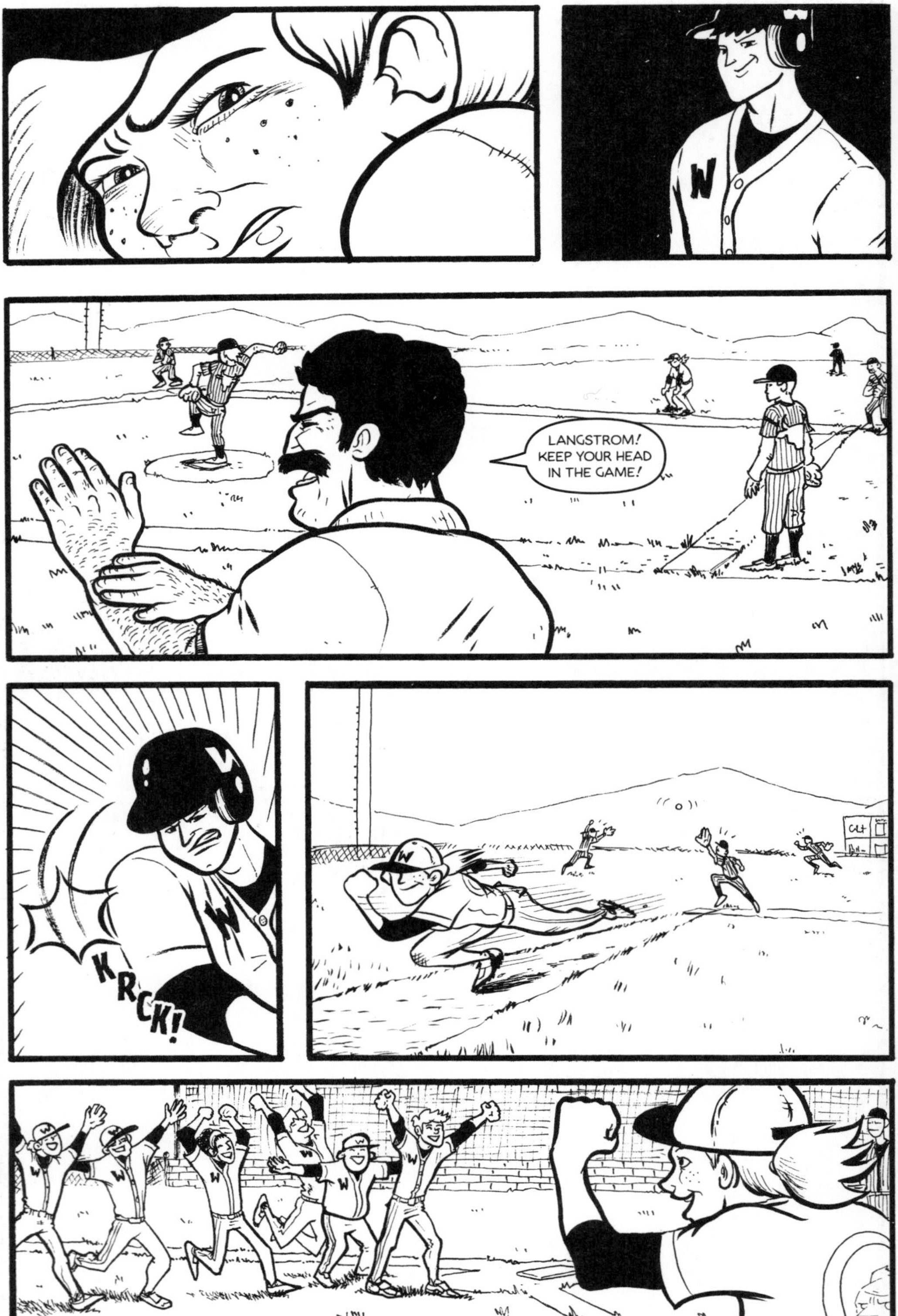
LANGSTROM! KEEP YOUR HEAD IN THE GAME!
KRCK!

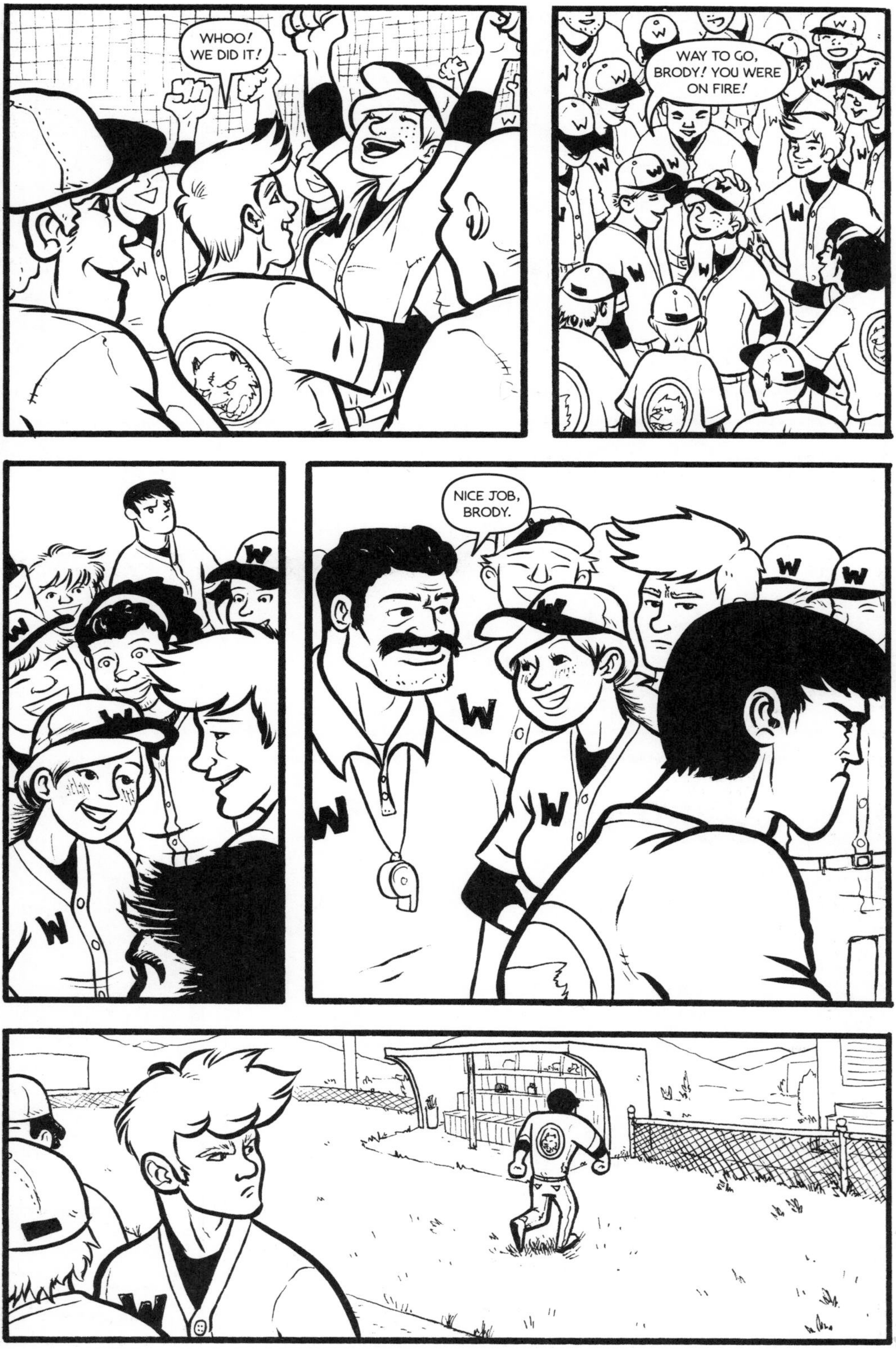
WHOO! WE DID IT!
WAY TO GO, BRODY! YOU WERE ON FIRE!
NICE JOB, BRODY.

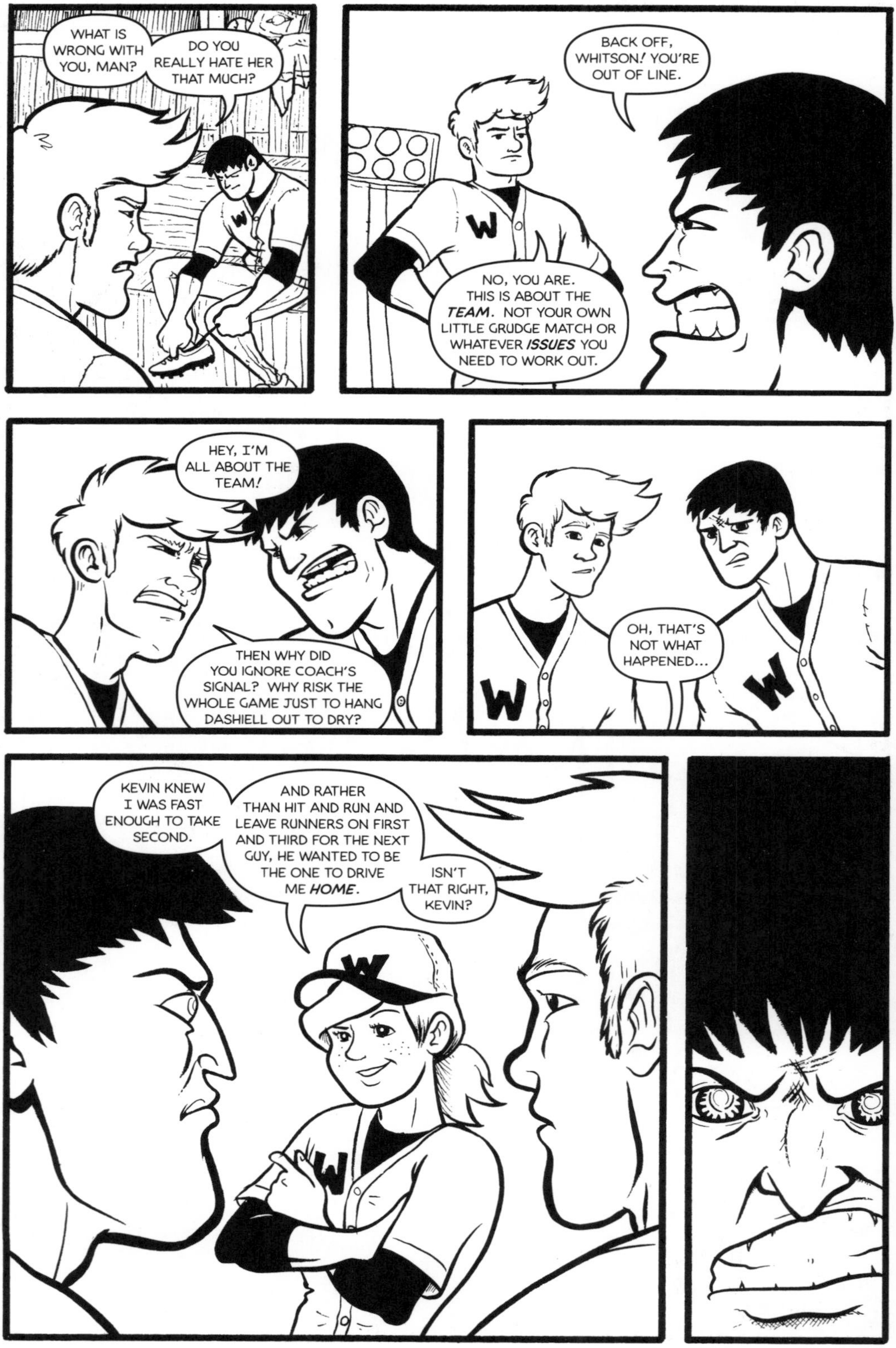
WHAT IS WRONG WITH YOU, MAN?
DO YOU REALLY HATE HER THAT MUCH?
BACK OFF, WHITSON! YOU'RE OUT OF LINE.
NO, YOU ARE. THIS IS ABOUT THE *TEAM*. NOT YOUR OWN LITTLE GRUDGE MATCH OR WHATEVER *ISSUES* YOU NEED TO WORK OUT.
HEY, I'M ALL ABOUT THE TEAM!
THEN WHY DID YOU IGNORE COACH'S SIGNAL? WHY RISK THE WHOLE GAME JUST TO HANG DASHIELL OUT TO DRY?
OH, THAT'S NOT WHAT HAPPENED...
KEVIN KNEW I WAS FAST ENOUGH TO TAKE SECOND.
AND RATHER THAN HIT AND RUN AND LEAVE RUNNERS ON FIRST AND THIRD FOR THE NEXT GUY, HE WANTED TO BE THE ONE TO DRIVE ME *HOME*.
ISN'T THAT RIGHT, KEVIN?

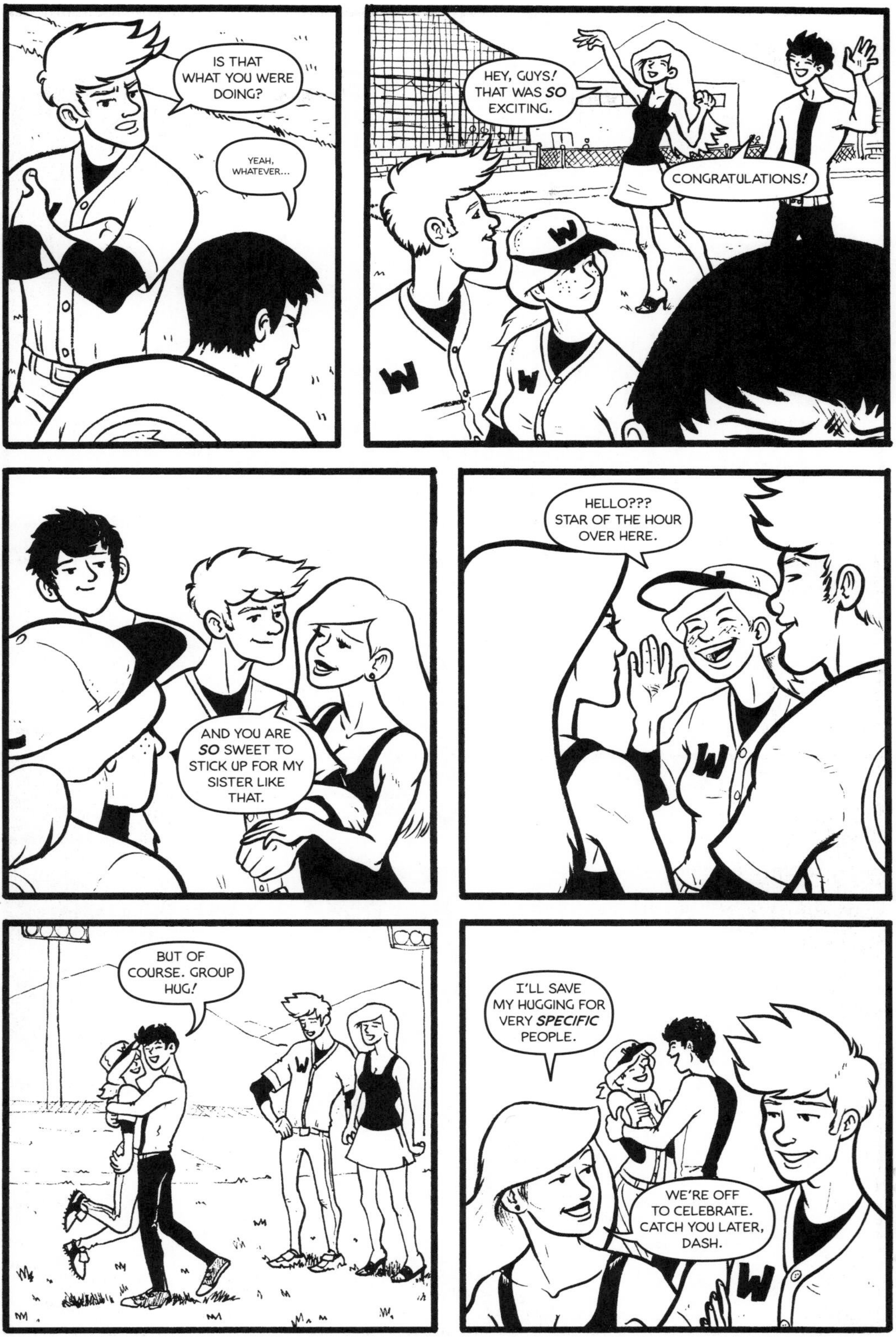
IS THAT WHAT YOU WERE DOING?
YEAH, WHATEVER...
HEY, GUYS! THAT WAS *SO* EXCITING.
CONGRATULATIONS!
AND YOU ARE *SO* SWEET TO STICK UP FOR MY SISTER LIKE THAT.
HELLO??? STAR OF THE HOUR OVER HERE.
BUT OF COURSE. GROUP HUG!
I'LL SAVE MY HUGGING FOR VERY *SPECIFIC* PEOPLE.
WE'RE OFF TO CELEBRATE. CATCH YOU LATER, DASH.

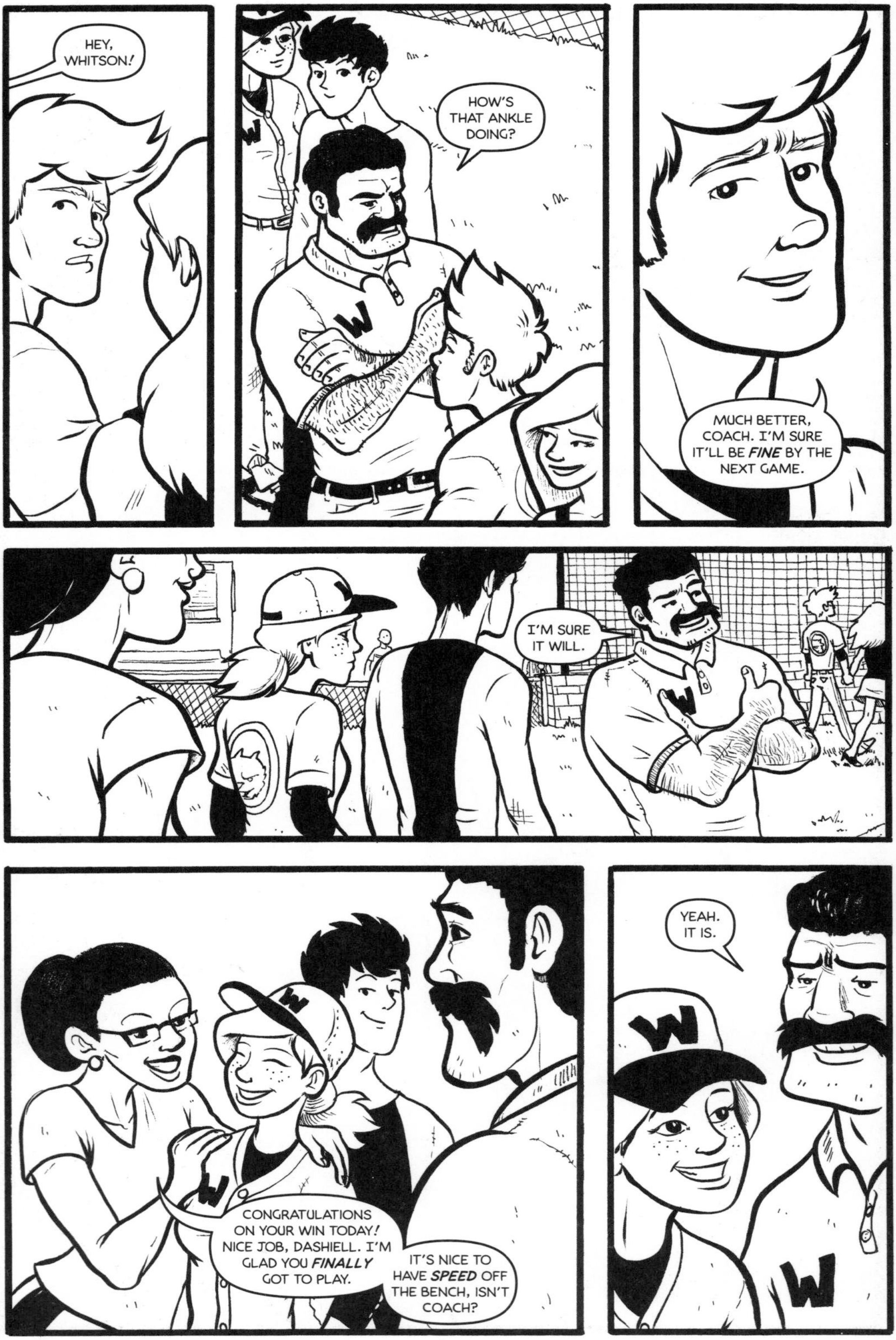
HEY, WHITSON!
HOW'S THAT ANKLE DOING?
MUCH BETTER, COACH. I'M SURE IT'LL BE *FINE* BY THE NEXT GAME.
I'M SURE IT WILL.
CONGRATULATIONS ON YOUR WIN TODAY! NICE JOB, DASHIELL. I'M GLAD YOU *FINALLY* GOT TO PLAY.
IT'S NICE TO HAVE *SPEED* OFF THE BENCH, ISN'T COACH?
YEAH. IT IS.

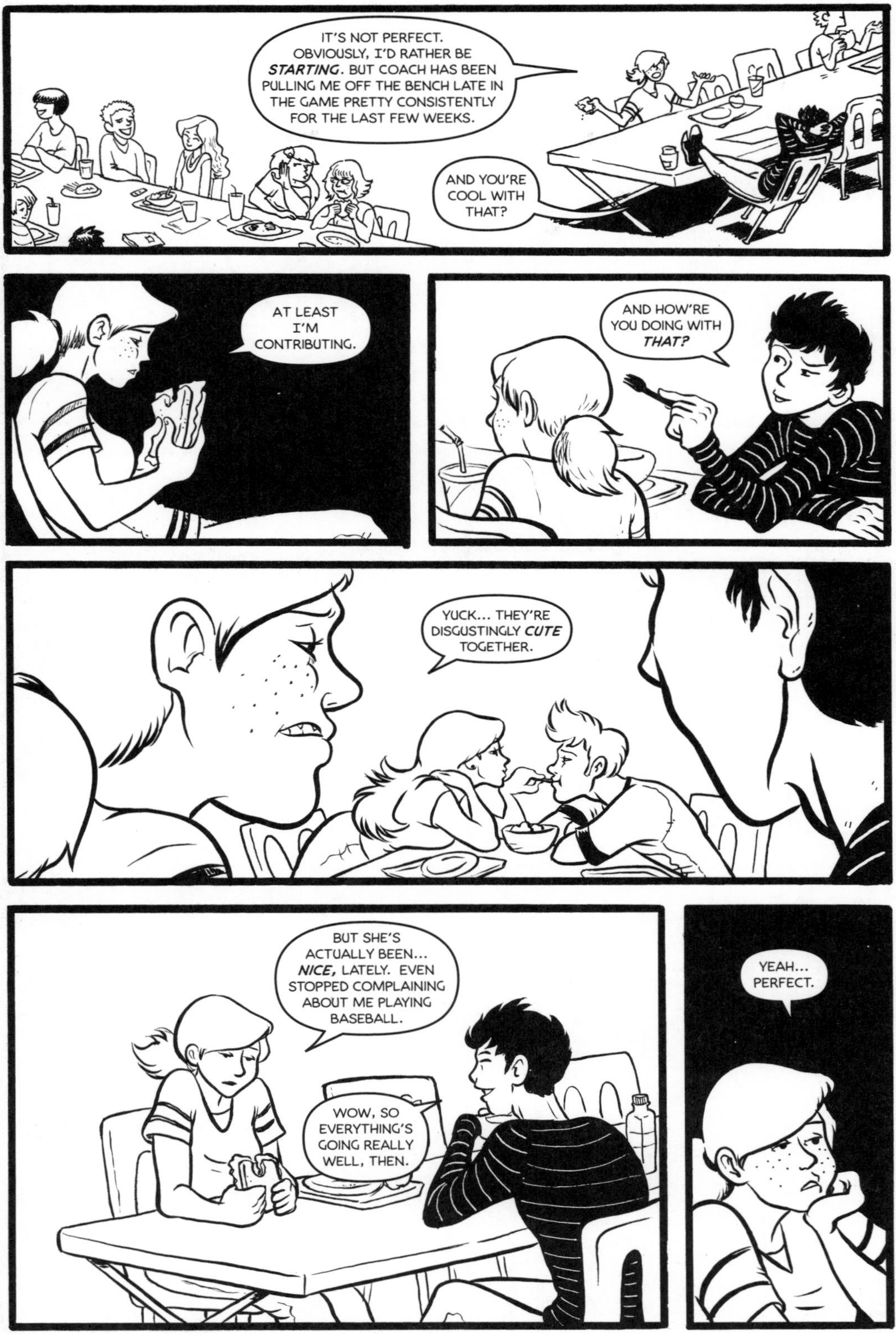
IT'S NOT PERFECT. OBVIOUSLY, I'D RATHER BE ***STARTING***. BUT COACH HAS BEEN PULLING ME OFF THE BENCH LATE IN THE GAME PRETTY CONSISTENTLY FOR THE LAST FEW WEEKS.
AND YOU'RE COOL WITH THAT?
AT LEAST I'M CONTRIBUTING.
AND HOW'RE YOU DOING WITH ***THAT?***
YUCK... THEY'RE DISGUSTINGLY ***CUTE*** TOGETHER.
BUT SHE'S ACTUALLY BEEN... ***NICE,*** LATELY. EVEN STOPPED COMPLAINING ABOUT ME PLAYING BASEBALL.
WOW, SO EVERYTHING'S GOING REALLY WELL, THEN.
YEAH... PERFECT.

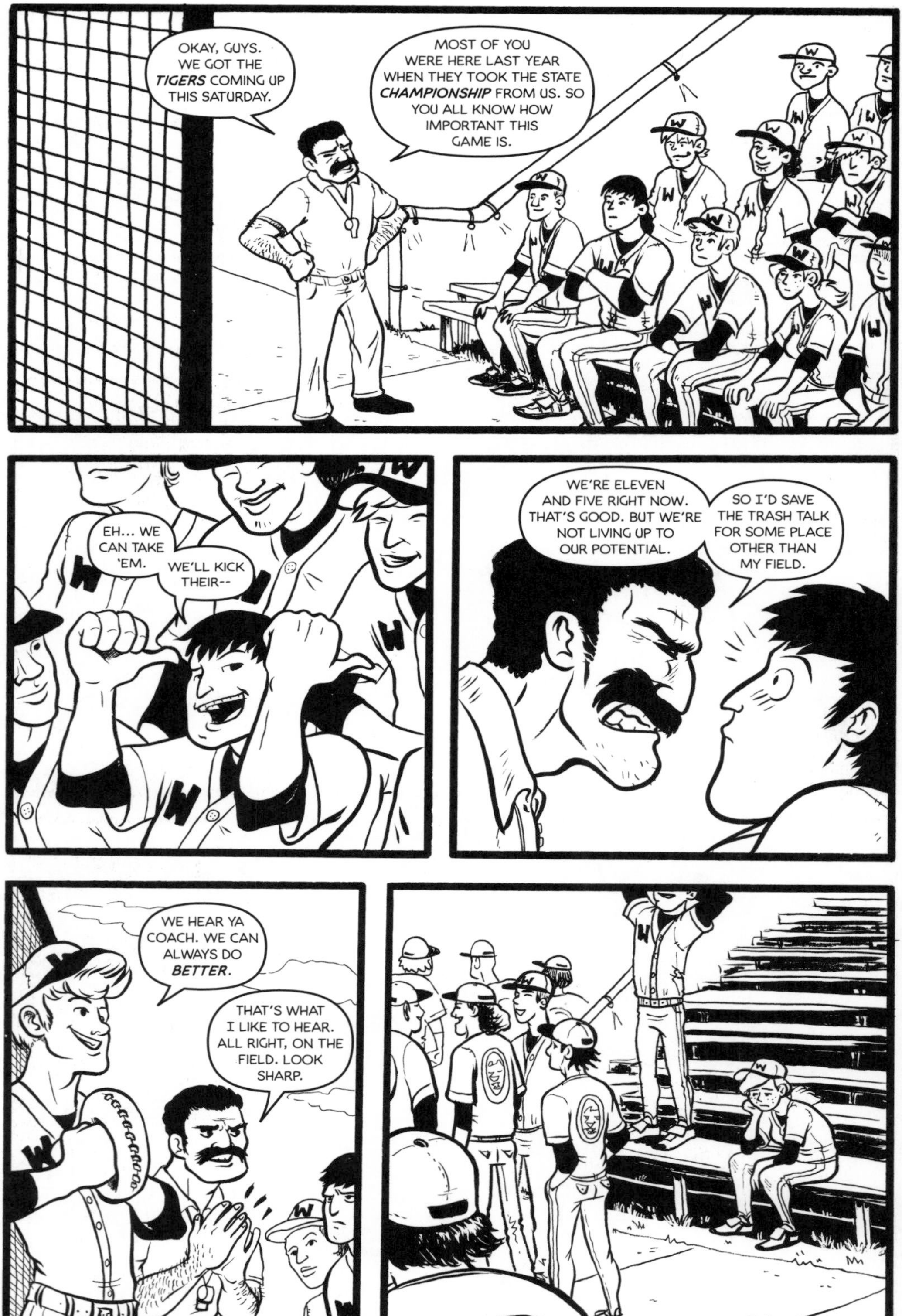
OKAY, GUYS. WE GOT THE TIGERS COMING UP THIS SATURDAY.
MOST OF YOU WERE HERE LAST YEAR WHEN THEY TOOK THE STATE CHAMPIONSHIP FROM US. SO YOU ALL KNOW HOW IMPORTANT THIS GAME IS.
EH... WE CAN TAKE 'EM.
WE'LL KICK THEIR--
WE'RE ELEVEN AND FIVE RIGHT NOW. THAT'S GOOD. BUT WE'RE NOT LIVING UP TO OUR POTENTIAL.
SO I'D SAVE THE TRASH TALK FOR SOME PLACE OTHER THAN MY FIELD.
WE HEAR YA COACH. WE CAN ALWAYS DO BETTER.
THAT'S WHAT I LIKE TO HEAR. ALL RIGHT, ON THE FIELD. LOOK SHARP.

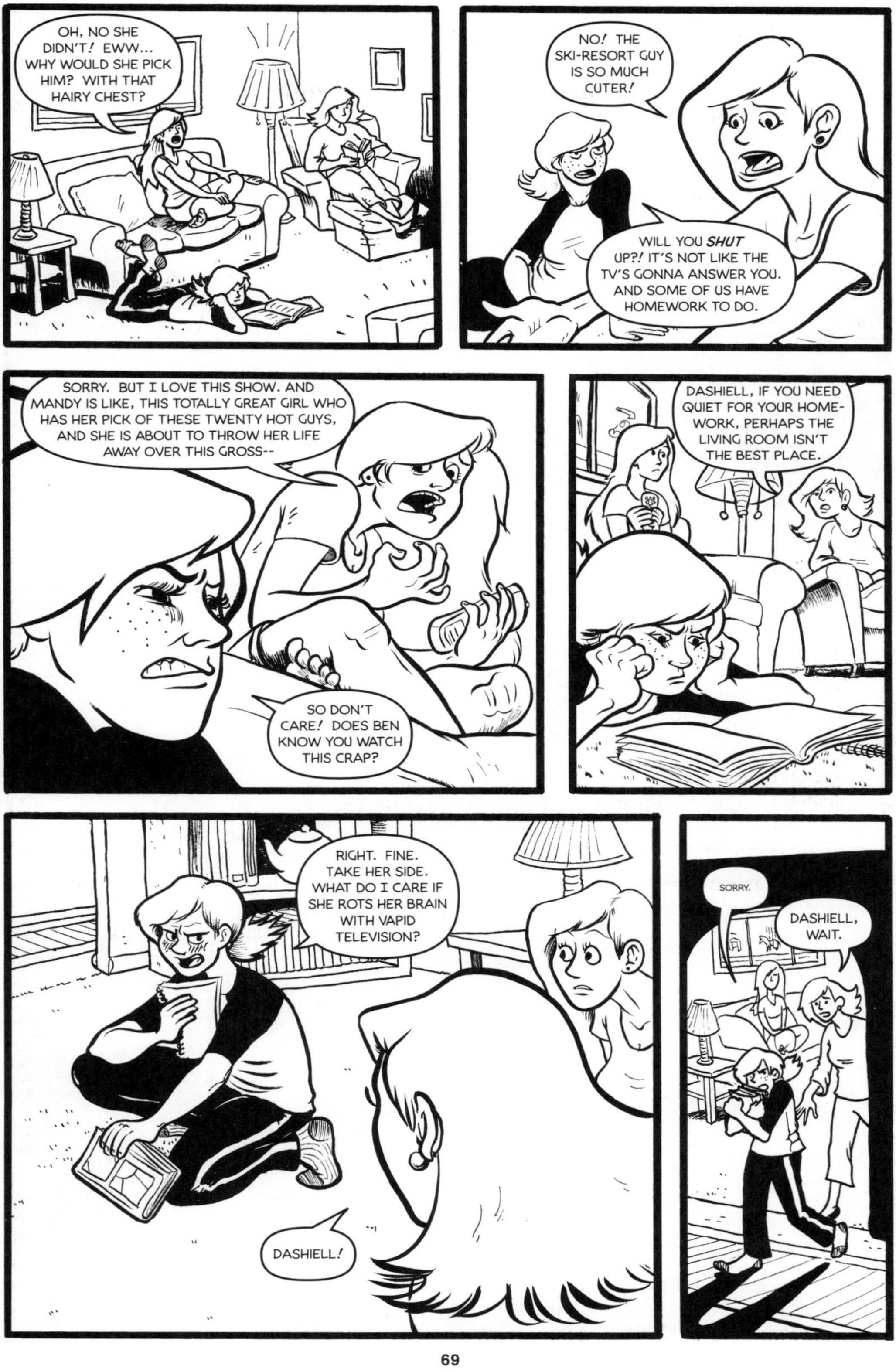
OH, NO SHE DIDN'T! EWW... WHY WOULD SHE PICK HIM? WITH THAT HAIRY CHEST?
NO! THE SKI-RESORT GUY IS SO MUCH CUTER!
WILL YOU SHUT UP?! IT'S NOT LIKE THE TV'S GONNA ANSWER YOU. AND SOME OF US HAVE HOMEWORK TO DO.
SORRY. BUT I LOVE THIS SHOW. AND MANDY IS LIKE, THIS TOTALLY GREAT GIRL WHO HAS HER PICK OF THESE TWENTY HOT GUYS, AND SHE IS ABOUT TO THROW HER LIFE AWAY OVER THIS GROSS--
SO DON'T CARE! DOES BEN KNOW YOU WATCH THIS CRAP?
DASHIELL, IF YOU NEED QUIET FOR YOUR HOME-WORK, PERHAPS THE LIVING ROOM ISN'T THE BEST PLACE.
RIGHT. FINE. TAKE HER SIDE. WHAT DO I CARE IF SHE ROTS HER BRAIN WITH VAPID TELEVISION?
DASHIELL!
SORRY.
DASHIELL, WAIT.

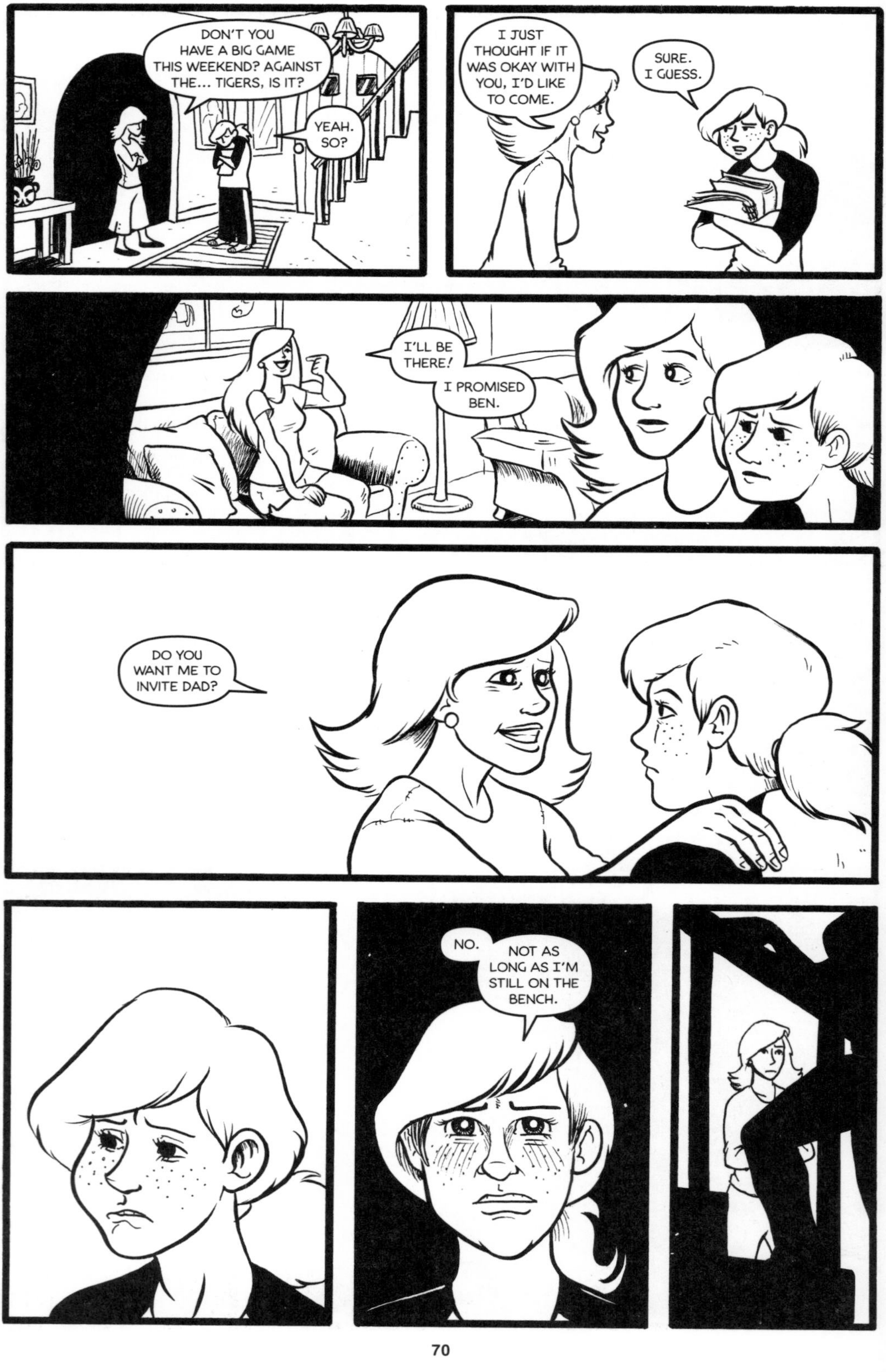
DON'T YOU HAVE A BIG GAME THIS WEEKEND? AGAINST THE... TIGERS, IS IT?
YEAH. SO?
I JUST THOUGHT IF IT WAS OKAY WITH YOU, I'D LIKE TO COME.
SURE. I GUESS.
I'LL BE THERE!
I PROMISED BEN.
DO YOU WANT ME TO INVITE DAD?
NO.
NOT AS LONG AS I'M STILL ON THE BENCH.

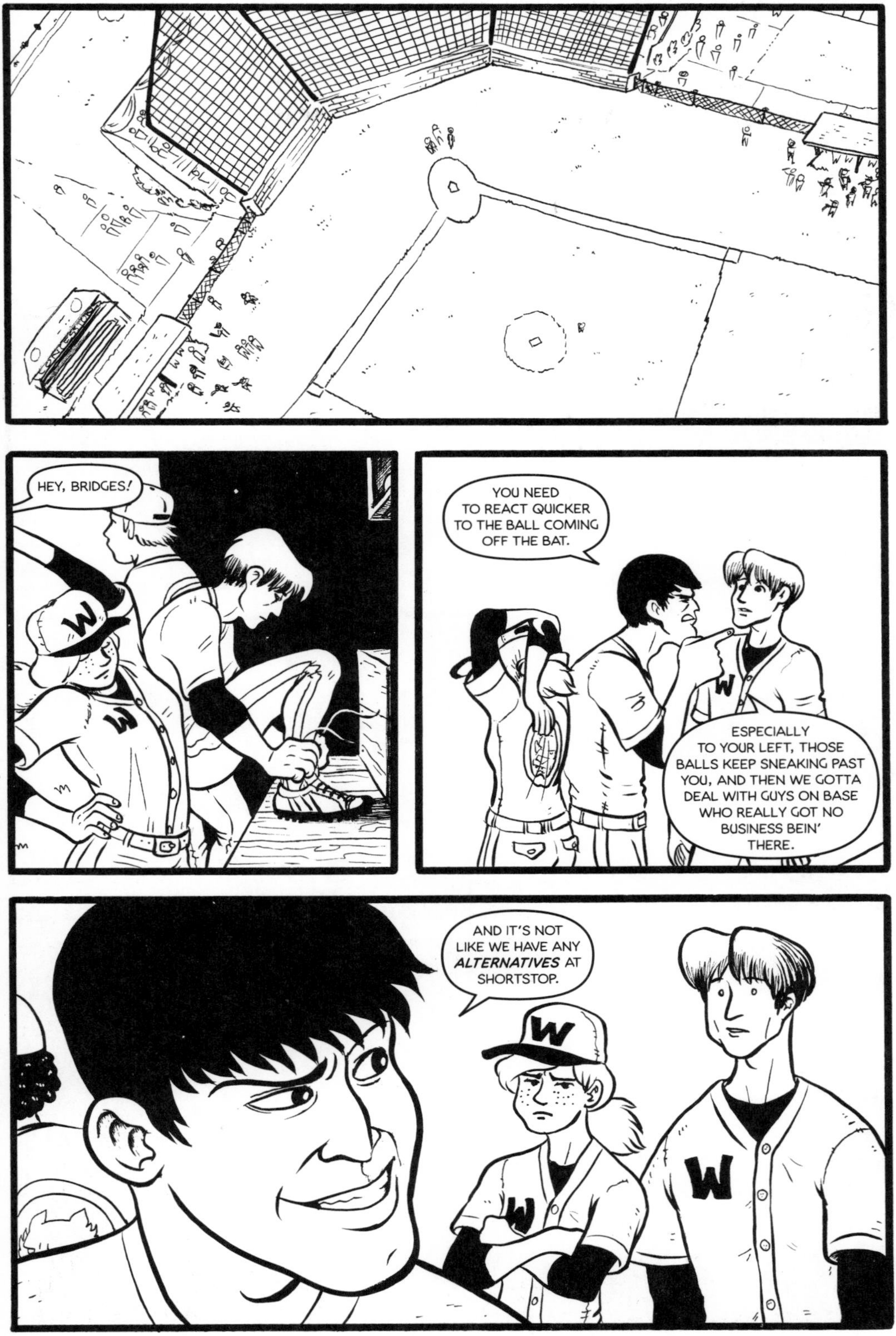
HEY, BRIDGES!
YOU NEED TO REACT QUICKER TO THE BALL COMING OFF THE BAT.
ESPECIALLY TO YOUR LEFT, THOSE BALLS KEEP SNEAKING PAST YOU, AND THEN WE GOTTA DEAL WITH GUYS ON BASE WHO REALLY GOT NO BUSINESS BEIN' THERE.
AND IT'S NOT LIKE WE HAVE ANY ***ALTERNATIVES*** AT SHORTSTOP.

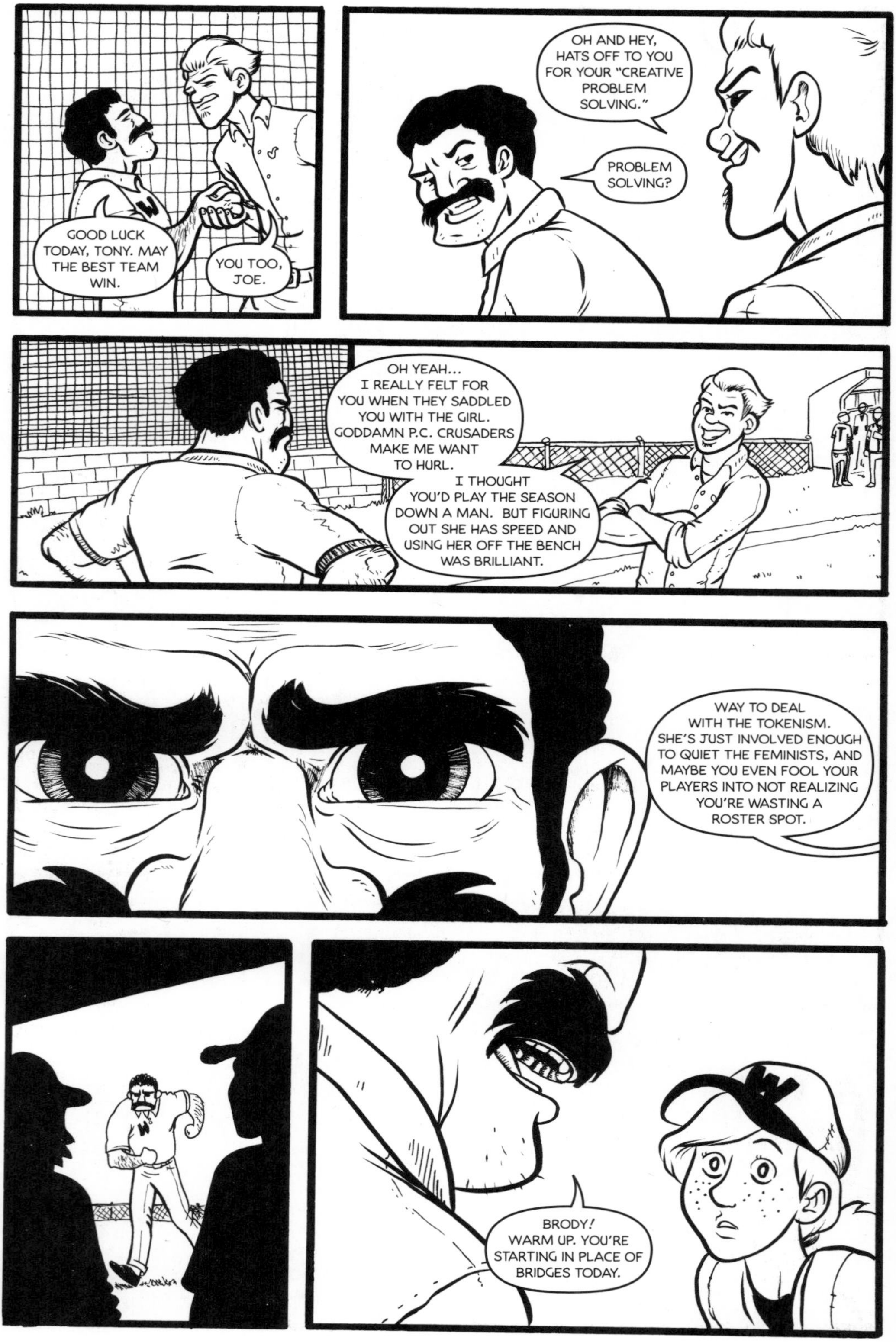
GOOD LUCK TODAY, TONY. MAY THE BEST TEAM WIN.
YOU TOO, JOE.
OH AND HEY, HATS OFF TO YOU FOR YOUR "CREATIVE PROBLEM SOLVING."
PROBLEM SOLVING?
OH YEAH... I REALLY FELT FOR YOU WHEN THEY SADDLED YOU WITH THE GIRL. GODDAMN P.C. CRUSADERS MAKE ME WANT TO HURL.
I THOUGHT YOU'D PLAY THE SEASON DOWN A MAN. BUT FIGURING OUT SHE HAS SPEED AND USING HER OFF THE BENCH WAS BRILLIANT.
WAY TO DEAL WITH THE TOKENISM. SHE'S JUST INVOLVED ENOUGH TO QUIET THE FEMINISTS, AND MAYBE YOU EVEN FOOL YOUR PLAYERS INTO NOT REALIZING YOU'RE WASTING A ROSTER SPOT.
BRODY! WARM UP. YOU'RE STARTING IN PLACE OF BRIDGES TODAY.

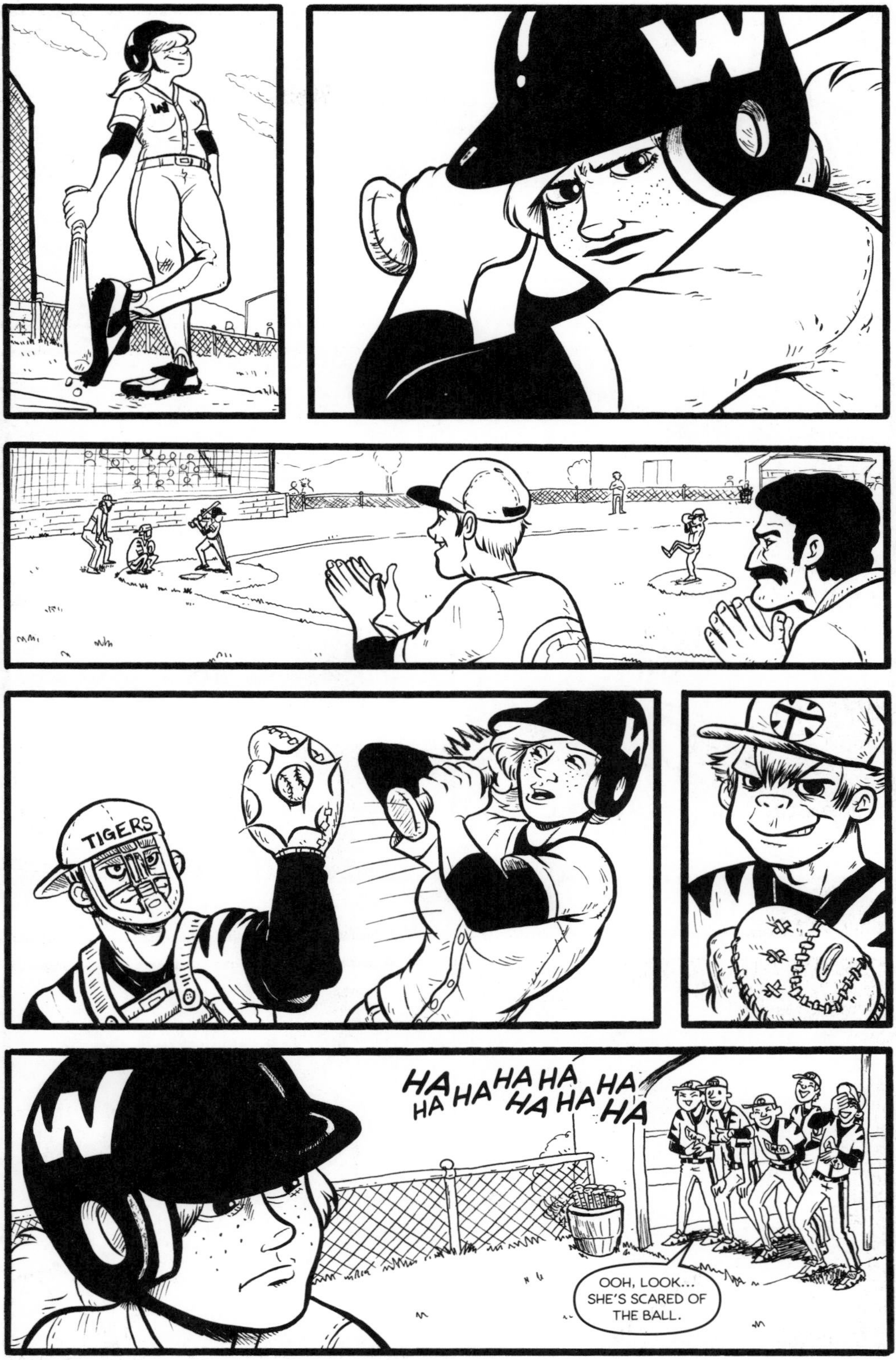
TIGERS
HA HA HA HA HA HA HA HA HA HA
OOH, LOOK... SHE'S SCARED OF THE BALL.

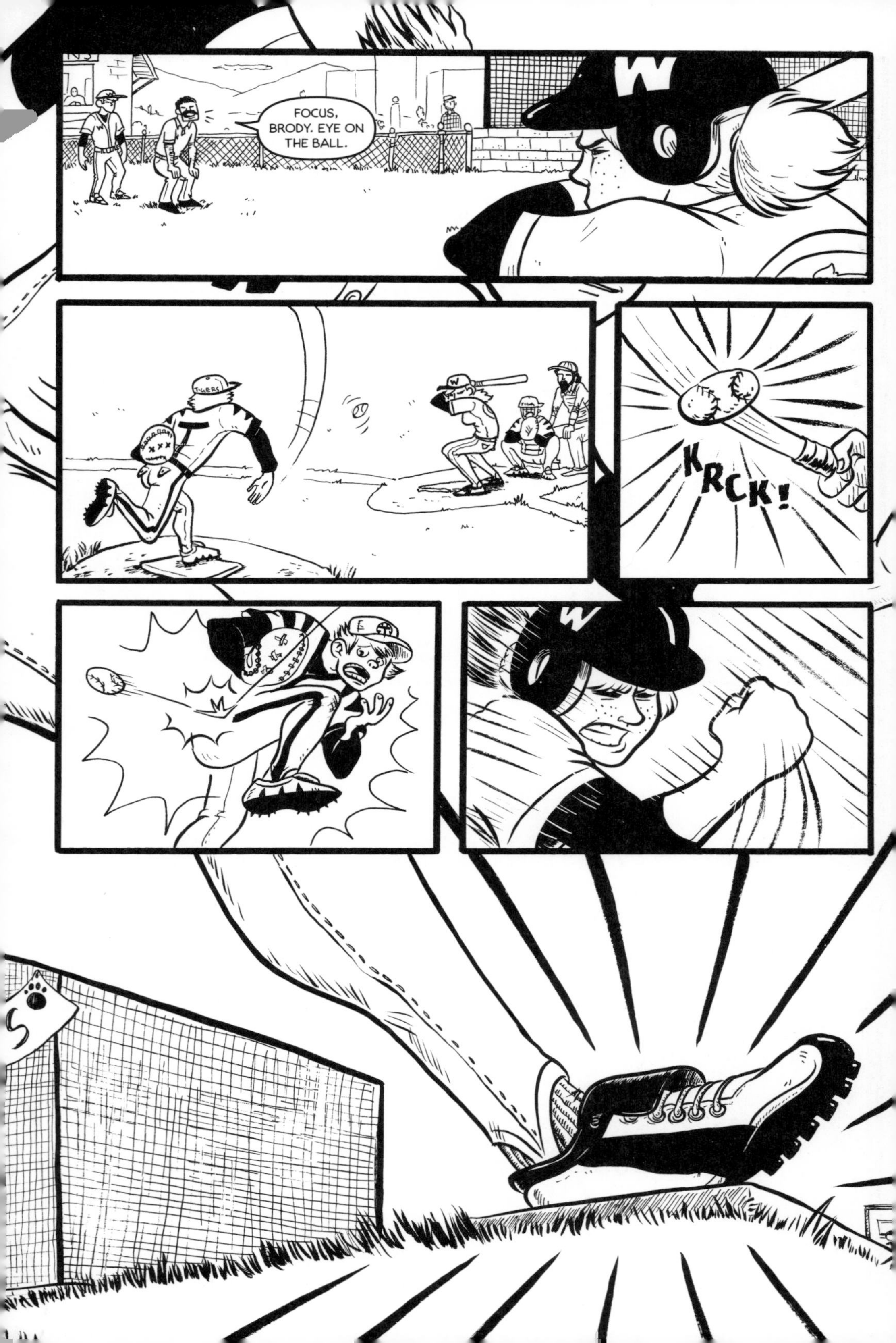
FOCUS, BRODY. EYE ON THE BALL.
TIGERS
KRCK!

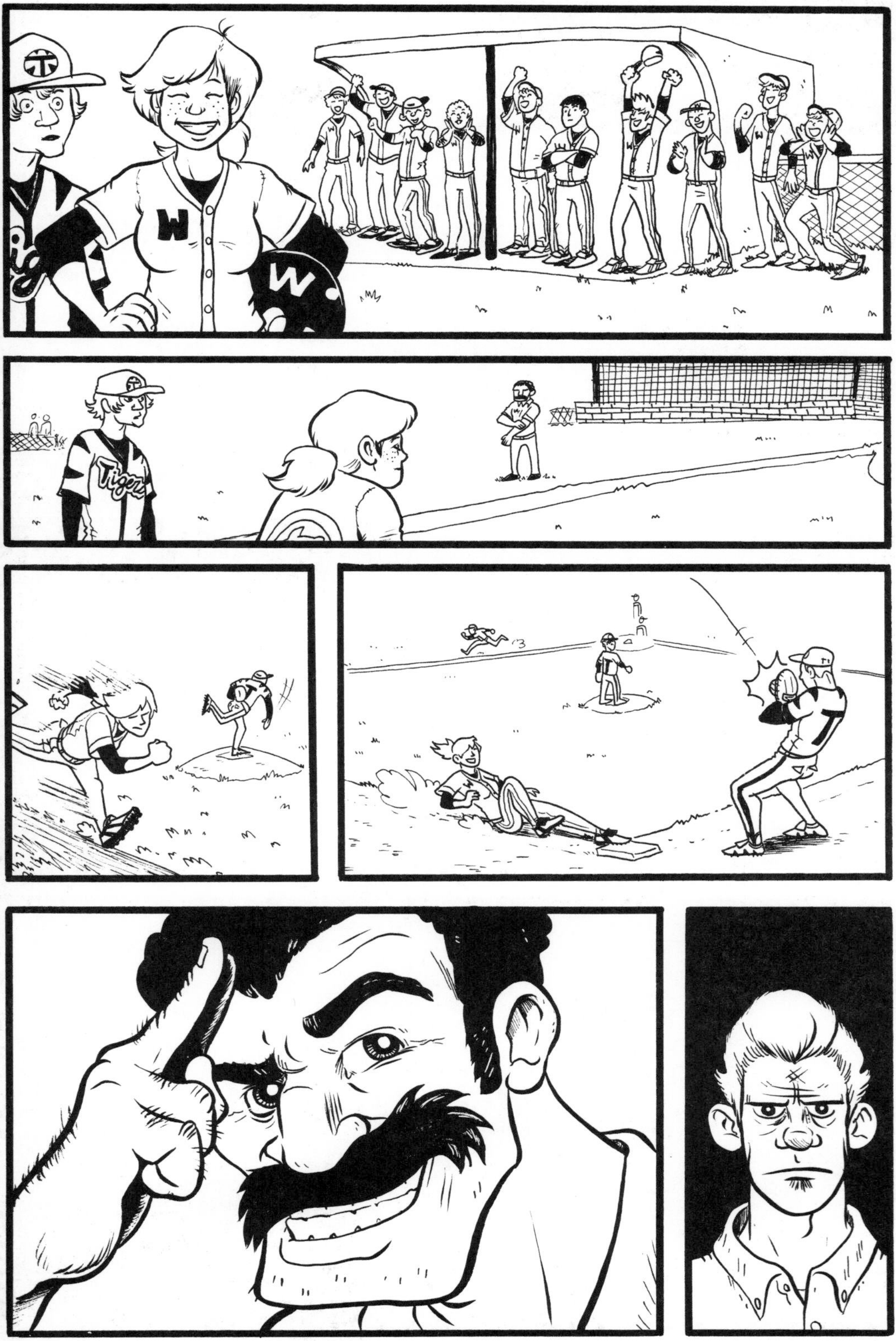

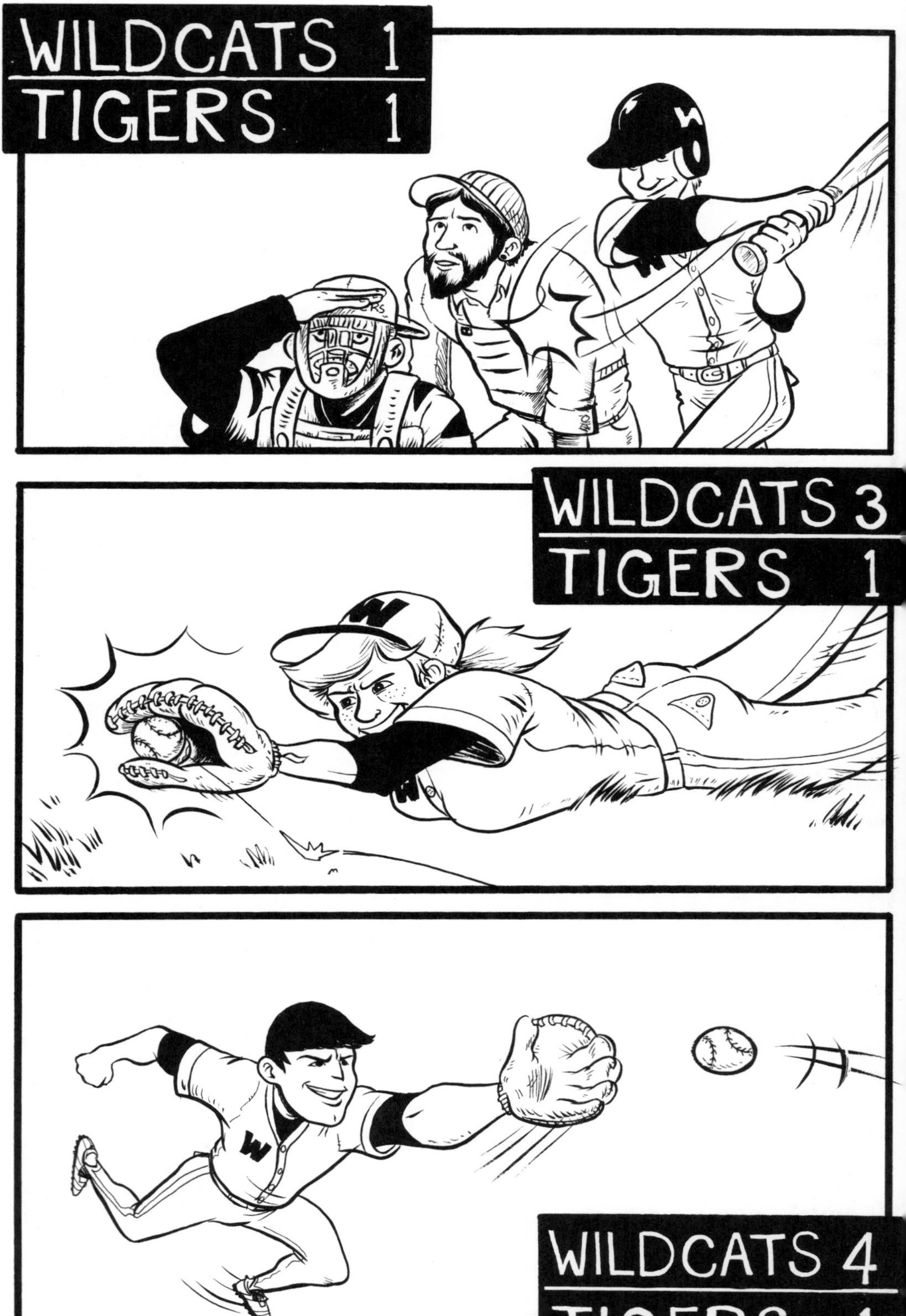
WILDCATS 1
TIGERS 1
WILDCATS 3
TIGERS 1
WILDCATS 4
TIGERS 1

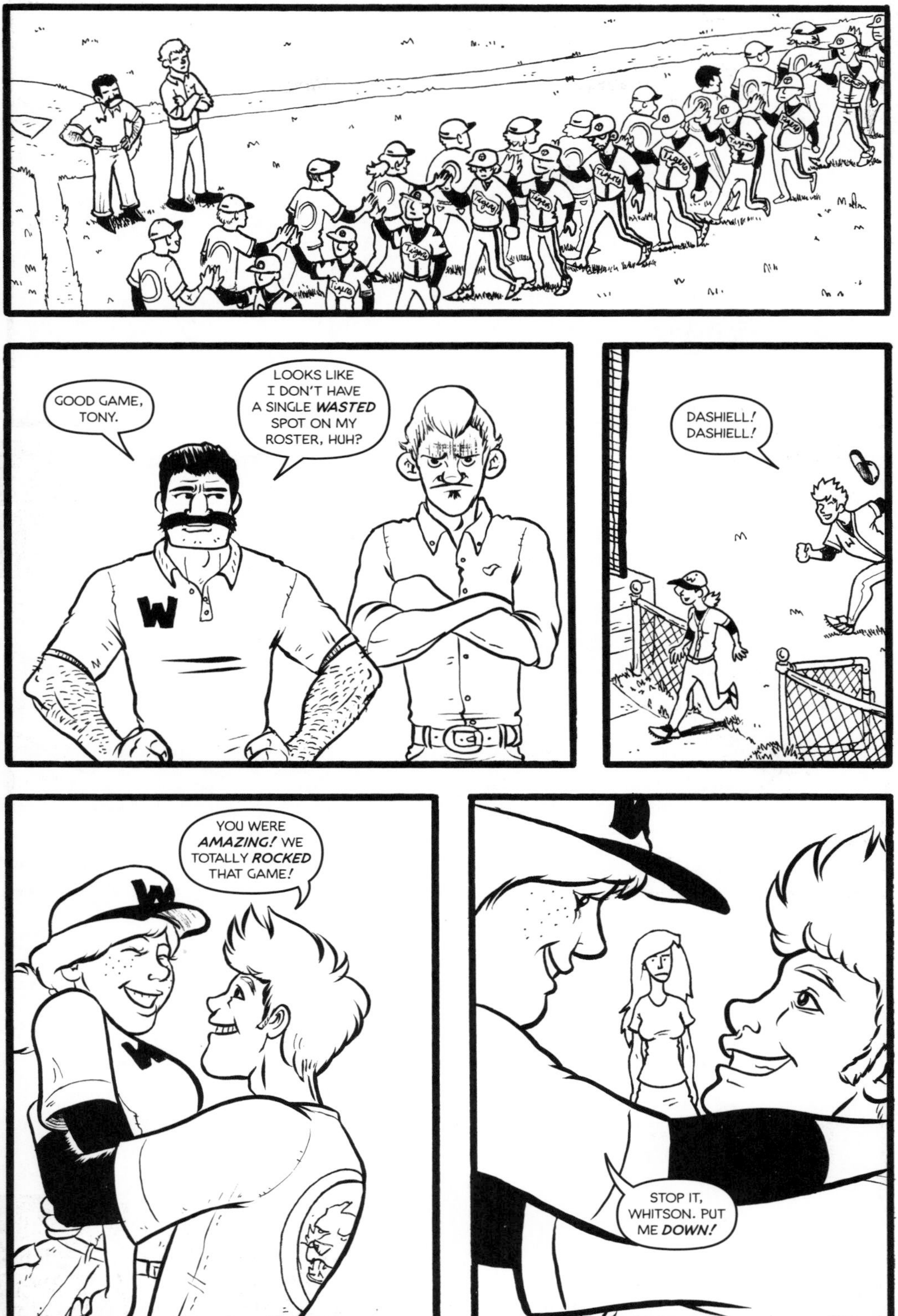
GOOD GAME, TONY.
LOOKS LIKE I DON'T HAVE A SINGLE **WASTED** SPOT ON MY ROSTER, HUH?
DASHIELL! DASHIELL!
YOU WERE **AMAZING!** WE TOTALLY **ROCKED** THAT GAME!
STOP IT, WHITSON. PUT ME **DOWN!**

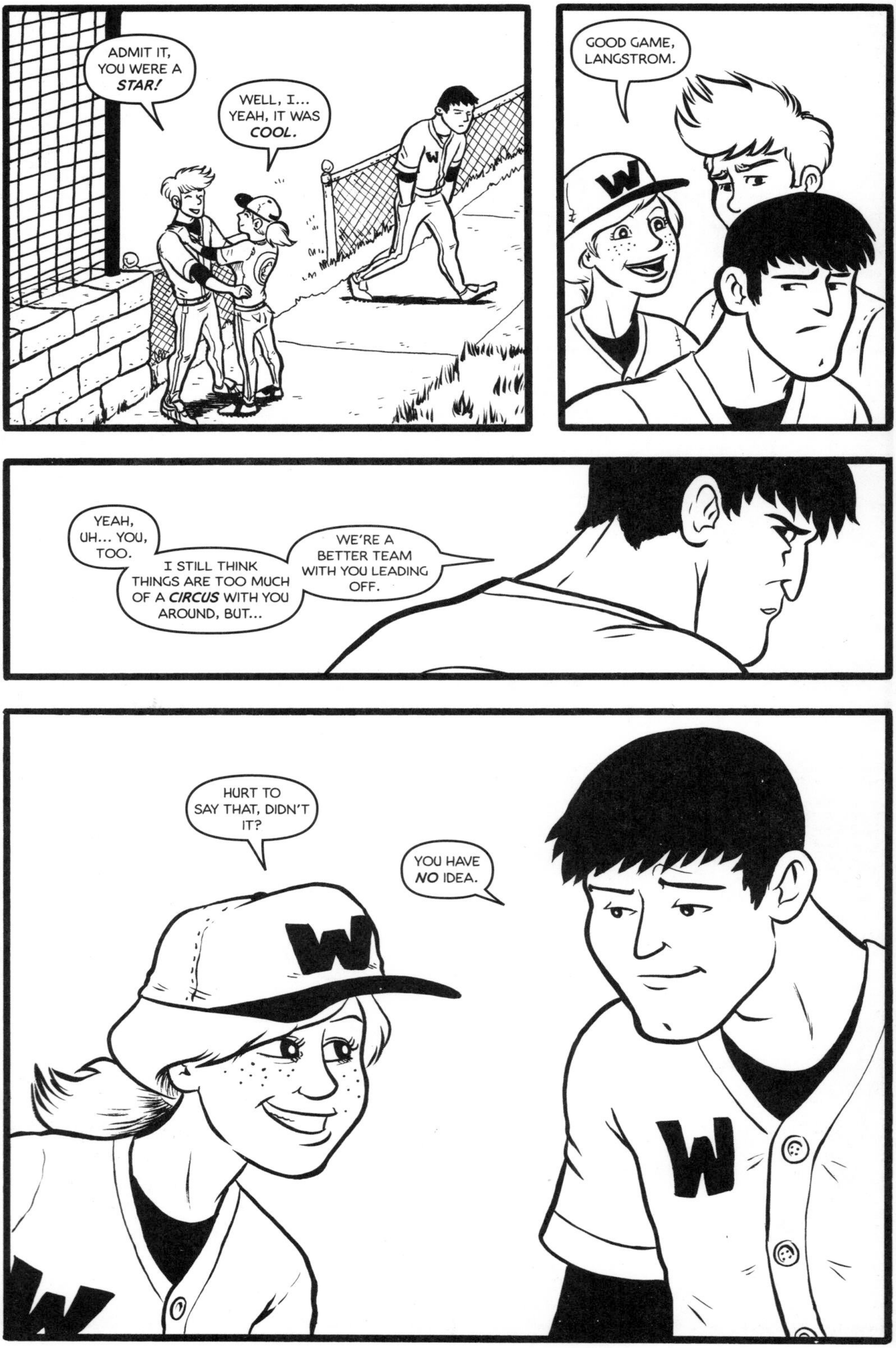
ADMIT IT, YOU WERE A *STAR!*
WELL, I... YEAH, IT WAS *COOL.*
GOOD GAME, LANGSTROM.
YEAH, UH... YOU, TOO.
I STILL THINK THINGS ARE TOO MUCH OF A *CIRCUS* WITH YOU AROUND, BUT...
WE'RE A BETTER TEAM WITH YOU LEADING OFF.
HURT TO SAY THAT, DIDN'T IT?
YOU HAVE *NO* IDEA.

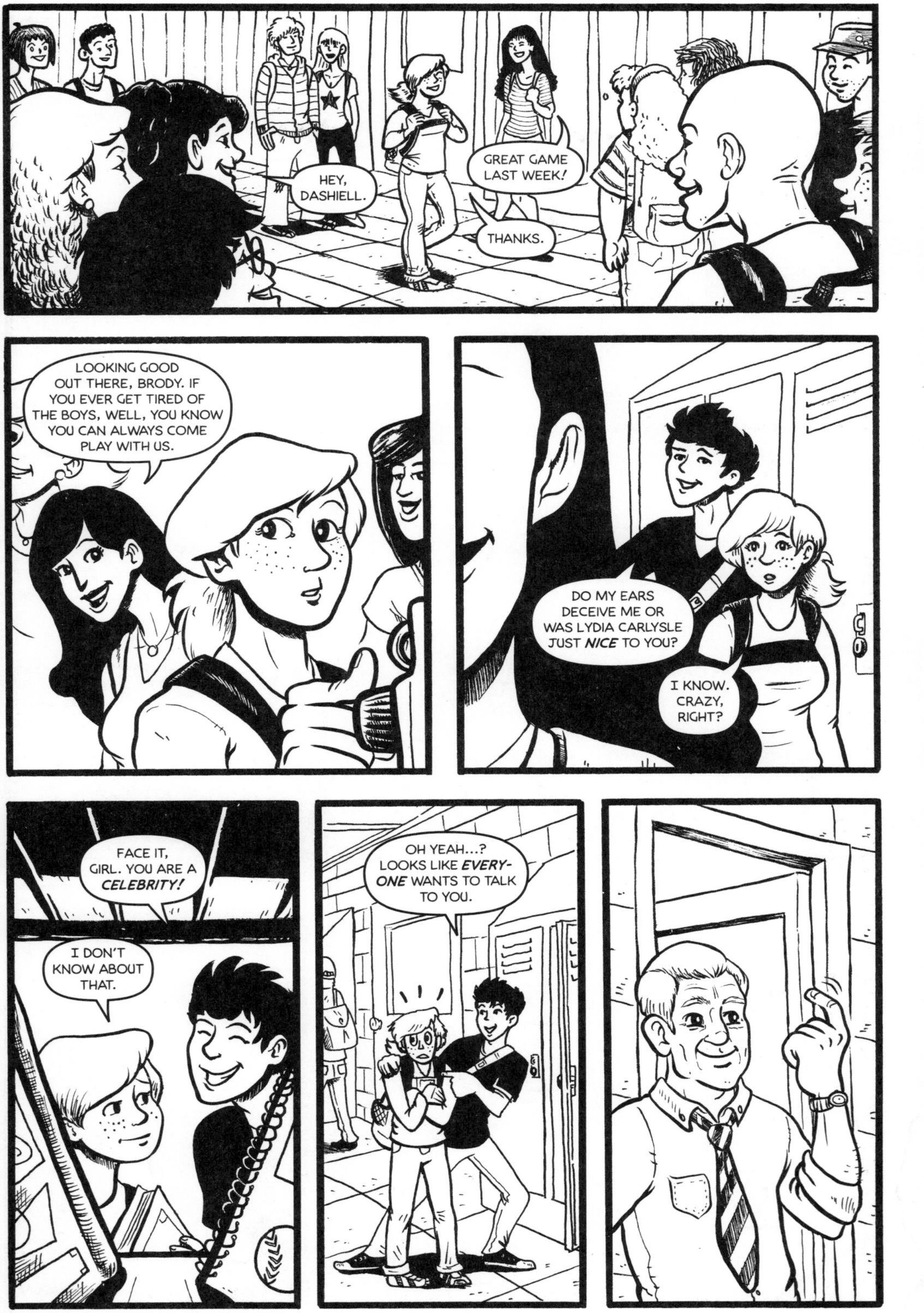
HEY, DASHIELL.
GREAT GAME LAST WEEK!
THANKS.
LOOKING GOOD OUT THERE, BRODY. IF YOU EVER GET TIRED OF THE BOYS, WELL, YOU KNOW YOU CAN ALWAYS COME PLAY WITH US.
DO MY EARS DECEIVE ME OR WAS LYDIA CARLYSLE JUST *NICE* TO YOU?
I KNOW. CRAZY, RIGHT?
FACE IT, GIRL. YOU ARE A *CELEBRITY!*
I DON'T KNOW ABOUT THAT.
OH YEAH...? LOOKS LIKE *EVERY-ONE* WANTS TO TALK TO YOU.

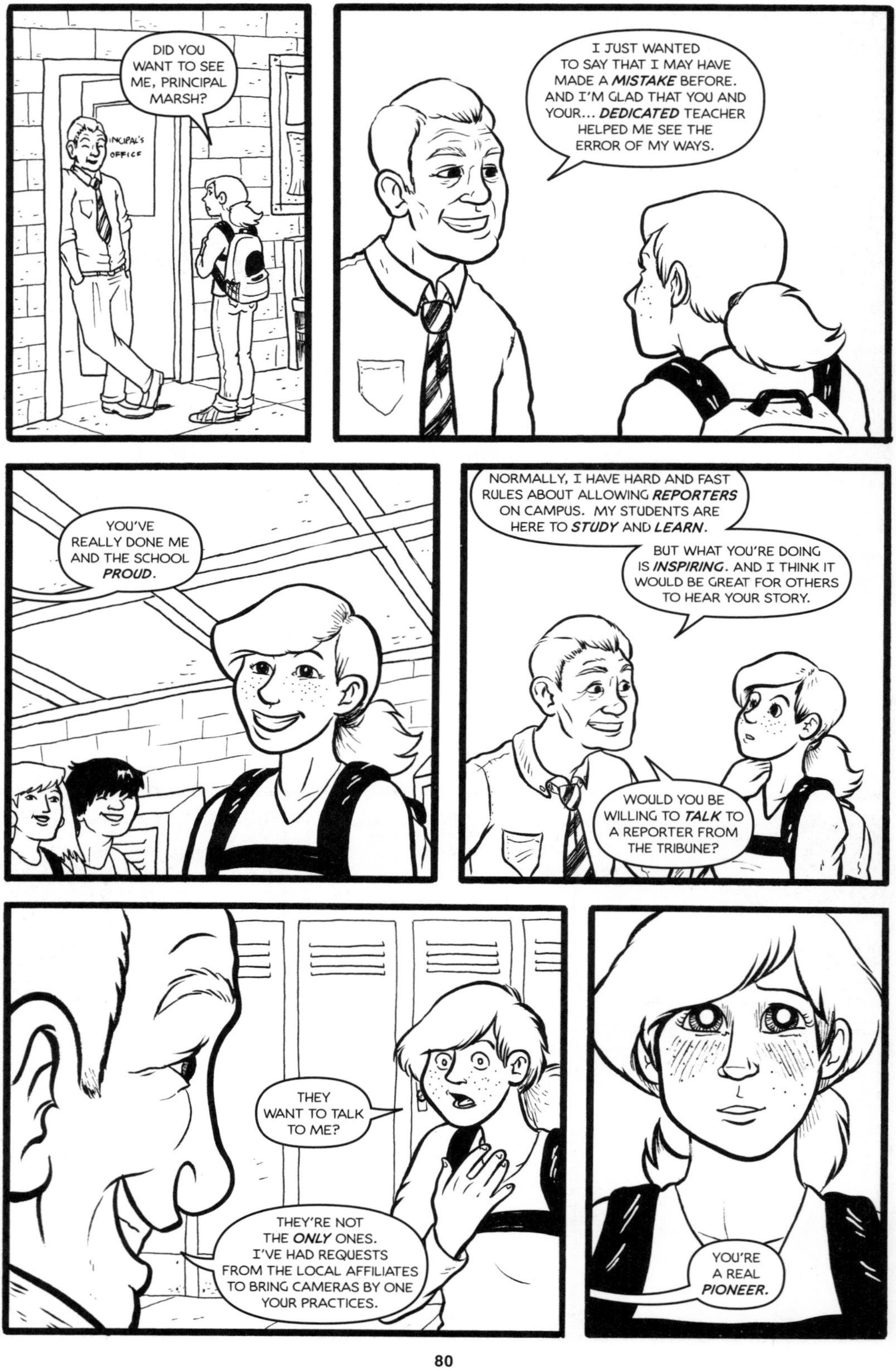
DID YOU WANT TO SEE ME, PRINCIPAL MARSH?
INCIPAL'S OFFICE
I JUST WANTED TO SAY THAT I MAY HAVE MADE A **MISTAKE** BEFORE. AND I'M GLAD THAT YOU AND YOUR... **DEDICATED** TEACHER HELPED ME SEE THE ERROR OF MY WAYS.
YOU'VE REALLY DONE ME AND THE SCHOOL **PROUD**.
NORMALLY, I HAVE HARD AND FAST RULES ABOUT ALLOWING **REPORTERS** ON CAMPUS. MY STUDENTS ARE HERE TO **STUDY** AND **LEARN**.
BUT WHAT YOU'RE DOING IS **INSPIRING**. AND I THINK IT WOULD BE GREAT FOR OTHERS TO HEAR YOUR STORY.
WOULD YOU BE WILLING TO **TALK** TO A REPORTER FROM THE TRIBUNE?
THEY WANT TO TALK TO ME?
THEY'RE NOT THE **ONLY** ONES. I'VE HAD REQUESTS FROM THE LOCAL AFFILIATES TO BRING CAMERAS BY ONE YOUR PRACTICES.
YOU'RE A REAL **PIONEER**.

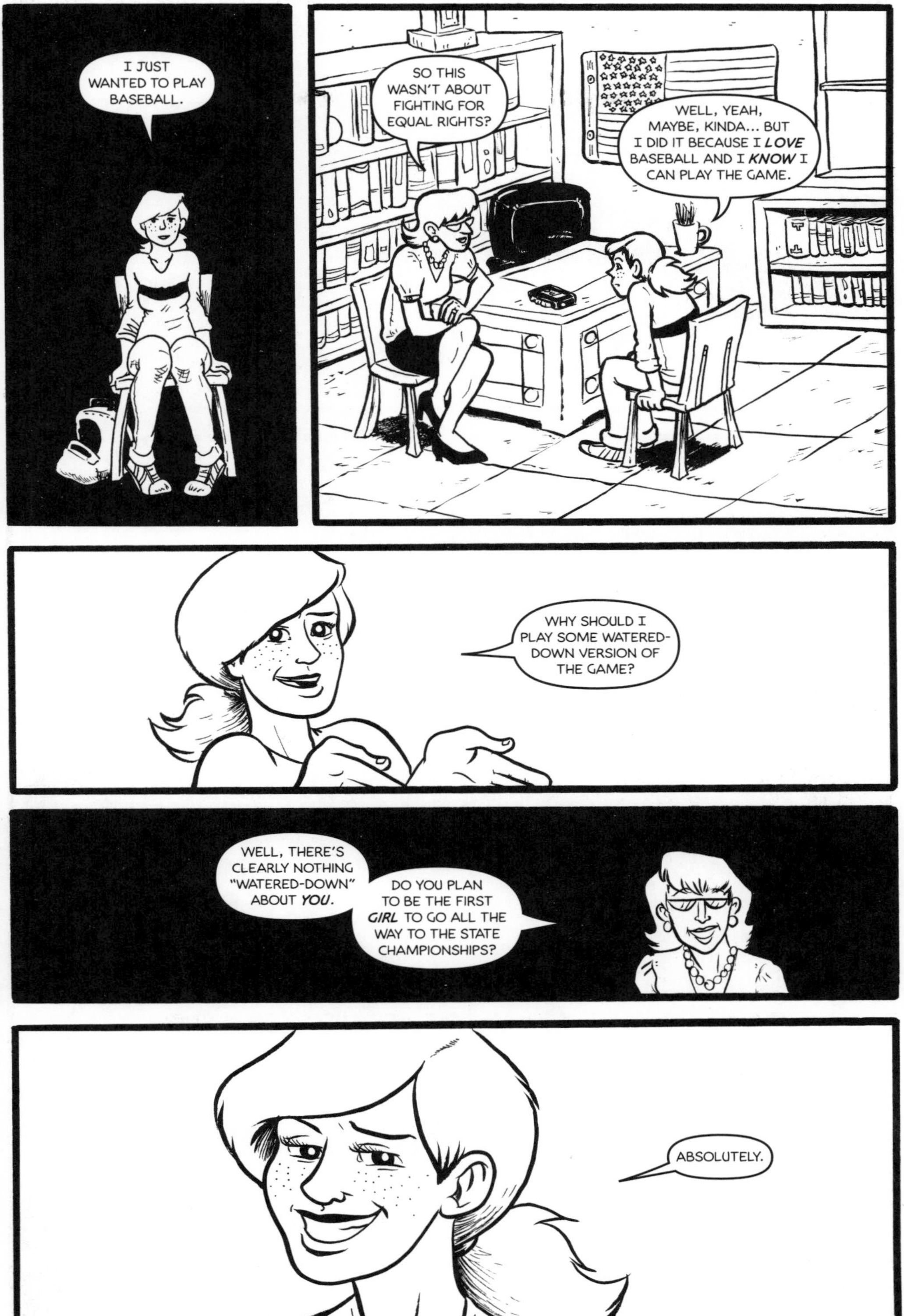
I JUST WANTED TO PLAY BASEBALL.
SO THIS WASN'T ABOUT FIGHTING FOR EQUAL RIGHTS?
WELL, YEAH, MAYBE, KINDA... BUT I DID IT BECAUSE I ***LOVE*** BASEBALL AND I ***KNOW*** I CAN PLAY THE GAME.
WHY SHOULD I PLAY SOME WATERED-DOWN VERSION OF THE GAME?
WELL, THERE'S CLEARLY NOTHING "WATERED-DOWN" ABOUT ***YOU***.
DO YOU PLAN TO BE THE FIRST ***GIRL*** TO GO ALL THE WAY TO THE STATE CHAMPIONSHIPS?
ABSOLUTELY.

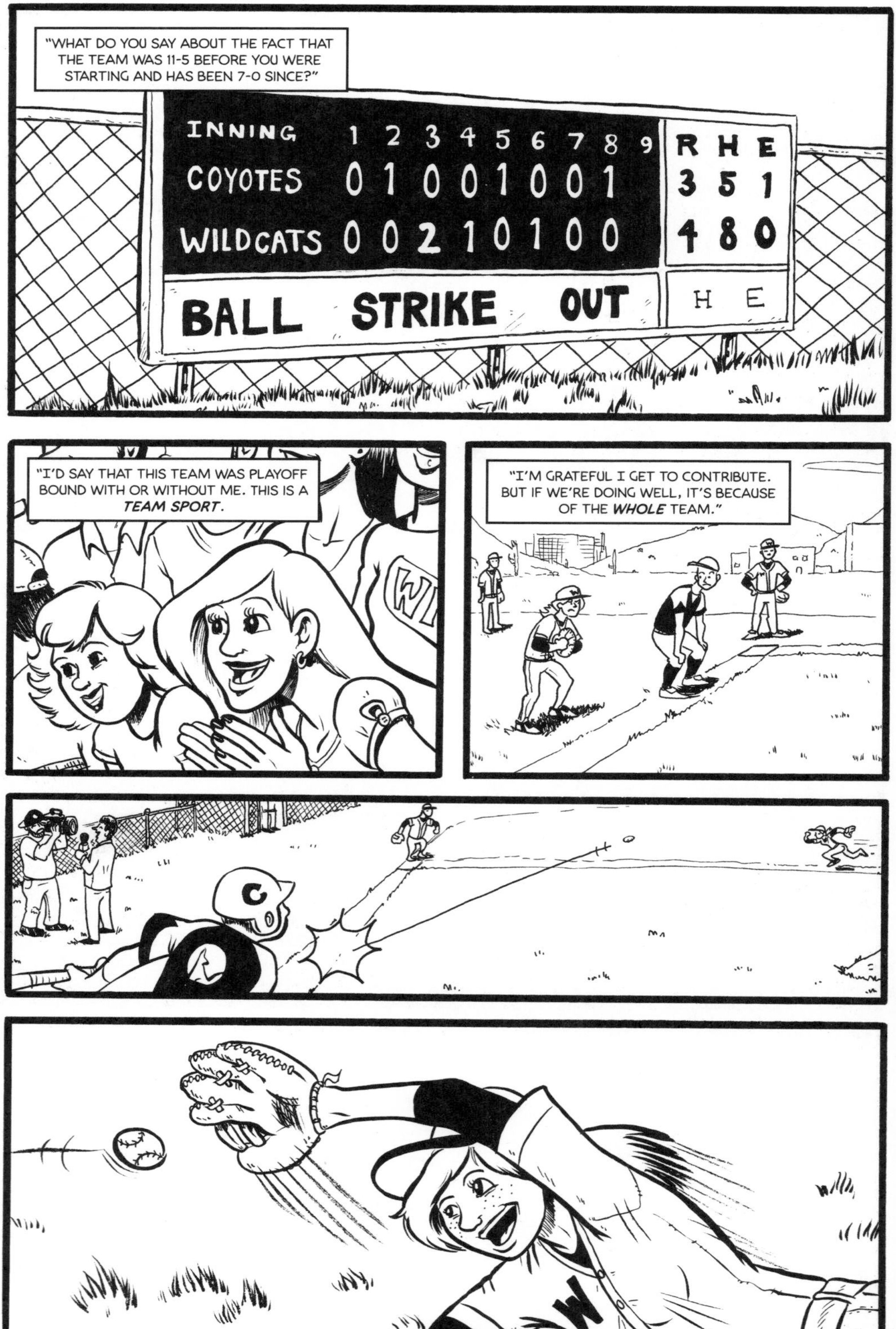
"WHAT DO YOU SAY ABOUT THE FACT THAT THE TEAM WAS 11-5 BEFORE YOU WERE STARTING AND HAS BEEN 7-0 SINCE?"
INNING 1 2 3 4 5 6 7 8 9 R H E
COYOTES 0 1 0 0 1 0 0 1 3 5 1
WILDCATS 0 0 2 1 0 1 0 0 4 8 0
BALL STRIKE OUT H E
"I'D SAY THAT THIS TEAM WAS PLAYOFF BOUND WITH OR WITHOUT ME. THIS IS A *TEAM SPORT*.
"I'M GRATEFUL I GET TO CONTRIBUTE. BUT IF WE'RE DOING WELL, IT'S BECAUSE OF THE ***WHOLE*** TEAM."

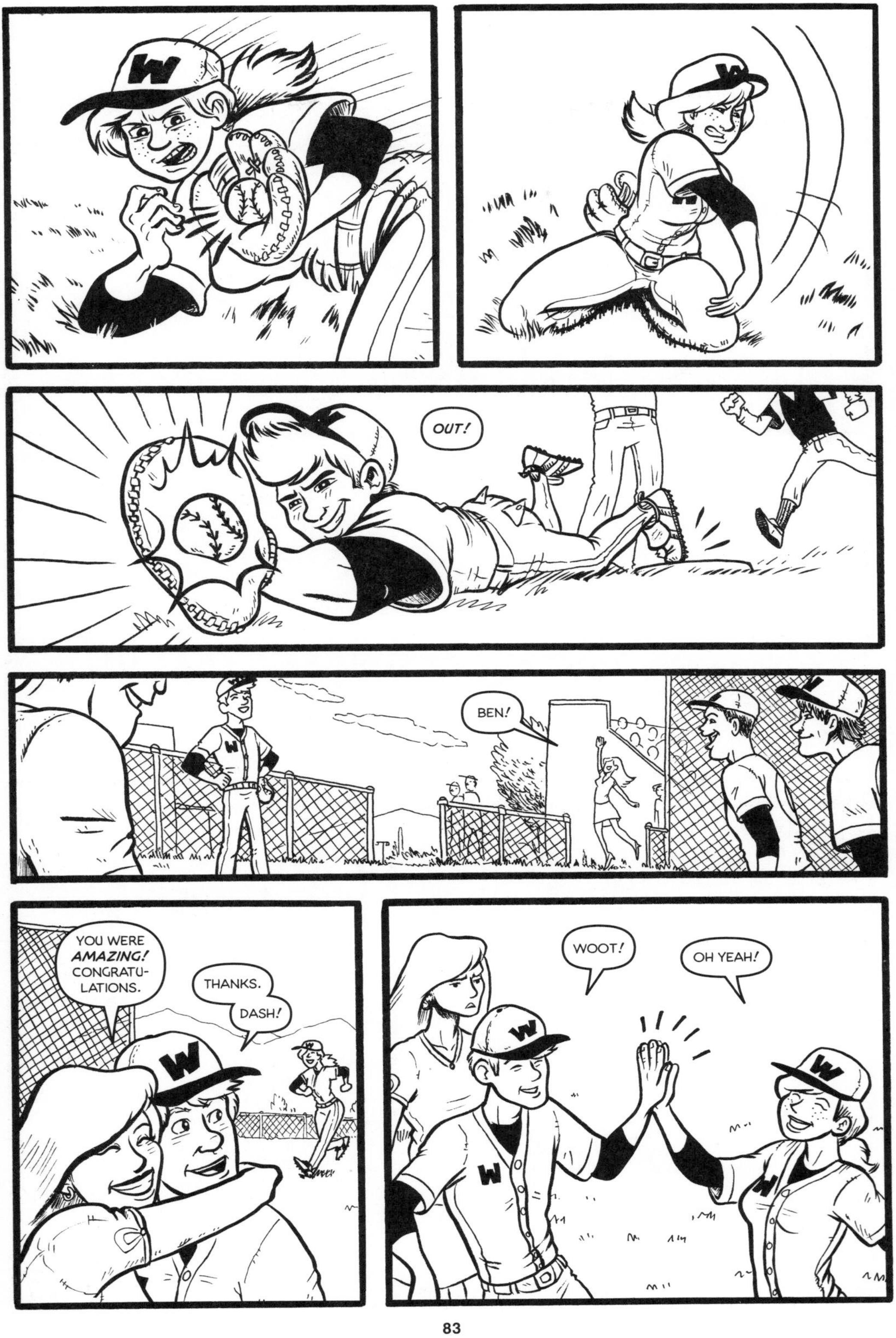
OUT!
BEN!
YOU WERE AMAZING! CONGRATU-LATIONS.
THANKS.
DASH!
WOOT!
OH YEAH!

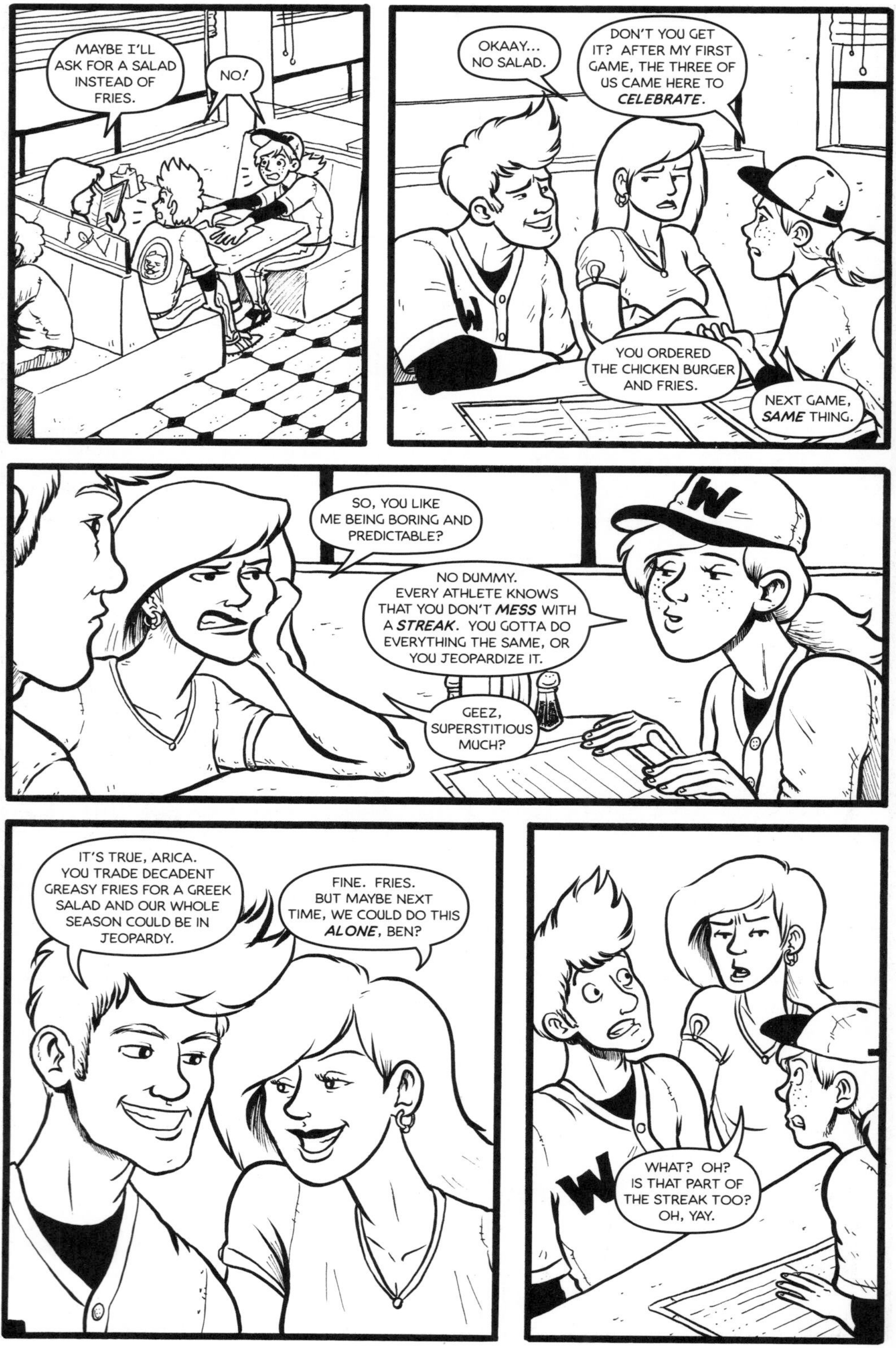
MAYBE I'LL ASK FOR A SALAD INSTEAD OF FRIES.
NO!
OKAAY... NO SALAD.
DON'T YOU GET IT? AFTER MY FIRST GAME, THE THREE OF US CAME HERE TO CELEBRATE.
YOU ORDERED THE CHICKEN BURGER AND FRIES.
NEXT GAME, SAME THING.
SO, YOU LIKE ME BEING BORING AND PREDICTABLE?
NO DUMMY. EVERY ATHLETE KNOWS THAT YOU DON'T MESS WITH A STREAK. YOU GOTTA DO EVERYTHING THE SAME, OR YOU JEOPARDIZE IT.
GEEZ, SUPERSTITIOUS MUCH?
IT'S TRUE, ARICA. YOU TRADE DECADENT GREASY FRIES FOR A GREEK SALAD AND OUR WHOLE SEASON COULD BE IN JEOPARDY.
FINE. FRIES. BUT MAYBE NEXT TIME, WE COULD DO THIS ALONE, BEN?
WHAT? OH? IS THAT PART OF THE STREAK TOO? OH, YAY.

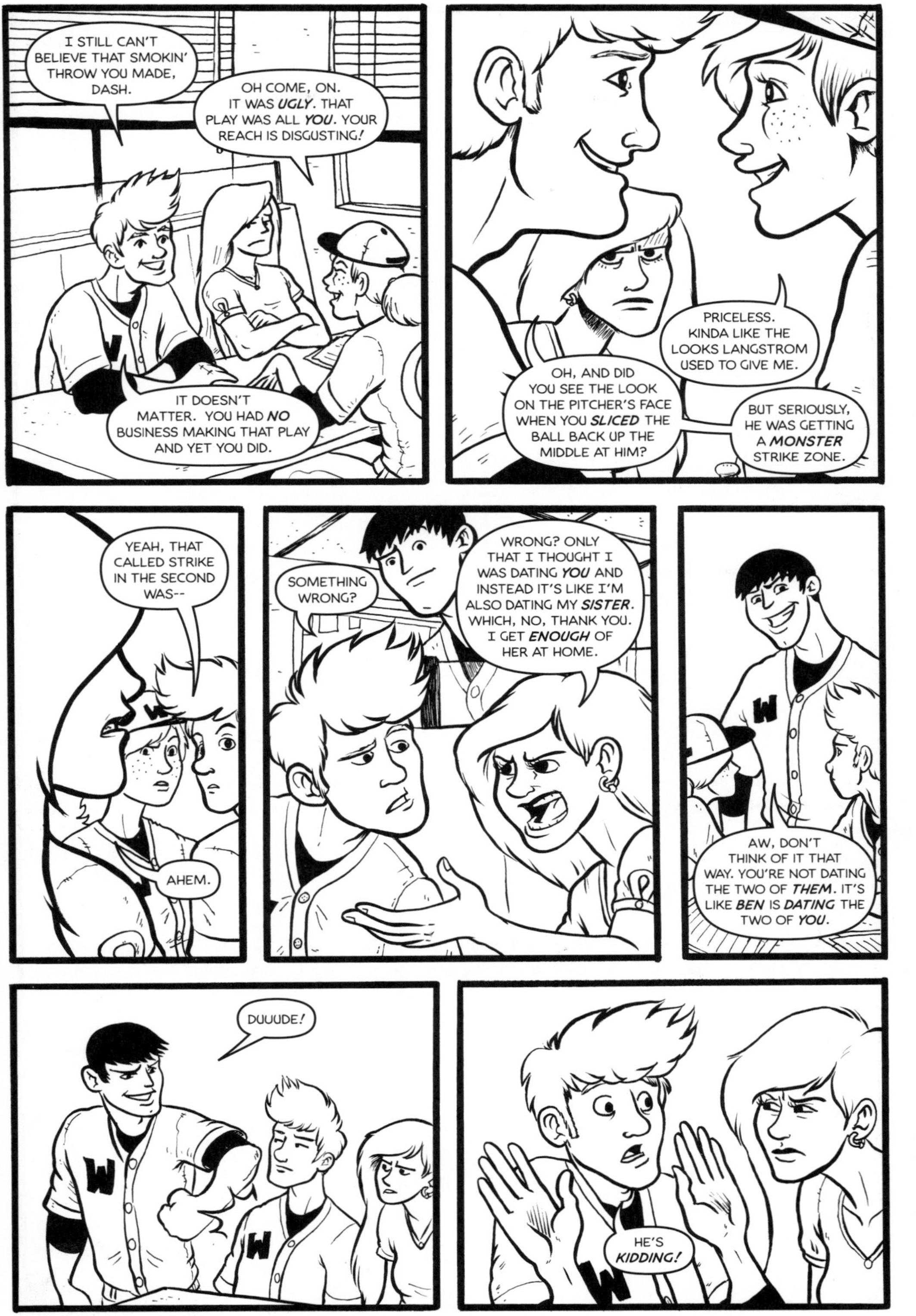
I STILL CAN'T BELIEVE THAT SMOKIN' THROW YOU MADE, DASH.
OH COME, ON. IT WAS UGLY. THAT PLAY WAS ALL YOU. YOUR REACH IS DISGUSTING!
IT DOESN'T MATTER. YOU HAD NO BUSINESS MAKING THAT PLAY AND YET YOU DID.
OH, AND DID YOU SEE THE LOOK ON THE PITCHER'S FACE WHEN YOU SLICED THE BALL BACK UP THE MIDDLE AT HIM?
PRICELESS. KINDA LIKE THE LOOKS LANGSTROM USED TO GIVE ME.
BUT SERIOUSLY, HE WAS GETTING A MONSTER STRIKE ZONE.
YEAH, THAT CALLED STRIKE IN THE SECOND WAS--
AHEM.
SOMETHING WRONG?
WRONG? ONLY THAT I THOUGHT I WAS DATING YOU AND INSTEAD IT'S LIKE I'M ALSO DATING MY SISTER. WHICH, NO, THANK YOU. I GET ENOUGH OF HER AT HOME.
AW, DON'T THINK OF IT THAT WAY. YOU'RE NOT DATING THE TWO OF THEM. IT'S LIKE BEN IS DATING THE TWO OF YOU.
DUUUDE!
HE'S KIDDING!

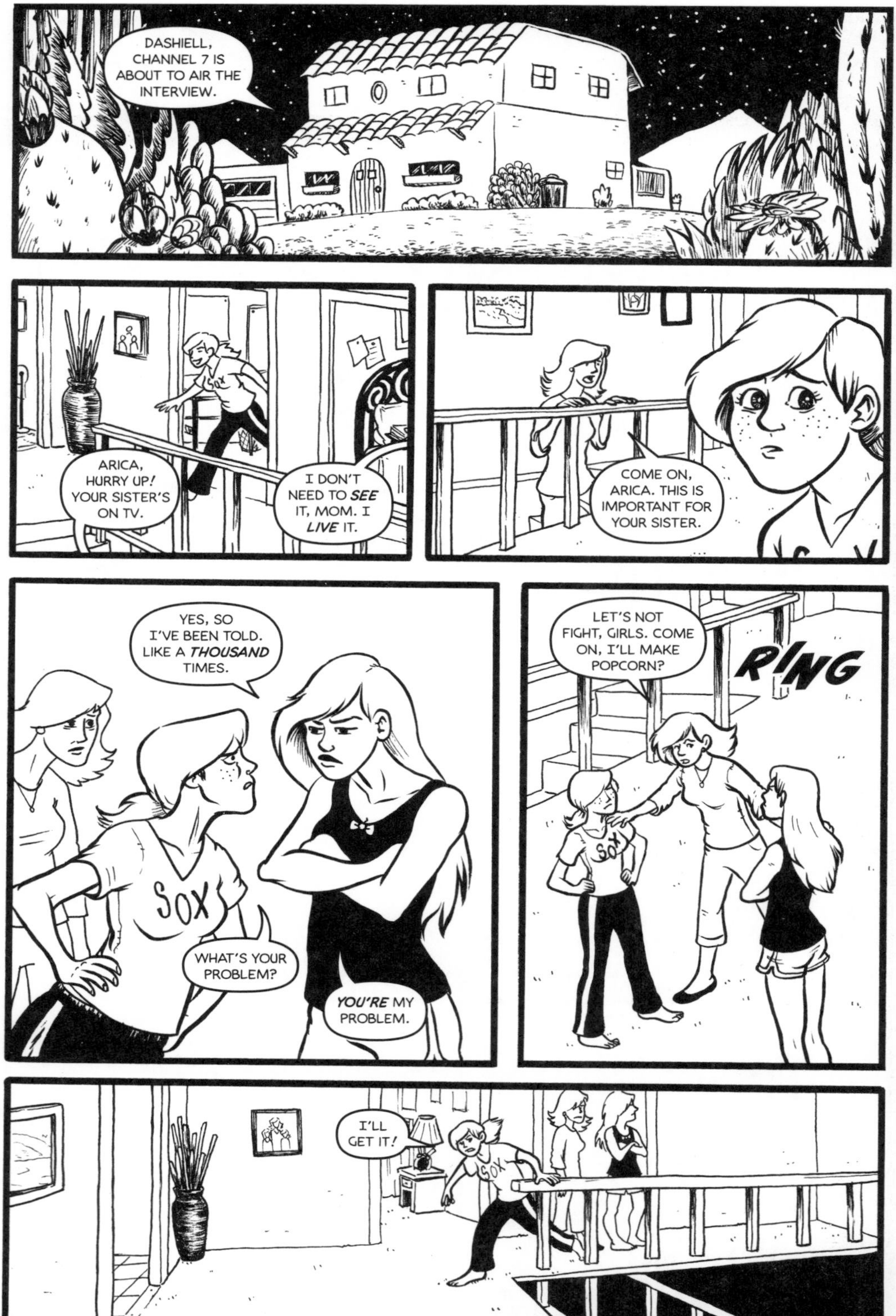
DASHIELL, CHANNEL 7 IS ABOUT TO AIR THE INTERVIEW.
ARICA, HURRY UP! YOUR SISTER'S ON TV.
I DON'T NEED TO *SEE* IT, MOM. I *LIVE* IT.
COME ON, ARICA. THIS IS IMPORTANT FOR YOUR SISTER.
YES, SO I'VE BEEN TOLD. LIKE A *THOUSAND* TIMES.
WHAT'S YOUR PROBLEM?
YOU'RE MY PROBLEM.
LET'S NOT FIGHT, GIRLS. COME ON, I'LL MAKE POPCORN?
RING
I'LL GET IT!

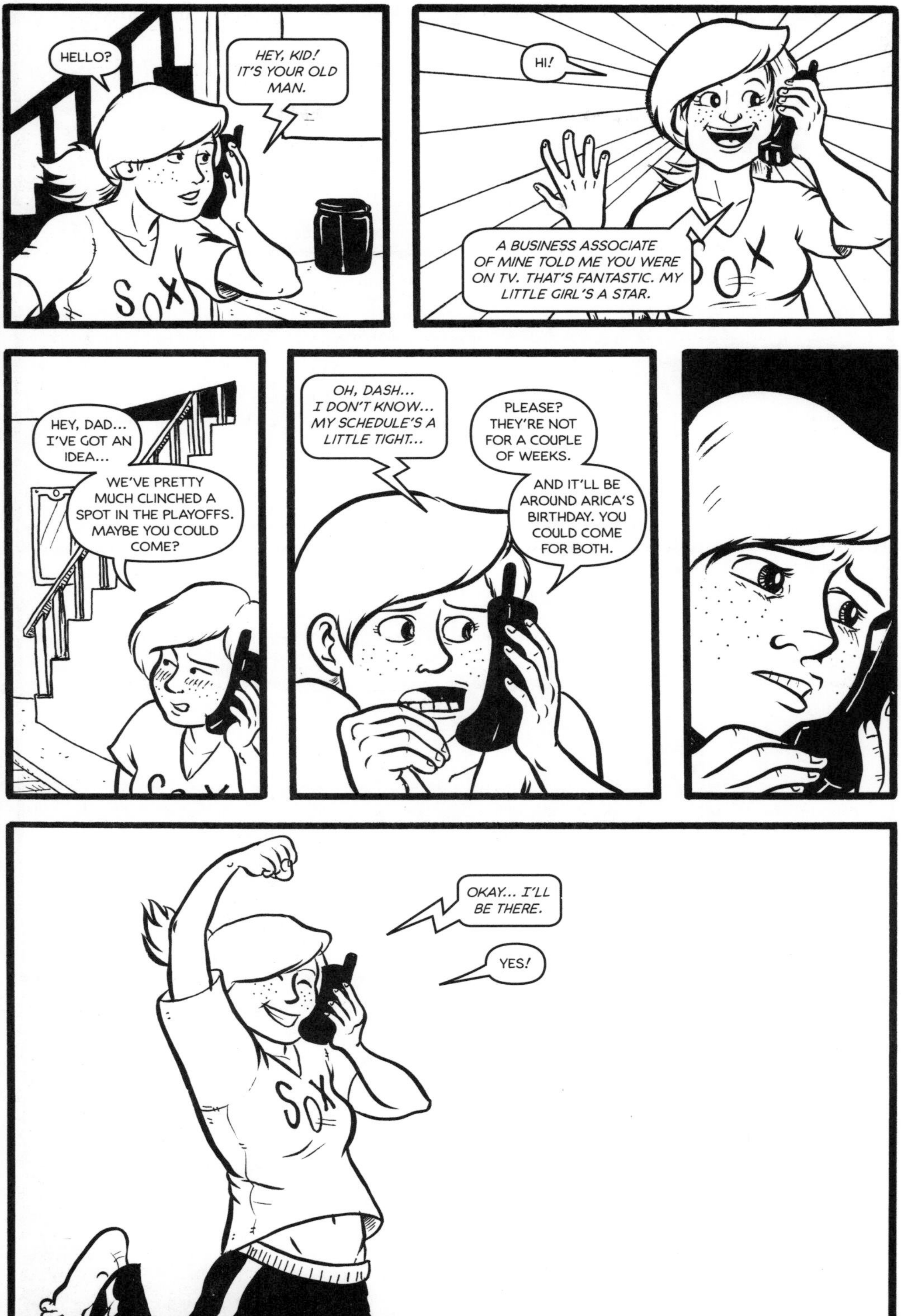
HELLO?
HEY, KID! IT'S YOUR OLD MAN.
HI!
A BUSINESS ASSOCIATE OF MINE TOLD ME YOU WERE ON TV. THAT'S FANTASTIC. MY LITTLE GIRL'S A STAR.
HEY, DAD... I'VE GOT AN IDEA...
WE'VE PRETTY MUCH CLINCHED A SPOT IN THE PLAYOFFS. MAYBE YOU COULD COME?
OH, DASH... I DON'T KNOW... MY SCHEDULE'S A LITTLE TIGHT...
PLEASE? THEY'RE NOT FOR A COUPLE OF WEEKS.
AND IT'LL BE AROUND ARICA'S BIRTHDAY. YOU COULD COME FOR BOTH.
OKAY... I'LL BE THERE.
YES!
SOX

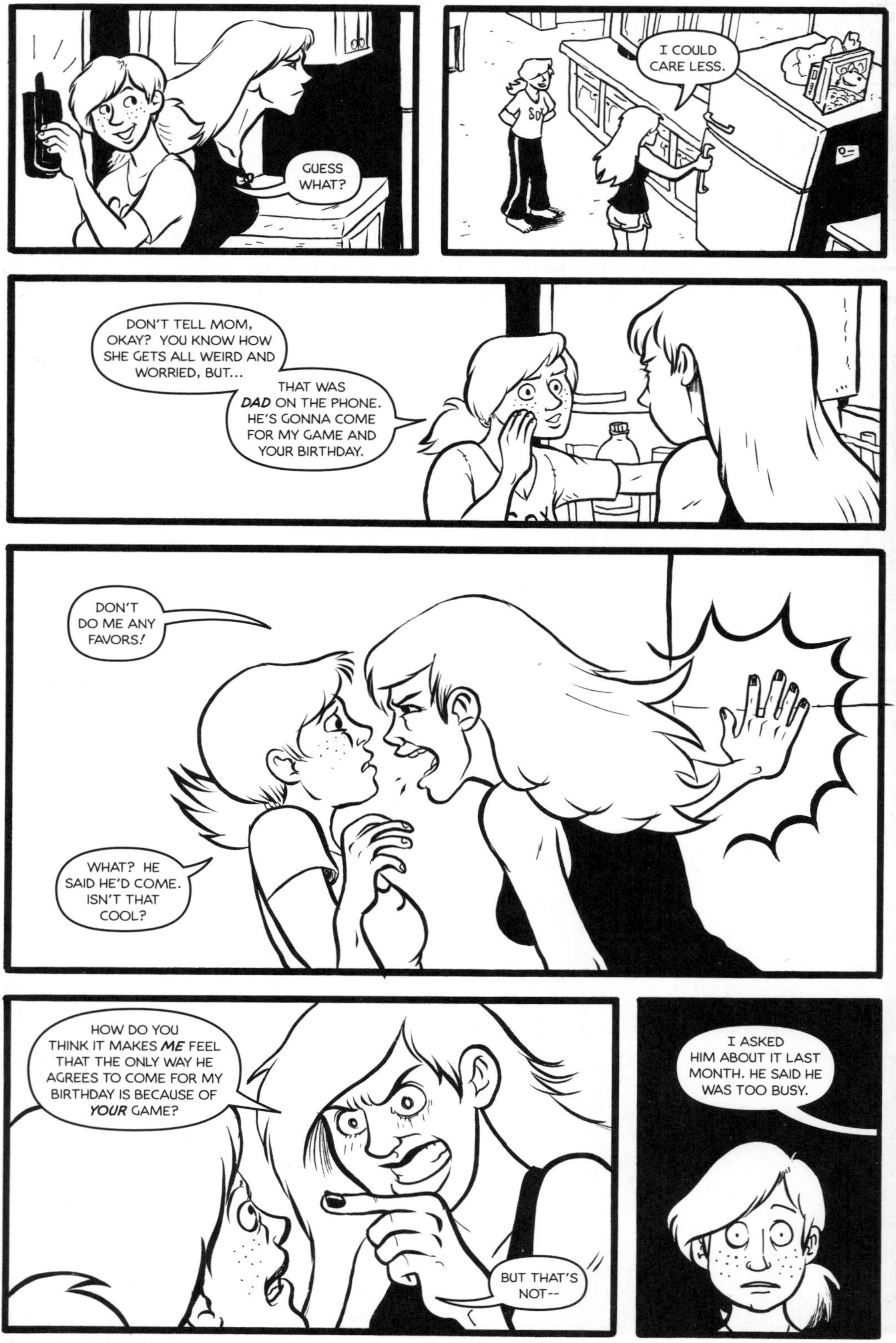
GUESS WHAT?
I COULD CARE LESS.
DON'T TELL MOM, OKAY? YOU KNOW HOW SHE GETS ALL WEIRD AND WORRIED, BUT...
THAT WAS DAD ON THE PHONE. HE'S GONNA COME FOR MY GAME AND YOUR BIRTHDAY.
DON'T DO ME ANY FAVORS!
WHAT? HE SAID HE'D COME. ISN'T THAT COOL?
HOW DO YOU THINK IT MAKES ME FEEL THAT THE ONLY WAY HE AGREES TO COME FOR MY BIRTHDAY IS BECAUSE OF YOUR GAME?
BUT THAT'S NOT--
I ASKED HIM ABOUT IT LAST MONTH. HE SAID HE WAS TOO BUSY.

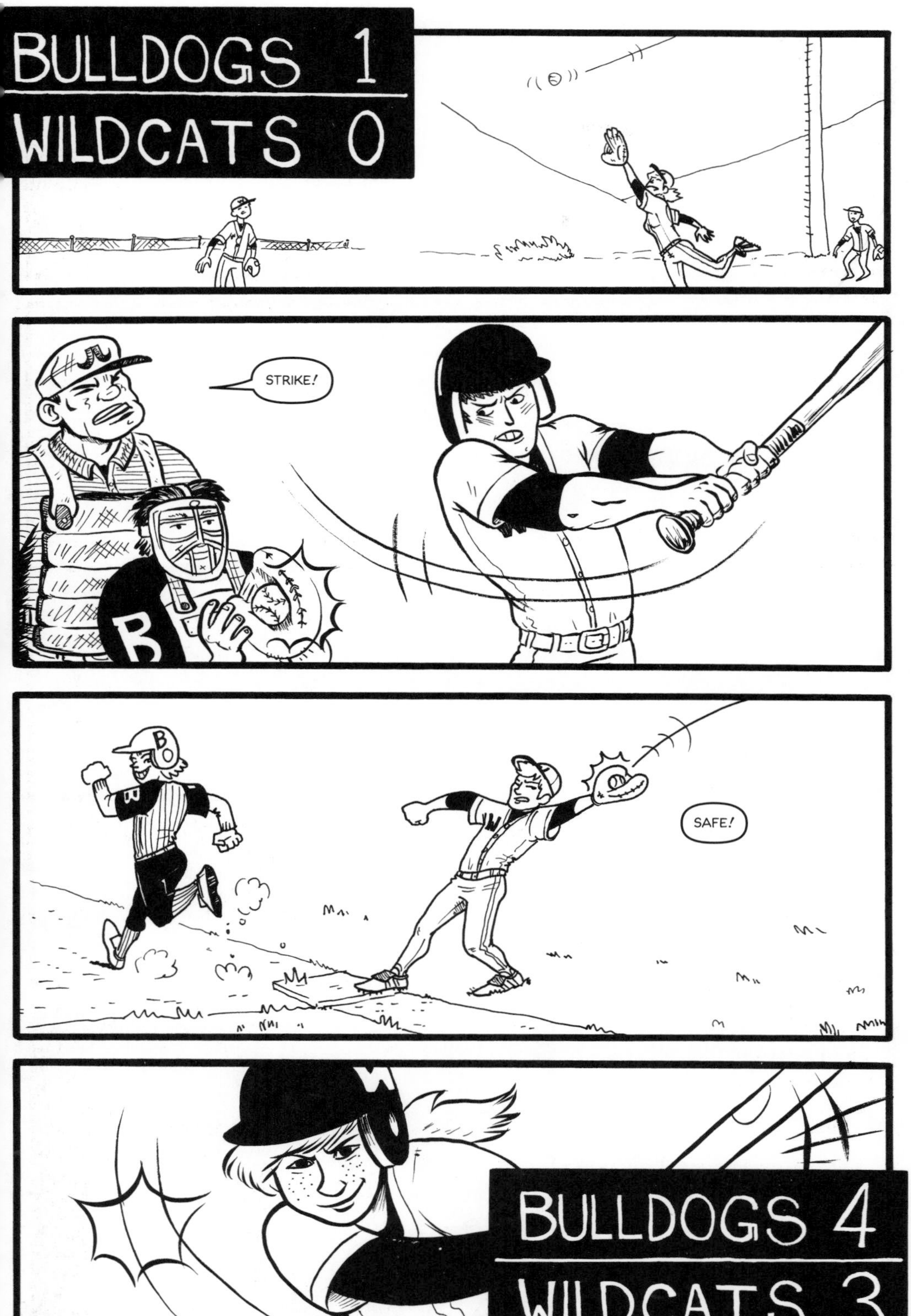
BULLDOGS 1
WILDCATS 0
STRIKE!
SAFE!
BULLDOGS 4
WILDCATS 3

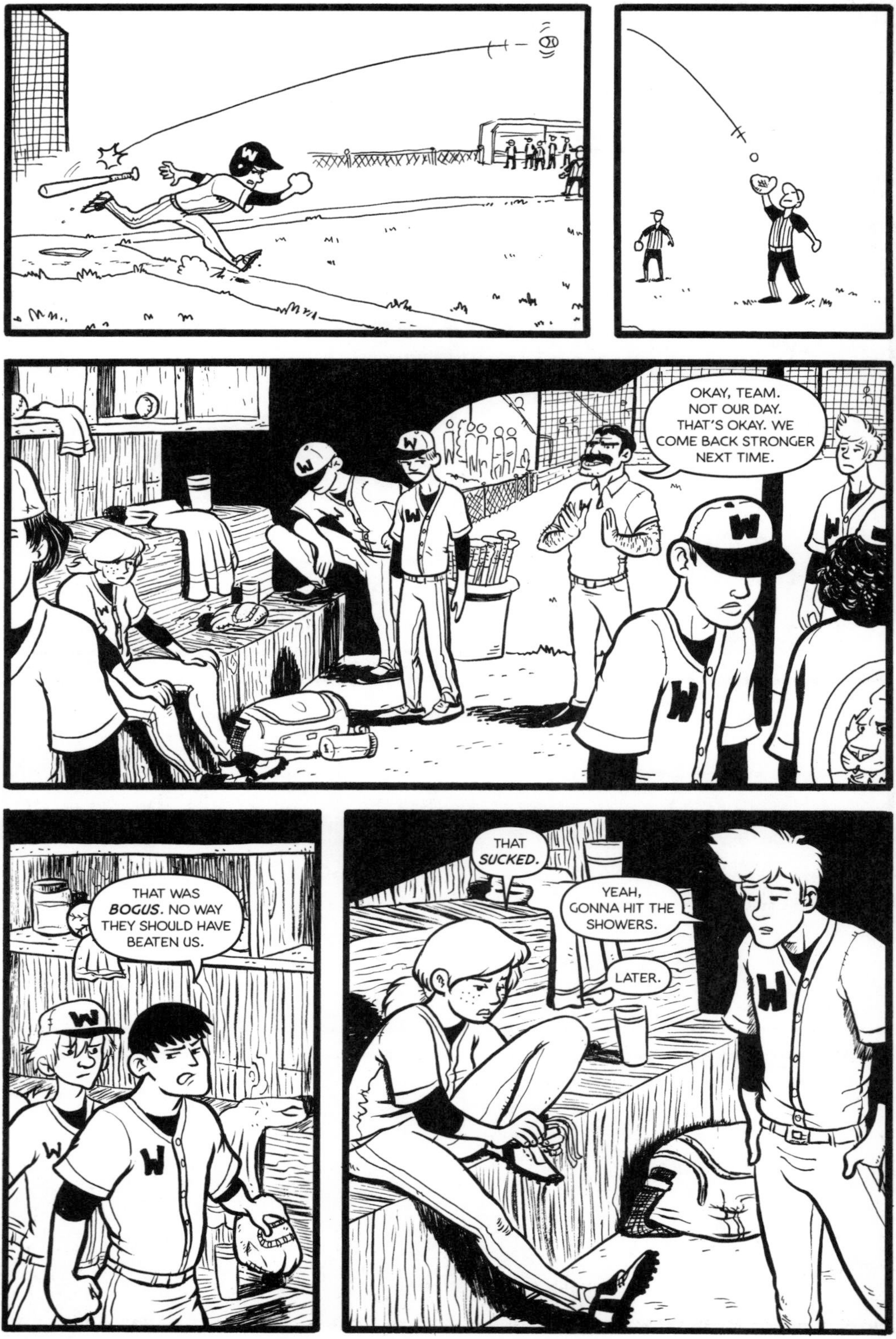
OKAY, TEAM. NOT OUR DAY. THAT'S OKAY. WE COME BACK STRONGER NEXT TIME.
THAT WAS *BOGUS*. NO WAY THEY SHOULD HAVE BEATEN US.
THAT *SUCKED*.
YEAH, GONNA HIT THE SHOWERS.
LATER.

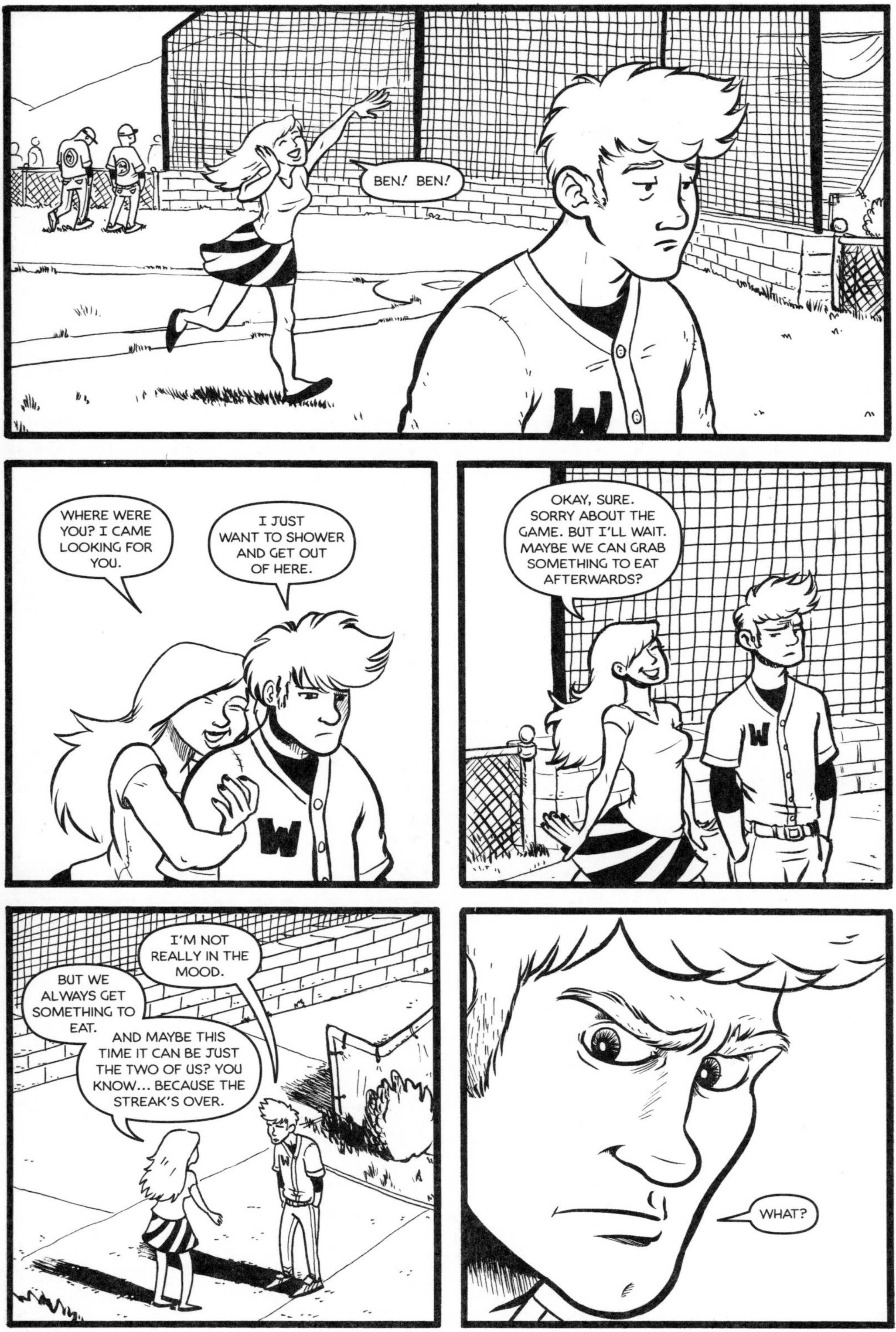
BEN! BEN!
WHERE WERE YOU? I CAME LOOKING FOR YOU.
I JUST WANT TO SHOWER AND GET OUT OF HERE.
OKAY, SURE. SORRY ABOUT THE GAME. BUT I'LL WAIT. MAYBE WE CAN GRAB SOMETHING TO EAT AFTERWARDS?
I'M NOT REALLY IN THE MOOD.
BUT WE ALWAYS GET SOMETHING TO EAT.
AND MAYBE THIS TIME IT CAN BE JUST THE TWO OF US? YOU KNOW... BECAUSE THE STREAK'S OVER.
WHAT?

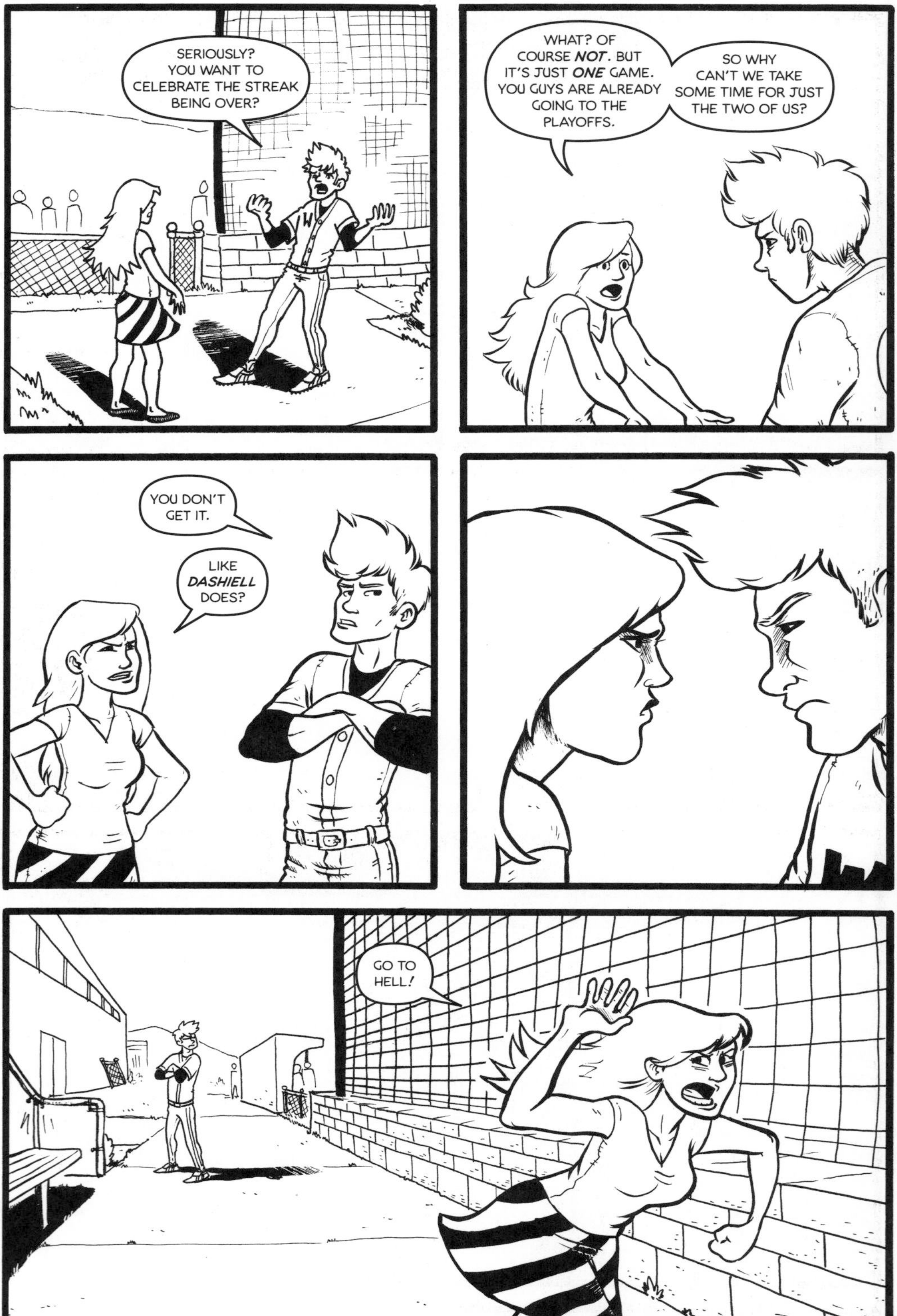
SERIOUSLY? YOU WANT TO CELEBRATE THE STREAK BEING OVER?
WHAT? OF COURSE **NOT**. BUT IT'S JUST **ONE** GAME. YOU GUYS ARE ALREADY GOING TO THE PLAYOFFS.
SO WHY CAN'T WE TAKE SOME TIME FOR JUST THE TWO OF US?
YOU DON'T GET IT.
LIKE **DASHIELL** DOES?
GO TO HELL!

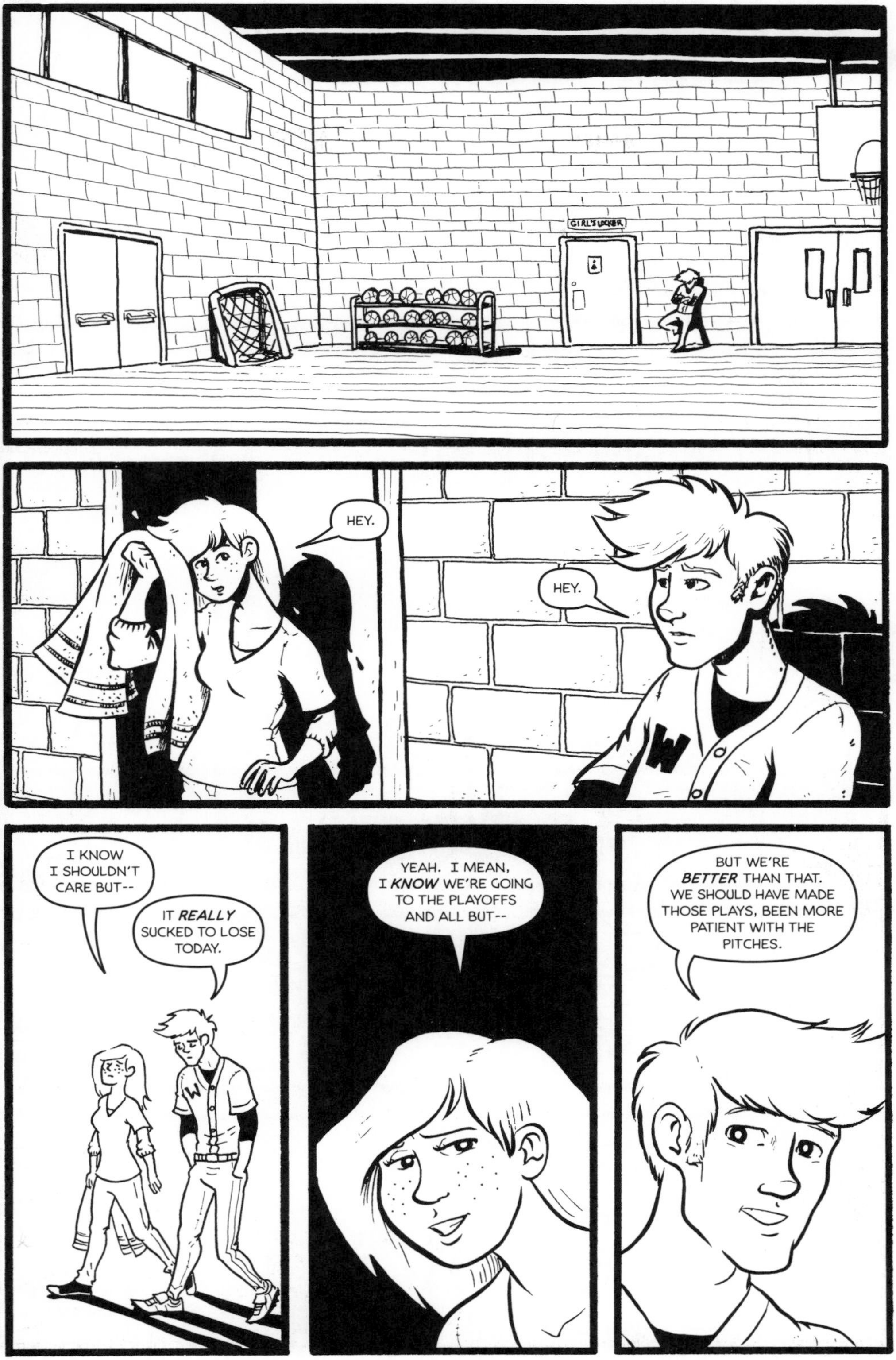
GIRL'S LOCKER
HEY.
HEY.
I KNOW I SHOULDN'T CARE BUT--
IT *REALLY* SUCKED TO LOSE TODAY.
YEAH. I MEAN, I *KNOW* WE'RE GOING TO THE PLAYOFFS AND ALL BUT--
BUT WE'RE *BETTER* THAN THAT. WE SHOULD HAVE MADE THOSE PLAYS, BEEN MORE PATIENT WITH THE PITCHES.

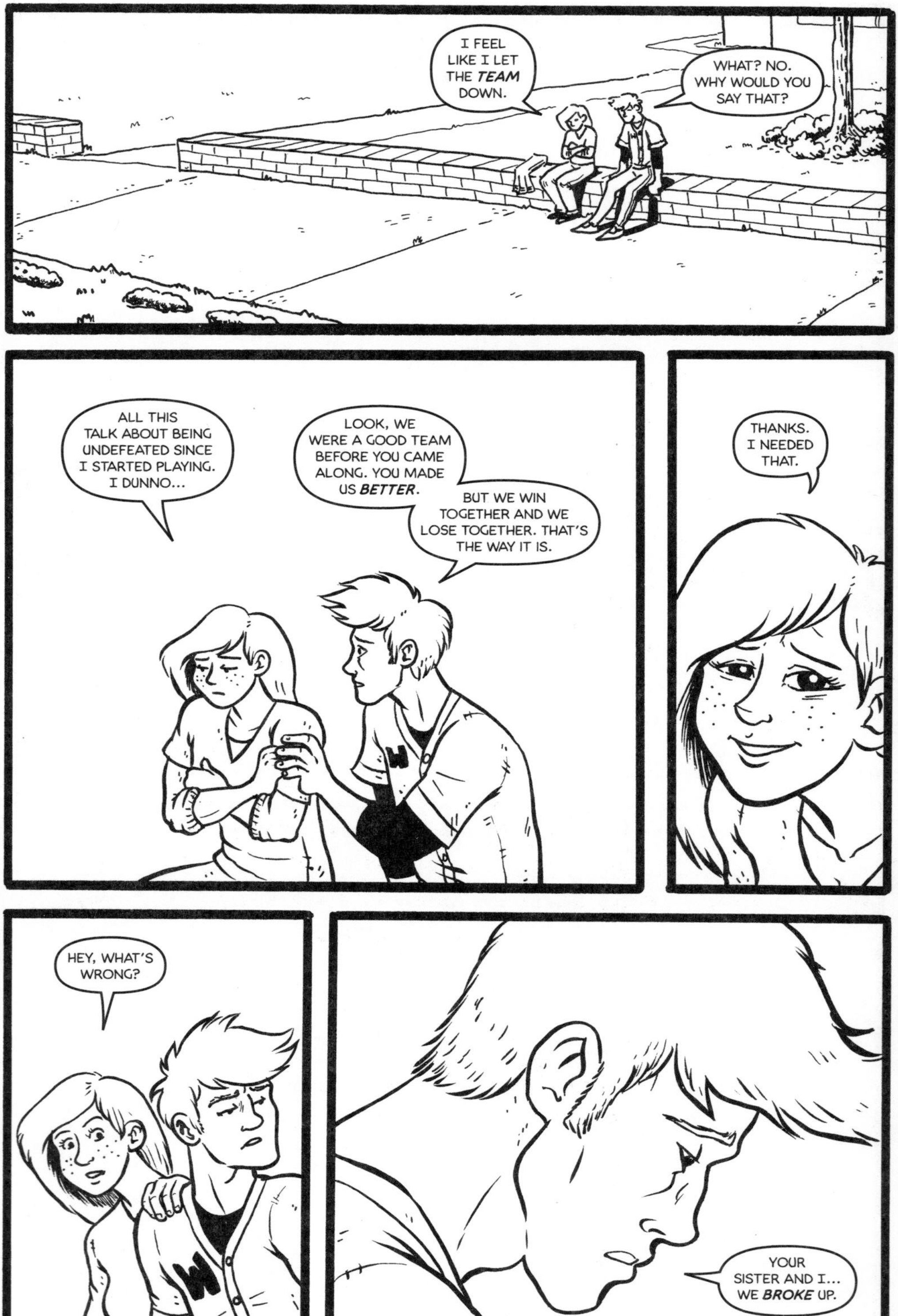
I FEEL LIKE I LET THE *TEAM* DOWN.
WHAT? NO. WHY WOULD YOU SAY THAT?
ALL THIS TALK ABOUT BEING UNDEFEATED SINCE I STARTED PLAYING. I DUNNO...
LOOK, WE WERE A GOOD TEAM BEFORE YOU CAME ALONG. YOU MADE US *BETTER*.
BUT WE WIN TOGETHER AND WE LOSE TOGETHER. THAT'S THE WAY IT IS.
THANKS. I NEEDED THAT.
HEY, WHAT'S WRONG?
YOUR SISTER AND I... WE *BROKE* UP.

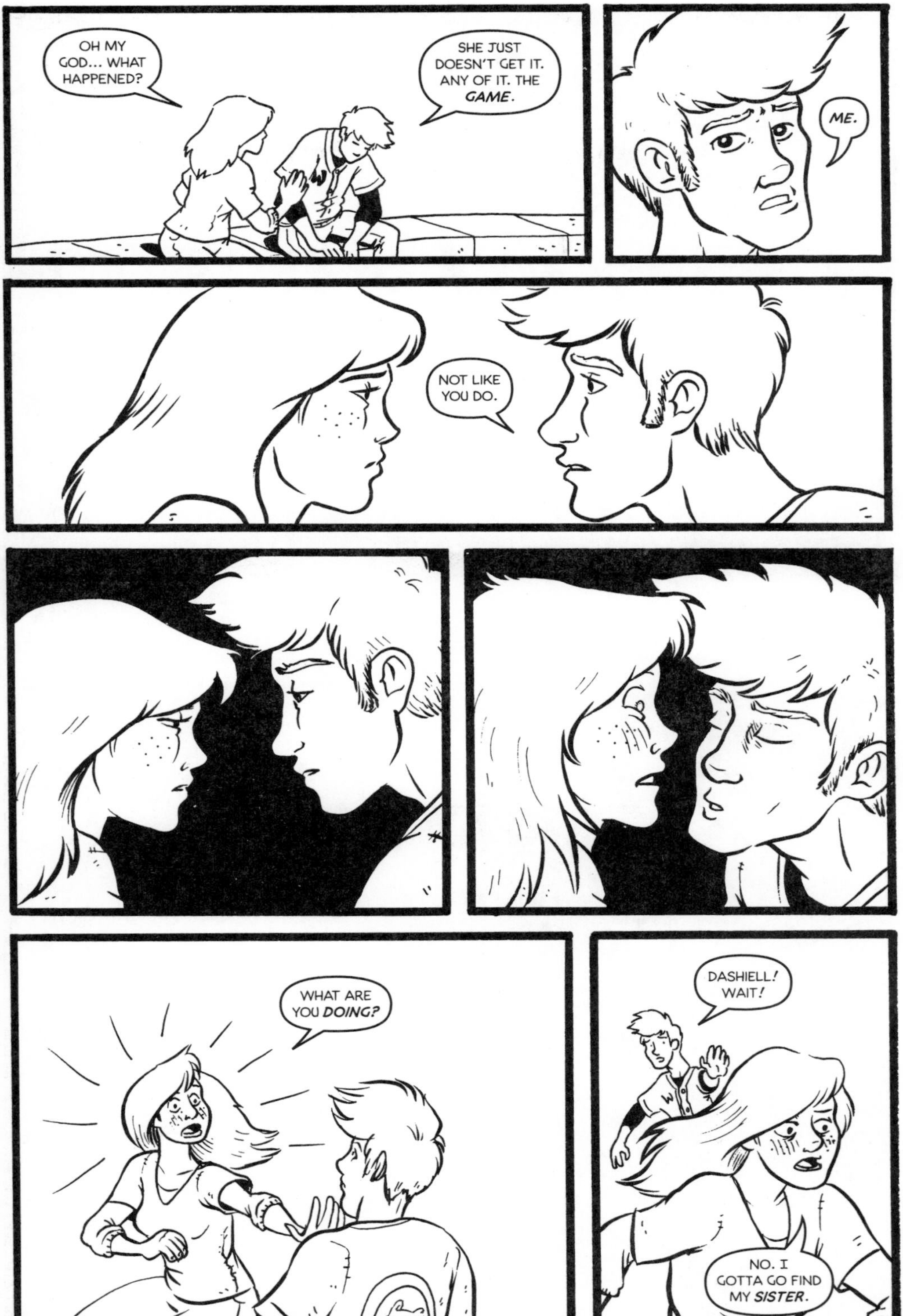
OH MY GOD... WHAT HAPPENED?
SHE JUST DOESN'T GET IT. ANY OF IT. THE *GAME*.
ME.
NOT LIKE YOU DO.
WHAT ARE YOU *DOING?*
DASHIELL*!* WAIT*!*
NO. I GOTTA GO FIND MY *SISTER*.

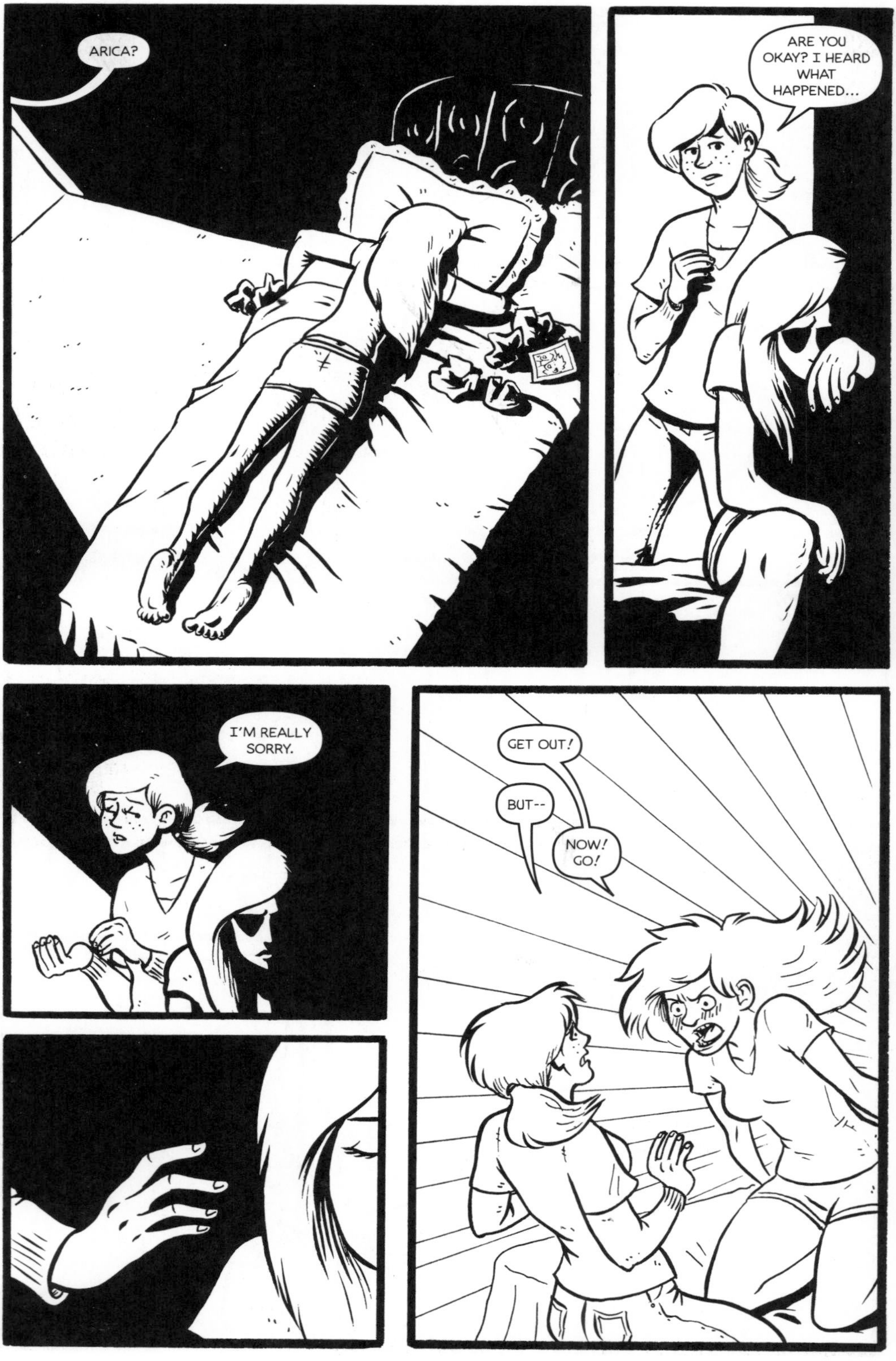
ARICA?
ARE YOU OKAY? I HEARD WHAT HAPPENED...
I'M REALLY SORRY.
GET OUT!
BUT--
NOW! GO!

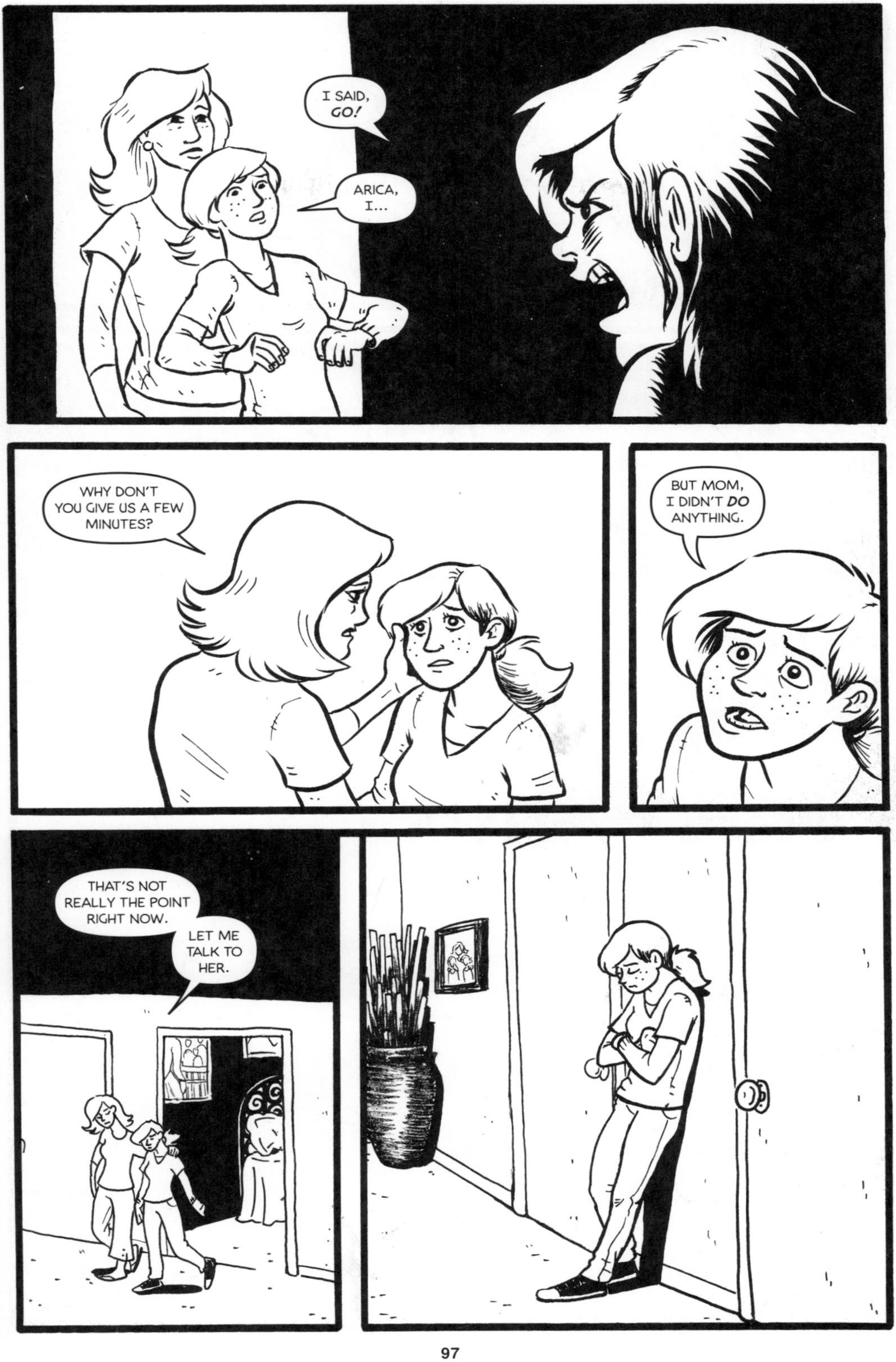
I SAID, *GO!*
ARICA, I...
WHY DON'T YOU GIVE US A FEW MINUTES?
BUT MOM, I DIDN'T *DO* ANYTHING.
THAT'S NOT REALLY THE POINT RIGHT NOW.
LET ME TALK TO HER.

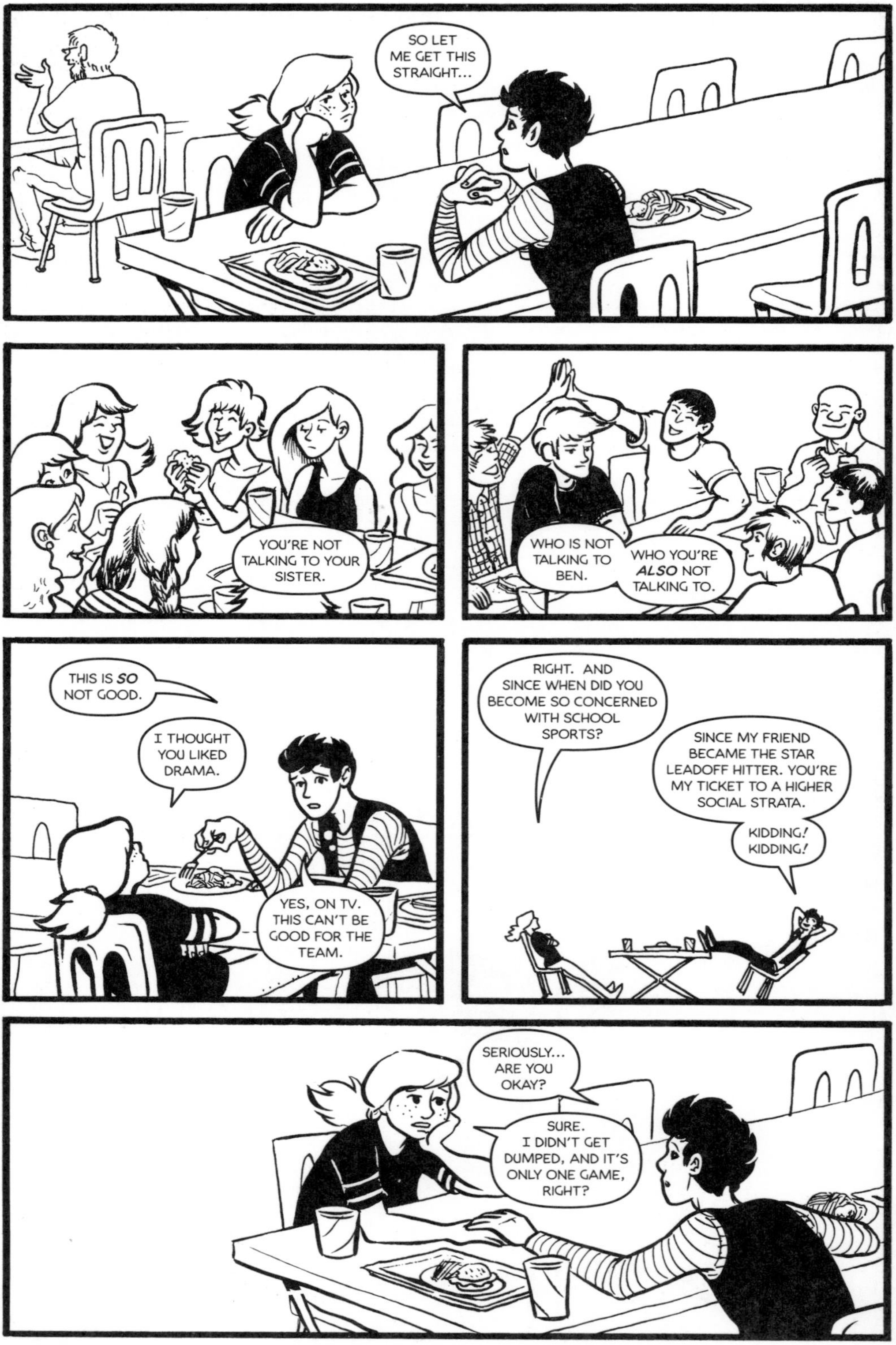
SO LET ME GET THIS STRAIGHT...
YOU'RE NOT TALKING TO YOUR SISTER.
WHO IS NOT TALKING TO BEN.
WHO YOU'RE ALSO NOT TALKING TO.
THIS IS SO NOT GOOD.
I THOUGHT YOU LIKED DRAMA.
YES, ON TV. THIS CAN'T BE GOOD FOR THE TEAM.
RIGHT. AND SINCE WHEN DID YOU BECOME SO CONCERNED WITH SCHOOL SPORTS?
SINCE MY FRIEND BECAME THE STAR LEADOFF HITTER. YOU'RE MY TICKET TO A HIGHER SOCIAL STRATA.
KIDDING! KIDDING!
SERIOUSLY... ARE YOU OKAY?
SURE. I DIDN'T GET DUMPED, AND IT'S ONLY ONE GAME, RIGHT?

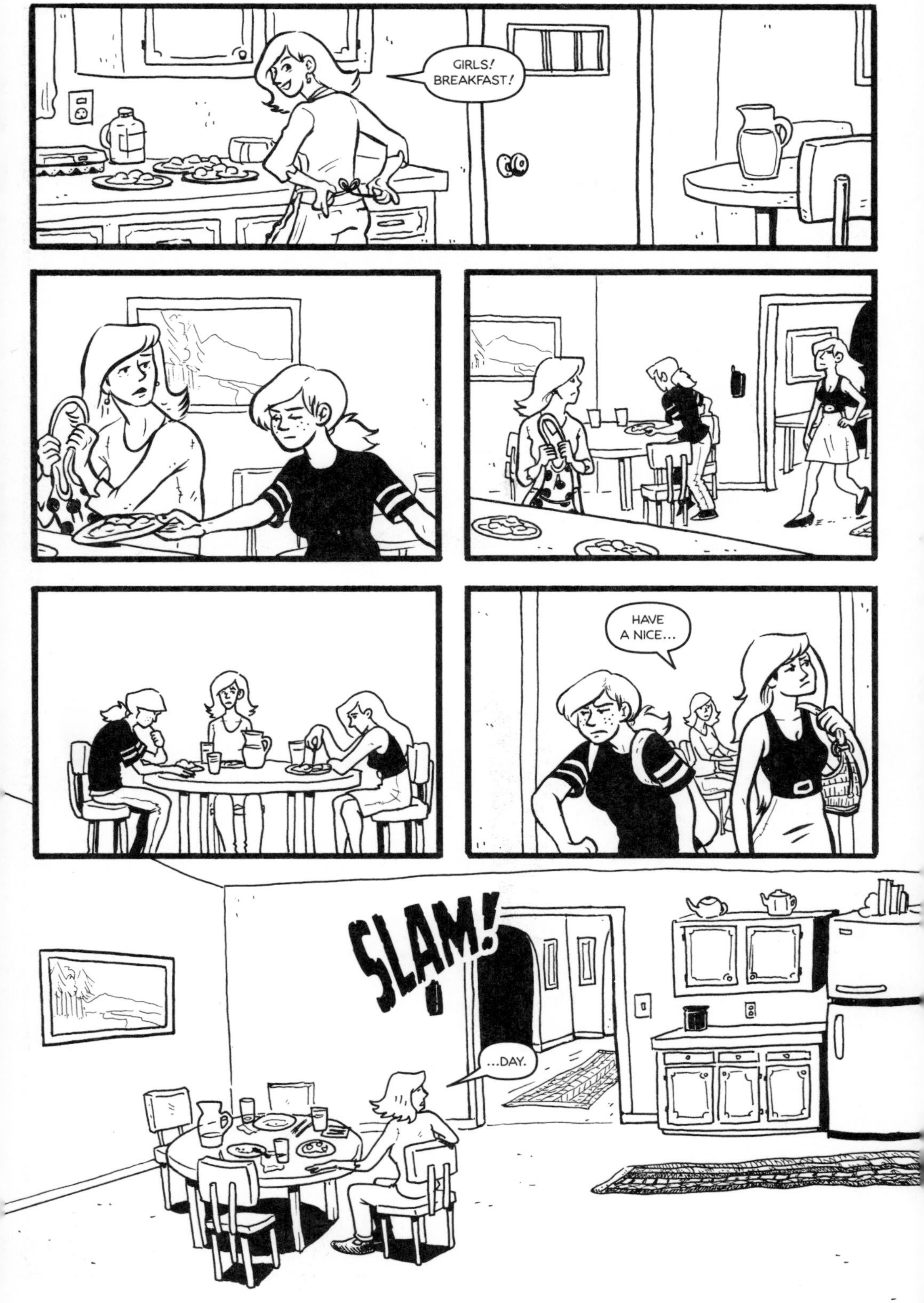
GIRLS! BREAKFAST!
HAVE A NICE...
SLAM!
...DAY.

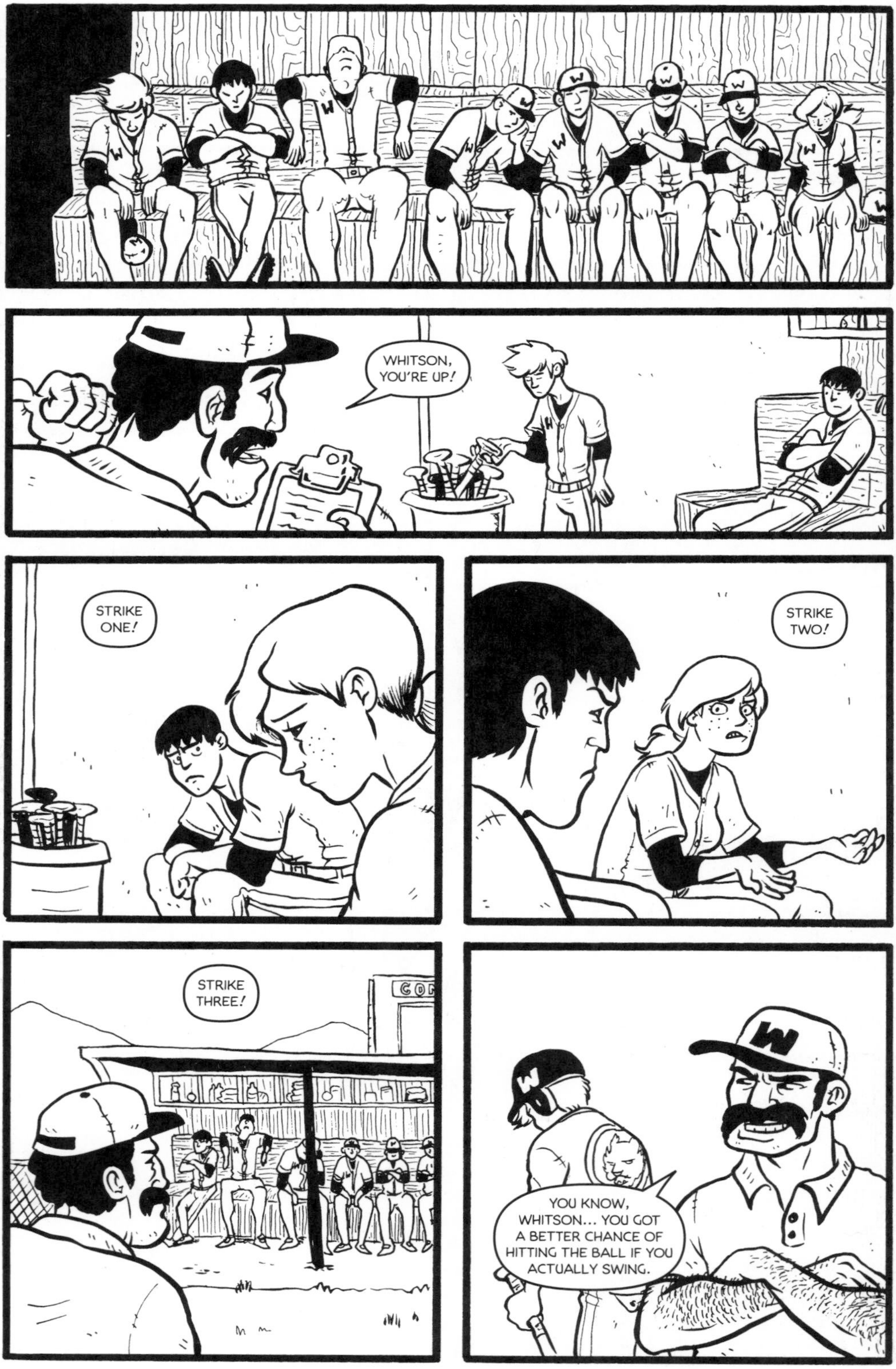
WHITSON, YOU'RE UP!
STRIKE ONE!
STRIKE TWO!
STRIKE THREE!
YOU KNOW, WHITSON... YOU GOT A BETTER CHANCE OF HITTING THE BALL IF YOU ACTUALLY SWING.

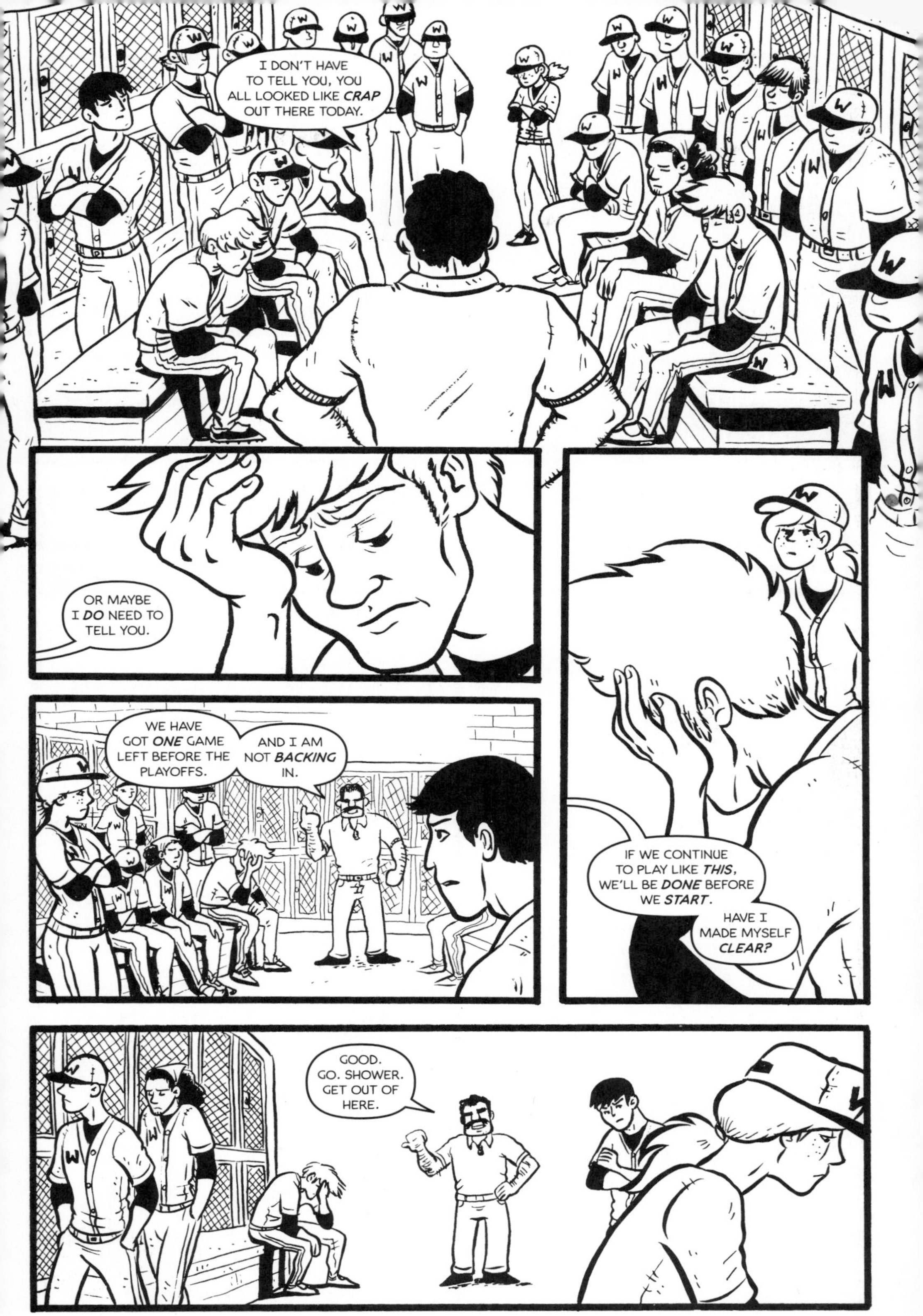
I DON'T HAVE TO TELL YOU, YOU ALL LOOKED LIKE *CRAP* OUT THERE TODAY.
OR MAYBE I *DO* NEED TO TELL YOU.
WE HAVE GOT *ONE* GAME LEFT BEFORE THE PLAYOFFS.
AND I AM NOT *BACKING* IN.
IF WE CONTINUE TO PLAY LIKE *THIS*, WE'LL BE *DONE* BEFORE WE *START*.
HAVE I MADE MYSELF *CLEAR?*
GOOD. GO. SHOWER. GET OUT OF HERE.

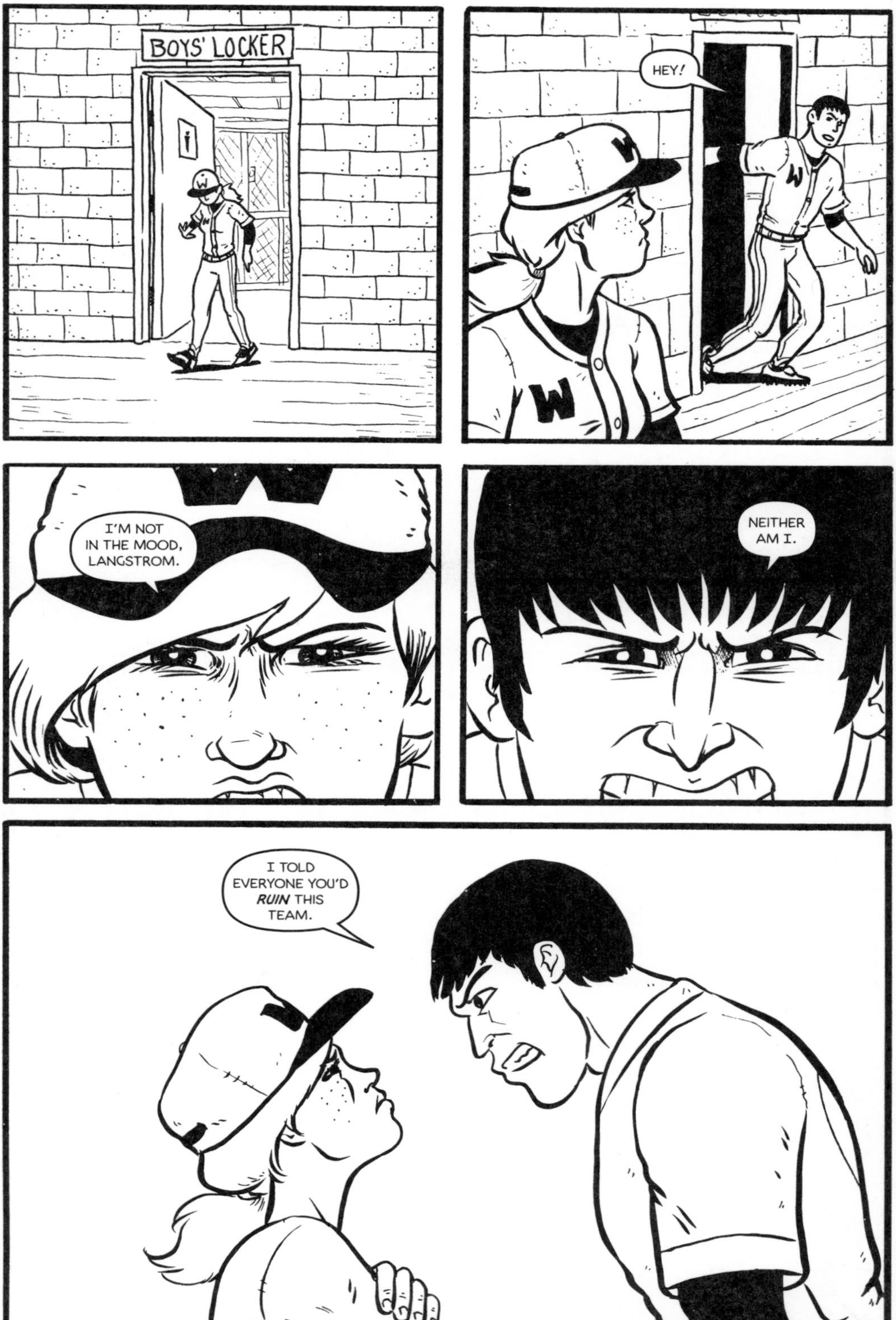

BOYS' LOCKER
HEY!
I'M NOT IN THE MOOD, LANGSTROM.
NEITHER AM I.
I TOLD EVERYONE YOU'D *RUIN* THIS TEAM.

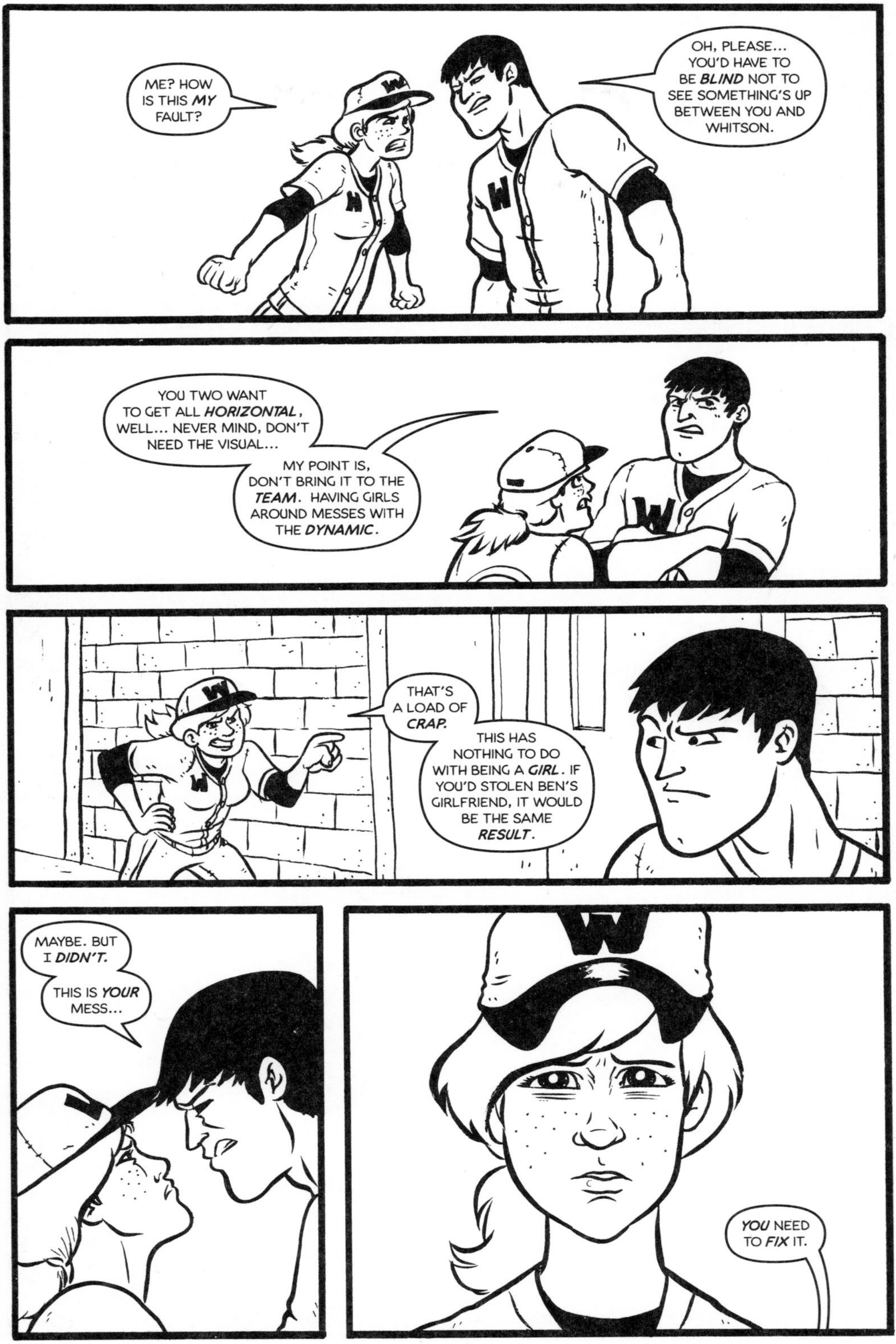
ME? HOW IS THIS *MY* FAULT?
OH, PLEASE... YOU'D HAVE TO BE *BLIND* NOT TO SEE SOMETHING'S UP BETWEEN YOU AND WHITSON.
YOU TWO WANT TO GET ALL *HORIZONTAL*, WELL... NEVER MIND, DON'T NEED THE VISUAL...
MY POINT IS, DON'T BRING IT TO THE *TEAM*. HAVING GIRLS AROUND MESSES WITH THE *DYNAMIC*.
THAT'S A LOAD OF *CRAP*.
THIS HAS NOTHING TO DO WITH BEING A *GIRL*. IF YOU'D STOLEN BEN'S GIRLFRIEND, IT WOULD BE THE SAME *RESULT*.
MAYBE. BUT I *DIDN'T*.
THIS IS *YOUR* MESS...
YOU NEED TO *FIX* IT.

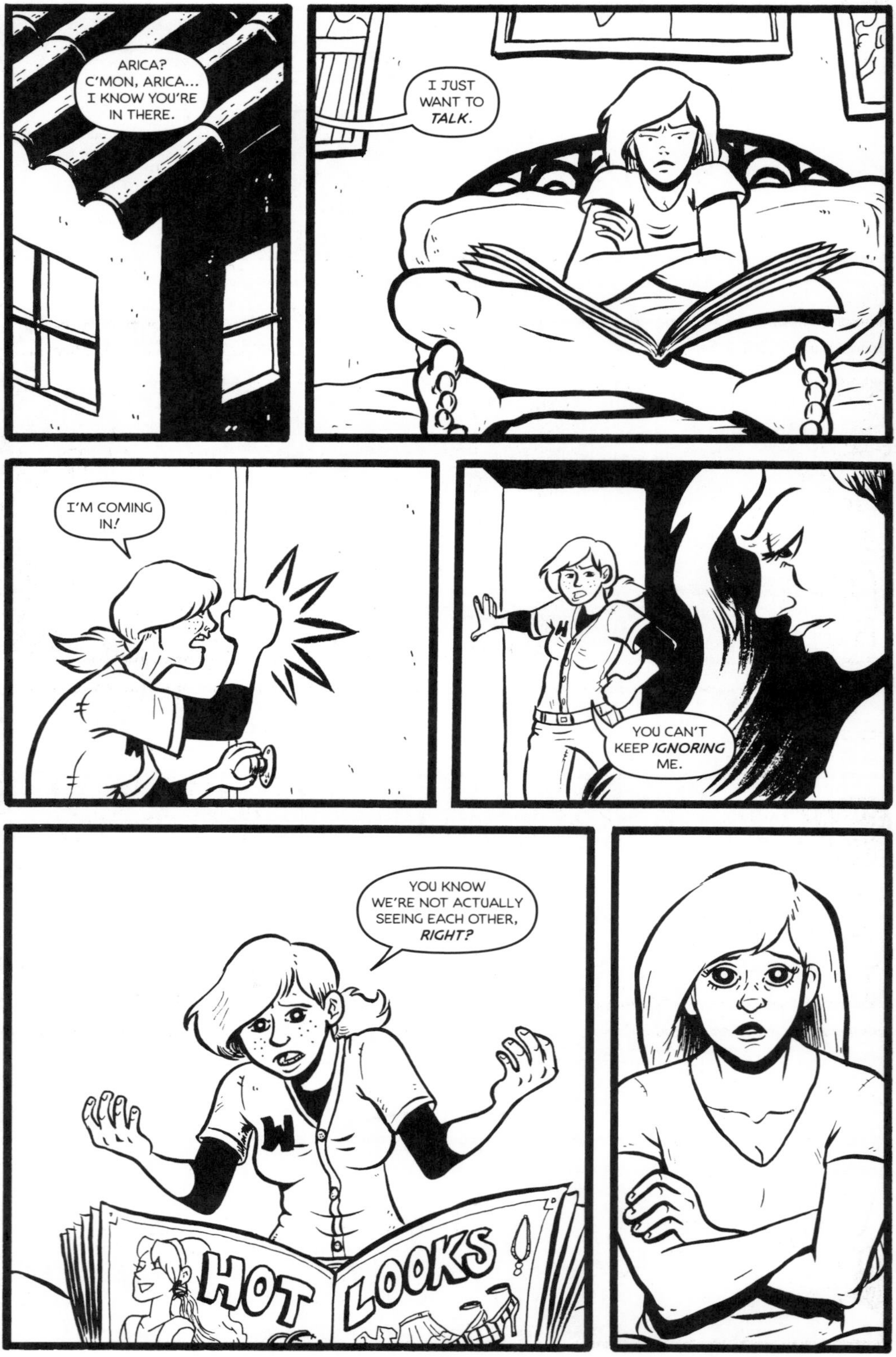
ARICA? C'MON, ARICA... I KNOW YOU'RE IN THERE.
I JUST WANT TO *TALK*.
I'M COMING IN!
YOU CAN'T KEEP *IGNORING* ME.
YOU KNOW WE'RE NOT ACTUALLY SEEING EACH OTHER, *RIGHT?*
HOT LOOKS

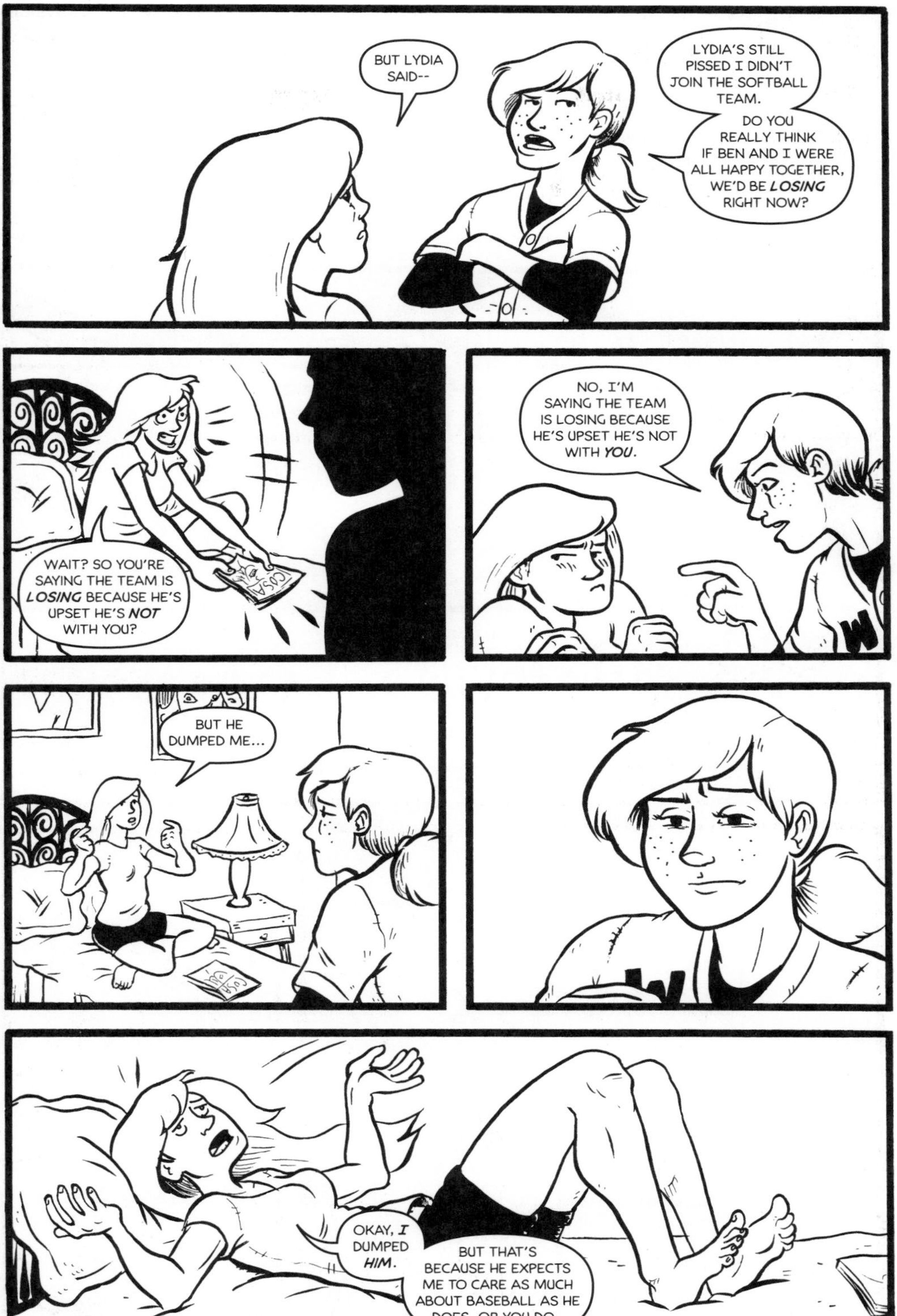
BUT LYDIA SAID--
LYDIA'S STILL PISSED I DIDN'T JOIN THE SOFTBALL TEAM.
DO YOU REALLY THINK IF BEN AND I WERE ALL HAPPY TOGETHER, WE'D BE ***LOSING*** RIGHT NOW?
WAIT? SO YOU'RE SAYING THE TEAM IS ***LOSING*** BECAUSE HE'S UPSET HE'S ***NOT*** WITH YOU?
NO, I'M SAYING THE TEAM IS LOSING BECAUSE HE'S UPSET HE'S NOT WITH ***YOU***.
BUT HE DUMPED ME...
OKAY, ***I*** DUMPED ***HIM***.
BUT THAT'S BECAUSE HE EXPECTS ME TO CARE AS MUCH ABOUT BASEBALL AS HE DOES. OR YOU DO.

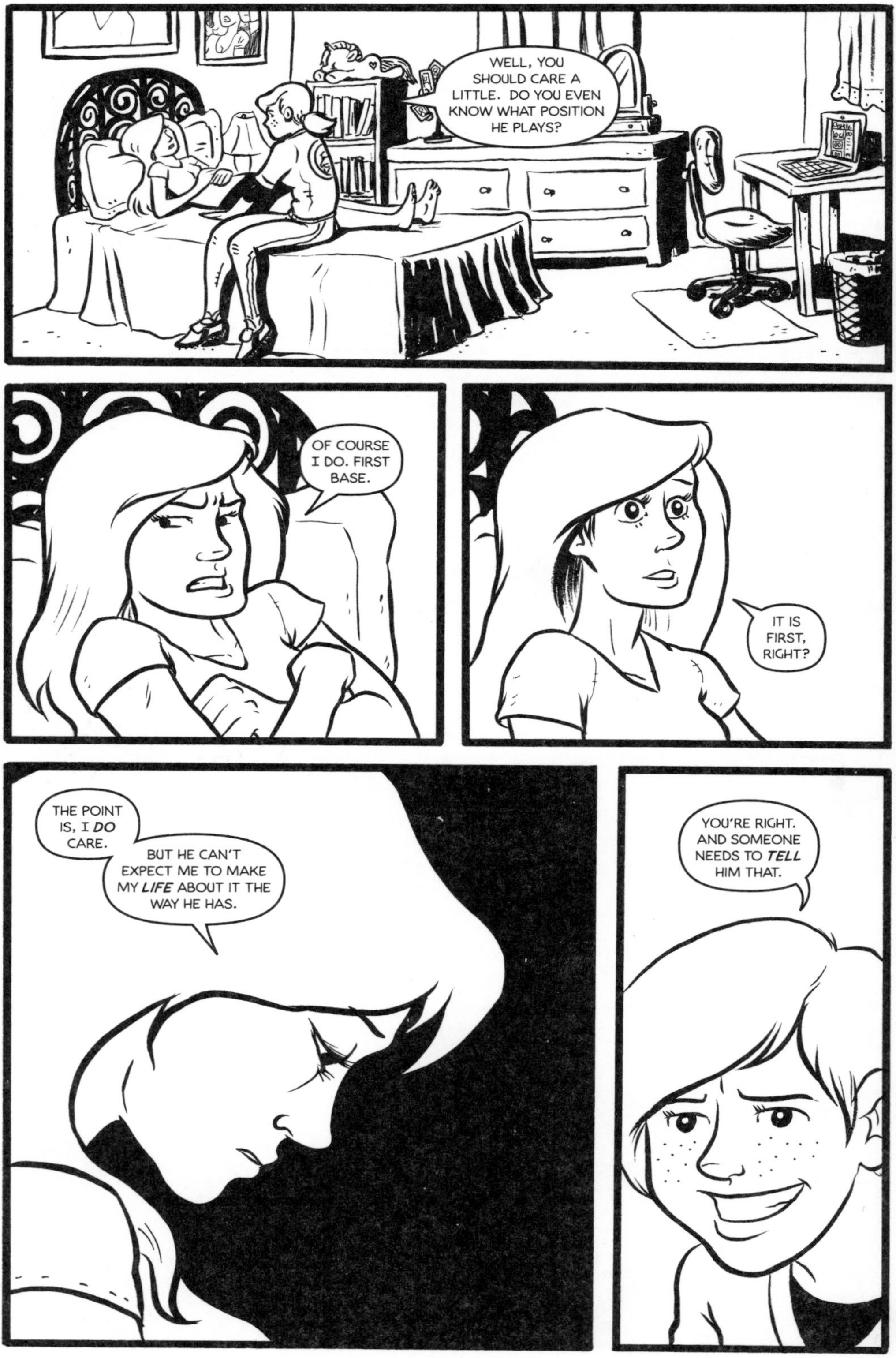
WELL, YOU SHOULD CARE A LITTLE. DO YOU EVEN KNOW WHAT POSITION HE PLAYS?
OF COURSE I DO. FIRST BASE.
IT IS FIRST, RIGHT?
THE POINT IS, I *DO* CARE.
BUT HE CAN'T EXPECT ME TO MAKE MY *LIFE* ABOUT IT THE WAY HE HAS.
YOU'RE RIGHT. AND SOMEONE NEEDS TO *TELL* HIM THAT.

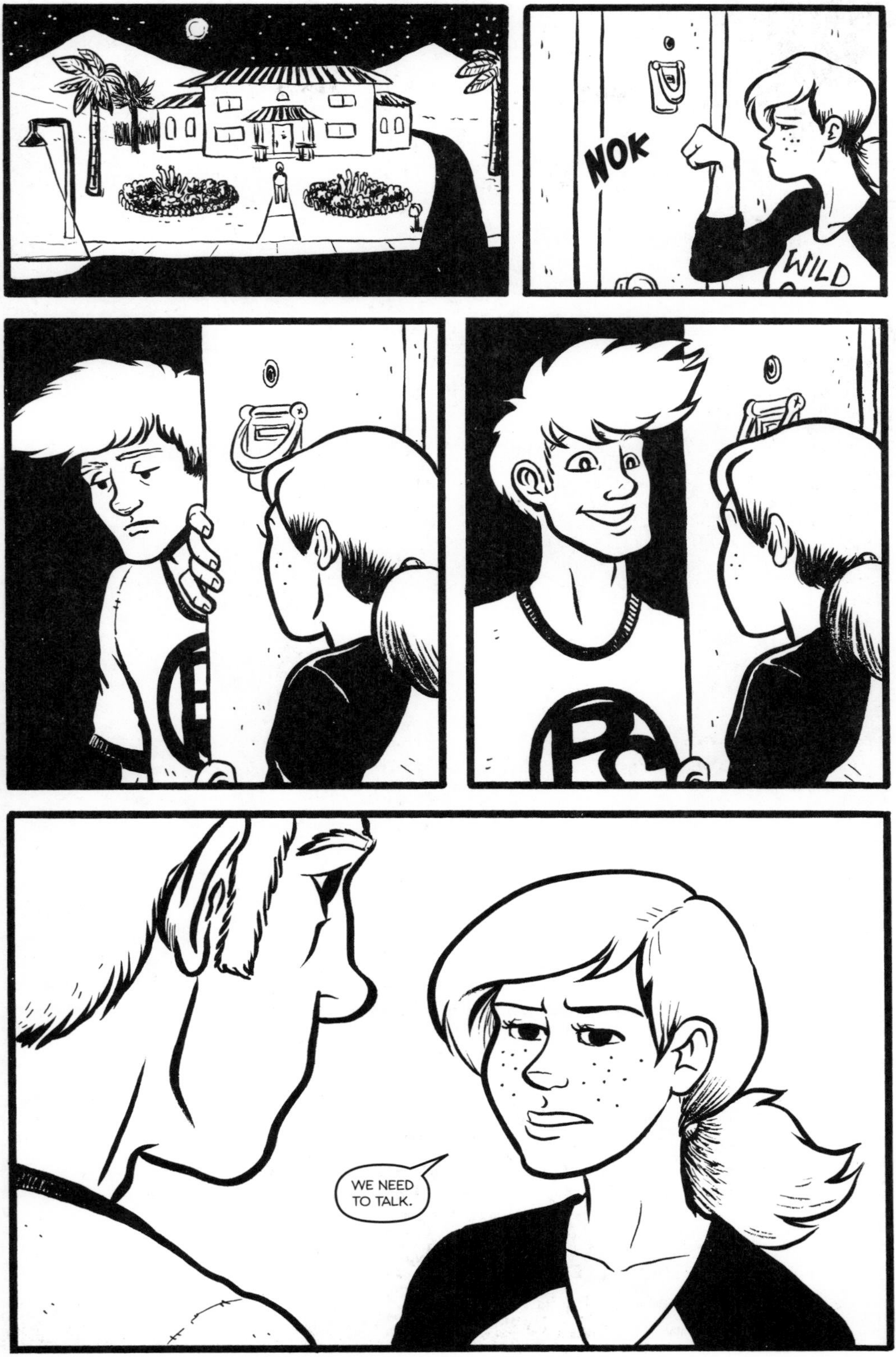
NOK
WILD
WE NEED TO TALK.

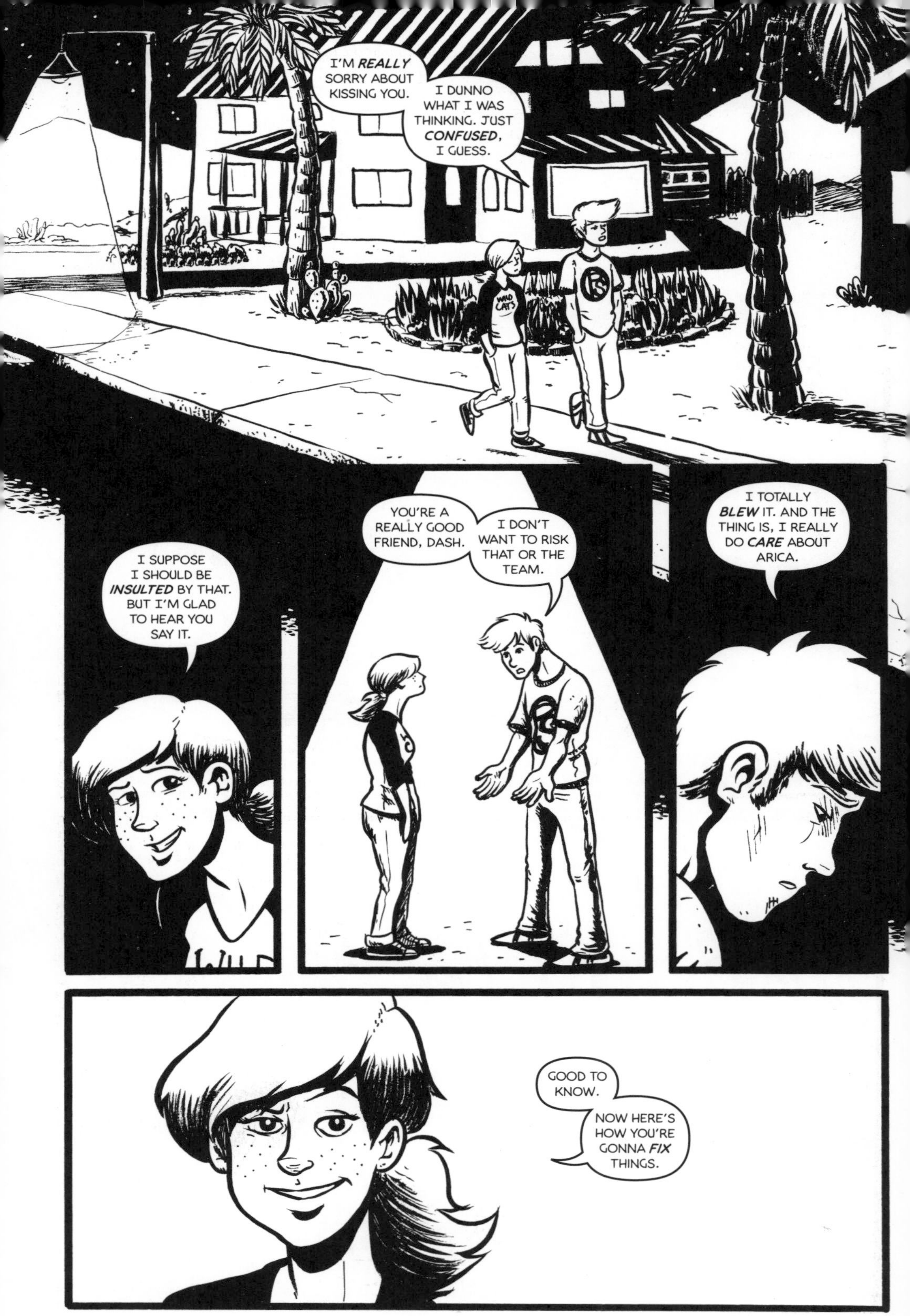
I'M REALLY SORRY ABOUT KISSING YOU.
I DUNNO WHAT I WAS THINKING. JUST CONFUSED, I GUESS.
I SUPPOSE I SHOULD BE INSULTED BY THAT. BUT I'M GLAD TO HEAR YOU SAY IT.
YOU'RE A REALLY GOOD FRIEND, DASH.
I DON'T WANT TO RISK THAT OR THE TEAM.
I TOTALLY BLEW IT. AND THE THING IS, I REALLY DO CARE ABOUT ARICA.
GOOD TO KNOW.
NOW HERE'S HOW YOU'RE GONNA FIX THINGS.

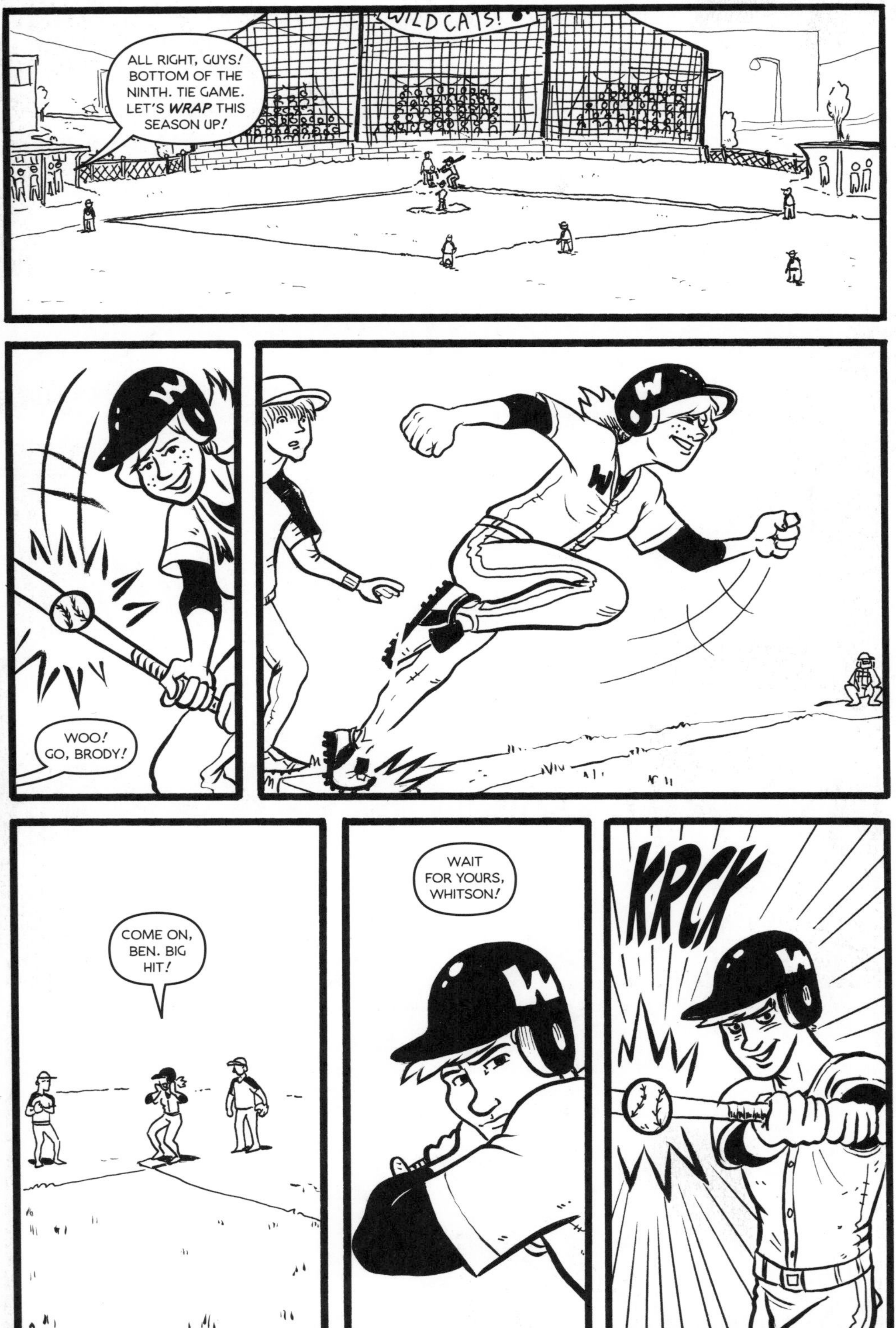
WILDCATS!
ALL RIGHT, GUYS! BOTTOM OF THE NINTH. TIE GAME. LET'S **WRAP** THIS SEASON UP!
WOO! GO, BRODY!
COME ON, BEN. BIG HIT!
WAIT FOR YOURS, WHITSON!
KRCK

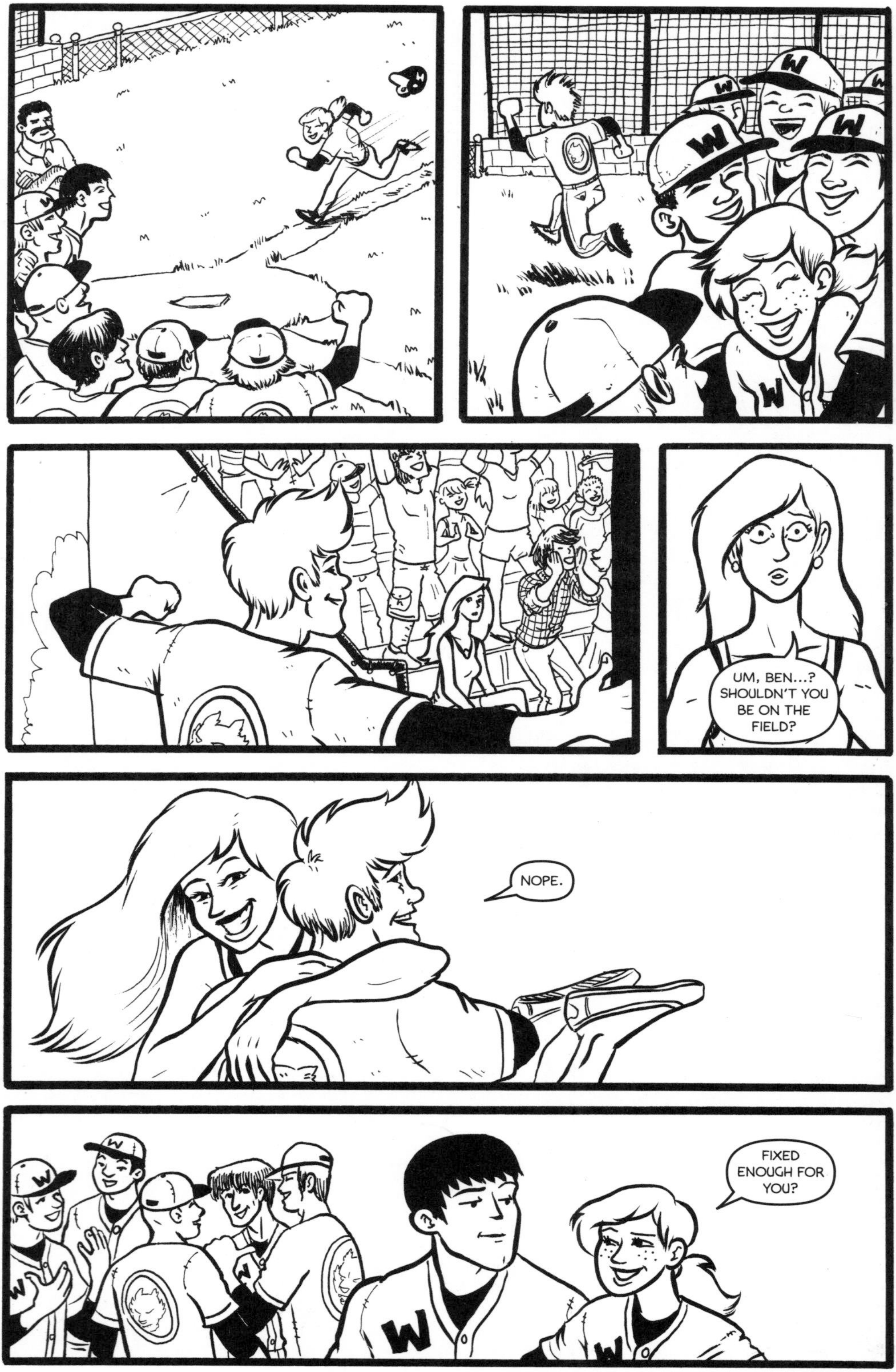
UM, BEN...? SHOULDN'T YOU BE ON THE FIELD?
NOPE.
FIXED ENOUGH FOR YOU?

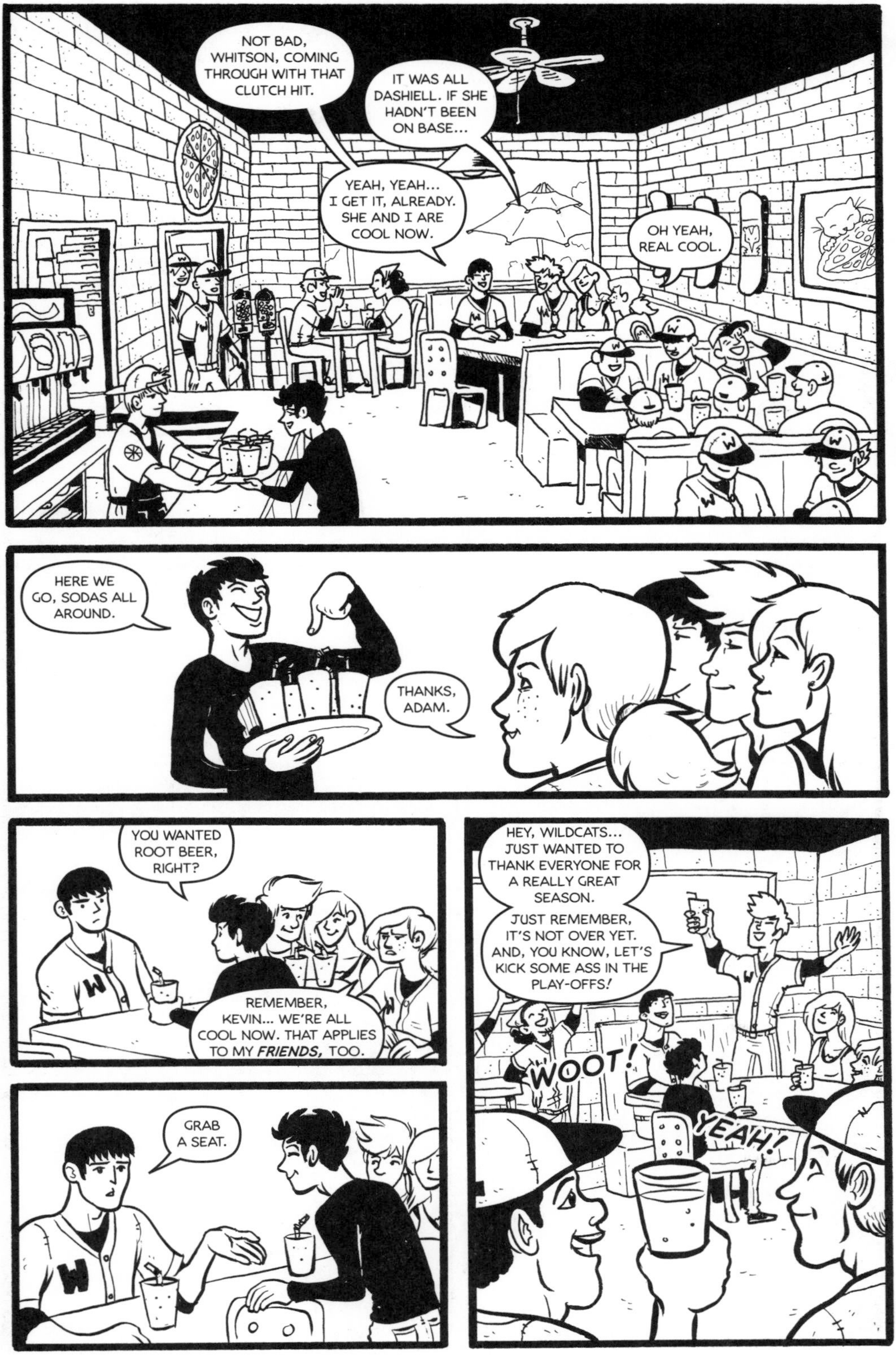
NOT BAD, WHITSON, COMING THROUGH WITH THAT CLUTCH HIT.
IT WAS ALL DASHIELL. IF SHE HADN'T BEEN ON BASE...
YEAH, YEAH... I GET IT, ALREADY. SHE AND I ARE COOL NOW.
OH YEAH, REAL COOL.
HERE WE GO, SODAS ALL AROUND.
THANKS, ADAM.
YOU WANTED ROOT BEER, RIGHT?
REMEMBER, KEVIN... WE'RE ALL COOL NOW. THAT APPLIES TO MY *FRIENDS,* TOO.
GRAB A SEAT.
HEY, WILDCATS... JUST WANTED TO THANK EVERYONE FOR A REALLY GREAT SEASON.
JUST REMEMBER, IT'S NOT OVER YET. AND, YOU KNOW, LET'S KICK SOME ASS IN THE PLAY-OFFS!
WOOT!
YEAH!

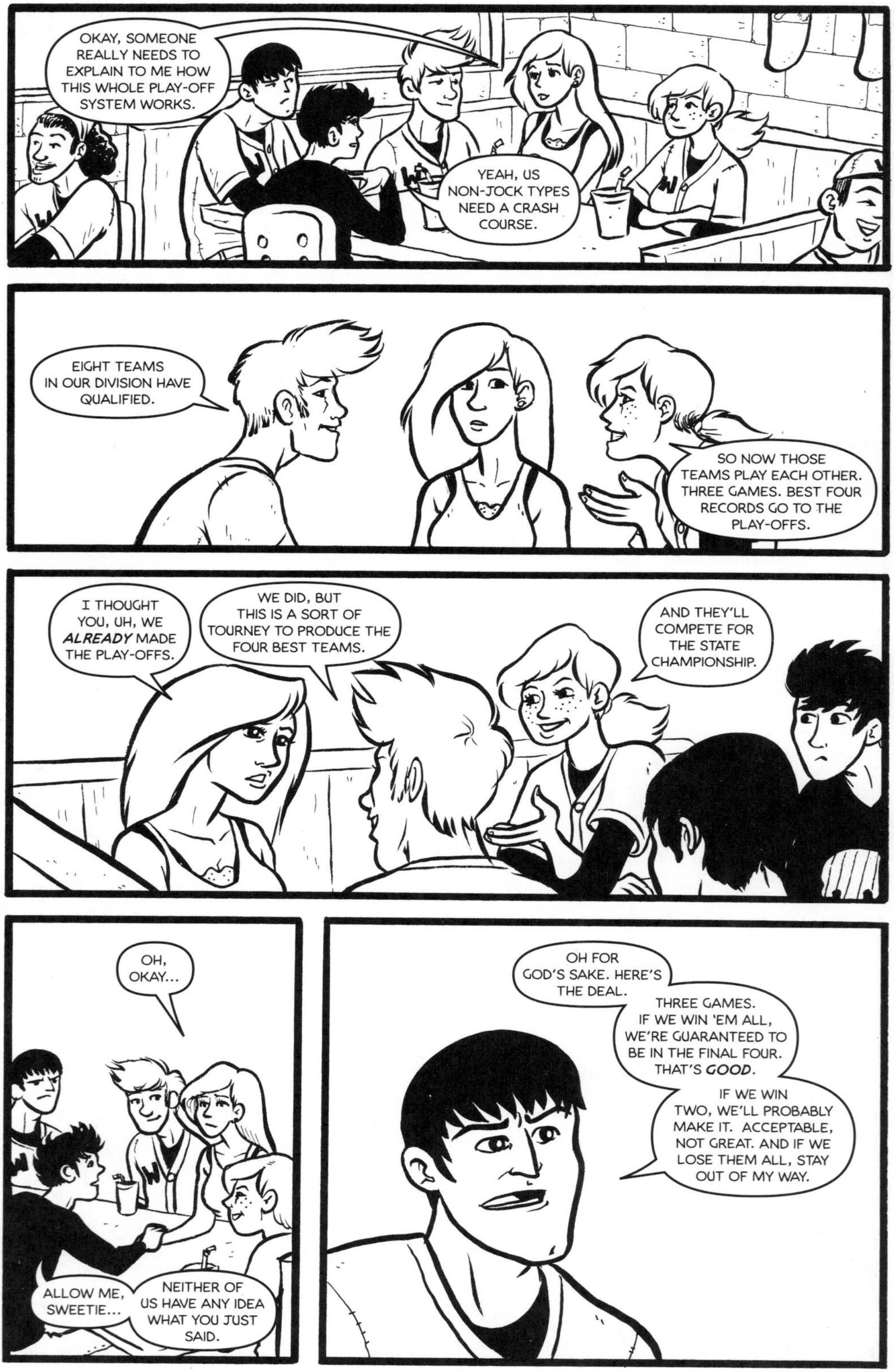
OKAY, SOMEONE REALLY NEEDS TO EXPLAIN TO ME HOW THIS WHOLE PLAY-OFF SYSTEM WORKS.
YEAH, US NON-JOCK TYPES NEED A CRASH COURSE.
EIGHT TEAMS IN OUR DIVISION HAVE QUALIFIED.
SO NOW THOSE TEAMS PLAY EACH OTHER. THREE GAMES. BEST FOUR RECORDS GO TO THE PLAY-OFFS.
I THOUGHT YOU, UH, WE *ALREADY* MADE THE PLAY-OFFS.
WE DID, BUT THIS IS A SORT OF TOURNEY TO PRODUCE THE FOUR BEST TEAMS.
AND THEY'LL COMPETE FOR THE STATE CHAMPIONSHIP.
OH, OKAY...
ALLOW ME, SWEETIE...
NEITHER OF US HAVE ANY IDEA WHAT YOU JUST SAID.
OH FOR GOD'S SAKE. HERE'S THE DEAL.
THREE GAMES. IF WE WIN 'EM ALL, WE'RE GUARANTEED TO BE IN THE FINAL FOUR. THAT'S *GOOD*.
IF WE WIN TWO, WE'LL PROBABLY MAKE IT. ACCEPTABLE, NOT GREAT. AND IF WE LOSE THEM ALL, STAY OUT OF MY WAY.

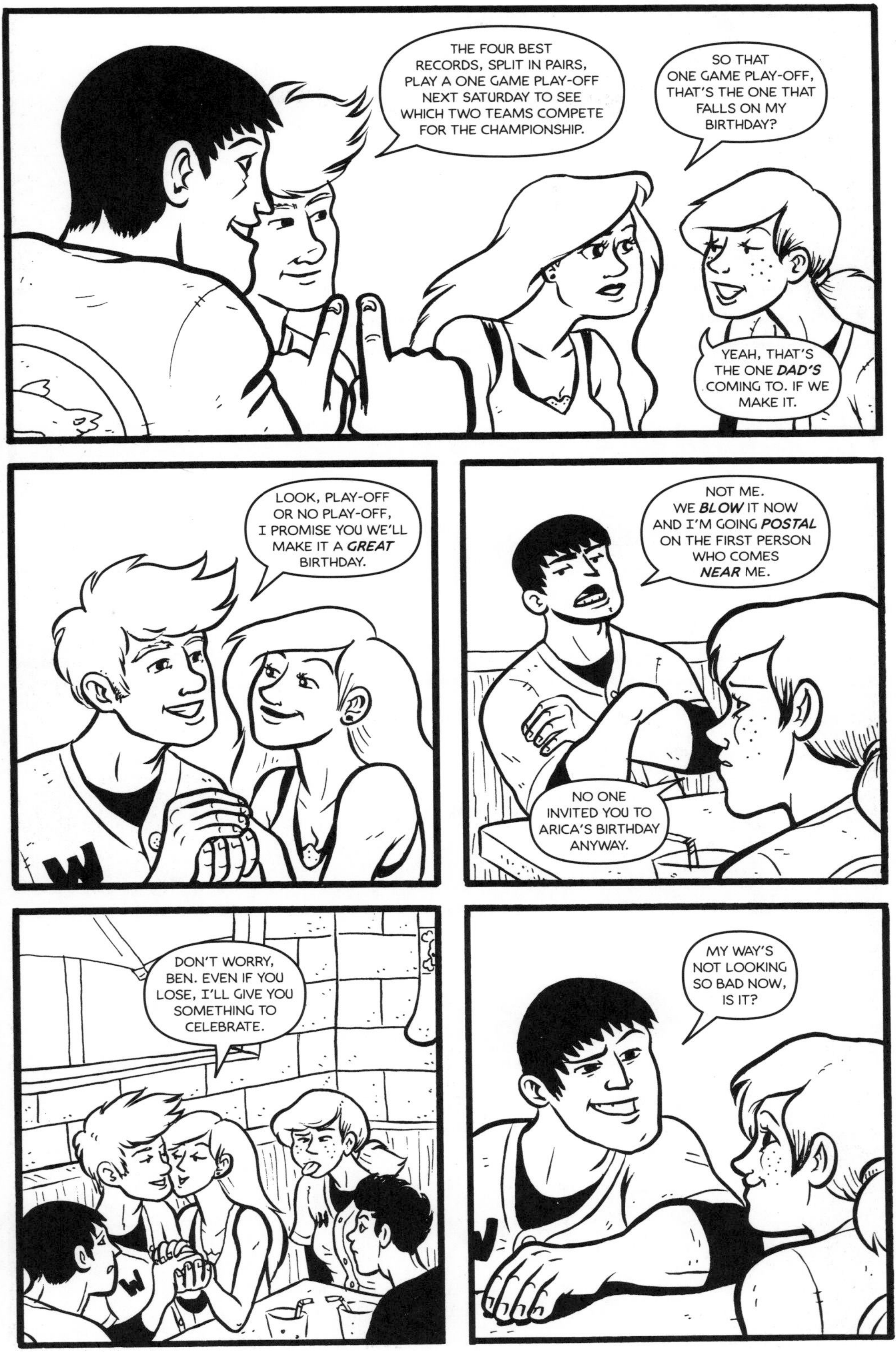
THE FOUR BEST RECORDS, SPLIT IN PAIRS, PLAY A ONE GAME PLAY-OFF NEXT SATURDAY TO SEE WHICH TWO TEAMS COMPETE FOR THE CHAMPIONSHIP.
SO THAT ONE GAME PLAY-OFF, THAT'S THE ONE THAT FALLS ON MY BIRTHDAY?
YEAH, THAT'S THE ONE ***DAD'S*** COMING TO. IF WE MAKE IT.
LOOK, PLAY-OFF OR NO PLAY-OFF, I PROMISE YOU WE'LL MAKE IT A ***GREAT*** BIRTHDAY.
NOT ME. WE ***BLOW*** IT NOW AND I'M GOING ***POSTAL*** ON THE FIRST PERSON WHO COMES ***NEAR*** ME.
NO ONE INVITED YOU TO ARICA'S BIRTHDAY ANYWAY.
DON'T WORRY, BEN. EVEN IF YOU LOSE, I'LL GIVE YOU SOMETHING TO CELEBRATE.
MY WAY'S NOT LOOKING SO BAD NOW, IS IT?

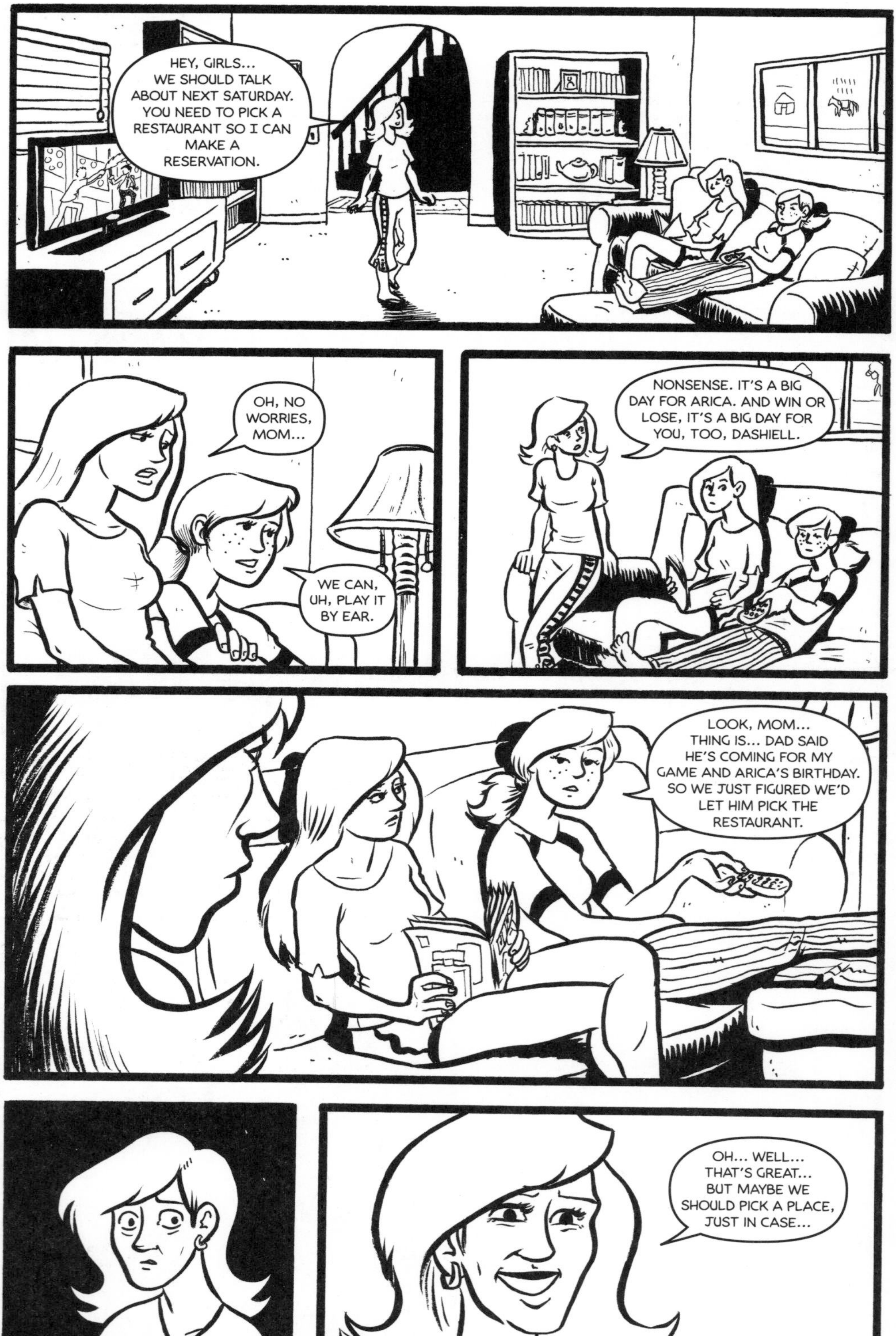
HEY, GIRLS... WE SHOULD TALK ABOUT NEXT SATURDAY. YOU NEED TO PICK A RESTAURANT SO I CAN MAKE A RESERVATION.
OH, NO WORRIES, MOM...
WE CAN, UH, PLAY IT BY EAR.
NONSENSE. IT'S A BIG DAY FOR ARICA. AND WIN OR LOSE, IT'S A BIG DAY FOR YOU, TOO, DASHIELL.
LOOK, MOM... THING IS... DAD SAID HE'S COMING FOR MY GAME AND ARICA'S BIRTHDAY. SO WE JUST FIGURED WE'D LET HIM PICK THE RESTAURANT.
OH... WELL... THAT'S GREAT... BUT MAYBE WE SHOULD PICK A PLACE, JUST IN CASE...

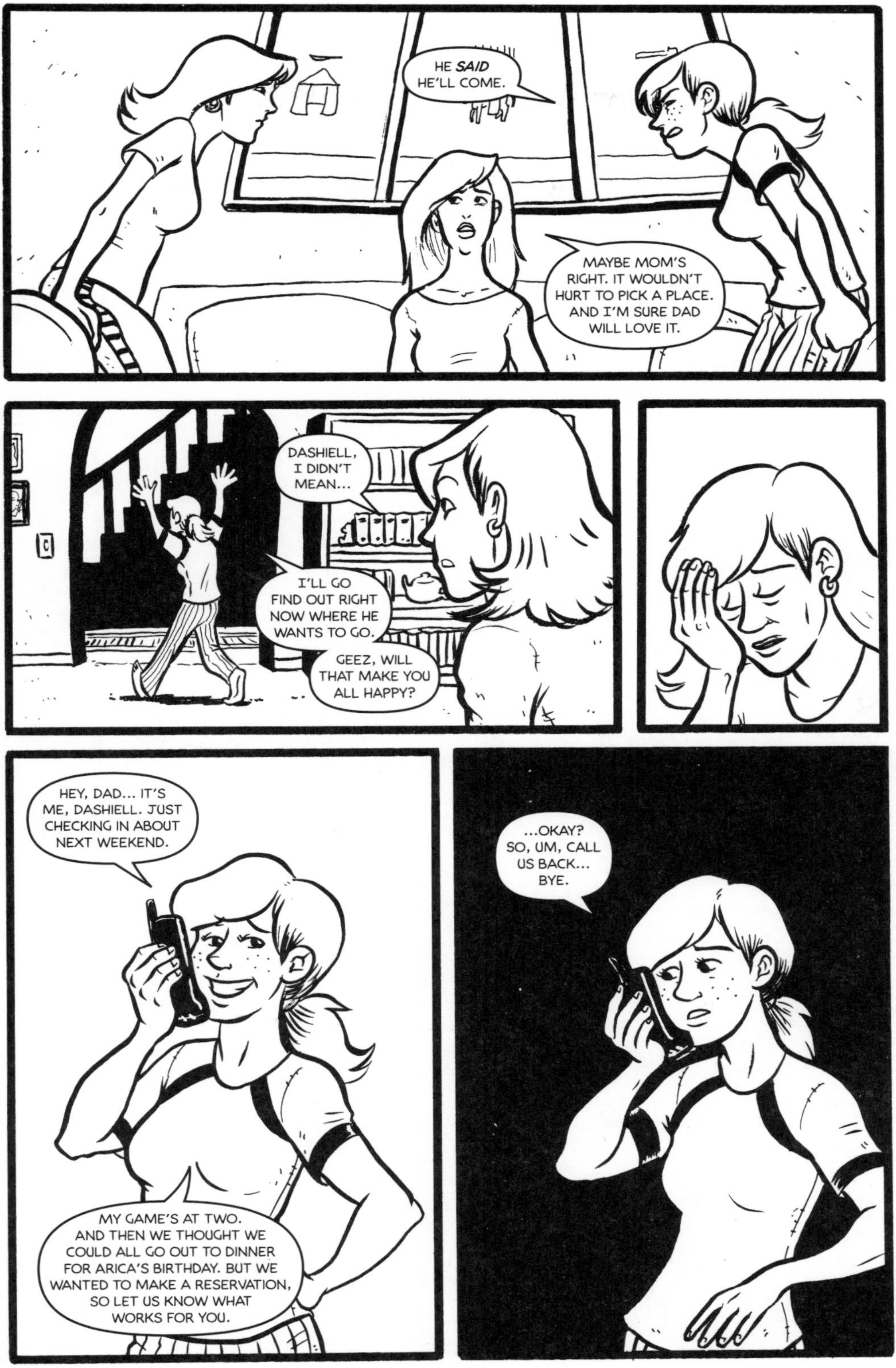
HE *SAID* HE'LL COME.
MAYBE MOM'S RIGHT. IT WOULDN'T HURT TO PICK A PLACE. AND I'M SURE DAD WILL LOVE IT.
DASHIELL, I DIDN'T MEAN...
I'LL GO FIND OUT RIGHT NOW WHERE HE WANTS TO GO.
GEEZ, WILL THAT MAKE YOU ALL HAPPY?
HEY, DAD... IT'S ME, DASHIELL. JUST CHECKING IN ABOUT NEXT WEEKEND.
MY GAME'S AT TWO. AND THEN WE THOUGHT WE COULD ALL GO OUT TO DINNER FOR ARICA'S BIRTHDAY. BUT WE WANTED TO MAKE A RESERVATION, SO LET US KNOW WHAT WORKS FOR YOU.
...OKAY? SO, UM, CALL US BACK... BYE.

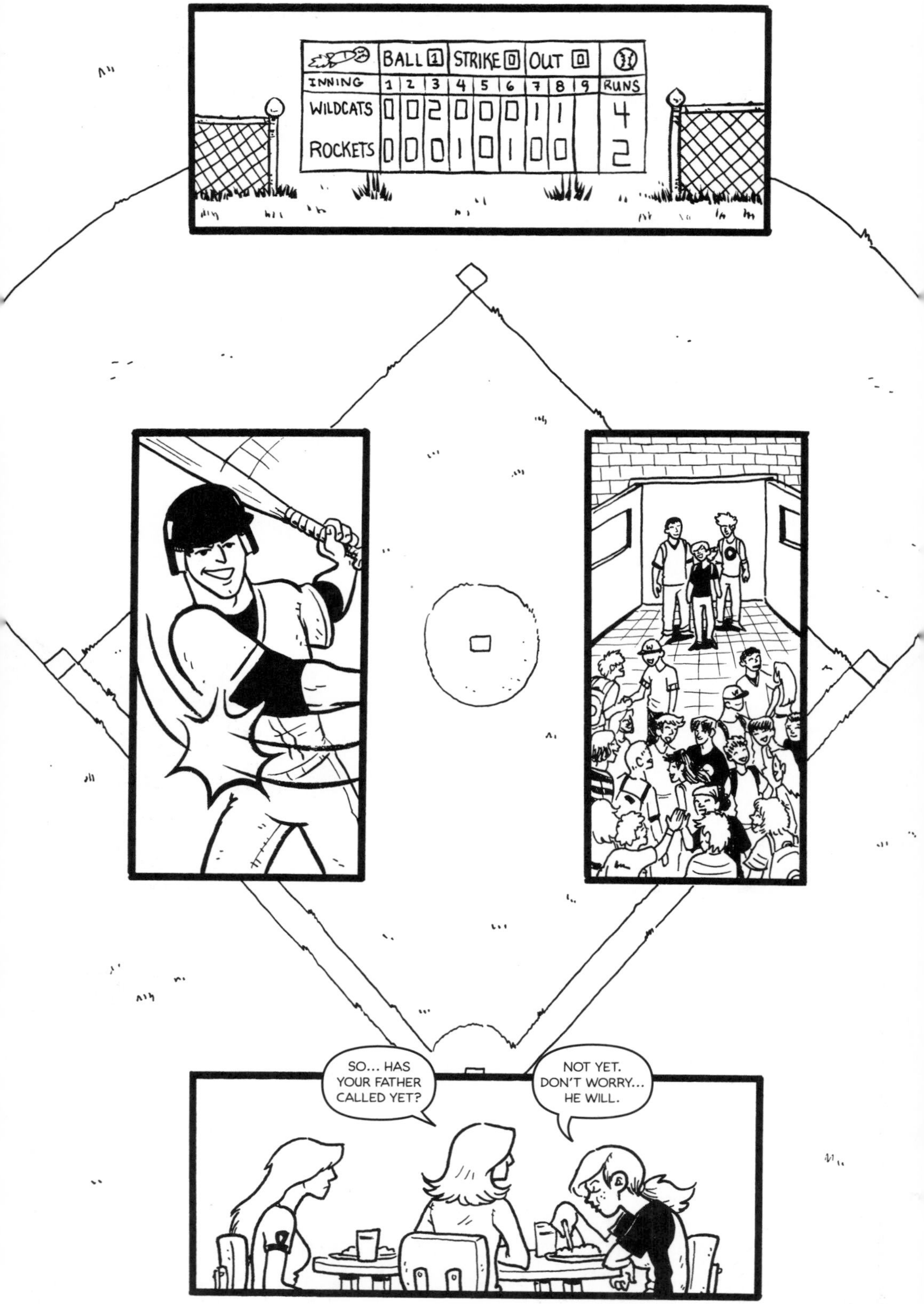
BALL 1 STRIKE 0 OUT 0
INNING 1 2 3 4 5 6 7 8 9 RUNS
WILDCATS 0 0 2 0 0 0 1 1 4
ROCKETS 0 0 0 1 0 1 0 0 2
SO... HAS YOUR FATHER CALLED YET?
NOT YET. DON'T WORRY... HE WILL.

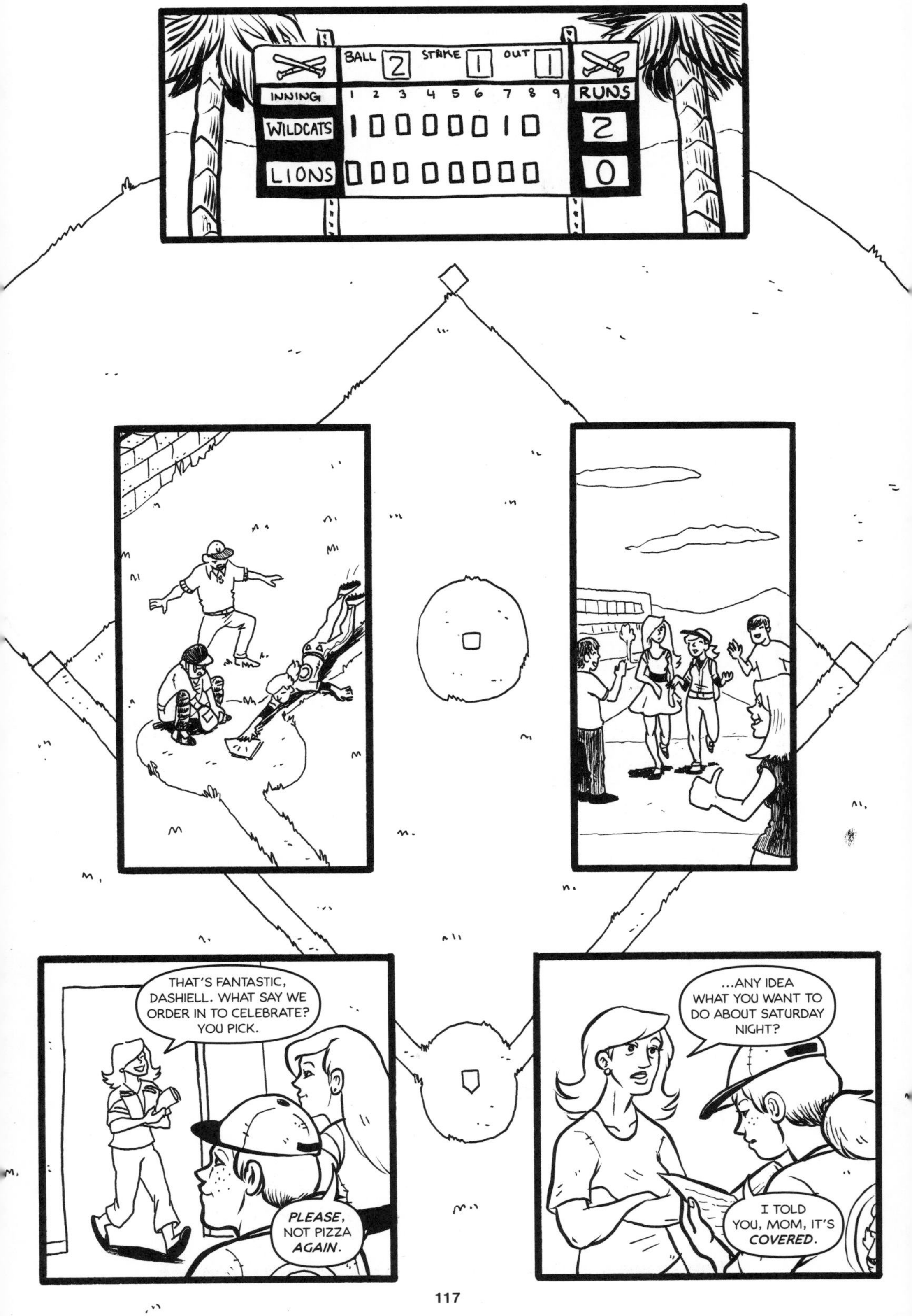
BALL 2 STRIKE 1 OUT 1
INNING 1 2 3 4 5 6 7 8 9 RUNS
WILDCATS 1 0 0 0 0 0 1 0 2
LIONS 0 0 0 0 0 0 0 0 0
THAT'S FANTASTIC, DASHIELL. WHAT SAY WE ORDER IN TO CELEBRATE? YOU PICK.
PLEASE, NOT PIZZA *AGAIN*.
...ANY IDEA WHAT YOU WANT TO DO ABOUT SATURDAY NIGHT?
I TOLD YOU, MOM, IT'S *COVERED*.

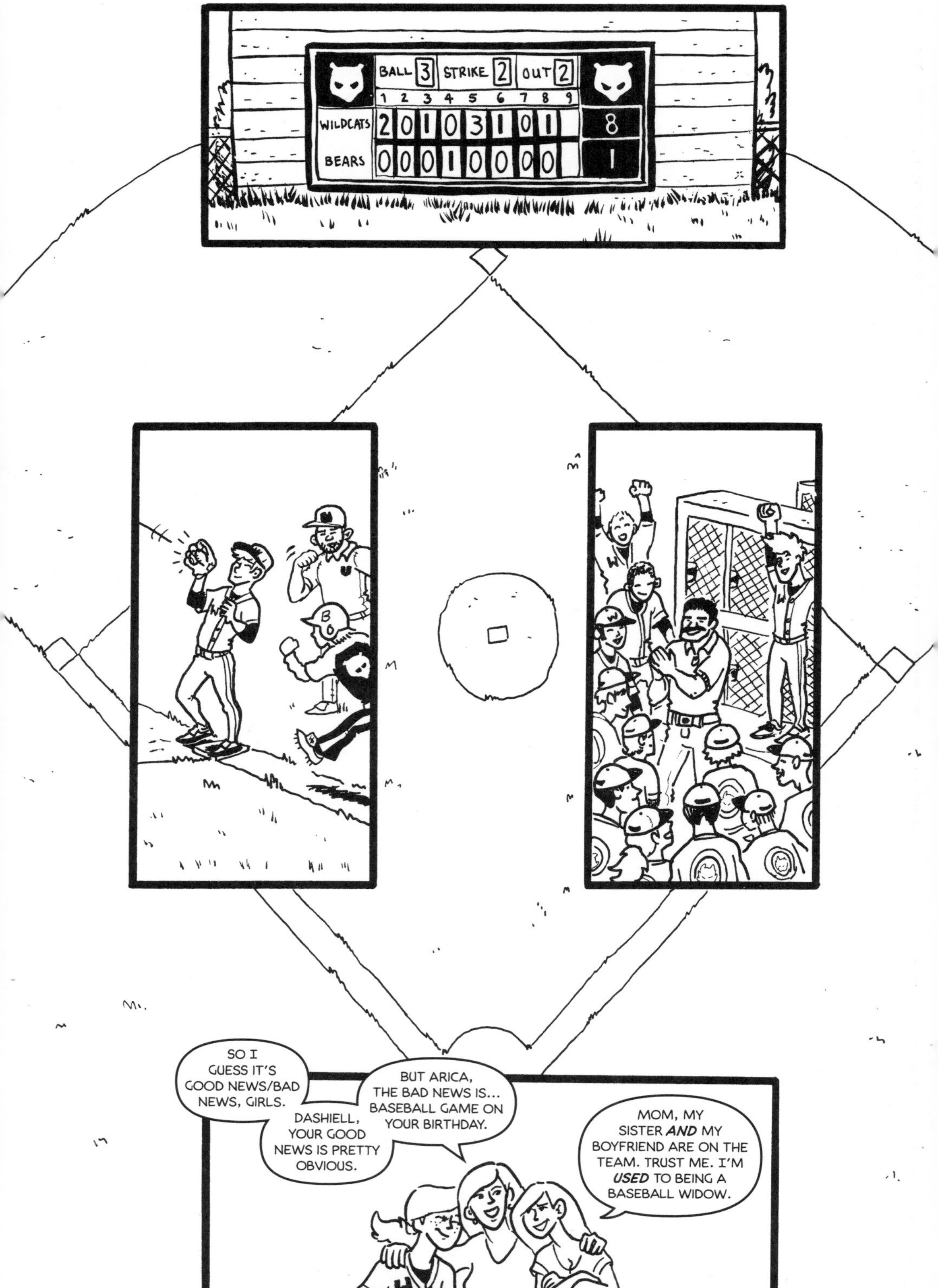
BALL 3 STRIKE 2 OUT 2
1 2 3 4 5 6 7 8 9
WILDCATS 2 0 1 0 3 1 0 1 8
BEARS 0 0 0 1 0 0 0 0 1
SO I GUESS IT'S GOOD NEWS/BAD NEWS, GIRLS.
DASHIELL, YOUR GOOD NEWS IS PRETTY OBVIOUS.
BUT ARICA, THE BAD NEWS IS... BASEBALL GAME ON YOUR BIRTHDAY.
MOM, MY SISTER ***AND*** MY BOYFRIEND ARE ON THE TEAM. TRUST ME. I'M ***USED*** TO BEING A BASEBALL WIDOW.

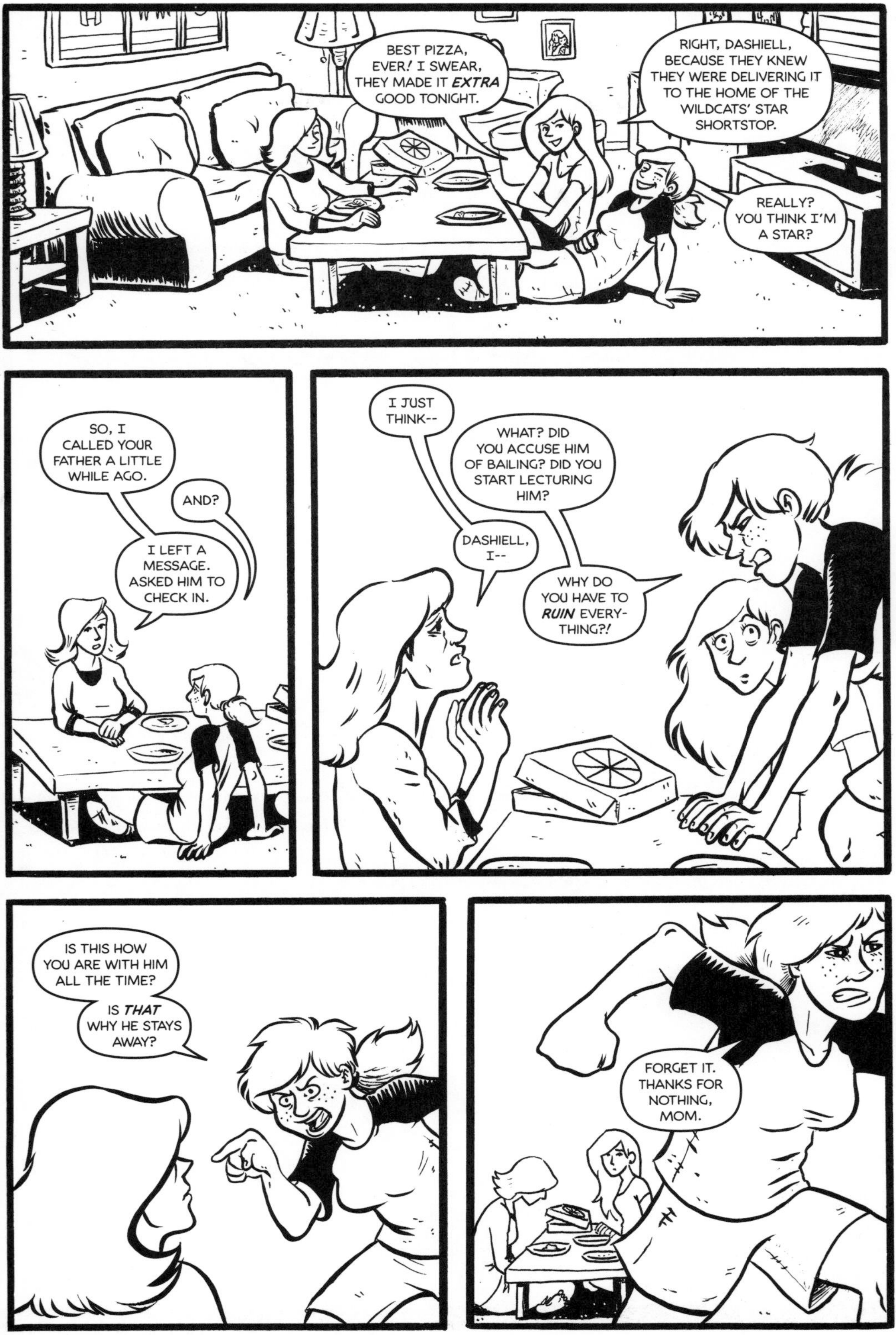
BEST PIZZA, EVER! I SWEAR, THEY MADE IT *EXTRA* GOOD TONIGHT.
RIGHT, DASHIELL, BECAUSE THEY KNEW THEY WERE DELIVERING IT TO THE HOME OF THE WILDCATS' STAR SHORTSTOP.
REALLY? YOU THINK I'M A STAR?
SO, I CALLED YOUR FATHER A LITTLE WHILE AGO.
AND?
I LEFT A MESSAGE. ASKED HIM TO CHECK IN.
I JUST THINK--
WHAT? DID YOU ACCUSE HIM OF BAILING? DID YOU START LECTURING HIM?
DASHIELL, I--
WHY DO YOU HAVE TO *RUIN* EVERYTHING?!
IS THIS HOW YOU ARE WITH HIM ALL THE TIME?
IS *THAT* WHY HE STAYS AWAY?
FORGET IT. THANKS FOR NOTHING, MOM.

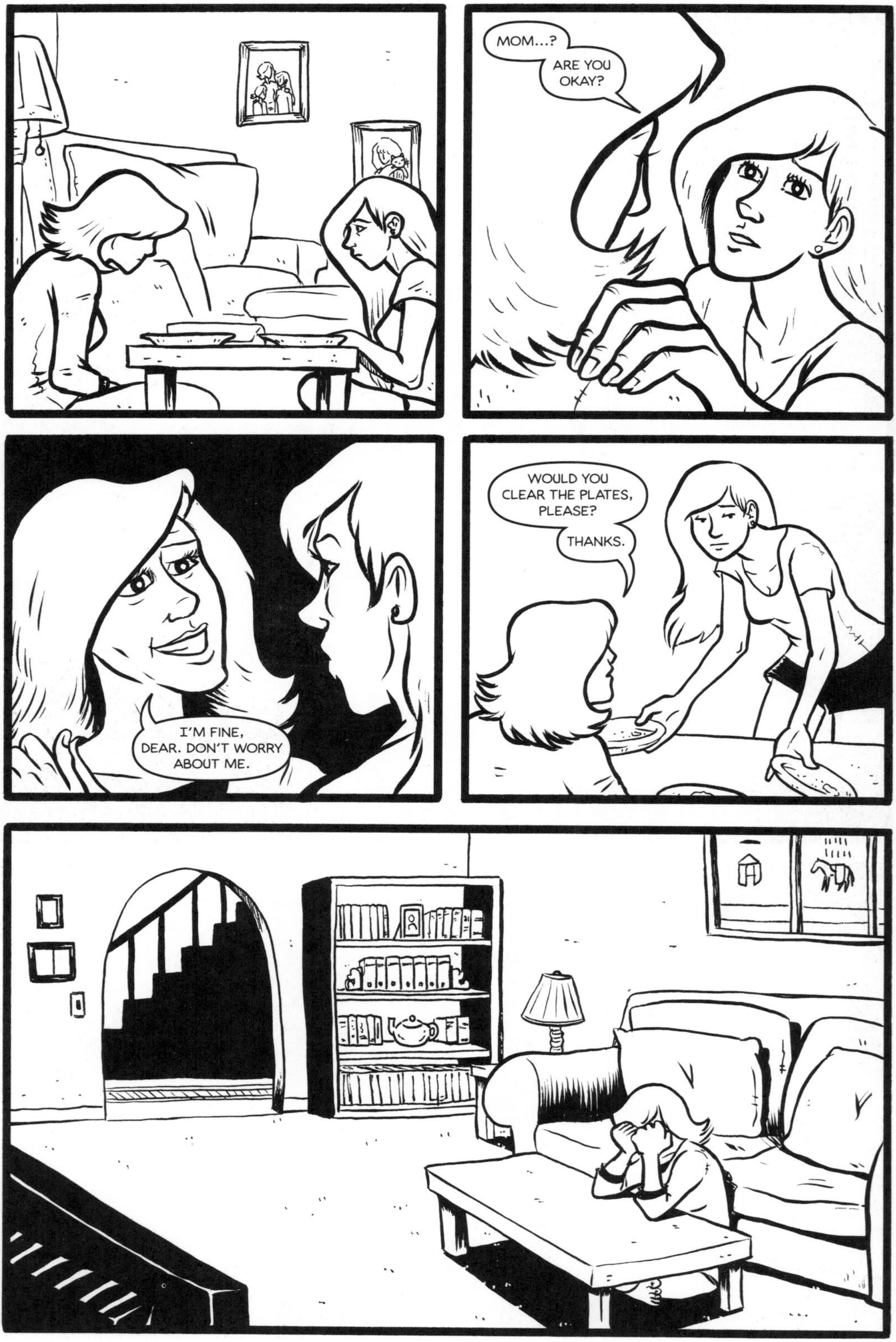
MOM...?
ARE YOU OKAY?
I'M FINE, DEAR. DON'T WORRY ABOUT ME.
WOULD YOU CLEAR THE PLATES, PLEASE?
THANKS.

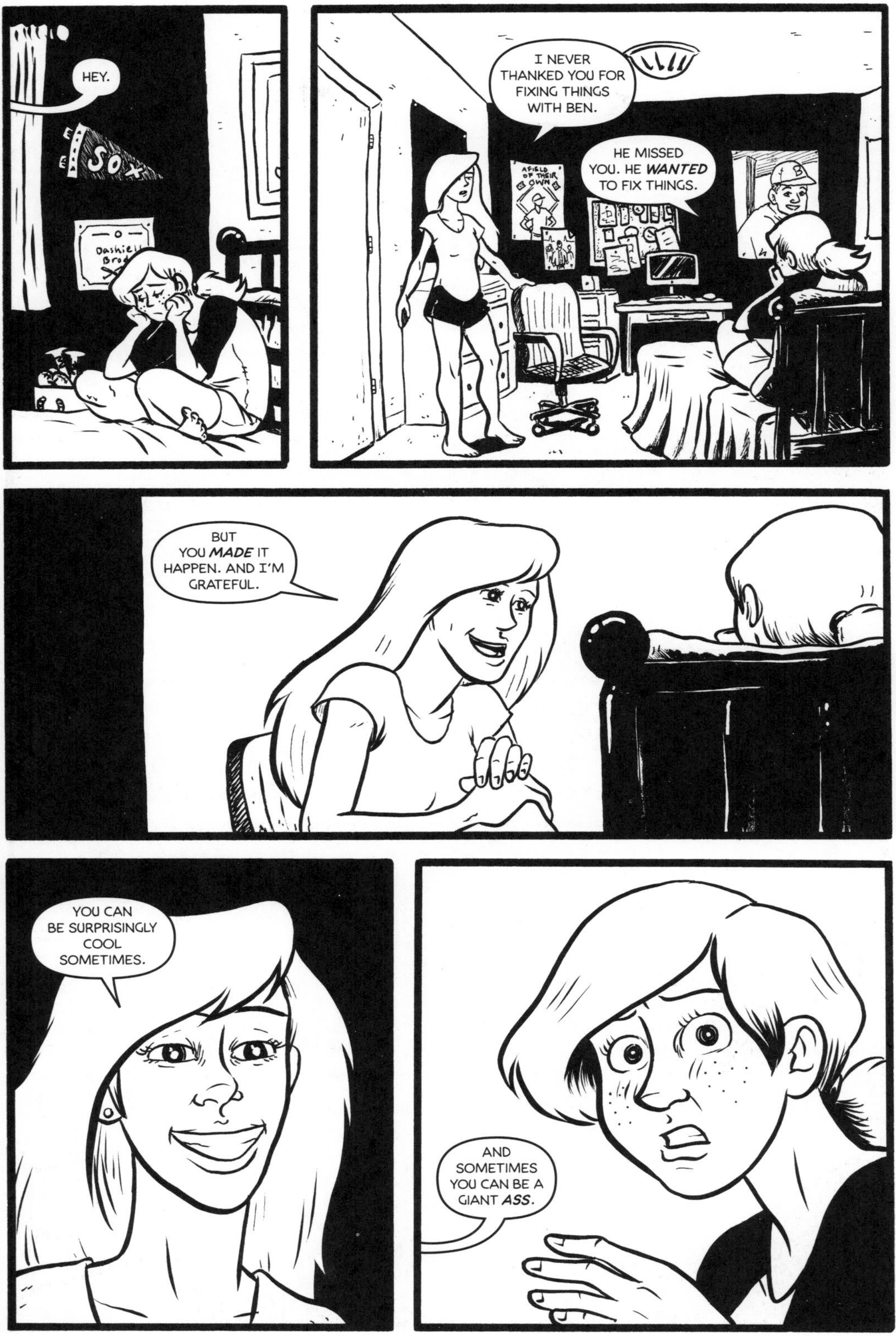
HEY.
I NEVER THANKED YOU FOR FIXING THINGS WITH BEN.
HE MISSED YOU. HE *WANTED* TO FIX THINGS.
BUT YOU *MADE* IT HAPPEN. AND I'M GRATEFUL.
YOU CAN BE SURPRISINGLY COOL SOMETIMES.
AND SOMETIMES YOU CAN BE A GIANT *ASS*.

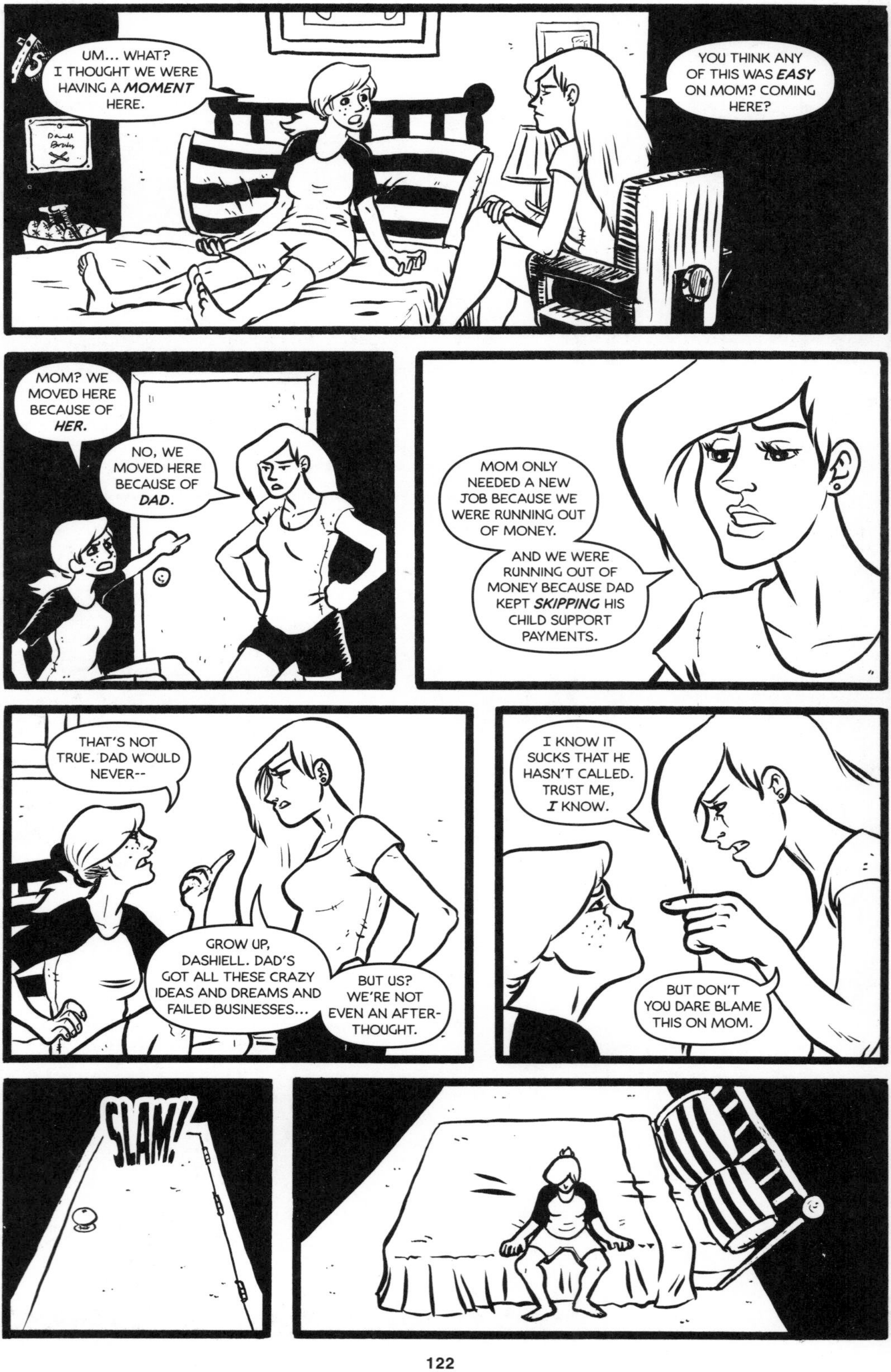
UM... WHAT? I THOUGHT WE WERE HAVING A *MOMENT* HERE.
YOU THINK ANY OF THIS WAS *EASY* ON MOM? COMING HERE?
MOM? WE MOVED HERE BECAUSE OF *HER.*
NO, WE MOVED HERE BECAUSE OF *DAD*.
MOM ONLY NEEDED A NEW JOB BECAUSE WE WERE RUNNING OUT OF MONEY.
AND WE WERE RUNNING OUT OF MONEY BECAUSE DAD KEPT *SKIPPING* HIS CHILD SUPPORT PAYMENTS.
THAT'S NOT TRUE. DAD WOULD NEVER--
GROW UP, DASHIELL. DAD'S GOT ALL THESE CRAZY IDEAS AND DREAMS AND FAILED BUSINESSES...
BUT US? WE'RE NOT EVEN AN AFTER-THOUGHT.
I KNOW IT SUCKS THAT HE HASN'T CALLED. TRUST ME, *I* KNOW.
BUT DON'T YOU DARE BLAME THIS ON MOM.
SLAM!

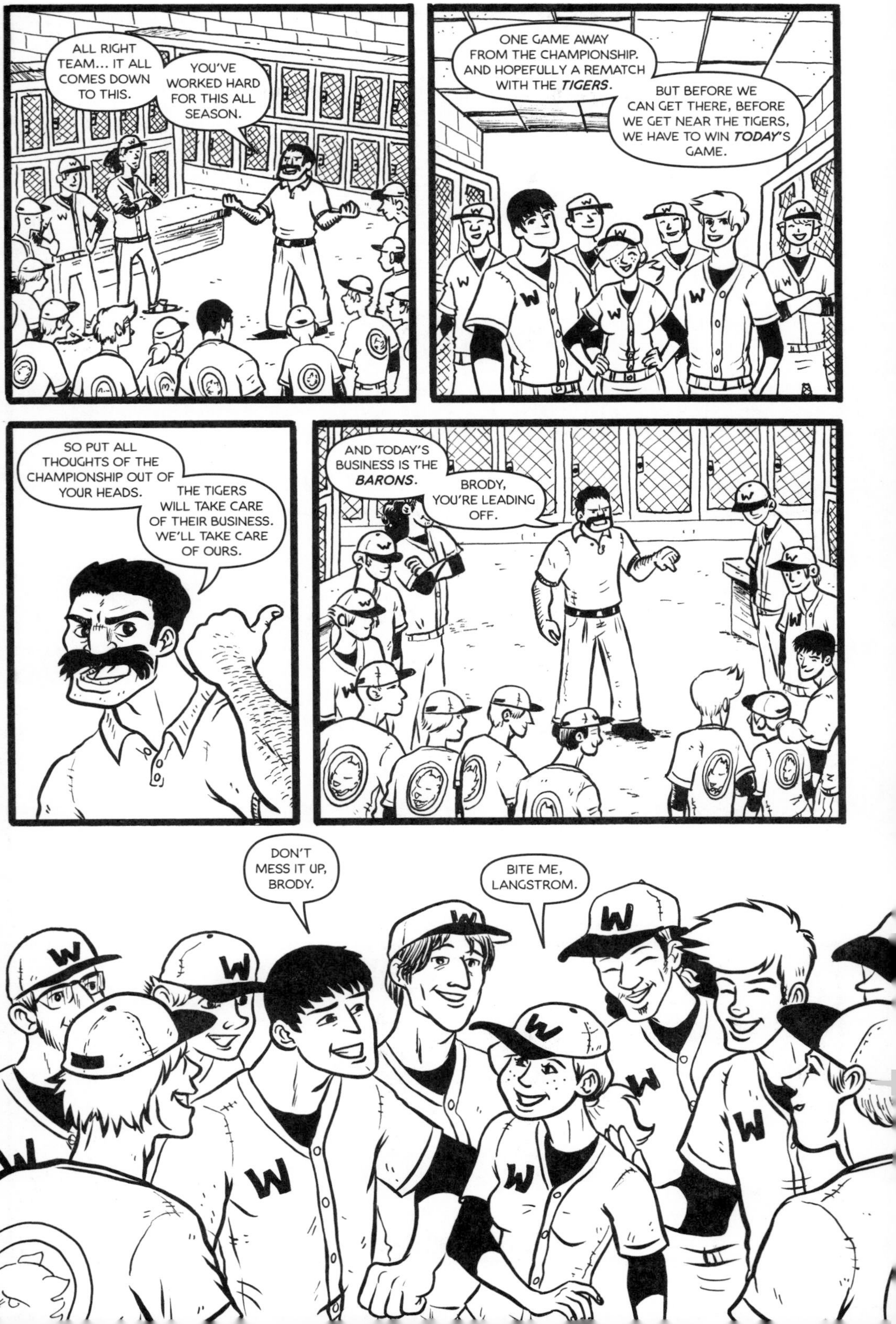
ALL RIGHT TEAM... IT ALL COMES DOWN TO THIS.
YOU'VE WORKED HARD FOR THIS ALL SEASON.
ONE GAME AWAY FROM THE CHAMPIONSHIP. AND HOPEFULLY A REMATCH WITH THE *TIGERS*.
BUT BEFORE WE CAN GET THERE, BEFORE WE GET NEAR THE TIGERS, WE HAVE TO WIN *TODAY*'S GAME.
SO PUT ALL THOUGHTS OF THE CHAMPIONSHIP OUT OF YOUR HEADS.
THE TIGERS WILL TAKE CARE OF THEIR BUSINESS. WE'LL TAKE CARE OF OURS.
AND TODAY'S BUSINESS IS THE *BARONS*.
BRODY, YOU'RE LEADING OFF.
DON'T MESS IT UP, BRODY.
BITE ME, LANGSTROM.

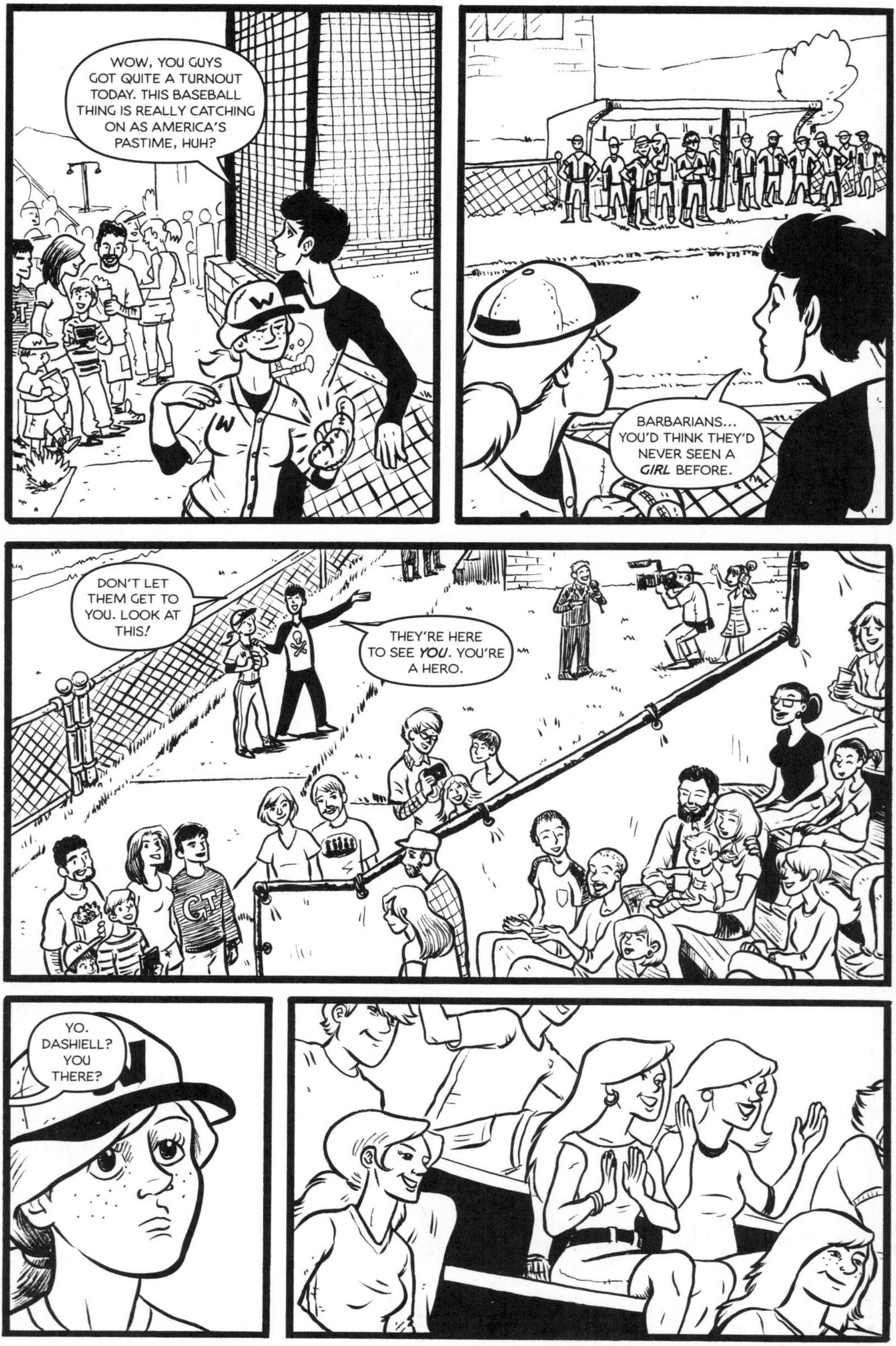
WOW, YOU GUYS GOT QUITE A TURNOUT TODAY. THIS BASEBALL THING IS REALLY CATCHING ON AS AMERICA'S PASTIME, HUH?
BARBARIANS... YOU'D THINK THEY'D NEVER SEEN A *GIRL* BEFORE.
DON'T LET THEM GET TO YOU. LOOK AT THIS!
THEY'RE HERE TO SEE *YOU*. YOU'RE A HERO.
YO. DASHIELL? YOU THERE?

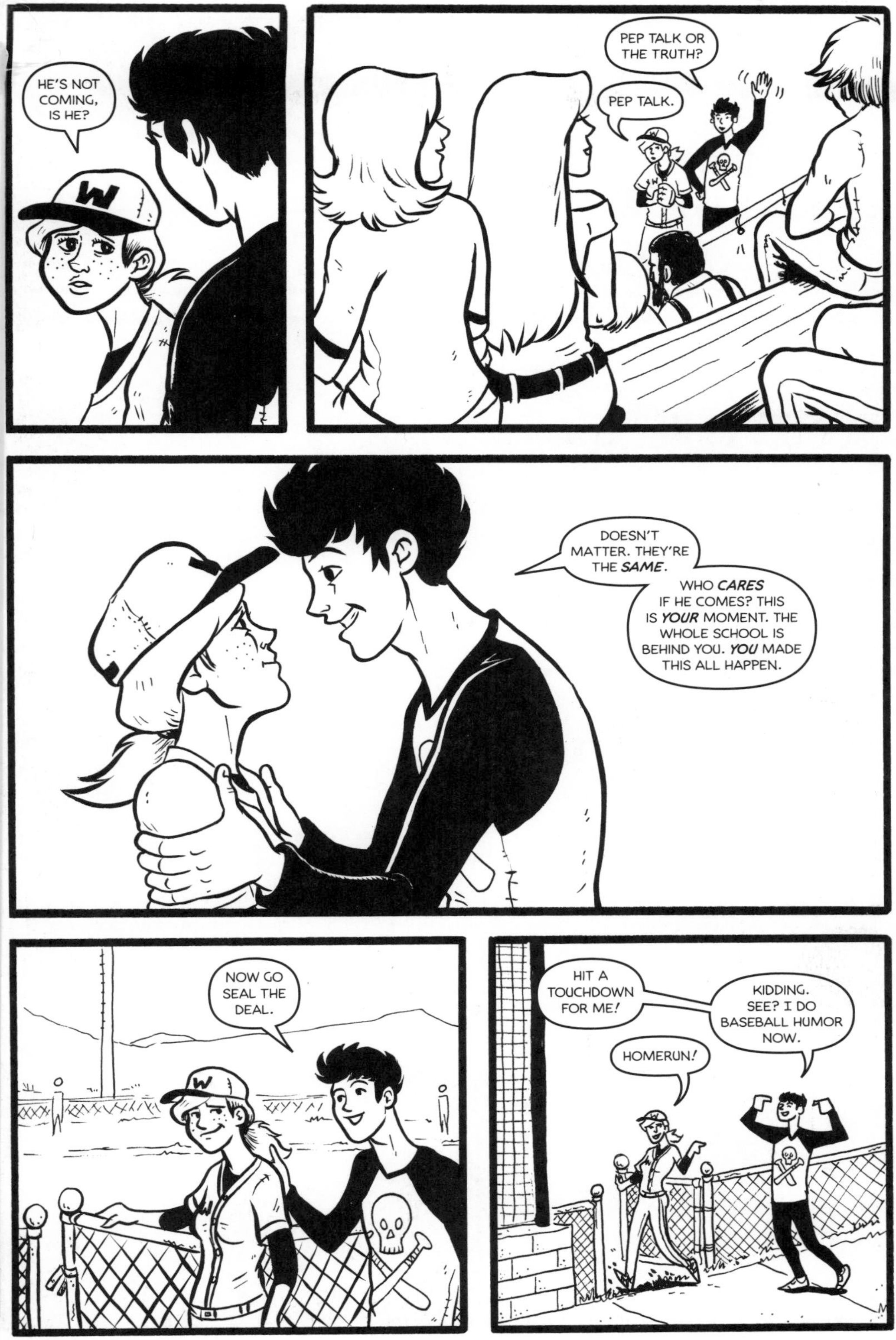
HE'S NOT COMING, IS HE?
PEP TALK OR THE TRUTH?
PEP TALK.
DOESN'T MATTER. THEY'RE THE *SAME*.
WHO *CARES* IF HE COMES? THIS IS *YOUR* MOMENT. THE WHOLE SCHOOL IS BEHIND YOU. *YOU* MADE THIS ALL HAPPEN.
NOW GO SEAL THE DEAL.
HIT A TOUCHDOWN FOR ME!
HOMERUN!
KIDDING. SEE? I DO BASEBALL HUMOR NOW.

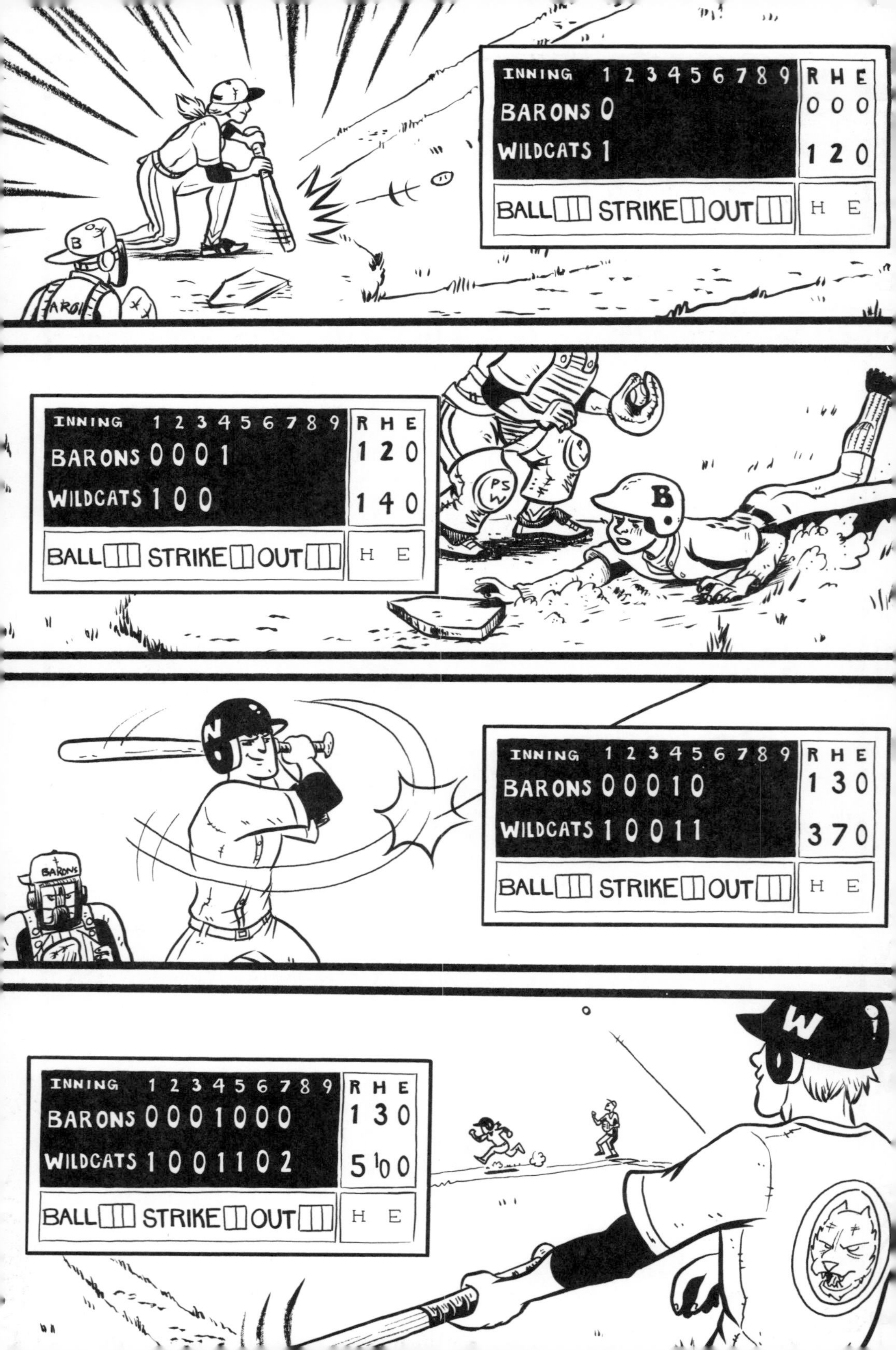
INNING 1 2 3 4 5 6 7 8 9 R H E
BARONS 0 0 0 0
WILDCATS 1 1 2 0
BALL STRIKE OUT H E
INNING 1 2 3 4 5 6 7 8 9 R H E
BARONS 0 0 0 1 1 2 0
WILDCATS 1 0 0 1 4 0
BALL STRIKE OUT H E
INNING 1 2 3 4 5 6 7 8 9 R H E
BARONS 0 0 0 1 0 1 3 0
WILDCATS 1 0 0 1 1 3 7 0
BALL STRIKE OUT H E
INNING 1 2 3 4 5 6 7 8 9 R H E
BARONS 0 0 0 1 0 0 0 1 3 0
WILDCATS 1 0 0 1 1 0 2 5 10 0
BALL STRIKE OUT H E

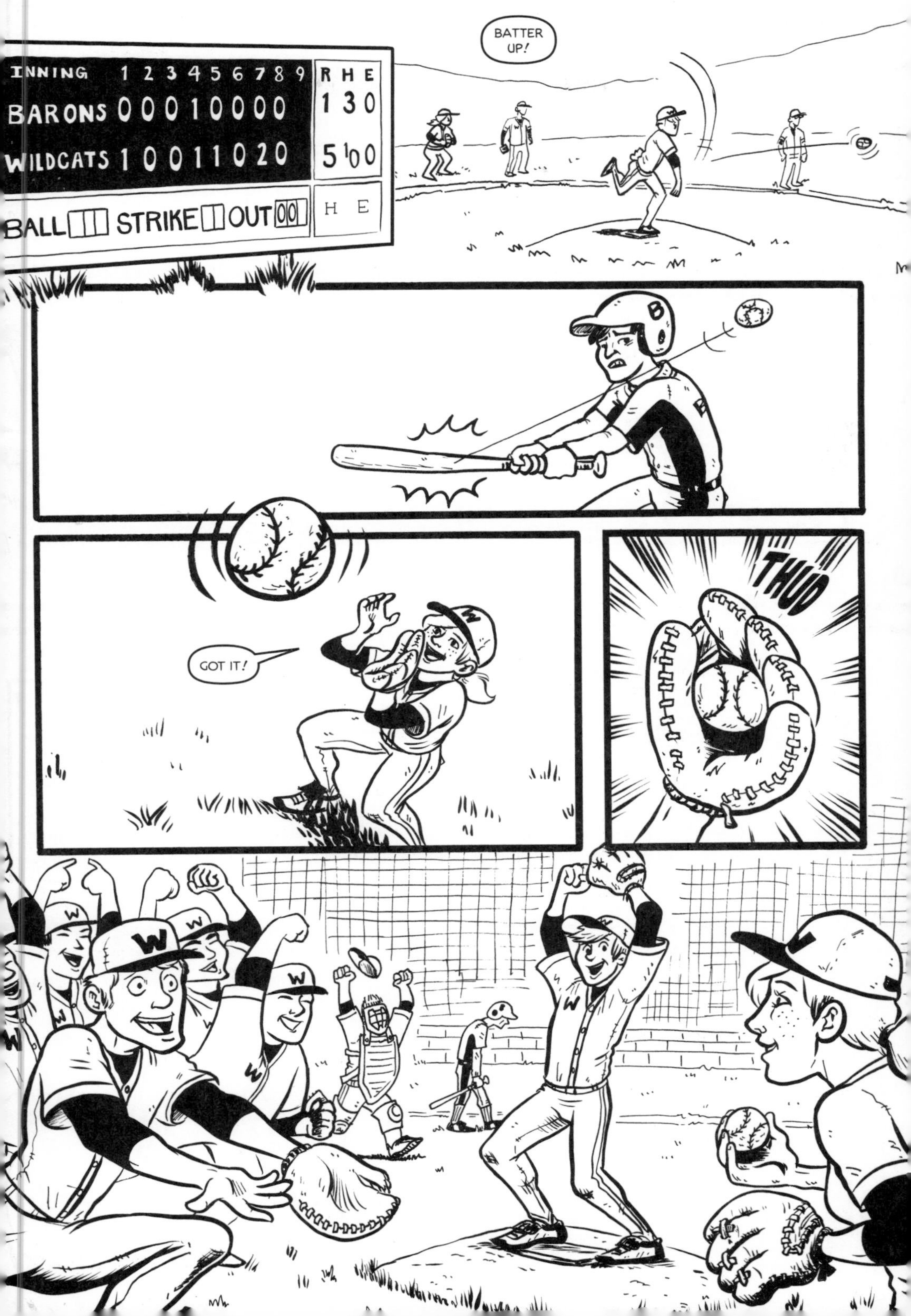
INNING 1 2 3 4 5 6 7 8 9 R H E
BARONS 0 0 0 1 0 0 0 0 1 3 0
WILDCATS 1 0 0 1 1 0 2 0 5 10 0
BALL STRIKE OUT H E
BATTER UP!
GOT IT!
THUD

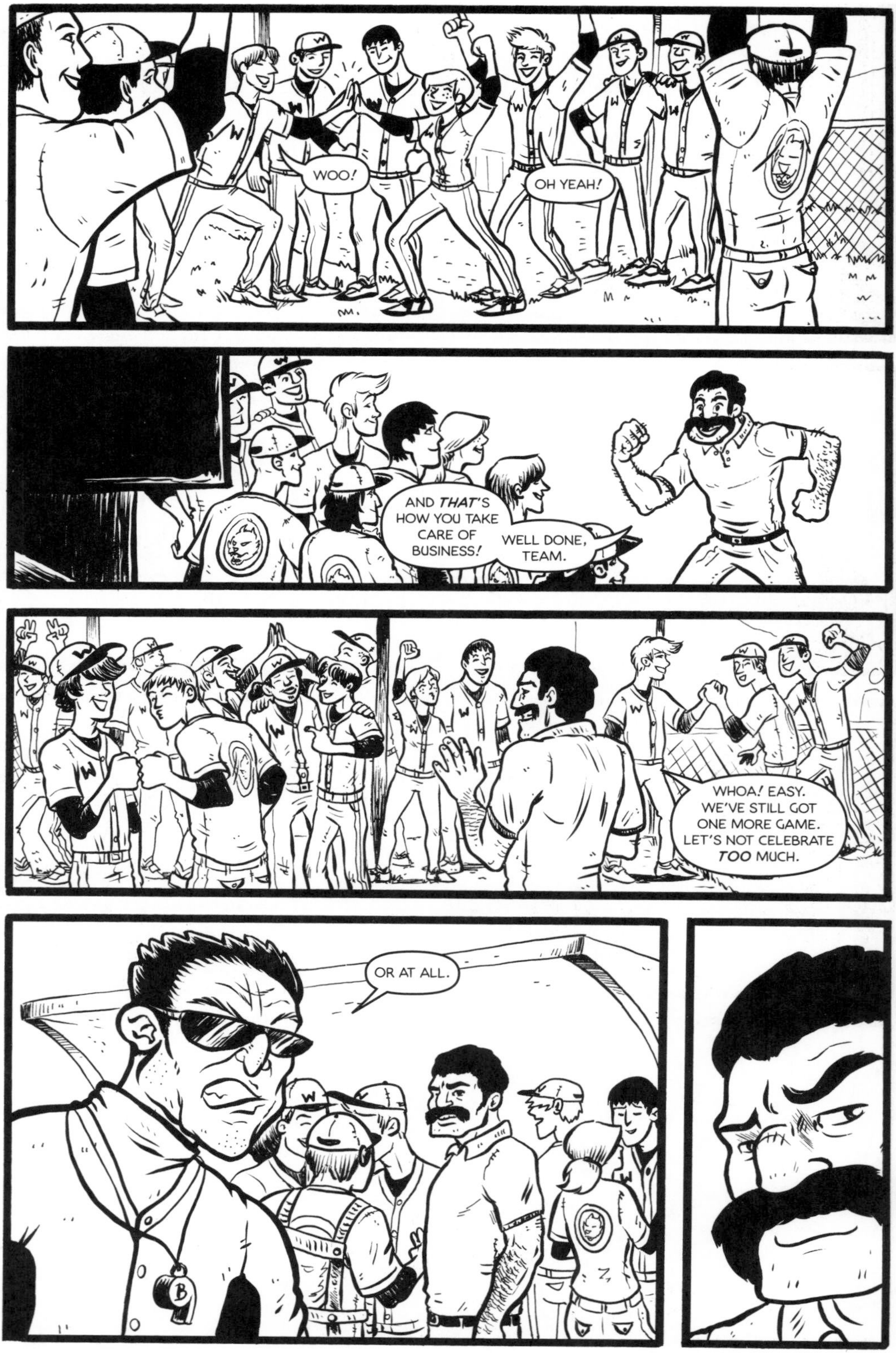
WOO!
OH YEAH!
AND *THAT*'S HOW YOU TAKE CARE OF BUSINESS!
WELL DONE, TEAM.
WHOA! EASY. WE'VE STILL GOT ONE MORE GAME. LET'S NOT CELEBRATE ***TOO*** MUCH.
OR AT ALL.

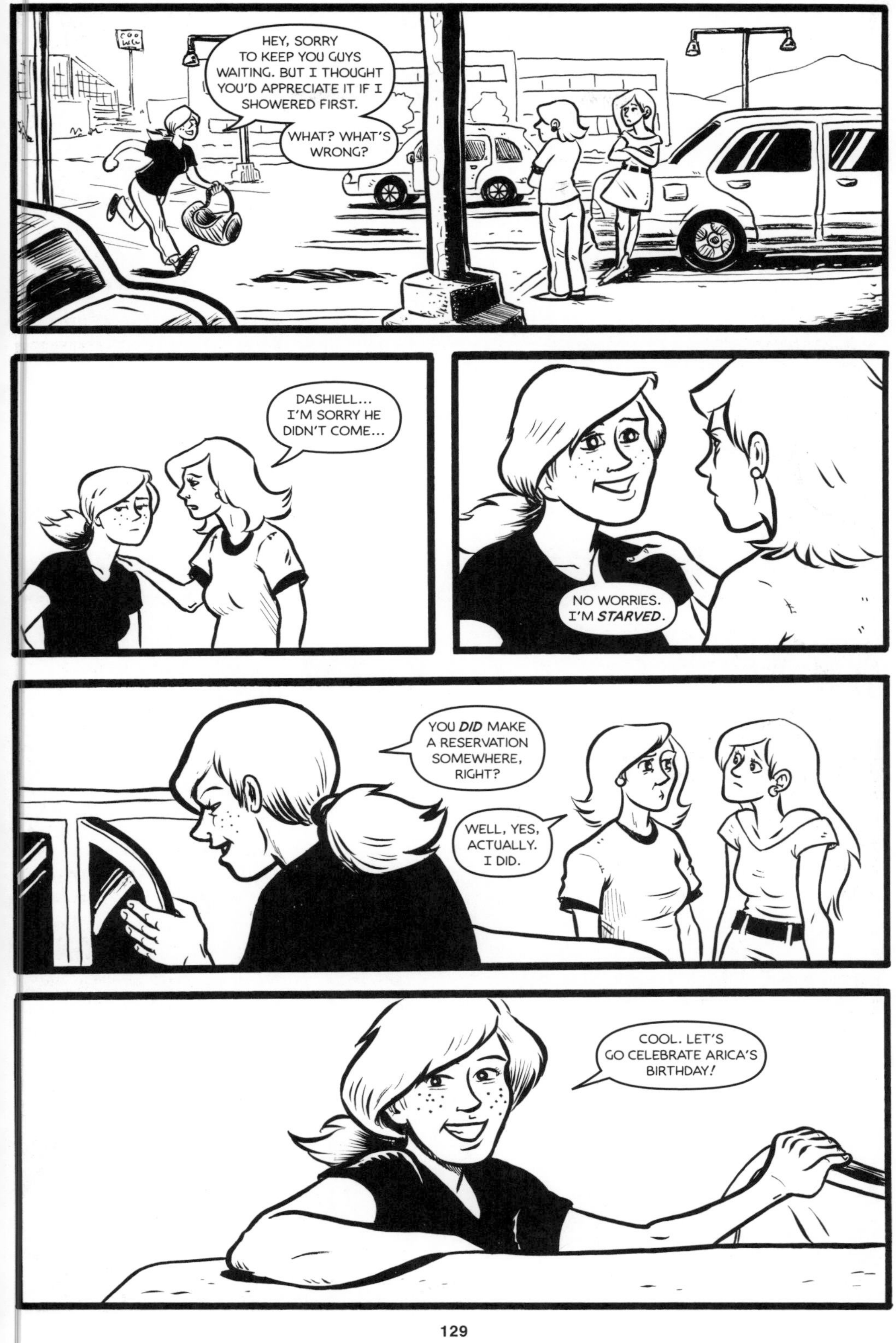
HEY, SORRY TO KEEP YOU GUYS WAITING. BUT I THOUGHT YOU'D APPRECIATE IT IF I SHOWERED FIRST.
WHAT? WHAT'S WRONG?
DASHIELL... I'M SORRY HE DIDN'T COME...
NO WORRIES. I'M *STARVED*.
YOU *DID* MAKE A RESERVATION SOMEWHERE, RIGHT?
WELL, YES, ACTUALLY. I DID.
COOL. LET'S GO CELEBRATE ARICA'S BIRTHDAY*!*

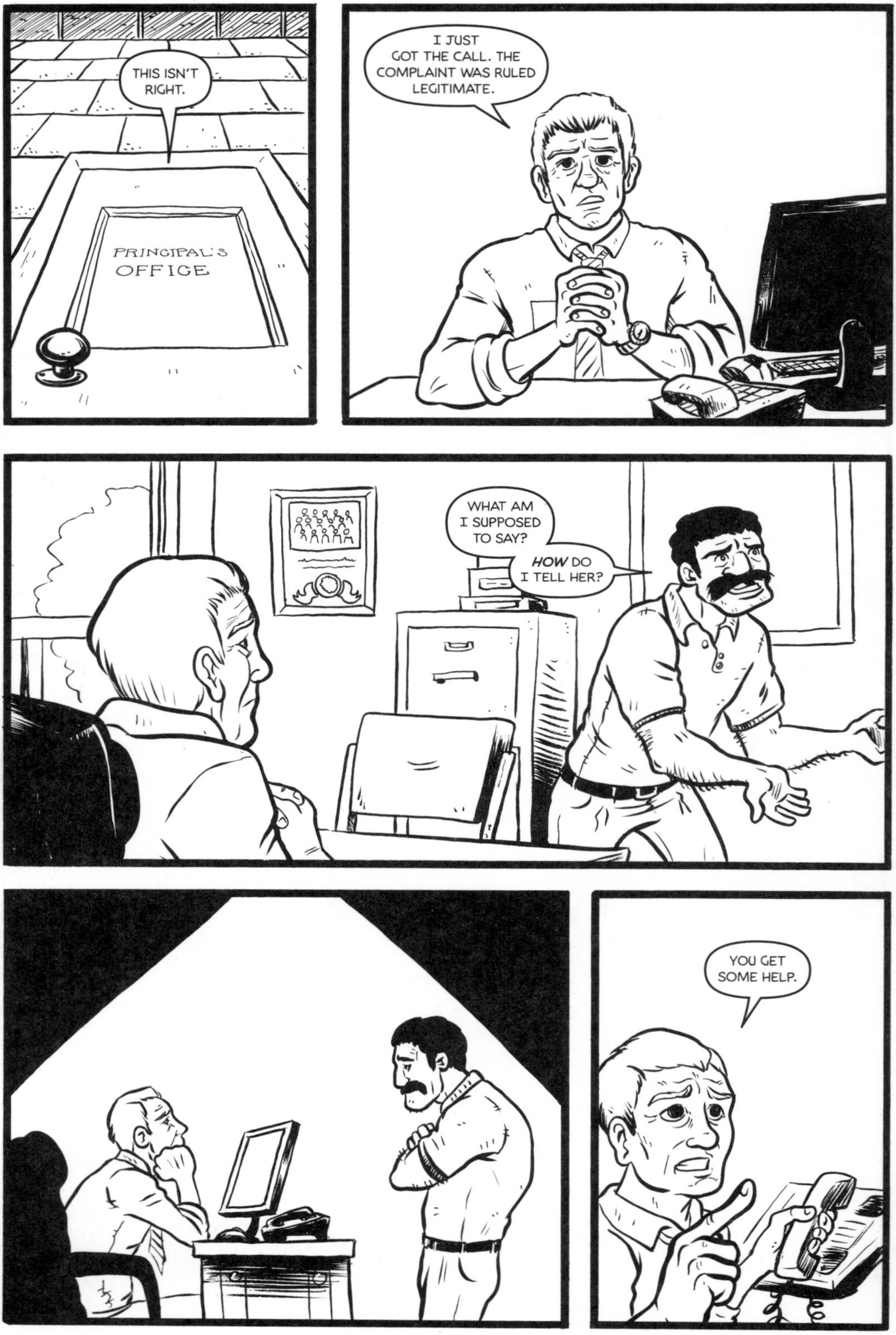
THIS ISN'T RIGHT.
PRINCIPAL'S OFFICE
I JUST GOT THE CALL. THE COMPLAINT WAS RULED LEGITIMATE.
WHAT AM I SUPPOSED TO SAY?
HOW DO I TELL HER?
YOU GET SOME HELP.

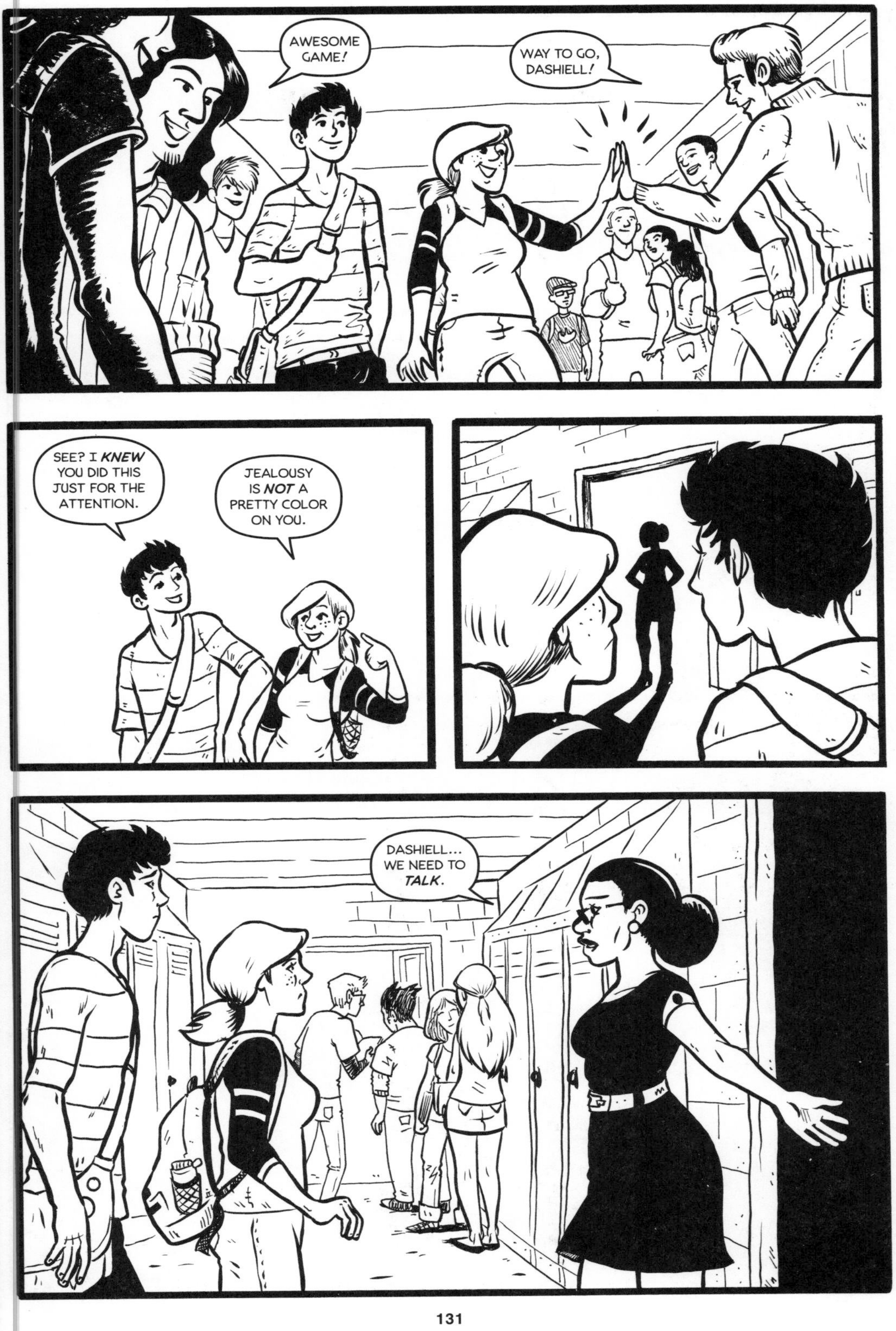
AWESOME GAME!
WAY TO GO, DASHIELL!
SEE? I KNEW YOU DID THIS JUST FOR THE ATTENTION.
JEALOUSY IS NOT A PRETTY COLOR ON YOU.
DASHIELL... WE NEED TO TALK.

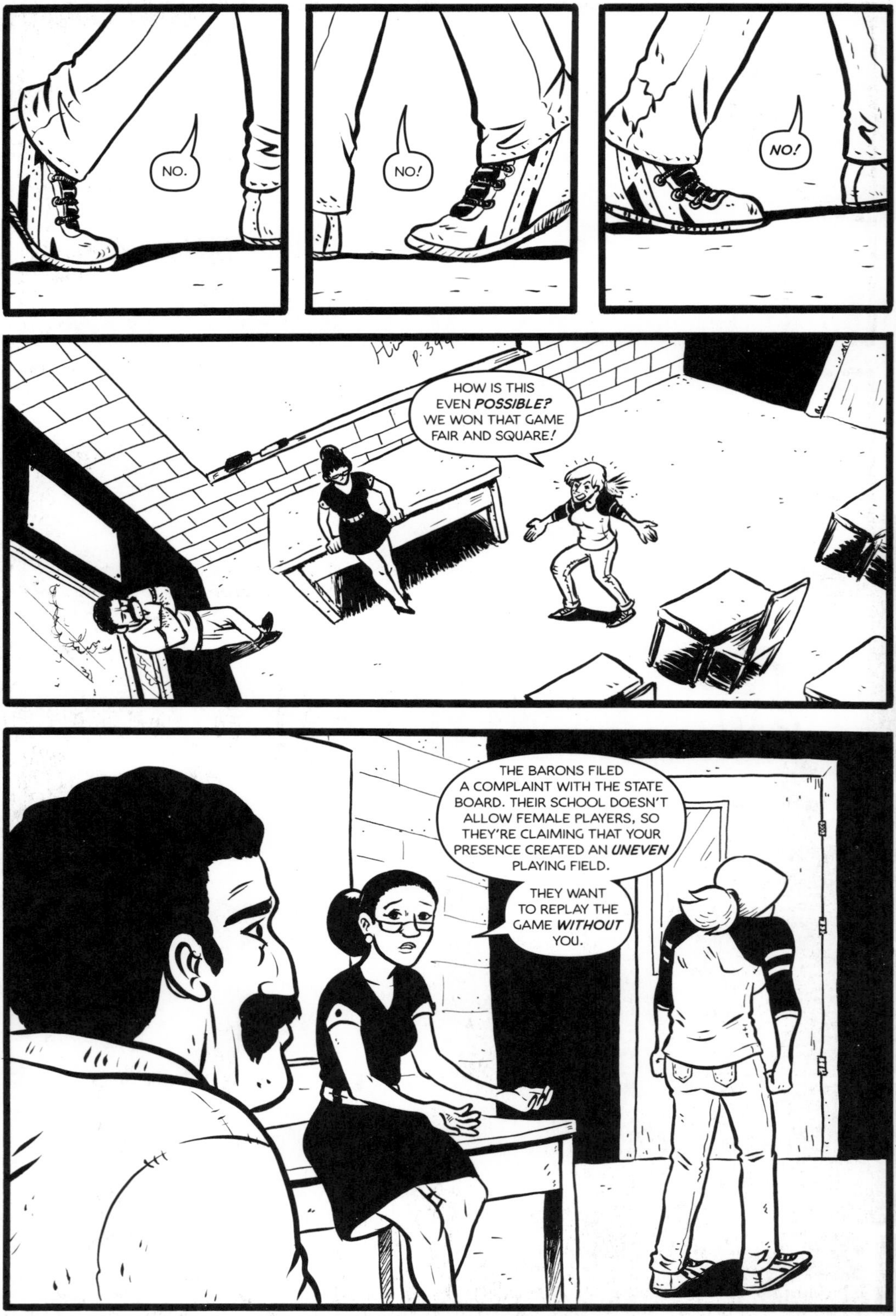
NO.
NO!
NO!
HOW IS THIS EVEN POSSIBLE? WE WON THAT GAME FAIR AND SQUARE!
THE BARONS FILED A COMPLAINT WITH THE STATE BOARD. THEIR SCHOOL DOESN'T ALLOW FEMALE PLAYERS, SO THEY'RE CLAIMING THAT YOUR PRESENCE CREATED AN UNEVEN PLAYING FIELD.
THEY WANT TO REPLAY THE GAME WITHOUT YOU.

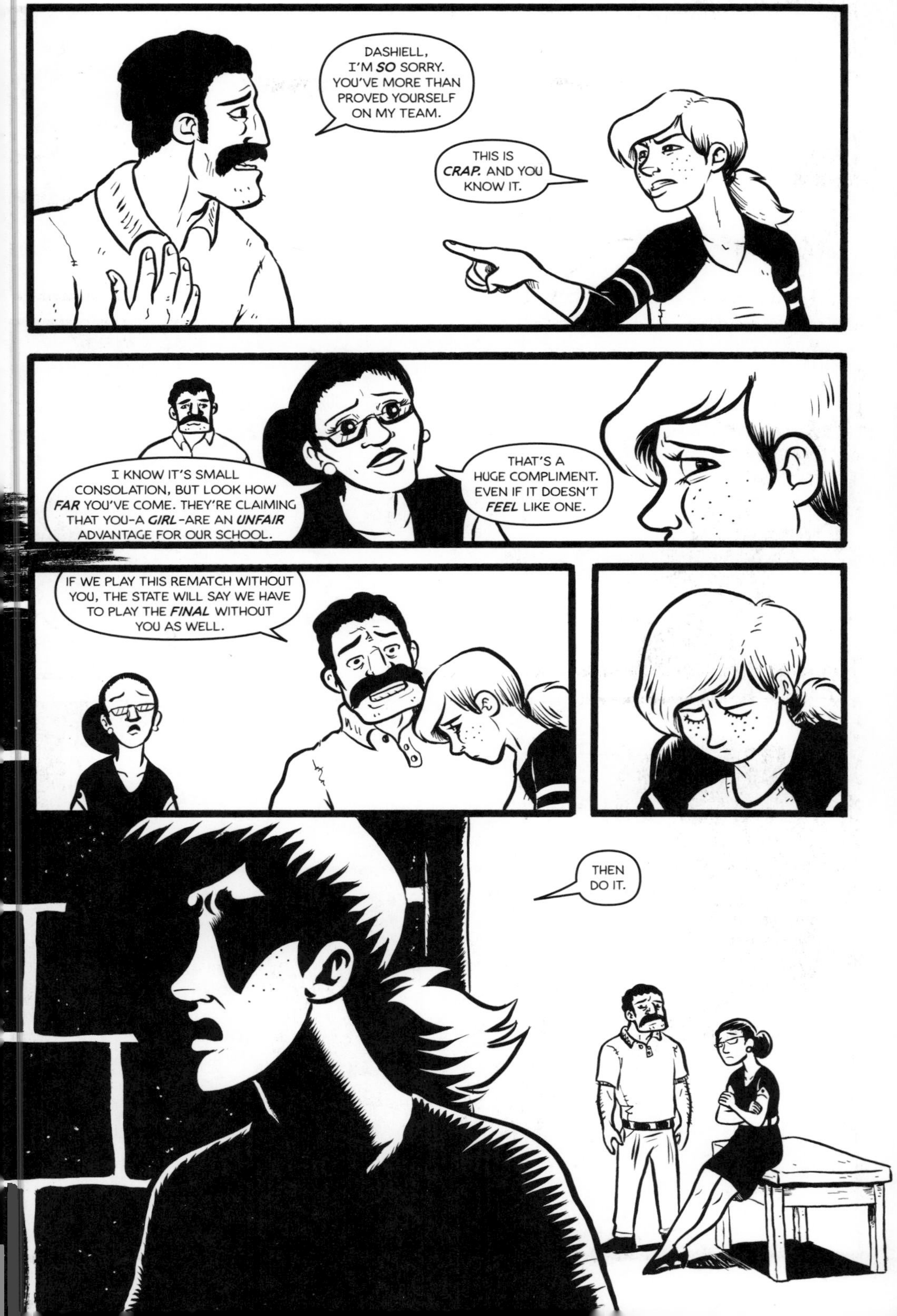
DASHIELL, I'M SO SORRY. YOU'VE MORE THAN PROVED YOURSELF ON MY TEAM.
THIS IS CRAP. AND YOU KNOW IT.
I KNOW IT'S SMALL CONSOLATION, BUT LOOK HOW FAR YOU'VE COME. THEY'RE CLAIMING THAT YOU-A GIRL-ARE AN UNFAIR ADVANTAGE FOR OUR SCHOOL.
THAT'S A HUGE COMPLIMENT. EVEN IF IT DOESN'T FEEL LIKE ONE.
IF WE PLAY THIS REMATCH WITHOUT YOU, THE STATE WILL SAY WE HAVE TO PLAY THE FINAL WITHOUT YOU AS WELL.
THEN DO IT.

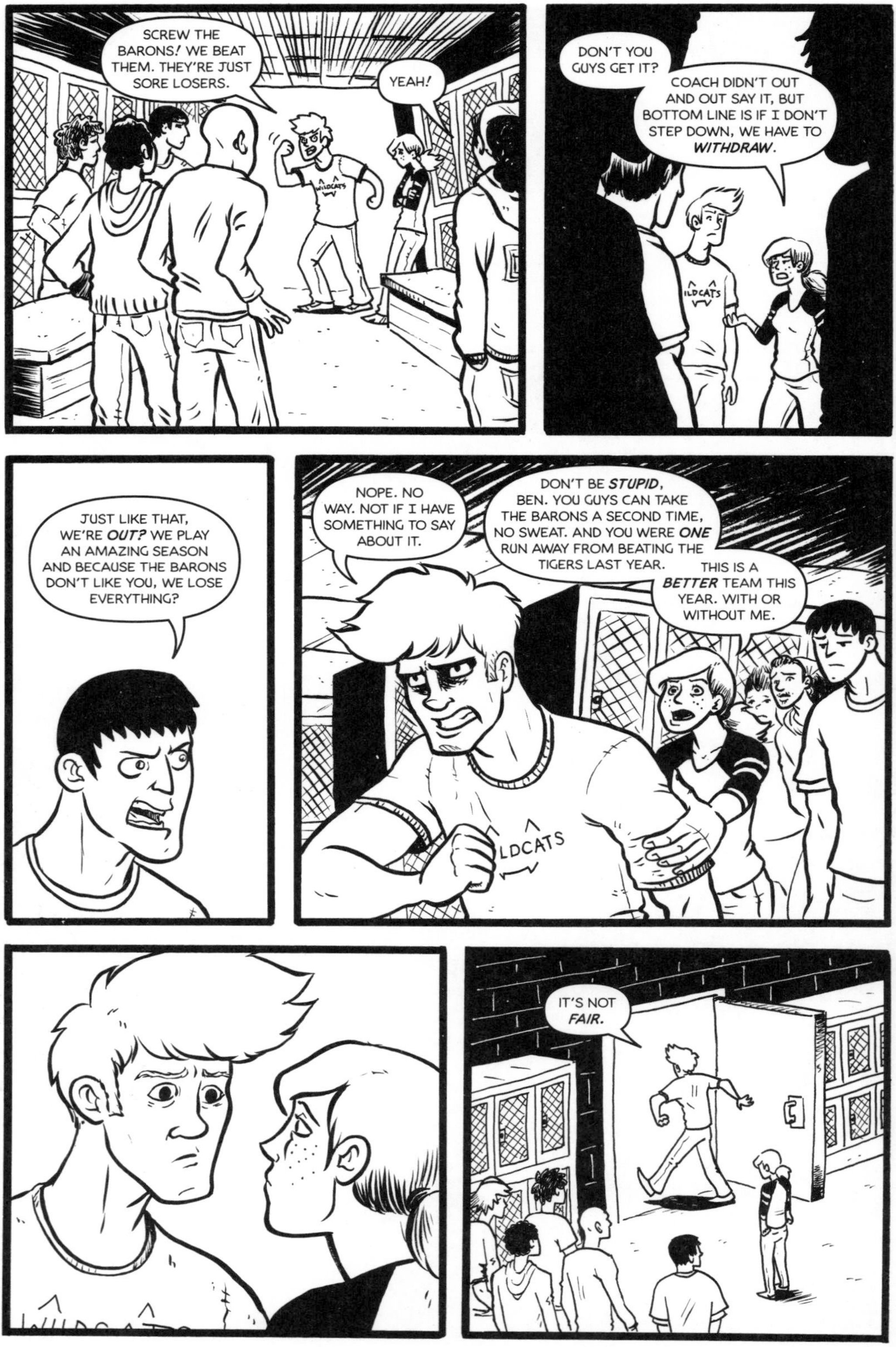
SCREW THE BARONS! WE BEAT THEM. THEY'RE JUST SORE LOSERS.
YEAH!
DON'T YOU GUYS GET IT?
COACH DIDN'T OUT AND OUT SAY IT, BUT BOTTOM LINE IS IF I DON'T STEP DOWN, WE HAVE TO *WITHDRAW*.
JUST LIKE THAT, WE'RE *OUT?* WE PLAY AN AMAZING SEASON AND BECAUSE THE BARONS DON'T LIKE YOU, WE LOSE EVERYTHING?
NOPE. NO WAY. NOT IF I HAVE SOMETHING TO SAY ABOUT IT.
DON'T BE *STUPID*, BEN. YOU GUYS CAN TAKE THE BARONS A SECOND TIME, NO SWEAT. AND YOU WERE *ONE* RUN AWAY FROM BEATING THE TIGERS LAST YEAR.
THIS IS A *BETTER* TEAM THIS YEAR. WITH OR WITHOUT ME.
IT'S NOT *FAIR.*

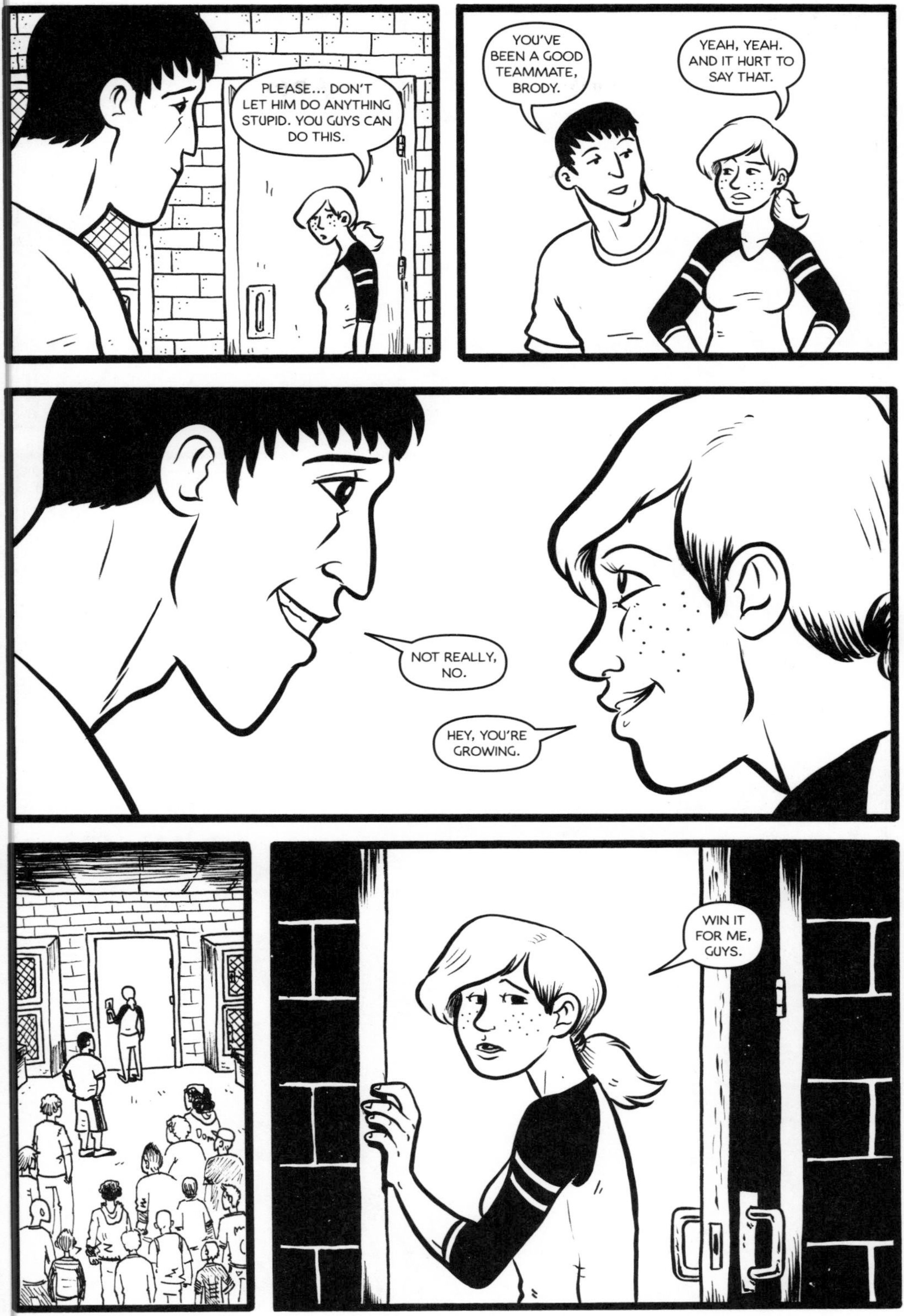
PLEASE... DON'T LET HIM DO ANYTHING STUPID. YOU GUYS CAN DO THIS.
YOU'VE BEEN A GOOD TEAMMATE, BRODY.
YEAH, YEAH. AND IT HURT TO SAY THAT.
NOT REALLY, NO.
HEY, YOU'RE GROWING.
WIN IT FOR ME, GUYS.

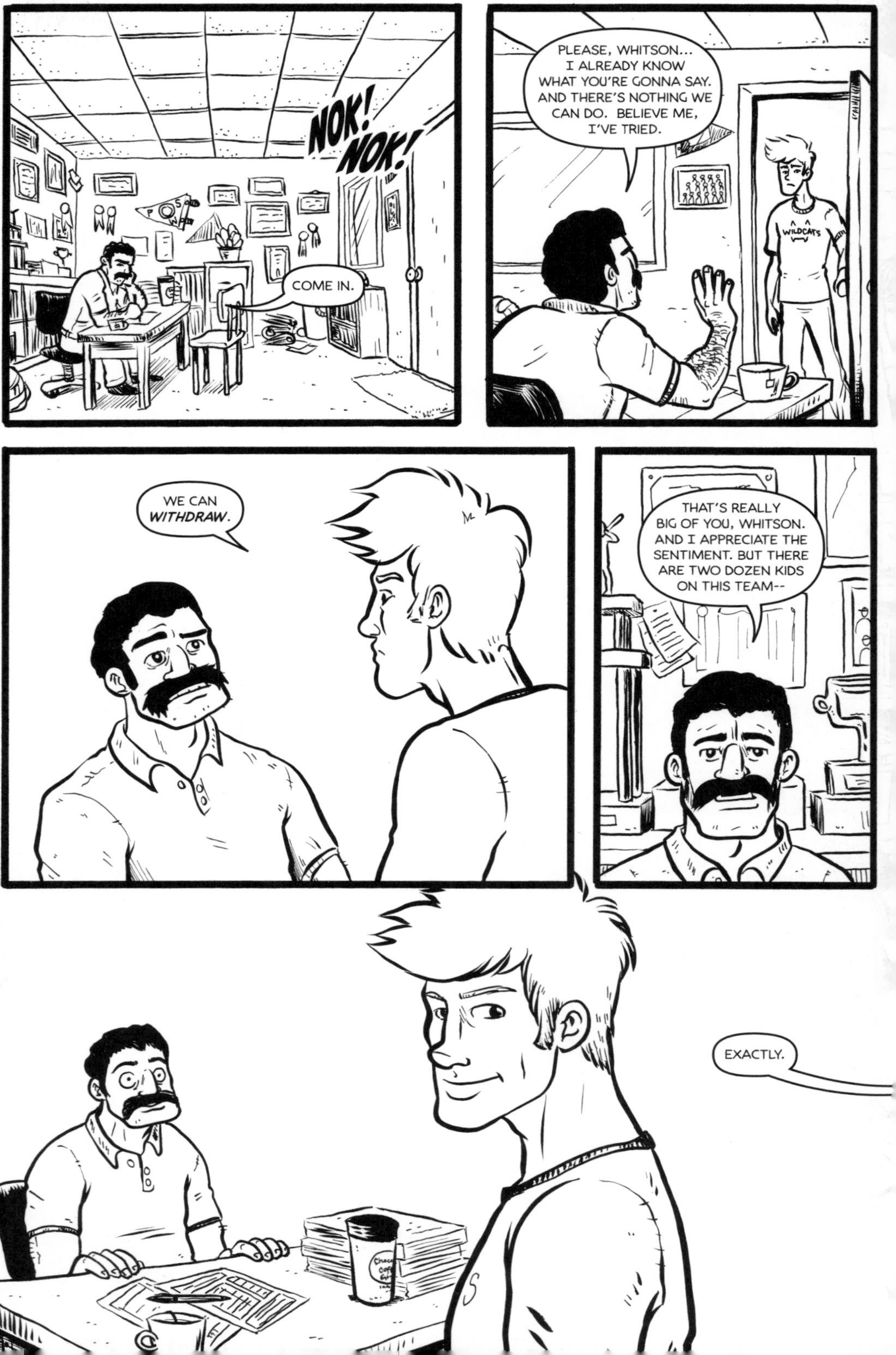
NOK! NOK!
COME IN.
PLEASE, WHITSON... I ALREADY KNOW WHAT YOU'RE GONNA SAY. AND THERE'S NOTHING WE CAN DO. BELIEVE ME, I'VE TRIED.
WILDCATS
WE CAN *WITHDRAW*.
THAT'S REALLY BIG OF YOU, WHITSON. AND I APPRECIATE THE SENTIMENT. BUT THERE ARE TWO DOZEN KIDS ON THIS TEAM--
EXACTLY.

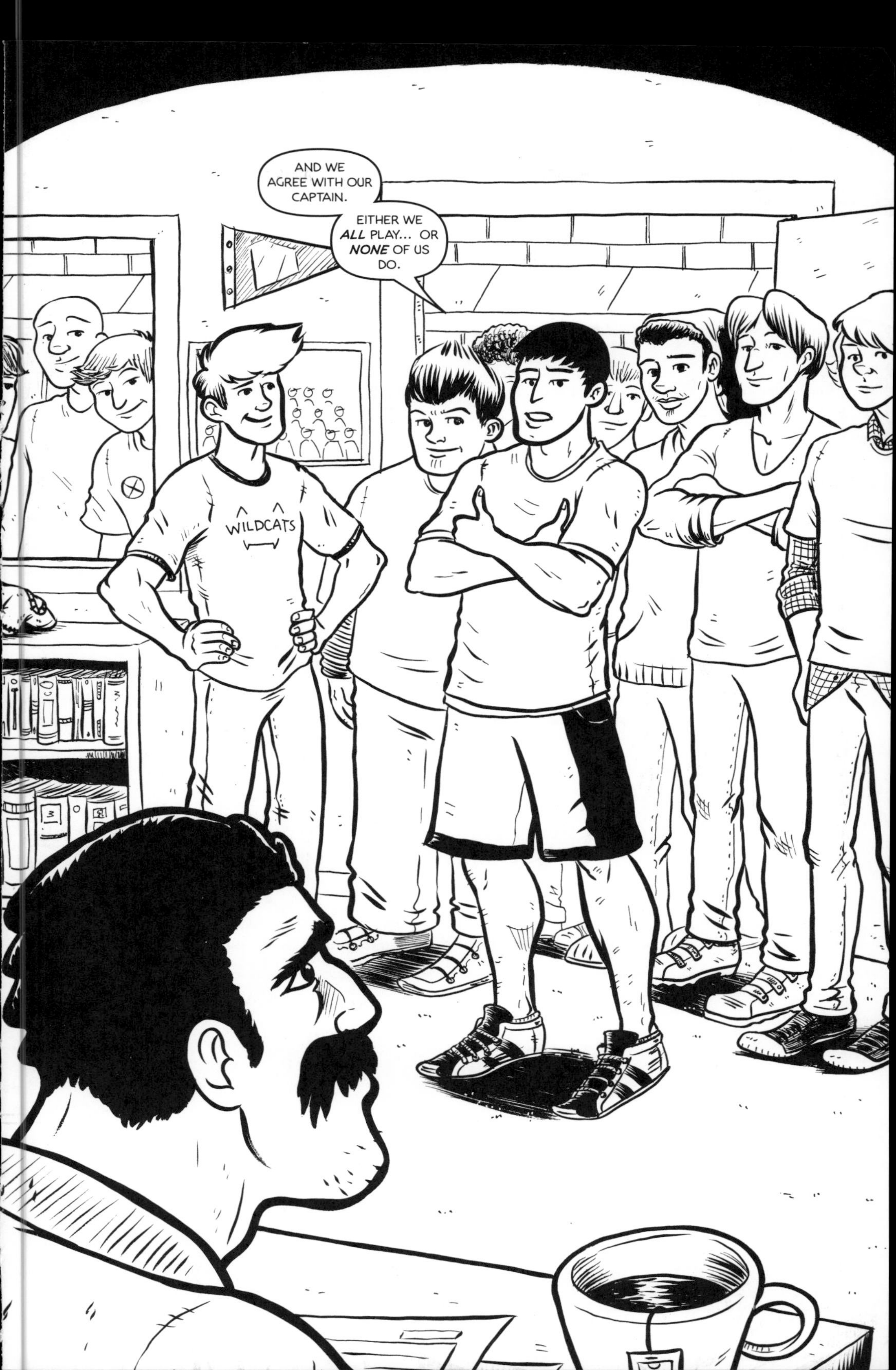
AND WE AGREE WITH OUR CAPTAIN.
EITHER WE *ALL* PLAY... OR *NONE* OF US DO.
WILDCATS

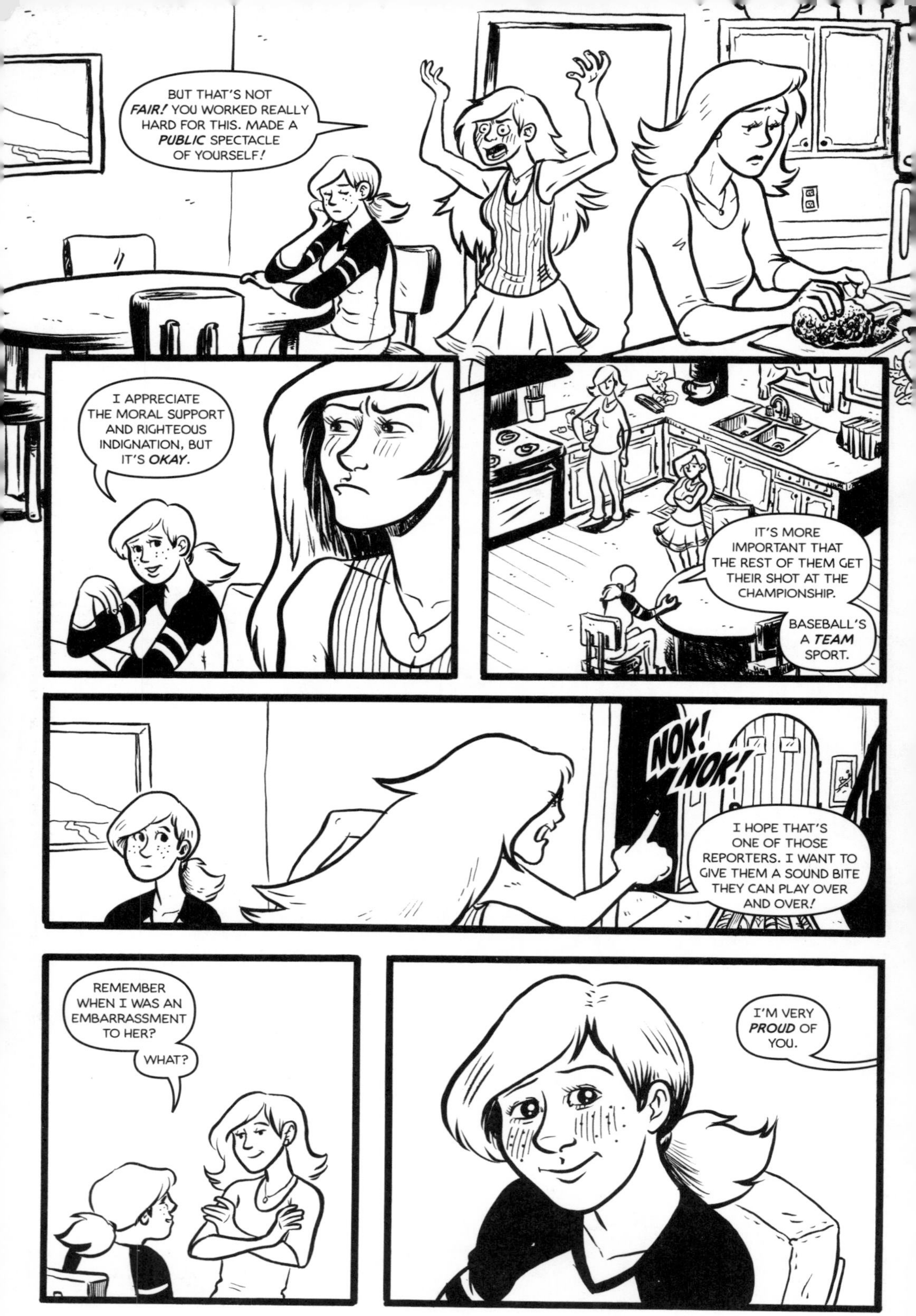
BUT THAT'S NOT *FAIR!* YOU WORKED REALLY HARD FOR THIS. MADE A *PUBLIC* SPECTACLE OF YOURSELF!
I APPRECIATE THE MORAL SUPPORT AND RIGHTEOUS INDIGNATION, BUT IT'S *OKAY*.
IT'S MORE IMPORTANT THAT THE REST OF THEM GET THEIR SHOT AT THE CHAMPIONSHIP.
BASEBALL'S A *TEAM* SPORT.
NOK! NOK!
I HOPE THAT'S ONE OF THOSE REPORTERS. I WANT TO GIVE THEM A SOUND BITE THEY CAN PLAY OVER AND OVER!
REMEMBER WHEN I WAS AN EMBARRASSMENT TO HER?
WHAT?
I'M VERY *PROUD* OF YOU.

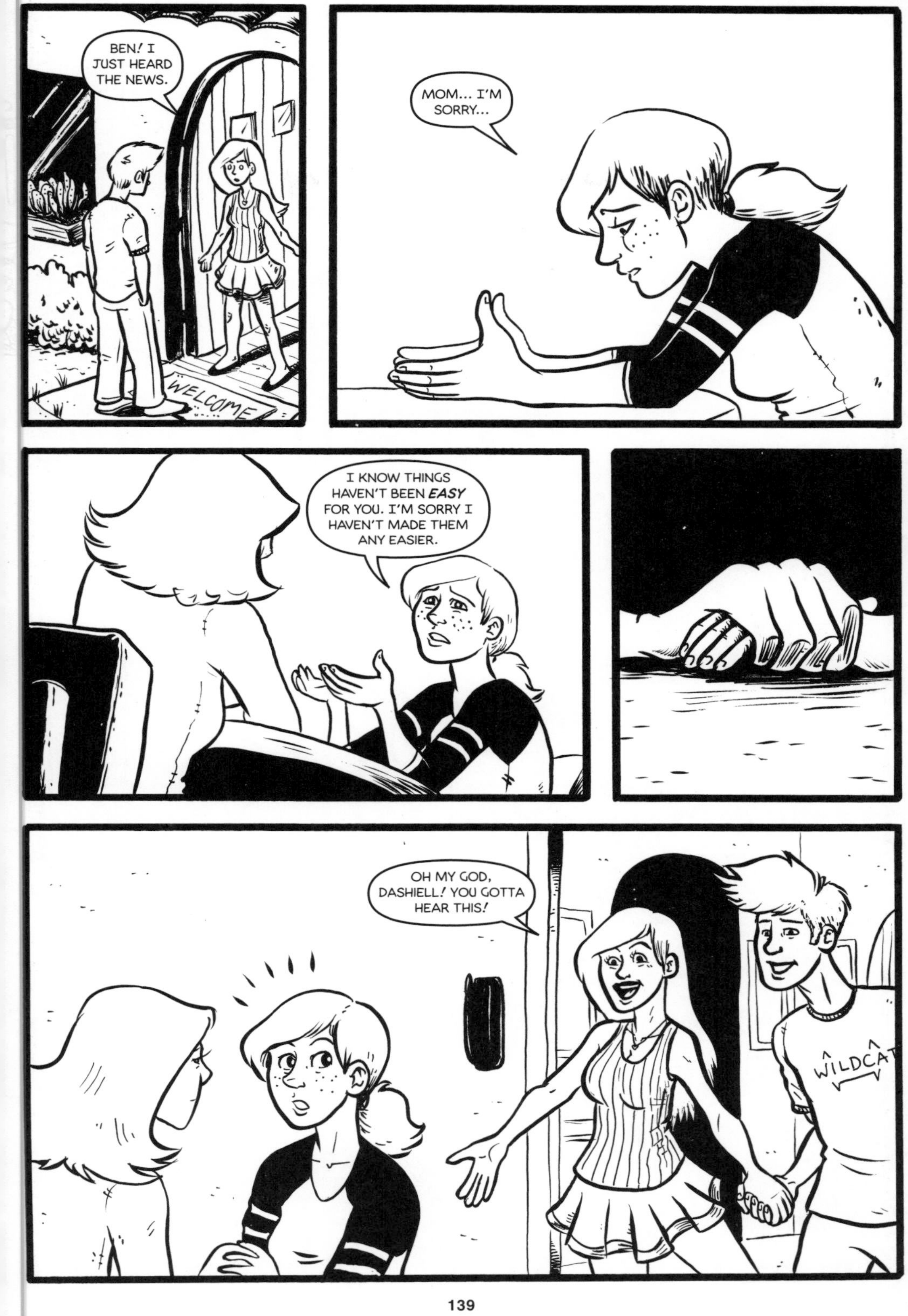
BEN! I JUST HEARD THE NEWS.
MOM... I'M SORRY...
I KNOW THINGS HAVEN'T BEEN EASY FOR YOU. I'M SORRY I HAVEN'T MADE THEM ANY EASIER.
OH MY GOD, DASHIELL! YOU GOTTA HEAR THIS!
WILDCAT

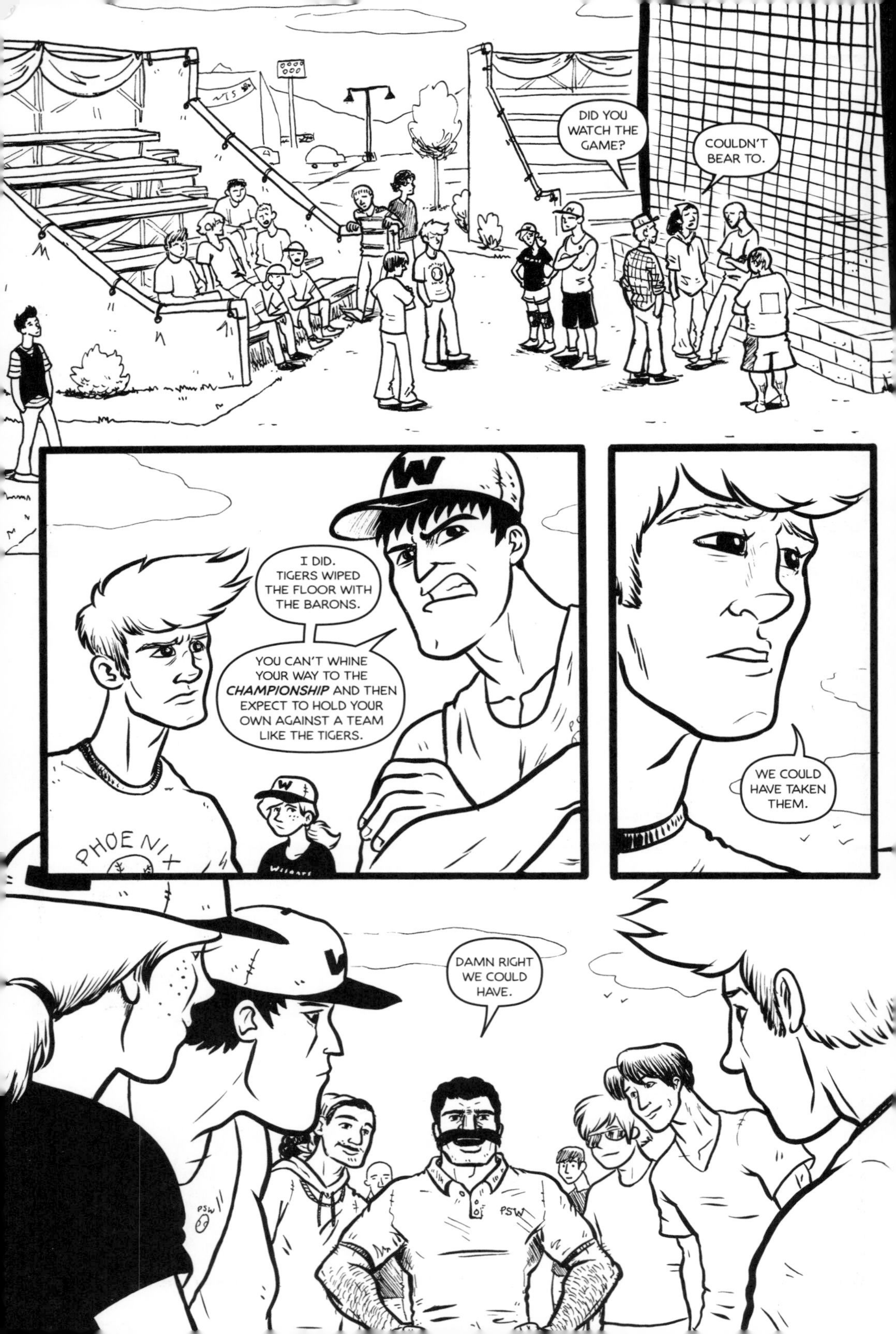
DID YOU WATCH THE GAME?
COULDN'T BEAR TO.
I DID. TIGERS WIPED THE FLOOR WITH THE BARONS.
YOU CAN'T WHINE YOUR WAY TO THE *CHAMPIONSHIP* AND THEN EXPECT TO HOLD YOUR OWN AGAINST A TEAM LIKE THE TIGERS.
PHOENIX
WE COULD HAVE TAKEN THEM.
DAMN RIGHT WE COULD HAVE.

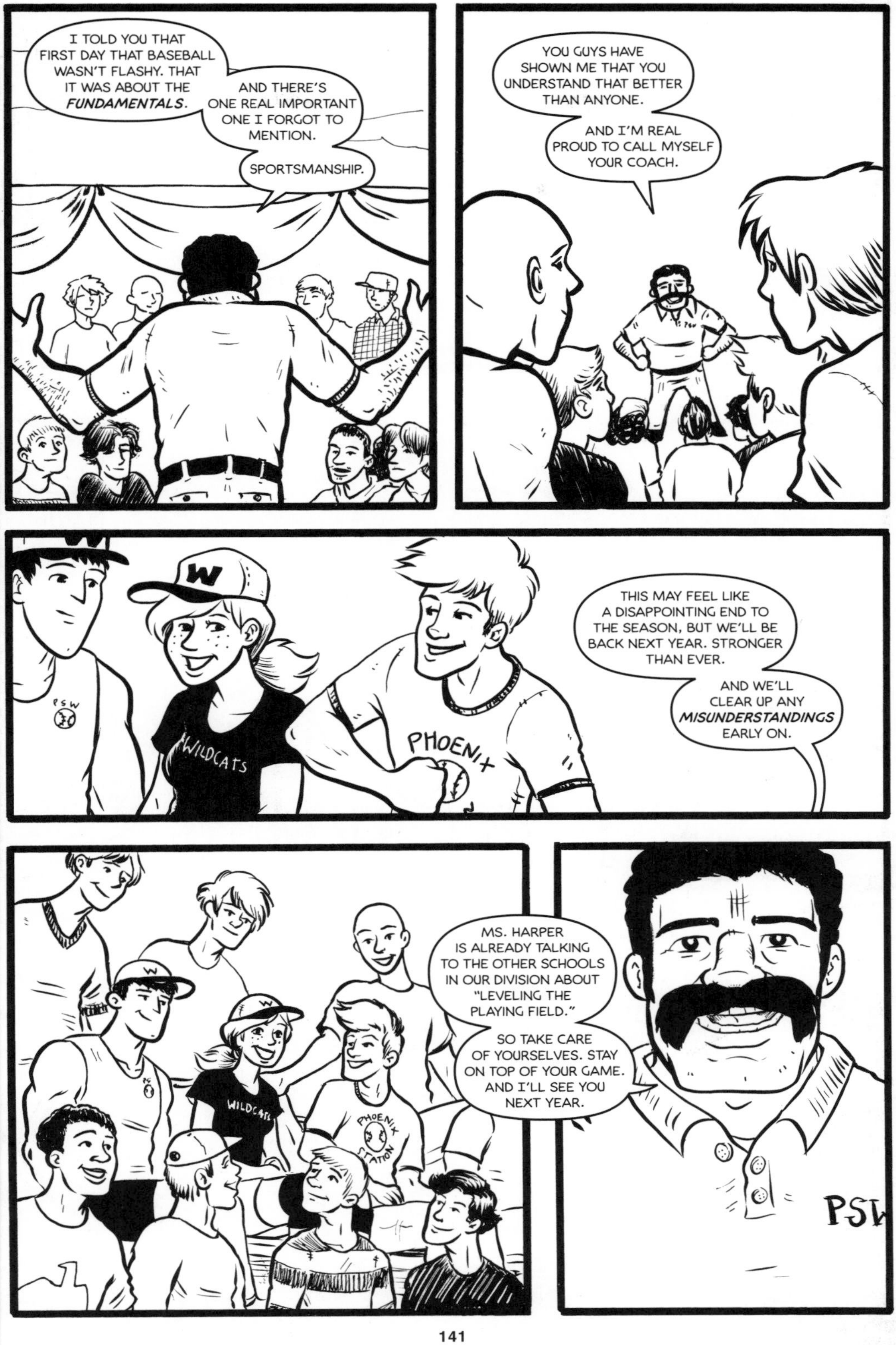
I TOLD YOU THAT FIRST DAY THAT BASEBALL WASN'T FLASHY. THAT IT WAS ABOUT THE ***FUNDAMENTALS***.
AND THERE'S ONE REAL IMPORTANT ONE I FORGOT TO MENTION.
SPORTSMANSHIP.
YOU GUYS HAVE SHOWN ME THAT YOU UNDERSTAND THAT BETTER THAN ANYONE.
AND I'M REAL PROUD TO CALL MYSELF YOUR COACH.
PSW
PSW
WILDCATS
PHOENIX
THIS MAY FEEL LIKE A DISAPPOINTING END TO THE SEASON, BUT WE'LL BE BACK NEXT YEAR. STRONGER THAN EVER.
AND WE'LL CLEAR UP ANY ***MISUNDERSTANDINGS*** EARLY ON.
WILDCATS
PHOENIX STATION
MS. HARPER IS ALREADY TALKING TO THE OTHER SCHOOLS IN OUR DIVISION ABOUT "LEVELING THE PLAYING FIELD."
SO TAKE CARE OF YOURSELVES. STAY ON TOP OF YOUR GAME. AND I'LL SEE YOU NEXT YEAR.
PSW

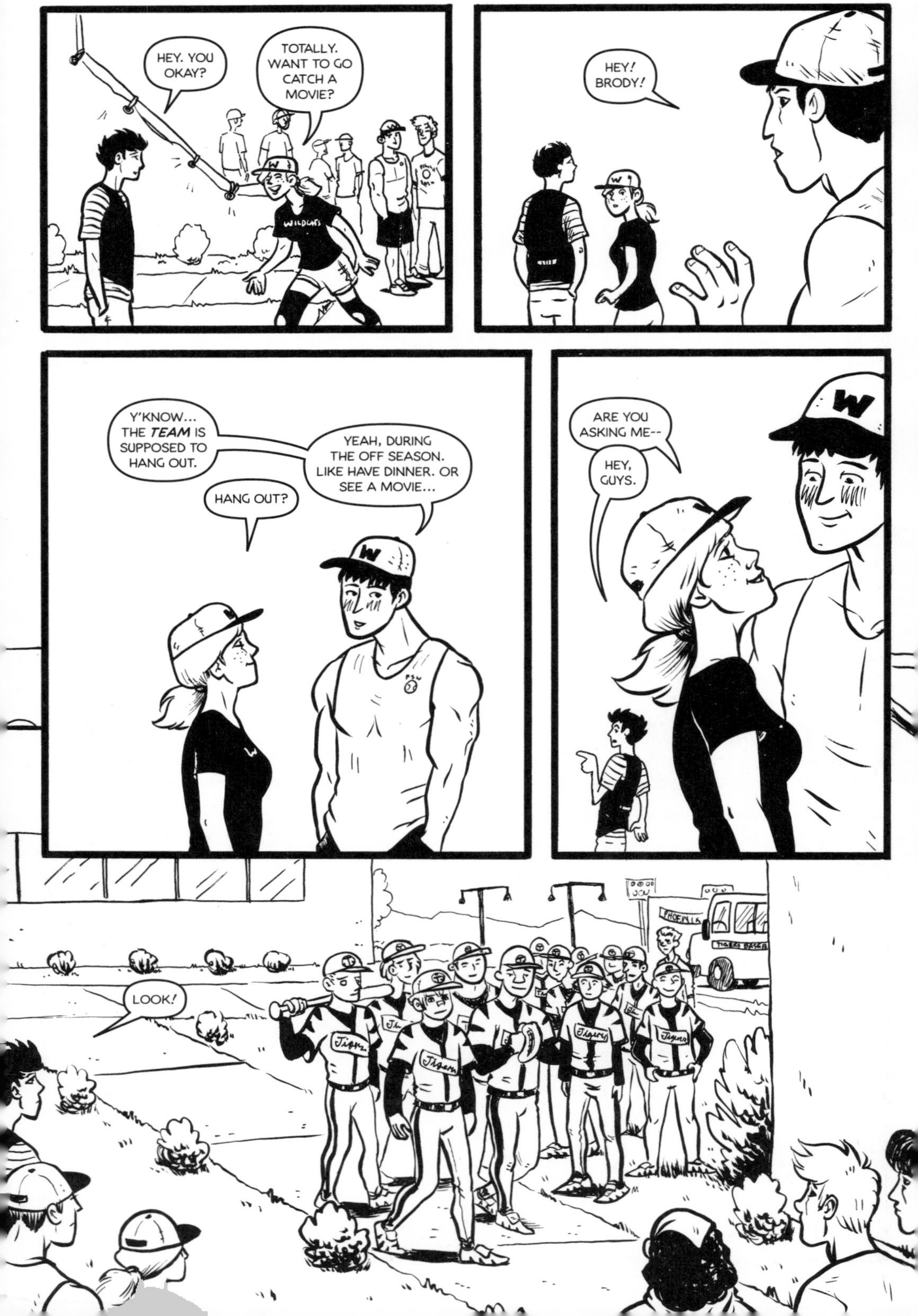
HEY. YOU OKAY?
TOTALLY. WANT TO GO CATCH A MOVIE?
WILDCATS
HEY! BRODY!
Y'KNOW... THE **TEAM** IS SUPPOSED TO HANG OUT.
HANG OUT?
YEAH, DURING THE OFF SEASON. LIKE HAVE DINNER. OR SEE A MOVIE...
ARE YOU ASKING ME--
HEY, GUYS.
LOOK!

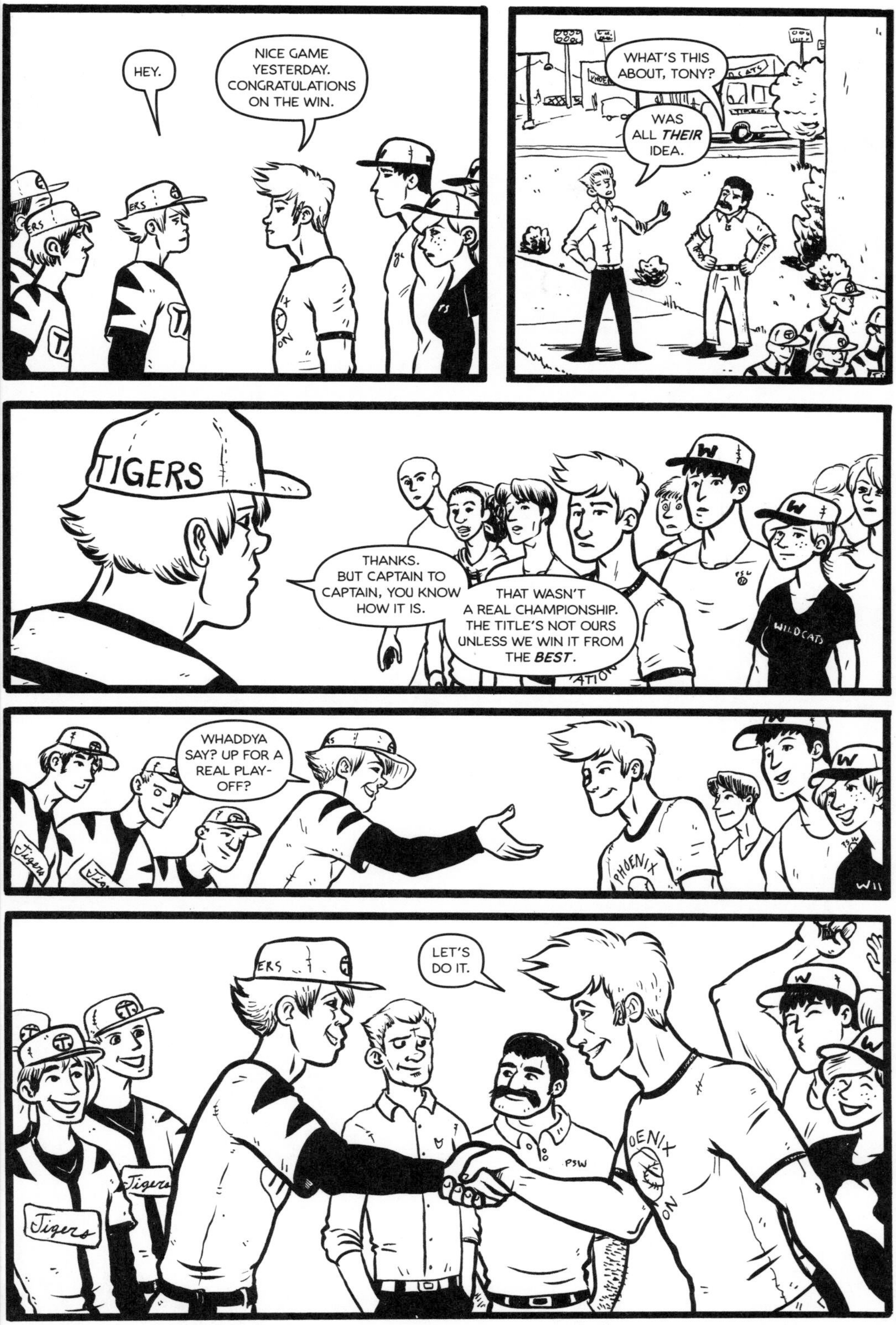
HEY.
NICE GAME YESTERDAY. CONGRATULATIONS ON THE WIN.
WHAT'S THIS ABOUT, TONY?
WAS ALL *THEIR* IDEA.
TIGERS
THANKS. BUT CAPTAIN TO CAPTAIN, YOU KNOW HOW IT IS.
THAT WASN'T A REAL CHAMPIONSHIP. THE TITLE'S NOT OURS UNLESS WE WIN IT FROM THE *BEST*.
WILDCATS
WHADDYA SAY? UP FOR A REAL PLAY-OFF?
PHOENIX
LET'S DO IT.

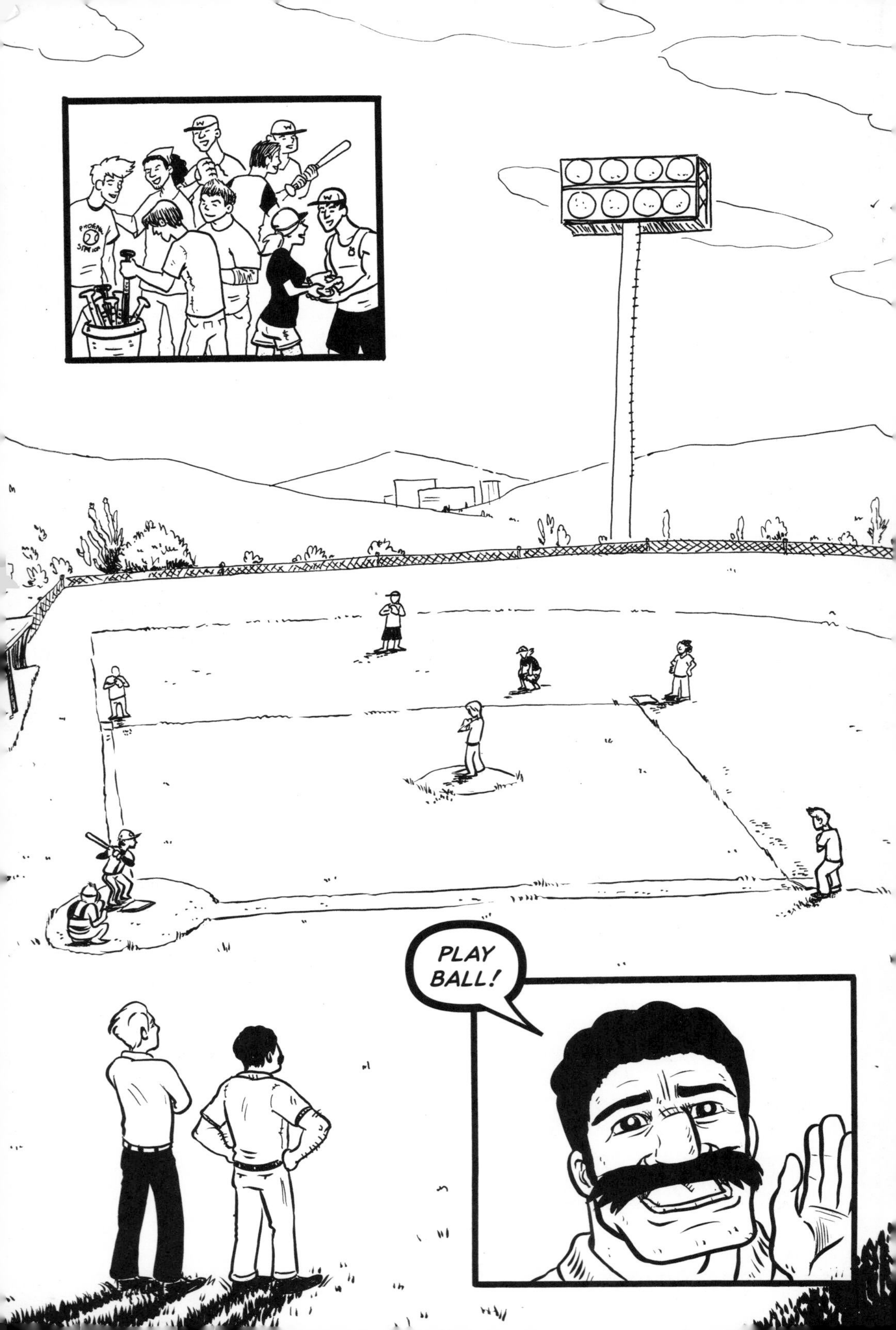
PLAY BALL!

NUNZIO DEFILIPPIS and CHRISTINA WEIR are a writing team trained as screenwriters. They have worked in television, on and off, for the last ten years. They were on the writing staff of HBO's ARLISS for two seasons, and worked on Disney's KIM POSSIBLE. They have also written an independent film called PARADISE SPRINGS that is in development.

In comics, they have primarily made their home at Oni Press, who have let them write books in a wide array of genres, including SKINWALKER, THREE STRIKES, MARIA'S WEDDING, THE TOMB, FRENEMY OF THE STATE, and THE AMY DEVLIN MYSTERIES.

They have also written superhero comics like NEW MUTANTS, NEW X-MEN, ADVENTURES OF SUPERMAN, and BATMAN CONFIDENTIAL, and have worked in the field of manga, adapting numerous series for Del Rey. They created three Original English Language Manga series for Seven Seas Entertainment: AMAZING AGENT LUNA, DRACULA EVERLASTING, and DESTINY'S HAND, with a two-volume Luna spinoff called AMAZING AGENT JENNIFER currently underway.

Currently, Nunzio and Christina have a graphic novel called AVALON CHRONICLES and an ongoing series called BAD MEDICINE, both set for release in 2012. Both projects are with Oni Press. They also just completed their first prose novel, a young adult thriller called MIND DANCE, and are at work writing a second novel and a new screenplay.

weirdefillipis.com

JACKIE LEWIS grew up in Atlanta, and she's still living there, so it must be a pretty awesome place. A graduate of Emory University and a recent graduate of SCAD Atlanta, Jackie is a smart and attractive young woman with a strong drive to make comics. She loves cats, books, knitting, and anything cuddly. She wears a lot of cardigans, and when it's too hot to wear cardigans, she wears them anyway, just to show the weather who's boss.

She'd like to send out a big thanks to her awesome friends who have been there for her every step of the way on her path to awesomeness, especially John, Jen, Courtney, Geoff, Jonas, Dan, Cara, Erin, Falynn, Schweizer, Nolan, Robin, and Doug. She'd like to thank Shawn Crystal for his tutelage and dedication, and Alex for his friendship and support.

jackiemakescomics.blogspot.com

ALSO BY DEFILIPPIS AND WEIR:

THE AMY DEVLIN MYSTERIES: PAST LIES
By Nunzio DeFilippis, Christina Weir &
Christopher Mitten
168 pages · Hardcover · B&W
$19.99 US · ISBN 978-1-934964-39-2

THE AMY DEVLIN MYSTERIES: ALL SAINTS DAY
By Nunzio DeFilippis, Christina Weir, Dove McHargue
& Kate Kasenow
168 pages · Hardcover · B&W
$19.99 US · ISBN: 978-1-934964-23-1

THE AVALON CHRONICLES, VOLUME 1:
ONCE IN A BLUE MOON
By Nunzio DeFilippis, Christina Weir & Emma Vieceli
168 pages · Hardcover · B&W
$19.99 US · ISBN: 978-1-934964-75-0

FRENEMY OF THE STATE
By Rashida Jones, Nunzio DeFilippis, Christina Weir,
Jeff Wamester & Chris Johnson
144 pages · Standard · Color
$19.99 US · ISBN: 978-1-934964-75-0

OTHER BOOKS FROM ONI PRESS!

HOPELESS SAVAGES, GREATEST HITS 2000-2010
By Jen Van Meter, Christine Norrie,
Bryan Lee O'Malley, Chynna Clugston-Flores & More
392 pages · Digest · B&W
$19.99 US · ISBN 978-1-934964-48-4

JAM! TALES FROM THE WORLD OF ROLLER DERBY
Eric Powell, Ray Fawkes & More!
192 pages · 6"x9" · Color
$19.95 US · ISBN 978-1-934964-14-9

POLLY AND THE PIRATES, VOL. 1
By Ted Naifeh
176 pages · Digest · B&W
$11.95 US · ISBN 978-1-932664-46-1

SCOOTER GIRL
By Chynna Clugston-Flores
168 pages · Digest · B&W
$14.95 US · ISBN 978-1-929998-88-3

For more information on these and other fine Oni Press
comic books and graphic novels, visit www.onipress.com.

To find a comic specialty store in your area, call
1-888-COMICBOOK or visit www.comicshops.us.

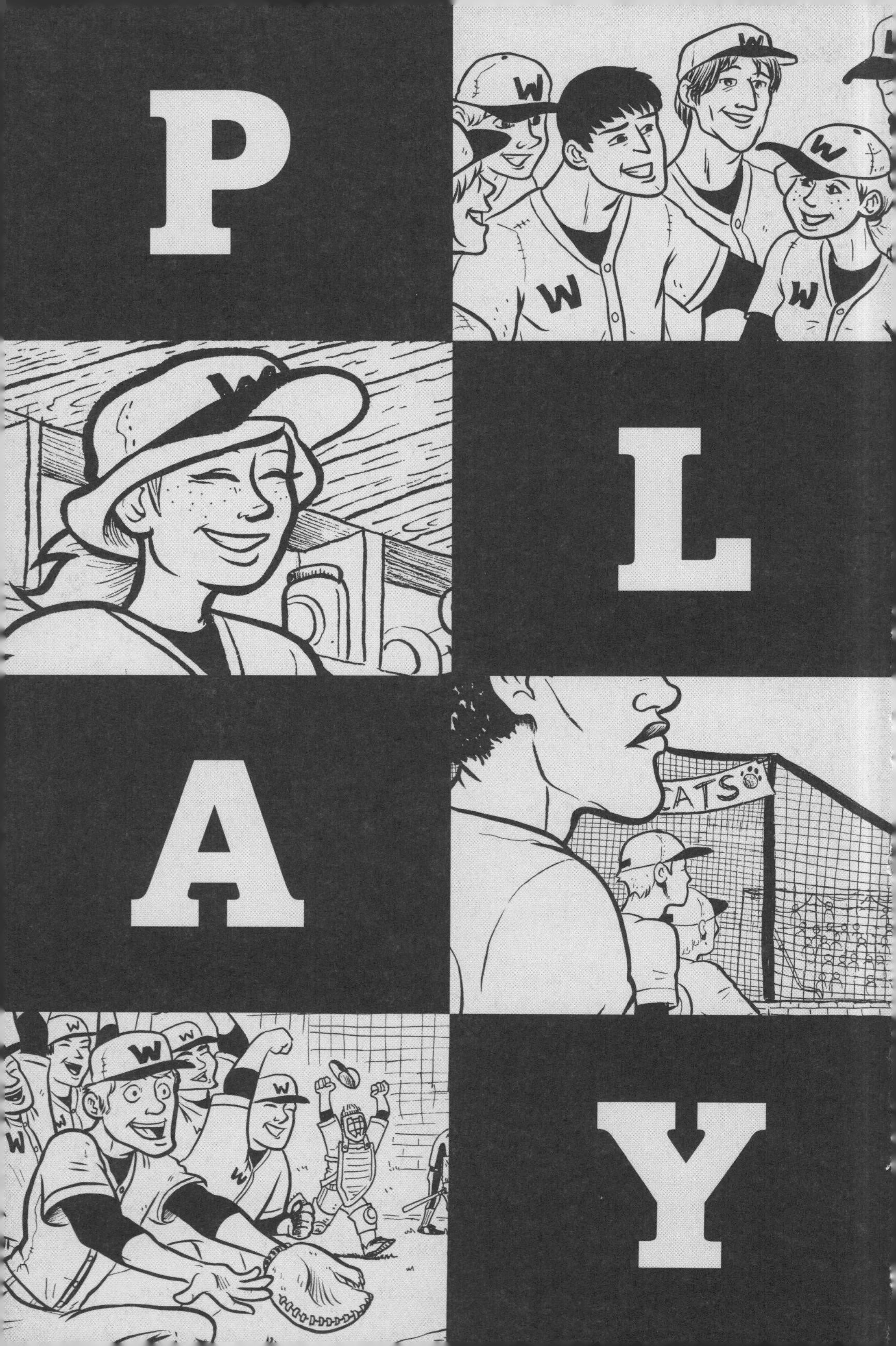
P
L
A
CATS
Y